BEST SERMONS

EDITED BY G. PAUL BUTLER

BEST
SERMONS

1946 EDITION

NEW YORK AND LONDON

HARPER & BROTHERS PUBLISHERS

TO
MY
THIRD
SON

JOLYAN

CONTENTS

[*viii*]

[ix]

[x]

[xi]

And the Darkness Did Not Master It

FOREWORD

by

REVEREND RALPH W. SOCKMAN, D.D.,
Minister, Christ Church, Methodist, New York;
and Preacher on the National Radio Pulpit

THE PREACHER and Prometheus have one thing in common: Each must carry the divine fire to man. John Donne stirred his great congregations at old St. Paul's Cathedral by the power of his convictions and the combination of his poetic language and the Gospel story. A hundred years later, Jonathan Edwards held Sinners in the Hands of an Angry God over the brink of hell. In our own time, religion has kept alive the spiritual forces at home and went to war with the men and women of the armed services. Four thousand soldiers and sailors plan to enter the ministry, and chaplains, Protestant and Catholic, ministered to the defeated Nazi leaders at the Nürnberg trials. "Amid the darkness the light shone, but the darkness did not master it."

Religion touches the whole of life. And never was the wholeness of life in more imperative need of being restored than after a war which has shattered the unity of the world and broken the spirits of so many of its millions. The minister of religion faces a spiritual crisis marked by bewilderment. Some old trails are hidden from view. Some have shown themselves to be dead-end streets. Others have been followed far enough to be revealed as vicious cycles. The popular bewilderment opens the way to charlatans and demagogues in the religious world as well as in other professions. When people are confused any Pied Piper with some new ideology can mislead them in politics, in business and in religion. We have a revival of premillennial preaching in these days. We also have the fantastic interpretations of Scripture which pervert prophecy. We are seeing many others who, tired of trying to think their way through, are content with escapist psychology. In various ways confused people are trying to escape the challenge of hard, straight thinking which the true prophet of God is called to give. We must recognize that the good life is a quest as well as a conquest, and the Church must be a map maker as well as a path maker.

Ours is the task of trying to recover the clues to life's meaning for this generation. Our general philosophy of life comes down from the Hebrew-Christian tradition. We seek to keep this historic perspective to guide us through the maze of the present and into the remaking of a world which man has partly destroyed. Our political liberty is limited for the good of society. And the social good must be interpreted and reinforced by a better knowledge of our ethical and spiritual background. True religion should give to the mind of its adherents a viewpoint somewhat comparable to that which the chauffeur's mirror gives to the driver of a motor car. The mirror is so adjusted that the driver can see the road behind without taking his major gaze off the road ahead. It is important to see what is coming behind, for there is as much danger of being wrecked by collision from the rear as there is in front, and the most danger of all is when we turn left. Likewise, when we turn left, socially speaking, we need to know the movements behind us, lest our good intentions be wrecked by old fallacies carrying 1947 license plates.

There are hopeful signs that the ministry is trying to get this historic sense. Evidence is to be seen in our seminaries where there is a deepened interest in theology and social ethics.

When we attempt to illumine the bewilderment of our contemporaries, we confront a second situation which is that of ignorance in the realm of religion. We cannot assume on the part of the people we address any large content of religious knowledge. John Hutton once said that Scotland had a reputation for distinguished preaching because its congregations were so steeped in Scripture. In an atmosphere of Scriptural intelligence even mediocre preaching can strike a spark, whereas the lack of Biblical knowledge in contemporary American congregations handicaps even the best pulpit efforts. We ministers flog the wills of our parishioners but do not feed their minds. We lead crusades for community betterment but neglect the teaching of our people.

The teaching function of the ministry must be recaptured and re-emphasized if we are to leaven the sodden ignorance of our time. This effort will mean more use of our Bible. Many young ministers seem afraid to use the Bible in the pulpit. They realize that the Bible is not being widely read by their people; they assume, therefore, that it is not interesting to the pew. It is out of date to quote Jeremiah or Amos. It is up to date to quote Shalom Asch or Bertrand Russell. Hence the Bible is left closed and our pulpits turn to all sorts of secular literature for illustrations and instruction.

Overdue is a revival of expository preaching. Some of the expository sermons of our grandfathers would not hold the modern congregations. We preachers can spend too much time in giving the Hebrew and Greek roots of our texts. But if we start where people are thinking and then lead them back into those uplands of the soul which have been given us in the Old and New Testaments, we shall recover the springs of creative life for our people.

To fulfill this function of teaching will also mean a revival of doctrinal preaching. Doctrines can be deadly dry if we take them up in stereotyped form, but I believe the pulpit, if it will give itself to it, can find a way of making old doctrines live. The doctrinal preacher who takes the lasting teachings and brings them down to the present in living form is like the incandescent current that comes from a source far behind the light.

If these recoveries in preaching are reborn in the modern pulpit, we will find ourselves preaching to win souls, which is the highest function of the pulpit. The minister who is a living evangel will never have an empty church for long. John Wesley's scholarly preaching developed into truly evangelistic preaching after the fire of the Gospel entered his soul with new meaning at the Aldersgate meeting. When Dr. Sheldon began preaching *In His Steps* his Sunday evening congregations grew from a handful to a crowded church.

Preaching should be a sharing of ideas and experience rather than an effort to put across propaganda. The preacher who becomes too dogmatic eventually ceases to hold his thoughtful hearers. He must win the mind and the will and the emotions—the whole man. American congregations have grown up in these several hundred years with an independence new to the world and this liberty needs guidance. Uncharted liberty not only tires, but it can easily deteriorate into license and even into a crime wave as after World War I. We must make liberty safe for the world.

To win free minds the minister must prove himself such an expert in Christian thought and living that his people recognize him as a spiritual authority. They will see that his divine power comes not so much from the hands which were laid on him as from his ability to lay hands on the needs and wounds of the human spirit.

The minister of today faces the problem of specialization. It is a much more difficult task to serve a typical modern congregation made up of specialists in different lines of work than it was to preach in the simpler days of our great-grandfathers when the parishioners were less diversified in their interests and activities. We lack community of interest in our congregations and it is difficult therefore to create community of feeling in our congregations. This community of feeling is very important in religion. It is the preacher's problem and opportunity to lead these specialized minds back to the centers where they can see life steadily and see it whole. We in the pulpit stand where the specialities meet. We can keep our eyes on endangered human values and cry out when they are threatened even though we cannot make the prescription for their cure. Ours is the task of correcting the errors of experts. Religion is a matter of life and death, and the minister who is commissioned to serve the Lord of all life is obligated to preserve and present that wholeness of view which avoids the mistakes of the specialists.

The preacher must ever struggle to keep his energies from being dissipated by organizational activities and his prophetic voice from being muzzled by institutional interests. It is his task to bring personal virtues up to the new frontiers of social temptations. The true pastor-preacher must catch the flashes of divine spirit manifested even in the darkness of war and harness them for the time of greatness which we hope and pray will be tomorrow.

INTRODUCTION

BEST SERMONS seeks to present a cross section of the best spiritual thought and preaching of our time, with sermons of such universal appeal that they could have been delivered in any church. All of the fifty-two sermons were chosen for their religious message, homiletic value and application to the needs of men in our day. Each sermon is in the preacher's own words, with the full denominational flavor of his church.

Reading the great number of sermons submitted for volumes one and two (over eleven thousand for the two volumes) has brought a renewed realization that the preachers firmly believe in their message, that they understand the men of our own time, that they are conscious of the needs of men, women, and children, that they want to help the service men find their places back in civilian life. There is a fervor in preaching, a sense of the necessity of reaching the seventy million unchurched people in the United States, of the need of winning or *"making"* the peace if a third world war is to be prevented in another twenty years or less. There is a sincere effort to bring the Gospel of Christ to the people who need it and an absence of preaching of thinly spun treatises on useless trifles. Preachers are speaking on war and peace, on home and business, children and education, vocations and recreation, on time and eternity, and what God wants men to do about each of these things in their world. The best sermons have exciting power, a suspense, a stirring quality, promise something important, and fulfill that promise. Preaching is still the open door to men's hearts! And truly, all the wealth of fiction pales into insignificance beside the Gospel of Christ.

Some men, as Dean Sperry recently said, "live *to* preach"; others "live *and* preach." Some of the sermons included are like a river, rising in eternal springs, flowing through deserts, valleys, mountains, great cities, carrying passengers and freight, ending at last at the sea, but always having a beginning, a purpose and an ending. Others are like an excellent conversation, where the minister talks *with* the hearts and minds of his hearers and where he discusses what he knows about God and His Ways with men. Well may the writer of the great Epistle to the Hebrews have said, "He makes his angels spirits, and his ministers a flame of fire."

All of the 252 preaching denominations were invited to have a sermon or sermons read with a view to inclusion. Thousands of individual ministers were asked to send sermons for consideration. Over five thousand responded with from one to a half dozen sermons. The book makes no pretense at containing all the best sermons preached during the last eighteen months, but the search for the finest and best has been as wide and as thorough as possible.

As nearly as one can estimate there are about five million sermons preached in the United States alone by the country's 231,000 clergymen each year. Several of the sermons are so excellent that they need no word of commendation. A few others would not rank with the immortals, for the editor has tried to discover the best of some of the newer ministers and to give them a chance to be known, as well as to secure the best by those who are in the great pulpits. Some other excellent preachers, I am sure, did not send sermons for consideration because of their strong sense of modesty. Since all sermons are read in strictest confidence, and this is in no sense a contest, but a wide search, I hope even these men will feel free to send sermons to me for careful reading for volume three.

It was a rare opportunity to include many of the sermons in this collection. To rediscover Dr. Frank W. Boreham and his winged words for the Gospel, to bring Dr. Buttrick's message on faith through pain, to present Dr. Reinhold Niebuhr's brilliant philosophical interpretations, and other magnificent messages, gave the editor special pleasure. It was also a great privilege to include sermons by the three major faiths, Protestant, Catholic and Jewish and to give some lesser-known men a wider hearing.

The editor made the preliminary selections, but his advisory committee assisted in the final decision on sermons included. Protestant sermons were selected with the advice of Dr. Paul Scherer, Dr. Joseph R. Sizoo and Dr. Ralph W. Sockman. Catholic sermons were chosen with the aid of the Very Reverend Ignatius Smith and the Reverend Robert E. Holland (who assisted during the illness of Reverent Gerald G. Walsh). Jewish sermons were decided upon with the guidance of Dr. David DeSola Pool, Dr. Israel Bettan and Dr. Israel Goldstein. Sermons by Dr. Sizoo, Dr. Scherer and Dr. Bettan were included at the editor's special request and he assumes full responsibility for these three inclusions.

While the collection was planned primarily as an American book of sermons, great preaching from other lands was welcomed and I am glad to include distinguished sermons from Australia, Canada, Switzerland and England. In succeeding volumes I hope to have sermons from Scotland, Sweden, South America, South Africa, the Orient—anywhere, in fact, where great sermons can be discovered and secured for inclusion.

Best Sermons is now planned as an annual and work on the third volume is now under way. The book is fast coming to belong to the clergy rather than the editor. And to those who gave me the material for the book, I gratefully return this collection of sermons from the contemporary pulpit in the earnest hope that it may help to bring current religious life to more perfect flower.

G. PAUL BUTLER

New York and Fairlee Haven
March 1, 1946

ACKNOWLEDGMENTS

SO MANY ministers, priests and rabbis, book people and other friends helped with this second collection of *Best Sermons* that it is impossible to mention each by name, but I am deeply grateful to all for the interest and co-operation they gave so freely.

To denominational heads, officers of the Federal Council of the Churches of Christ in America, the National Catholic Welfare Conference, the National Council of Catholic Men, seminary heads, clergymen, bishops and archbishops, I express sincere thanks. To Dr. J. V. Moldenhawer, Dr. Samuel M. Cavert, Dr. Quinter Miller, Dr. Millard L. Robinson and Dr. Henry Smith Leiper, I am under a deep debt of gratitude. To His Eminence Francis Cardinal Spellman, Monsignor Francis X. Shea, Monsignor Thomas J. McDonnell, Father Robert I. Gannon, Father Gerald G. Walsh and Father Salvatore Piccirillo, a special word of appreciation is due.

To the members of my Advisory Committee, Dr. Joseph R. Sizoo, Dr. Paul E. Scherer, Dr. Ralph W. Sockman; the Very Reverend Ignatius Smith, Reverend Gerald G. Walsh, Reverend Robert E. Holland; and to Dr. Israel Goldstein, Dr. David DeSola Pool and Dr. Israel Bettan, I am happy to record my appreciation. Without the help of these ministers, who are themselves distinguished preachers, the book would not have been possible in its representative and ecumenical character.

Publishers have been most gracious in permitting quotations from their copyrighted volumes. I am glad to acknowledge such permissions from the following:

Mr. J. K. Anderson for the quotation from *The Wingless Victory*, by Maxwell Anderson.

The Catholic World, New York, for the poem, "The Guns Speak," by John Edward Spear.

Dodd, Mead & Company, Inc., New York, for the poem, "The Mystic's Prayer," by William Sharp, from *Poems and Dramas*.

Henry Holt and Company, Inc., New York, for the poem, "Let Me Flower As I Will," by Lew Sarett, from *The Box of God*.

Houghton Mifflin Company, Boston, for the poem, "Grant Us the Will," by John Drinkwater.

John Richard Moreland, for the poem, "His Hands."

The Pilgrim Press, Boston, for the poem, "The Cross at the Crossways," by John Oxenham, from *Gentlemen—The King!*

Charles Scribner's Sons, New York, for the quotation from "This Is My

Father's World," by Maltbie D. Babcock, and "Invictus," from *Poems by W. E. Henley.*

Willett, Clark & Company, Chicago, for the poem by E. W. Lyman, from *1,000 Quotable Poems*, compiled by T. C. Clark.

Ziff-Davis Publishing Company, Chicago, for permission to use all or part of the introductory notes for Dr. Moldenhawer, Father Gannon, Cardinal Spellman, Monsignor Sheen, Dr. Lynn Harold Hough and Archbishop Lucey from *Best Sermons: 1944 Edition.*

To Miss Elinor Inman of the Columbia Broadcasting System for recommending several of the best sermons on the Church of the Air program; to Mr. Robert Wilberforce, Mr. Gavin Casey, Thomas R. Birch, Gabriel Javsicas, Edward J. Heffron and Frank A. Hall, for their invaluable help in interdenominational and international details, I cannot express sufficient thanks. To my publishers for their understanding, patience and determination to make this volume a real contribution to the ministers of the country, I am truly grateful. To Erica Butler for her constant loyalty I wish I had words to say thank you. And to the booksellers throughout the country who also co-operated in making this book what it is, a special word of appreciation and good will is gladly given.

BEST SERMONS

BEST SERMONS

No Wedge Is Driven

REVEREND GEORGE ARTHUR BUTTRICK, D.D., LL.D., LITT.D.
Minister, Madison Avenue Presbyterian Church, New York

Dr. Buttrick is recognized as one of the great preachers of our day. His sermons have a freshness, a Lancashire independence of thought and expression, a vitality, and a sense of the eternal which businessmen, teachers, housewives and people of all walks of life find inspiring. Born in England in 1892, he was educated at Lancaster Independent College in Manchester and took honors in philosophy at Victoria University. His outstanding ability as a preacher and religious thinker has been recognized with the honorary doctorate by Hamilton, Middlebury, Yale, Miami, Princeton, Bethany and Albright.

He was ordained to the ministry of the Congregational Church of the United States in 1915 and was pastor of First Union Congregational Church, Quincy, Illinois from then until 1918. He served First Congregational Church, Rutland, Vermont from 1918 to 1921, when he was called to First Presbyterian Church, Buffalo, New York for six years. Since 1927 he has been minister of Madison Avenue Presbyterian Church, New York, and was president of the Federal Council of the Churches of Christ in America from 1938 to 1940.

Five books mark him as a writer of great ability, The Parables of Jesus, Jesus Came Preaching, The Christian Fact, Modern Doubt *and* Prayer, *which is almost a classic in the religious field. His newest book,* Christ and Man's Dilemma, *is an application of the Gospel of Christ to contemporary problems. In the next three or four years he will complete his work as editor in chief of a multivolume commentary,* The Interpreters Bible.

In the distinguished sermon which represents Dr. Buttrick here, he shows how one may grow through pain to faith, makes James Thomson's "City of Dreadful Night," and God's saving mystery full of new meaning. Dr. Buttrick uses the original Greek for his New Testament readings and frequently varies the text from the standard versions slightly to bring new light for our day.

Sermon One

TEXT: Who shall separate us from the love of Christ? Shall tribulation, or distress, or persecution, or famine, or nakedness, or peril, or sword? ROMANS 8:35

JAMES THOMSON, in the latter part of the last century, wrote a poem entitled, "The City of Dreadful Night." Casual readers have supposed that he meant London. Actually he meant life. He did not spend his whole life in London. He spent some time in Colorado, and was war-correspondent in Spain for the old *New York World*. He meant our planet. The poem comes to a climax in an atheistic sermon preached from a black pulpit to wretches moving in unholy gloom, counseling them to despair and suicide. Thomson once said that if he could not have made a better world than this world he would not be God for all God's power. That mood could easily become ours today. Our civilization seems one cruelty, our best brains are dedicated to swifter and more wholesale killing. "The City of Dreadful Night!"

We wonder and we wonder. Much of the pain comes of human sin; from all men's sin, not merely from the sins of rulers. The common folk consent to rulers of low mind; and either they like them, or they are too selfishly absorbed to pay the cost of ousting them. There is justice to much of our suffering. We ourselves would not wish to live in a world where wickedness is with impunity. The Japanese issue is for evidence. Many of the Japanese are pagans. There is only one sure way to change pagans; by the contagion of enlightened life. Where that way has been tried the Japanese are not pagans. But we did not often walk that way. We gave Japan our materialistic science, raised tariff walls to hug our standard of living, slapped Japan in the face in the Exclusion Act, shipped her arms (with which to kill Chinese); but did little to prove ourselves Christian. Then we were surprised when Japan sprang on us with pagan cunning and fury. Our sins come home to roost— in pain and death, and we would not wish to live in a world where fire-of-wrong does not burn.

But whole areas of suffering cannot be explained as due to our sin. What of Russian peasants caught in the tides of war? Or of parents who lose an only child? Or of saints martyred? What would you have said to the child who asked, "Why does God make us sad?" Our planet is the only one known to be inhabited, and only a few patches of our planet are fit for habitation. We are a tribe of hairless bipeds, clinging precariously to our shelter between tropic heat and arctic cold, between sand and ocean; and we wage a losing battle against time, weather, and aging flesh. Meanwhile our brand of self-consciousness, our memory and power of anticipation, enable us to borrow pain from past and future, and to give it a sharper edge of fear. "The City of Dreadful Night!"

> Nothing begins and nothing ends
> That is not paid with moan;
> For we are born in others' pain,
> And perish in our own.

The customary explanations do not explain. "There is compensation for every pain," says the preacher. This pulpit has not said it. Perhaps there is; perhaps not. Our eyes cannot tell. Compensation for the death of an only child? Compensation for the poor folk of Hamburg or Chungking who have lost all their children? It would have to be a large sum in happy peace! "The fire refines," says the preacher. So it does, sometimes. That picture of the blind Milton dictating poems that are like some embattled heaven is a heart-stirring sight. "The Song of the Blind Ploughman" is true of him:

> God who took away my eyes,
> That my soul might see.

Perhaps all suffering could refine. But does it? Torture can turn to despair, and sorrow to a rebel bitterness. A poetess has said that pain is like iron left in the fog: "Pain rusts into beauty too." But rust is still corrosion. In any event, bear me witness, when pain comes it is almost impossible for us to philosophize about it, and to say, "This will refine my dross."

So we wonder and we wonder. Most of us have some claim to talk about suffering—from experience, but many of us have not much claim. I have not had more than my share, except as I have tried to carry other people's burdens; and that was perhaps no more than my share. I cannot talk piously or heroically. I am not much of a stoic when pain comes, but as much a coward as my neighbor. But suppose a man should say, "Distress, tribulation, famine, persecution, nakedness, peril, sword." Suppose we found that he had met them all, in mind and body, in an age when anesthetics were not known. Suppose we knew that he did not deserve the piled-up pain. We would listen to that man. There had been a day when he had persecuted the Christians; there was martyr blood on his hands. But that had been so well repented that he could now write the hymn of Godly love: "Now abideth faith, hope, love; these three; and the greatest of these is love." He was that kind of man. But he had been seared in flesh and thought by the cruelty of men; and, so far as they were concerned, his only crime was that their selfishness was threatened by his truth. He states the stark fact: "We are accounted as sheep for the slaughter." We must listen to such a man.

His approach is new. "Who shall sunder us from the love of Christ?" It is as if he said: "The fact of pain is mysterious enough; but there is another fact just as sure, just as mysterious—the soul's bond with God." He is right.

[3]

It is a staggering surprise that in "The City of Dreadful Night" there should ever have arisen this feeling for a just God. Yet the word is on our lips, the fact is in our lives. We feel awe. The explanation that it arose from fear of the dead does not explain. *Why* do we fear the dead, when the dead have no power, being dead, to hurt us? Would it not be truer to say that when death visits our home we know that we "are in the hands of him with whom we have to do"? We feel obligation: "I ought." We feel guilt, because we fail to do as we ought. The explanation that this feeling comes from fear of tribal penalty for father-killing and incest does not explain. Why did the tribe think these acts wrong? Why, if they were not wrong? Why does the feeling persist, and become in saintly souls more pure? The primal sense of conscience is better argument than the too-fanciful theories of Dr. Freud. We are all like Wordsworth when as a boy he stole a boat. Poor lad!—the mountain from which he rowed rose up like a judgment:

> The grim shape
> Towered up between me and the stars, and still,
> For so it seemed, with purpose of its own
> And measured motion like a living thing,
> Strode after me.

We feel Compassion—like kindly steps across meadows. We feel Beauty— breathing through all lovely sights and sounds. We never escape God, and are never quite content without God. John Buchan, when he first went to London as a young lawyer, chose a room on the Thames where he could hear the birds crying at night as they flew from the ocean up the river. Always we yearn for the voice of the Ocean that beats on the shores of our mortality.

We feel God. We feel Christ—after the same fashion. He quickens our sense of awe, despite His humanness. He is like a living conscience. Nay, we can omit that "like": He is a living conscience. He forgave sins. That no one here would ever presume to do. We do not go to Sing-Sing, open the gates, and say, "Thy sins be forgiven thee." Pardon is the gift of the Holy God. But Jesus said it, in deep humility. For myself, I am sure Dr. C. S. Lewis is right when he declares of Jesus: "Either he is a raving lunatic of an unusually abominable type, or else he was, and is, precisely what he said." He said he was Son of man and Son of God. At any rate, people who ponder him have a feeling of reverence towards him. In many it amounts to worship.

In short, we believe in God. This belief is as stubborn as the mystery of pain, and even harder to explain. We doubt? Yes, often. But we could not doubt if we did not first believe. What we doubt is our faith. What else could we doubt? The faith persists. Even when misgivings throng, it persists. We may rail at pain, and declare with Thomson that life is a "city of dreadful night," but actually we do not carry our railing to the point of advocating universal despair and suicide. Despite our rebellion, we know that Job is a nobler person than his wife. In his utter extremity, she said, "Curse God, and die." But he said, "Though he slay me, yet will I trust him." We may bitterly insist, as we look out upon our world that it is an imbecile planet; but we do not live that lack of faith. Next day we are reasonably considerate. We pick German airmen from the sea, and feed once hostile cities. We rail, but soon recoil from our railing; and we would be ashamed to try to pervert the faith of Job. The bond with God remains. It is wonderful that it does, but it does. God is even harder to explain than the suffering.

Paul fixes his eyes on that bond. He says that pain seems to him like a wedge driven between the soul and God. Of a truth it has that appearance, however its appearance may change in retrospect. "Tribulation, distress, persecution, famine, nakedness, peril, and sword" rise up like so many angry foes trying to drive the wedge. "Who shall sunder us from the love of God?" That is the question! "What is the philosophic explanation of pain?" is not the question, for we would have to meet pain when all the pretty explanations had been made. "Can the bond between the soul and God be broken?" —that is the question. Life is full of separations: distance drives its wedge, and sickness, and misunderstanding, and death. How strong is the bond? That is what we need to know.

Paul found—in that age which had no anesthetics, in which he was as a sheep slaughtered—that nothing could sunder the soul from Christ. Yes, his courage was needed, but not more courage than he could summon. The new sustaining of God was more needed—and was given. So Dr. C. S. Lewis again: "A little courage helps more than much knowledge, a little human sympathy more than much courage, and the least tincture of the love of God more than all." Look at that great saying: "God so loved the world." It begins with God's love, and ends with the promise of eternal life to our world. But what comes in between? God's act in Christ, and our faith: "God so loved the world, that he gave his only-begotten Son, that whosoever believeth in him, should not perish, but have everlasting life." Paul found that as often as he "believed"—though blindly, though in tears—God gave again, in new gift, the grace of Jesus Christ. Samuel Rutherford told Lady Kenmore that as she met pain and death, if she would set foot in the river and walk, however timidly, "God will come in at the deepest part of the stream to lend you a hand." That is true. That has been our experience. That is what we need to know. It is all we need to know, or, at least, it is enough for earthly life. That was what Allan Gardiner found. He had gone with three others as missionaries to a savage land. The three died of hunger, and Gardiner survived them only by a few days. A ship touched on the bleak shore, and found their bones. Could any pain seem so needless and so wasted? Yet over the entrance to the cave he had painted a hand pointing downwards, as if to his grave; and under the hand the words, "My soul, trust thou still upon God." It is earth's best wisdom.

There is more to be said—but not much more at the time of pain's onset. Then all we can say is that if pain is a mystery, God (in a world of pain)

[5]

is a great and more saving mystery. Then we can only cling to God—and find that He has a stronger hold on us. Later we find that the rough hands which tried to break the strands between the soul and God are like fingers on harpstrings that make undying music. Milton did see more deeply because of blindness, and Tennyson did write more lastingly because his pen was dipped in tears, and Beethoven did give us more poignant harmonies because his gathering deafness robbed him of power to hear them—except in the soul. But that bright issue is not seen or understood at the onset of pain. That revelation comes later, when the onset has been met; and it comes, not from the pain alone (alone the pain only lacerates), but from the pain playing on a soul clinging to God made known in Christ. Maude Royden is right when she says that Christ does not give us reasons, at least not in the first instance: He gives us strength without telling us why the pain has come, and gives us the reasons only beyond the victory.

Pain is still a mystery. But God is a more saving mystery. Lay hold on God in the time of suffering, even if your grasp is not stronger than a prayer: you will find then that He has laid hold on you. The Knights of Saint Patrick had as their motto: *Quis separabit?* ("Who shall separate?"). It is a good motto. But it will not serve us if we keep questioning the pain, and keep ignoring the deeper fact of God. To set foot in the river and walk—that is the strategy. Then we shall find God coming to meet us, and lending us a hand, at the deepest part of the stream. Thus through pain we are nearer Him. Dr. H. C. G. Moule tells of reading this text as he looked at the Coliseum in Rome—that place of which some pope said: "Do you want a relic? Gather dust from the Coliseum: it is all martyrs." The word suddenly took on a life of silent fire: "Who shall separate us from the love of Christ? Shall tribulation, or distress, or persecution, or famine, or nakedness, or peril, or sword? As it is written, For thy sake we are killed all the day long; we are accounted as sheep for the slaughter. Nay, in all these things we are more than conquerors through him that loved us. For I am persuaded that neither life nor death, nor angels, nor principalities, nor powers, nor things present, nor things to come, nor height, nor depth, nor any other created thing shall be able to separate us from the love of God, which is in Christ Jesus our Lord."

The Loans of Life

REVEREND FRANK WILLIAM BOREHAM, D.D.
Baptist Minister, Victoria, Australia

For fifty years, Dr. Boreham has been preaching in Australia and New Zealand. He is highly respected as one of the leading figures of the Australian Baptist Church, a famous Australian essayist and a great sermonizer. Born in 1871 at Tunbridge Wells, England, he was educated in England, and in 1895 went to New Zealand as Minister of the Baptist Church at Mosgiel, where he remained for eleven years. For the following ten years he was Minister of the Hobart (Tasmania) Baptist Church, after which he transferred to the Armadale (Victoria) Baptist Church, where he remained until 1928.

Dr. Boreham, now retired from pastoral responsibilities, has added to his signal achievements by establishing a remarkable lunch-hour ministry at Scotch Church, Presbyterian, Melbourne, Victoria, where Thursday by Thursday he attracts a large and representative congregation of city people by his picturesque and lively preaching.

Dr. Boreham has made three preaching tours of England, Canada and the United States, in 1924, 1928, and 1936. He received the honorary D.D. from McMaster University, Toronto in 1928, and has published thirty books of essays and sermons, including A Handful of Stars, The Nest of Spears, My Pilgrimage, *and* The Ivory Spires.

In "The Loans of Life" his old power of coining phrases, of dressing the Gospel story in new words to catch the attention of the chance hearer, and his intense faith in Christ are clear and distinct. His figures of speech, the freshness of his language, and his ability to play on the human imagination with the Gospel story have made his sermons great literary works, religious gems, and an event to hear or read.

Sermon Two

TEXT: I am debtor. . . . ROMANS 1:14

WE ARE incorrigible borrowers, and, on the whole, we are none the worse for it. Most of us are borrowing, borrowing, borrowing all the time. We not only borrow from Peter to repay our debt to Paul, but we mortgage the Future in order to meet our obligations to the Past and borrow from one hemisphere in order that we may redress the balance of the other.

We seldom pay for anything we purchase, or, if we do, we pay only in part and, by hook or by crook, obtain credit for the rest. And such payments as we do make, we make, like Mr. Micawber, with an I.O.U. Everybody knows the story as Dickens tells it. Mr. Micawber was leaving London; but he owed Mr. Traddles forty-one pounds ten shillings and eleven pence half-penny.

"To leave this metropolis," said Mr. Micawber, "and my friend, Mr. Thomas Traddles, without acquitting myself of the pecuniary part of this obligation, would weigh upon my mind to an unsupportable extent. I have, therefore, prepared for my friend, Mr. Thomas Traddles, and I now hold in my hand, a document which accomplishes the desired object. I beg to hand to my friend, Mr. Thomas Traddles, my I.O.U. for forty-one, ten, eleven and a half, and I am happy to recover my moral dignity, and to know that I can once more walk erect before my fellow man!" If we took the trouble to analyze matters carefully, we should discover that most of us make our way through life in pretty much the same temper.

We began early. When making our preparations for invading this planet, we naturally came to the conclusion that our equipment would be lamentably incomplete unless we brought a body with us. But a body was the one thing that we did not happen to possess. A body is composed of certain chemical substances. It consists of so much iron, so much phosphate, so much salt, so much soda, and so on. Now here was a dilemma in which to be placed at the very outset! We could not very well begin without a body: a body required all these substances: and we did not chance to have any of them about us! What could we do?

Borrowing was inevitable. But from whom? It is begging the issue to say that we borrowed from our parents. They no more possessed these chemical ingredients in their own right than we did. If they had them, it was because they themselves had borrowed them. To the extent to which we borrowed from them, we merely borrowed what they, in their turn, had borrowed from us.

Iron, phosphate, salt, soda and all the other constituent elements in the human body belong, quite obviously, to the earth beneath our feet. Strictly speaking, therefore, it was from the earth that we borrowed them. *In the beginning*, the inspired record affirms, *the Lord God formed man from the dust of the ground.* That is what Paul means by saying of the corruptible body that it is of the earth, earthy. From the soil, then, the body sprang. *Ashes to ashes; dust to dust!* Ashes and dust inanimate to ashes and dust animate: ashes and dust below to ashes and dust above: ashes and dust lifeless and cold to ashes and dust living and warm!

It was distinctly a loan and not a gift. We had to pledge ourselves, by the most solemn and binding instruments, that, so soon as we had finished with the articles that were to be so useful to us, we would indubitably return them to the earth again. *Ashes to ashes; dust to dust!* The chemicals that we borrowed from the earth must all go back to the earth. Nature makes her generous advances only on the best security. She holds the mortgage in an inflexible clutch and will exact to the uttermost farthing all that she has advanced.

The same principle operates all through life. Never a day comes to us but some little thing reminds us of the incalculable debt that we owe to the parents who nourished and protected our infancy. It was not a case of love at first sight: they fell in love with us before they had even seen us. They knew that we were pitifully human, yet they idealized us until they made us almost divine. Dreaming of all the good things that we should do, they never for a moment fore-visaged the bad. Every day they persuaded themselves—the logic of love being such a hopelessly illogical thing—that they needed us, and never for a moment thought of our tremendous need of them. For our sakes they made life a constant struggle, a perpetual sacrifice; yet they endured it bravely, cheerfully, gratefully, a smile ever on their faces and a song ever in their hearts.

For a while we regard all this as a gift: it is only in the days of our maturity that we discover that, after all, it was but a loan. In due course we become surrounded by happy children of our own. These smaller hands outstretched to us are the hands that Nature has sent to demand the repayment of the earlier loan. With the arrival of our own offspring, the time has come to meet the obligation that we incurred a generation back: to the extent to which we repudiate that obligation we invite the stern faces of our creditor-parents to rise up in judgment against us.

Even amidst the ordinary commerce and traffic of life, the same law holds. Like Mr. Micawber, we pay all our bills, at least in part, with an I.O.U. The cash that crosses the counter never quite settles the score. James Nasmyth, the inventor of the steam hammer, tells us in his autobiography of the picturesque scenes he witnessed as a boy in the old fish market in Edinburgh. After a stormy night, he says, during which the husbands and sons had toiled at the risk of their lives to catch the fish, intending buyers would ask the usual question of the fishwives:

"Weel, Janet, and hoo's haddies the day?"

"Haddies, mem?" Janet would reply meaningly, "ou, haddies is men's lives the day!"

Janet was probably recalling the refrain of Lady Nairne's famous ballad:

> Wha'll buy my caller herrin'?
> They're no brought without brave darin',
>   Buy my caller herrin'!
>   Ye little know their worth
> Wha'll buy my caller herrin'?
> Ye may call them vulgar farin',
> Wives and mothers most despairin'
>   Call them lives of men!
>   Caller herrin'! Caller herrin'!

The shining fish would be sold for a few coppers; but did those few coppers discharge the debt? What of the miner who dares the perils of the shafts? However high the price of coal, and however munificent the miner's wages, there is still a balance owing. And what of the soldier who hazards, or surrenders, his very life in our defense? Do we dispose of our obligations to him by merely paying our taxes? "How little," exclaims Robert Louis Stevenson in *An Inland Voyage*, "how little we pay our way in life! Although we have our purses continually in our hand, the better part of service still goes unrewarded." We meet practically every demand, that is to say, with an I.O.U.

It comes, then, to this: from the moment at which, through my mother's travail, I first drew breath, my life has been sustained by the blood and agony and tears of others. Unless, therefore, I give back to the world something that costs me blood and agony and tears, I shall, when I quit the planet, be in the position of the man who slips out of the neighborhood without first discharging his just and honorable debts.

I knew a man once who thought it very wicked to borrow.

"My dear fellow," I said, "you can't get through life without!"

"Oh!" he answered, visibly shocked, "but doesn't the Bible exhort us to *owe no man anything?*"

"No," I replied, "the Bible says nothing of the kind. The Bible says, 'Owe no man anything, *but . . .*' —and that exception is the greatest exception to a general principle that has ever been stated in human language —'Owe no man anything, *but to love one another.*'" No man can walk the world with any consciousness of moral integrity unless he has done his best, by the grace of God, to meet that tremendous obligation.

But let us delve more deeply. We have so far only dealt with the debt in which we have become involved by the blood and agony and tears of men. But what of the debt in which we have become involved by the blood and agony and tears of God?

In one of the stateliest and most impressive autobiographical passages in all his epistles, Paul declares that the gospel of free grace and dying love by which his life has been transfigured has placed him under an obligation that it must be his ceaseless endeavor to discharge. *I am debtor,* he says, *both to the Greeks and to the Barbarians; both to the wise, and to the unwise. So, as much as in me is, I am ready to preach the gospel to you that are at Rome also.*

But how? In what way had either the Greeks or the Barbarians placed Paul in their debt? You might as well ask in what way my newly-born children had placed me in their debt. My obligation to my children was based on my indebtedness to my parents. Paul feels, and rightly feels, that the sheer immensity of that redeeming love, which had so amazingly enriched his own life, imperatively demanded that he should spend all his powers in making that gospel known to all kinds and conditions of men. He who has freely received must freely give. If the Son of God died for all men—and for me—I can no more discharge my debt to him personally than I can pay my parents for all that they did for me. But, since he died that all men might be saved, I can at least recognize my obligation to him by spreading the sensational tidings among all those for whom he gave His life.

It is the keynote of the New Testament. The best-known prayer in the world lays it down, in its central petition, that he who has been greatly forgiven must himself greatly forgive. It is the last word in the Bible. *The Spirit and the Bride say Come! And let him that heareth say Come!* The very fact that my ears have heard constitutes itself a demand that my tongue shall tell. He whose soul has been enchanted by the music of a lovely melody is in honor bound to do his best to set the whole world singing.

The Inclusive Name

REVEREND FREDERICK W. NORWOOD, D.D.
Minister, St. James United Church, Montreal, Canada

"The Inclusive Name" represents Dr. Norwood at his preaching best. By birth an Australian, he served several churches there, then left for World War I with Australian troops, 1914-18. After that he became minister of City Temple, London, the leading Congregational church of England,

and remained there for seventeen years. During that time he was chairman of the Congregational Union of England and Wales, president of the National Free Church Council, president of the London Free Church Council, and a member of many important boards.

In 1939 he decided to make Canada his home, and for nearly four years was minister of St. Andrews-Wesley Church, Vancouver, B. C. Recently he accepted an invitation to St. James United Church in Montreal, one of the oldest and perhaps the largest church of the United Church in Canada.

He has traveled a great deal as a preacher and lecturer, on one occasion taking sixteen months for a world tour throughout Africa, India, China, Japan, Australia, New Zealand, the United States and Canada. He has made at least twenty visits to the United States and has been a frequent summer preacher in New York at The Riverside Church and at Fifth Avenue Presbyterian Church.

In his books and sermons he has a force and fire that touch the spiritual life of man, as in "The Inclusive Name."

Sermon Three

I ONCE had a friend who was a famous and successful novelist.

He had in mind for several years to write the story of one family which would require three volumes for its telling. The dramatic events he intended to describe could not fall within the life of one man, or even of one generation.

There was to be one original character, of striking personality and amid fateful circumstances, who would stamp himself upon the future. He would die, then his children would follow him, and their children would follow them. But his tragic influence would go right down the line. His children would not be born when fate made him what he was; he would be dead when some of them would still be grappling with the secret forces that had shaped him. The point was that this man in his crisis had done the right as he saw it, but he did not see far enough. His descendants had to suffer for his lack of vision, but they held on to his principles and worked them through at last.

In short, my friend wrote a trilogy of books—three volumes setting forth the same drama, with different actors and at different times.

I remember my friend telling me that, as an author, he could not keep those three books separately in his mind.

Once he had done the groundwork of his lengthy plot, he could not keep the fences up. When he put his original character through some experiences, he found himself wondering how it would affect the people of the second or the third generation. Sometimes, in his notebooks, he worked that out in volume two or three while yet volume one was unfinished. Later, when he came specifically to the later volumes, he felt he had to reshape parts of volume one.

In the end he finished the three books at about the same time, though he published them at intervals. His readers must follow the path laid down for them; they could not sufficiently enter into the drama unless they shared the partial blindness of the actors on the stage.

My friend, who is dead now, came back to me, as I was pondering over a saying of Simon Peter's upon which I wish to speak. It is something that he said, as it were, in Book One of the Christian history, in the very beginning of the story. I seemed to see it cropping up again in Book Two, arousing entirely different feelings in my mind. And I am wondering if in some third book, as yet not fully written, whether it may not have an altogether different significance.

Here is the saying: "There is no salvation by anyone else, not even a second Name under heaven appointed for us men and our salvation."

If your minds worked like mine as you heard that old story a few minutes ago, you doubtless thrilled at first to the sheer courage and unhesitating conviction with which Peter first spoke those words. Then you began to recoil from what sounded like narrowness and intolerance. And perhaps we may be able to see together that they are not narrow but exceedingly broad; that they are not exclusive but inclusive words.

This claim, which Christians must make, that there is only one Name— the Name of Jesus.

This fear, this fearful possibility, that we may make that Name the symbol of narrow-mindedness and bigotry.

This hope, that it is big enough to include every worthwhile thing and yet not lose the drive, but give point and force without which neither we nor society can possibly be saved.

Let us put it this way:

Until you can put a Name to a thing, you do not really know it. The Name of Christ is the most descriptive syllable in the language. Without the Name of Christ, Christianity is only one among a million religions or philosophies. The greatest perversion is the attachment of Christ's Name to what is un-Christly. To carry forward the significance of that Name into every realm of life, in personal or social affairs, is the supreme need of the world.

I sat a long while in my study not long ago reading again that story of the arraignment of Simon Peter and his friend John before the authorities in Jerusalem.

I found it quite easy to visualize the scene—in the Acts of the Apostles it is so simple and so lucid.

I saw that imposing gathering of the influential religious authorities, the High Priest Caiaphas with Annas, John, Alexander, and all the relatives and dignitaries, the men who swayed things in old Jerusalem and who so easily held the lives of other citizens in their grasp. I saw the crowd, facile and uncertain, subject to many moods like the sea, who, by a mere word might be made friendly or might be lashed into a tempest.

I saw these two solitary men, Peter and John, standing at the foot of the steps before the council. The matter was not critical at the moment, though it was potentially dangerous. Nobody wished at that early stage to harm these followers of Christ. The thing was to stamp out a few verbal sparks before they lit a conflagration. All the authorities wanted of these two men was that they should be silent. "Say no more," said they, "about this Jesus and nothing will happen to you." They believed that if there were a brief interval of silence, this fantastic story would come to its end; this story of a crucified man who was alleged to be Divine, who was asserted to have risen from the dead. It would flicker out as a small fire does if it is not fed with inflammable sticks. The grim old realistic world would see to that. Let these men be silent and the danger would pass soon enough.

I saw in the eyes of the two men that they understood the situation very clearly. They knew that if they made just a few more speeches it would mean prison. It might be death. Why speak, then, in the teeth of a gale? I heard the voice of Peter ringing out clearly and distinctly, himself defiant of danger, restless of consequences, saying, "Whether it is right to obey men or God, judge ye. We cannot but speak the things that we have heard."

The question is, as we would say, whether these men would "go on the air" or "off the air" for a few short days or weeks. They would get a better and a safer chance by and by. There need not be permanent silence, only a judicious pause. What would that amount to in the long tale of history?

And then it was that Simon Peter revealed the finality of the conviction that was within him. He said, "There is no salvation by anyone else, not even a second Name under heaven appointed for us men and our salvation."

As I watched and listened I felt a tremendous admiration for Simon Peter and also at the same time I was conscious of a feeling of repugnance. One likes a brave man; one hates a bigot. There is nothing more noble or inspiring in this world than to see one man standing alone for a truth in which he believes. It is all the more noble when he can see nothing else than to declare it, against all caution, against all self-interest. There is nothing more impressive than to hear one man say, "Here stand I. I can do no other, God help me."

There are all kinds of courage in the world, but there is none that excels that. There is the courage that comes to men in a crowd, when many hearts beat as one. It is often irresistible, but all hail to the solitary man who can look the whole world in the face, take his life in his hands, and say what loyalty to truth sternly commands.

If ever we make that impossible, God help us—our society would deserve to perish.

Over and over again the fate of mankind has turned upon what one man has believed and dared to say. He ought to be wrong seeing he is alone. Such men are often half wrong, but an honest man half wrong is better than a bellwether to a flock of sheep, without conscience, compelled to be the soulless majority.

But I have said that I was conscious also of a feeling of repugnance. I do not like the tone of those words—they jar against something in my soul. "There is no salvation by anyone else, not even a second Name under heaven appointed for us men and our salvation."

I do not naturally like that kind of a speech. I cannot bear bigotry. I resent it with all my soul when any person or any institution says, "This is the truth and this alone, and all the rest is false." I resent it in religion more than I do in politics, and God knows any thoughful man ought to resent it in politics. We have seen it. The world is not safe from it. In whole countries no man has dared to differ from the authorities in our time.

I recoiled in thought from Simon Peter. It required some time, in spite of my extreme admiration for this gallant hero, to get on terms of sympathy with his arbitrary pronouncement which seemed to focus eternal truth upon a pin point.

I felt that after all Peter lived a long while ago in a remote little place before a thousand thousand things had come into being which are very real in the world today.

I wondered if he were here now, would he make the same assertion. I am sure if he did he would find himself up against a much greater number of authorities than he confronted in Jerusalem, authorities who would speak in the name of science and philosophy, in the name of political institutions, in the name of new learning and arbitrary forces imperfectly understood. I felt that those present-day challengers would not be so violent as the judges in old Jerusalem. They would be more supercilious, more contemptuous, more indifferent to the ignorant who withstood them—but much more decisive!

I looked around the rows of books in my study noting the names on the covers, names of great authority. It came to me how extraordinary it was that such a vast number of these books are really concerned with the things of Jesus. They may not mention his Name, but there does not seem to be anything in the world into which Jesus has not projected himself. His influence has penetrated into realms of thought and life where his feet never trod.

I reflected, as I looked around upon my books, that so many of the world's great ones have pronounced their verdicts upon Jesus. They have admired him; they have patronized him; the great ones with solemnity, the lesser ones with flippancy. But, sifted down to the bottom, they meant to say that he lived a long time ago when many things were not known which are known now. He launched a little boat on the Sea of Galilee that was

[15]

not built to weather the storms of the limitless ocean of destiny. To them it seemed fantastic to assert that amid a myriad of names and an unending succession of ideas there can be one Name only, one authoritative messenger only. Against this claim of Simon Peter's there would be a curling of the lips, no need for fiery denunciation. The voices of today assume that men will speak no more in the Name of Jesus, at least with finality.

Then it seemed to my imagination that Simon Peter himself walked into my room as if he were here with us now; as if, like some Rip Van Winkle who had slept through these nineteen centuries or more and was now a citizen of our time, looking out upon our world as he had looked out upon his own. I felt as if I were carrying on a conversation with him and I said to him, "Simon Peter, it was a very gallant thing you did and I revere you highly, but against the background of the world of today, would you say quite as confidently as you said, then, 'There is no salvation by anyone else, not even a second Name under heaven appointed for us men and our salvation'?" I had a feeling that he hesitated a moment, as if he confessed that there are many things in our world of which he had not been conscious in his time; as if admittedly strange things had happened during the long interval. Many great names have rung out across the earth. I felt as if he were pondering. I wondered if he had recalled, thinking back to his own life in Galilee, how once his friend John had said to the Master, "Master, we saw one casting out devils in thy name and he followeth not with us, and we forbade him because he followeth not with us." And the Master said, "Forbid him not. No man can cast out devils in my name and think lightly of me. He that is not against us is with us."

I wondered if he would remember how he himself had been reluctant to believe that a man like Cornelius, the Gentile soldier, could have the spirit of Christ in him. How he had needed to be startled out of his bigotry by a dream. How he had seen, as it were, a sheet let down from Heaven, a sheet containing creatures clean and unclean, and when bidden to eat he had said, "Never, I do not touch the unclean." I fancied that Simon Peter remembered that in his own lifetime he had had to learn charity. He was a singularly direct and simple man but he held his opinions with great tenacity and saw them through to the end.

I am sure he had to learn to widen his ideas during his own lifetime, and if he were with us today the necessity would be greater still.

Yet I had a feeling that after a moment he lifted himself up and looked me straight in the eye and said, "I said it then and I say it now—where is your second name? Whose name will you invoke? In all these nineteen or twenty centuries has any other man spoken as he spoke? Has any other man made the claims that he made? Has any other man died for our sins as he did? There have been many who have died because of our sins, but he died for them. Has any other man risen again from the dead as he did? Has any other man made credible such a claim?

"Do men say of any other man as they say of him, that God and he are one? Has any other man reached down into the depths of human sin or plumbed the abyss of human sorrow? Has any other man drawn men to God as he has done all down the centuries? I see no reason why I should obscure the splendor of his Name."

I thought he said, "I remember once when he faced us and said 'Who do men say that I am?' And my companions made their varying answers. Then he said again, more searchingly, 'But who do you say that I am?' And I said away there in Caesarea Philippi, 'Thou art the Christ.' And then, as some great surge of conviction came over me, I said, 'Thou art the Son of the Living God.' And having said that, how could I share his pre-eminence with anyone? What could I do but follow?"

Said Peter to me, or so I imagined: "The supreme question is whether God sent him. If God sent him, then it is with God you have to do. It is not your varying opinions. It is God. God is not forever improvising. He does not proceed by trial and error. Whatever he does, is done forever. You men must improvise. You try out part of the truth; find you went wrong; must try again. If not, the universe will convince you in the end. If God sent Christ, you must not seek to take him captive to all your changing whims. You must test them against the eternal rock of God's revealing. You had better explore the Christ, not exclude him."

Then I thought I said to him, "St. Peter, it was very simple for you. It is very difficult for us. You had that wonderful experience of long months of close fellowship with him. You looked into his eyes; his eyes looked into yours. What else could you say but, 'I will follow thee whithersoever thou goest'?

"But, St. Peter, people cannot see this Christ today. They cannot look into his eyes. They hear all manner of things said about him. His servants, his representatives, the theologians and churchmen—they say all manner of conflicting things about him, while in our modern world there are great disturbing things such as you never experienced in your day.

"The world has become strangely congested. It is the whole race of mankind we are dealing with now, not the people of Galilee on the shores of the little lake. Great mass movements, comprising millions of people who move like automats in obedience to world forces. The world we are living in is one where men have so imposed their organization that some ridiculously inadequate person can pull a lever and the whole machine throbs into life. After that we do our little bit of work by the moving belts, not knowing what we are making or whether it be good or evil. Why talk to us of personally following Jesus?

"St. Peter, it was simple for you. Folk now hardly know what to think about Jesus and they honestly do not know how to follow him. Many of them want to do it, but cannot make up their minds whether the things they must do are for him or against him."

And I thought he said, "I understand, but if you think it was simple for me because I saw him face to face, you are mistaken. I had scarcely said to him that day, 'Thou art the Christ the Son of the Living God,' when a few moments afterwards I said something that saddened and angered him so that he turned upon me and said, 'Get thee behind me, Satan, thou art an offense unto me. Thou savorest of the things of men, not the things of God.'

"It shocked me that day to be so persuaded of his divinity and yet to grieve him so soon afterwards. I remember too that we all forsook him when he was crucified and I cannot forget that I denied him three times when he had no friends in the world, when he stood, as I myself stood later on, alone with all the odds against him. Then it was I said, 'I never knew Him.' I said it three times.

"I had to learn. I had to find out what it meant to follow him. There were lots of occasions when I did not know . . . when the Gentiles were crowding into the church, outraging all my Jewish prejudice and protective care for sacred things. I did not know what to do to follow Christ. I had to find out just as people have to today. I knew that a light had shined upon me. I could never forget the light. No matter how often I stumbled, I did not turn back—I followed him only by hearkening to the voices that were deepest within my soul. I followed him often through darkness, through confusion, but I could not turn away from him.

"Once he said to us twelve, 'Will ye also go away?' And I said to him then, 'Lord, to whom shall we go? Thou hast the words of eternal life.' Believe me, it does not make as much difference as you think to have been close to Jesus, or to be as you are, far away from him, in terms of history. But if you know him as the light you must follow—and surely at no time in history has that been more necessary than now in your day—the time will come as surely as you are alive—it has almost come now, when the vast combinations will say to you, 'You must not challenge established order with your task of following Jesus.' You have seen it in Germany. You may see it elsewhere, even in your own country.

"There will come times when there will seem to be no way through but engaging in customs and practices that in your souls you loathe, and yet this light will keep burning in your souls. The time will come when you will say 'The forces are too great for us, we will extinguish the light.' Then you will become all that you hated, all that you fought against, because having fought successfully you finally surrendered to the essentially evil thing against which you fought. Now, believe me, as long as the world rolls on it will mean no other way to follow Jesus Christ than to be true to the light, even when it costs you what you are afraid to pay."

And I thought I said, "Ah, St. Peter, it must have been fine to be living when you were living with that little band of devoted disciples who changed the world by their courage and tenacity. What a church you had in your day! It had very little organization but was energized by loyal souls. If I only knew where to find them, how quickly I would link up with them;

how quickly! But in our day what we call churches are full of all sorts of people. We do not know why they are there or what they believe at all. They make of the Christ a shrine for their prejudices, a cover for their arrogance. It is very depressing in our day to link up with the church and be one of its members. Some of them are so narrow, some so uncharitable and nonprogressive."

I thought he said, "Do you think it was not like that in my day? Do you imagine everybody in the early church was utterly devoted? Have you forgotten that even among twelve there was one who betrayed him, or that even I at one time denied him?

"We were no more perfect in that day than men are in your day. Surely you have not read my letters if you think otherwise. Do you not remember, in what you call my second letter, some of the things I said in the violence of my emotion?

"I said to some of them, 'You are wells without water; you are like winds that blow over deserts; you are servants of iniquity.' I said once, so indignant was I, 'You are like dogs that return to their vomit; you are like sows that had been washed and have returned again to their wallowing in the mire.'

"I know that the church of that day was perfect no more than yours may be. If we had waited for a perfect church we would never have carried the message onward to you. You would never have known of him.

"You have got to follow the highest, and if you can find anything higher, follow it through to the end. If your Christ grows upon you as he ought, to follow him will mean something you had never dreamed of before. That is what he came for. He did not come to put over one fixed system upon the world. He came to bring a quickening spirit into the world—and we are to follow, even when we can barely see the way."

And I thought he said, with a radiant smile at last, "You object to my words because you think they express narrow bigotry. You think my claim was too exclusive. Christ's Name is all-inclusive. Every good thing in the world belongs to his Name. He is not against your science. He is against the application of your science to the degradation of mankind. He is not against your airplanes. He is against their dropping death upon helpless people. He would make them vehicles of mercy, truth and brotherhood. That is one name. It is one name because it is an inclusive name. It is the only name in your world of today that is all-inclusive. You even now build a new world which would unite all races for true salvation—and there is still no other name.

"Are the names of the great men whom today you revere sufficiently inclusive? No, they belong to one race, one nation, one class or one system which asserts itself against others. The Name of Christ belongs to any man—to your enemies as well as to your friends. You have more to do with them than just to exterminate them. Had you carried the Name and Spirit of Christ forward in your developing civilization, you might not have had now the situation that made a global war inevitable.

"The only Name even yet in your world that means the everlasting brotherhood of mankind, the absolute refusal to finally accept hate as the solvent of human woes; the so-called patriotic truth that denies the universal truth; the apocalypse of destruction for the revelation of salvation, is the name that I singled out back there in Jerusalem as the One and only Name. It is not bigotry; it is tolerance. It is not one exclusive ecclesiastical institution; it is one universal spirit. There is still no salvation except in the recovery and the widening application of that spirit."

Little old Jerusalem was a microcosm; the great seething world of today is a microcosm, and still the man counts who, standing before a tremendous destiny, can gather up his life, his labor, and his hope in the One indestructible NAME! that alone redeems them all.

He Came Too Soon, This Christ

REVEREND G. BROMLEY OXNAM, LITT.D., D.D., LL.D.
Resident Bishop, The Methodist Church, New York

Bishop Oxnam is one of the great religious statesmen of our time. A native of California, he studied at the University of Southern California, Boston University School of Theology, Harvard University, and Massachusetts Institute of Technology. He also did research in Japan, China and India.

His first pastorate was at Poplar, California, in 1916. In 1917 he founded the Church of All Nations in Los Angeles and developed there the leading social service institution on the Pacific Coast. He was elected Bishop of the Methodist Church at the 1936 General Conference and was assigned to the Omaha Area, where he served for three years. In 1939 he was assigned to the Boston Area, and in 1944, to New York. In addition to his episcopal duties, he is president of the Federal Council of the Churches of Christ in America and is a member of the Federal Council's Commission to study the bases of a just and durable peace. He is secretary of the Council of Bishops, president of the Foreign Division of the Board of Missions and Church Extension, vice-chairman of the Methodist Commission on Chaplains and of the General Commission on Army and Navy Chaplains, and has been serving the National War Labor Board as a special mediator in labor disputes.

Bishop Oxnam has been closely identified with education. During his pastorate at the Church of All Nations, he was professor of social ethics at the University of Southern California from 1919 to 1923. In 1927 he became

*a member of the faculty at Boston University School of Theology as professor
of practical theology and the city church, and was president of DePauw
University from 1928 to 1936.*

*The Bishop's travels have led him into most of the countries of Europe
and Asia. He was a member of the American Delegation to Russia in 1926,
of the Japanese Education Commission of the International Missionary
Council in 1932, and a delegate to the World Conferences at Edinburgh
and Oxford in 1937. Among his written works are* The Mexican in Los
Angeles, Social Principles of Jesus, Russian Impressions, Youth and the
New America, The Ethical Ideals of Jesus in a Changing World, Behold
Thy Mother, Preaching in a Revolutionary Age, Labor and Tomorrow's
World.

*In 1940 he gave the Enoch Pond Lectures at Bangor Seminary, the
Merrick Lectures at Ohio Wesleyan University in 1941, lectures at Florida
Southern College School of Religion in 1941, the Fondren Lectures at
Southern Methodist University in 1944, the Lyman Beecher Lectures on
Preaching at Yale University in 1944, and the Earl Lectures at the Pacific
School of Religion in 1945.*

Sermon Four

IN HIS play, *The Wingless Victory*, Maxwell Anderson has written a
tragedy that strangely enough may be called beautiful. It is phrased in
the strong, simple English of Elizabethan days, and speaks of the terrible
nemesis that forever pursues intolerance. The scene is laid in Salem, Massachusetts, about the year 1800. Nathaniel McQueston and his wife Oparre
are the central characters. He is a sea captain who left Salem in poverty to
return in wealth. Oparre is a Malay princess, who had saved his life. They
return with their two children, to meet the bitter rebuff of racial prejudice, a
rebuff in this instance made the more bitter by the covetous spirit of the
self-righteous who envied his possessions.

Oparre, once a worshiper of the tribal gods of revenge and blood, is drawn
to the gentle, kindly Christ. She seeks to win the love of her husband's
people; but they are cruel in their intolerance, even though, in pleading
declaration, they hear her say, "Still carrying in my heart the secret Christ
by whom you live, I answer, I am your friend." But she warns them, "Dark
as your words have been, dark as your looks at me, evil as you may think
you are, your evil is as the play of children to the world we two have left
behind." But they will have none of her, nor her children. They would ruin
her husband. At last she speaks to her husband's brother, a clergyman, whose
prejudice is the more terrible because of the very passion of religion: "Sir,
if this winter coast is tarnished by our footsteps in the snow, as I fear it

might be; if the Christ you worship gives sanctuary only to his own lest they be polluted, say this at once, and we shall rouse the children and be away. I came only with a hope."

They have their way with her, and in a moment of awful trial her husband falters, broken by the overwhelming pressure of the community. Knowing that she must leave, and leave alone, save for her children and a faithful servant, she repudiates the Christ, rejects all; turns once again to the gods of earth and blood. She boards the ship, resolved to die and to take her little ones with her. She speaks of "unwanted babes" and of the "drink of darkness." Taking the poison, with broken heart, we hear her say, "We shall sleep and turn to nameless ground." Awaiting the end, she kneels to utter a prayer, her last. It is addressed to the gods she knew.

> The earth rolls toward the dark, and men begin to sleep. God of the children, god of the lesser children of the earth, the black, the unclean, the vengeful, you are mine now as when I was a child. He came too soon, this Christ of peace. Men are not ready yet. Another hundred thousand years they must drink your potion of tears and blood. . . .[1]

"He came too soon, this Christ of peace. Men are not ready yet. Another hundred thousand years. . . ." "He came too soon, this Christ."

Paul, the apostle, believed Christ had come in the fullness of time. Oparre, the Malay princess, thought he had come too soon. A court, charged with decision, might conclude that the evidence justifies the contention of Oparre rather than of Paul.

It is written that the common people heard him gladly; but he was despised and rejected. The long-awaited Messiah had come too soon. Barabbas was released. Jesus was crucified. It was not the recitation of a line from a predestined drama. It was the crucifixion of a poor Galilean, who had come too soon. Surely the Garden of Gethsemane was more than a predetermined scene from the pen of the Eternal Playwright.

Did the brokenhearted young Christ who would have the cup pass from him, who feared the Father had forsaken him, believe he had come too soon? There was so much more he desired to tell them; but he said, "Ye cannot bear it now."

> When Jesus came to Golgotha
> They hanged Him on a tree
> They drove great nails through hand and feet,
> And made a Calvary;
> They crowned Him with a crown of thorns,
> Red were His wounds and deep,
> For those were crude and cruel days
> And human flesh was cheap.
> —G. A. Studdert-Kennedy[2]

[1] From *The Wingless Victory*, by Maxwell Anderson.
[2] "Indifference," from *The Sorrows of God*, by G. A. Studdert-Kennedy. Harper & Brothers, publishers.

He had come too soon!

Oparre might well call upon the court to note the many centuries of struggle, unfortunately not yet concluded, wherein man lived the fighting way of life. The warrior was king. There are those who yet believe that strength comes through struggle. They insist that man is ruled by an inner urge to survive. They argue that nature is red in tooth and claw, and if man would survive he must be fit, physically fit. They tell us this is the fundamental reality beneath the thin veneer which man hypocritically calls civilization. Did Christ come too soon? Is our biological heritage too strong? Is this talk of the strong bearing the burdens of the weak, of laying down a life for a friend, of finding life in losing it, the demand of a poor dreamer? Are we fated to struggle on, until at last the groups that have survived because they have learned to co-operate in fighting against their environment develop enough of the co-operative spirit to realize at last that mutual aid must be carried into all the activities of men? Oparre would not be alone in that courtroom. Regardless of the millions who bow before cross or crucifix, there are many millions more who argue, "This Christ came too soon." His teachings, we are told, are but the evanescent pictures of perfectionist ethics projected upon a silver screen. They insist that the Christ who came too soon must be taught the futility of the distant ideal.

A Chinese Christian said, "You cannot teach men to love their enemies in the twinkling of an eye." It is still an eye for an eye. The fighting way of life carries on; and grows more brutal in the very refinement of the money-making way of life. Here the financier is king. Sidney Lanier, poet of the South, tells us that "Trade is war grown miserly."

You came too soon, Galilean, too soon to talk of the second mile, the cloak, the cup of cold water—too soon to tell of houses builded on the sand, of new barns, and Mammon—too soon for Matthew and Zacchaeus, for broken alabaster and forgiven sins. Puritanical codes justify flinging the first and the last stone. Too soon to behold Mary of the streets become Mary of the saints! We are still in the fighting way of life, the money-making way of life, it is argued. Jesus dreamed of a personality-making way of life in which the suffering servant would be king. But we are forced, Oparre might say, to be awake to the realities, the realities of the fighting way of life, of the money-making way of life. Were this poor Malay princess addressing the court, with what overwhelming argument might she build her case! She would repeat it, "Your Christ came too soon, I say. Look, if you will, to the Eternal City. Was it not upon a rock your church was built? Is it not called Saint Peter's Church? Did not the man Paul who was so sure that Jesus came in the fullness of time, did he not lie in prison there? Did he not die there? I know that he wrote:

> I may speak with the tongues of men and of angels,
>   but if I have no love,
>   I am a noisy gong or a clanging cymbal;

I may prophesy, fathom all mysteries and secret lore,
I may have such absolute faith that I can move
   hills from their place,
   but if I have no love,
     I count for nothing;
I may distribute all I possess in charity,
I may give up my body to be burnt,
   but if I have no love,
     I make nothing of it.

Love is very patient, very kind. Love knows no
jealousy; love makes no parade, gives itself no
airs, is never rude, never selfish, never irritated,
never resentful; love is never glad when others go
wrong, love is gladdened by goodness, always slow to
expose, always eager to believe the best, always
hopeful, always patient. Love never disappears. . . .

Thus 'faith and hope and love last on, these three,'
but the greatest of all is love."[3]

But he, like his Lord, came too soon. The ancient Roman was ready for the Christ of Empire. He could envision the Empire that was to be, the Holy Roman Empire. The Roman conqueror could understand killing in the name of the very cross upon which Jesus had been killed—"By this sign conquer." No, he was not too soon for the empire builders, this Empire Christ. But the Christ of Love, the peasant who had no place to lay his head, he came too soon. They were ready, these medieval theologians, for the Christ of Dogma. With what delight did they create the formula to explain him! Actually, they buried him in another tomb. They bound him with creedal graveclothes. He was not too soon, this Christ of the Councils. But the Christ who declared, "I am the way, the truth and the life," this Jesus who knew the truth would make us free, he came too soon.

The woes that Jesus uttered were directed to the Scribes and Pharisees. Were they uttered too soon? "You are all brothers . . . for One is your Heavenly Father." Moffatt translates the next verse; "One is your leader, even the Christ." You came too soon, Christ; we have other leaders. He who would be greatest among you must become the servant of all. It is to laugh. Whoever humbles himself will be uplifted—absurd! And is there not a danger in the Church itself? Some churchmen have become so enamored with the very idea of the Church that they regard the Church as an end in itself rather than as a means to create the Kingdom. Will we say he came too soon, with his insistence upon finding life by losing it? When he scathingly denounced the Pharisees, did he not refer to swearing by the sanctuary, the altar, the gift? Did he not talk of tithes of mint and anise and cumin? Is there not danger that we, too, may forget the weightier matters of the law?

[3] I Cor. 13:1-13. From *The Bible: A New Translation*, by James Moffatt. Harper & Brothers, publishers.

"He came too soon, this Christ. Men are not ready yet. Another hundred thousand years. . . ."? Or is the Church to be one in declaring, "Now is the accepted time"? Not "Now is the appointed time," but "Now is the accepted time."

Now is the time to cease postponing the idea of brotherhood. Now is the time to take it and enthrone it. Let us not associate the idea of holy love with altar alone, but relate it to mill and mine and market. Let us take the idea of a Father of all mankind and translate that idea into instruments that make for a brotherly world. Let us have done once and for all with the atheism that lies in pagan statements bandied about by nominal Christians who declare, "Self-interest is the only sufficient motive to drive men to real achievement"; "moral right must bow to economic necessity"; "war is inevitable." Now is the accepted time. Christ did not come too soon. We came to Christ too late.

I make bold to relate an incident, once again news, when Constitution Hall is denied to artists who are black. It was not the Daughters of the Confederacy—no, it was the Daughters of the American Revolution—who refused Marian Anderson the right to sing in Constitution Hall. Let us forget that and turn rather to the expression of an Americanism worthy of the founders of this Republic—I refer to the concert given there upon the steps of the Lincoln Memorial on a prewar Sunday—it seems but yesterday. I saw men and women of the South, distinguished leaders of this nation, among the great who had come to pay tribute to a voice. I saw them sitting there while she sang. I can see her now, black against the white marble. There he sat "With malice toward none" dreaming of government "of the people, by the people, and for the people." And she sang *America*. "My country, 'tis of thee, Sweet land of liberty." And then we heard *Ave Maria* ("Hail Mary"). A black girl—Hail Mary, a Jewish girl. Send that message across the sea, and let them know One is our leader, even Christ. And as she sang that day, I realized full well that now is the accepted time to take our conceptions of justice and of brotherhood and translate them into actualities.

The Inescapable Christ

REVEREND BENJAMIN E. MAYS, PH.D.
*A Minister of the Baptist Church; President, Morehouse College,
Atlanta, Georgia*

Dr. Mays was educated at South Carolina State College, at Bates College in
Maine and at the University of Chicago. He has served in various capacities:
pastor of the Shiloh Baptist Church of Atlanta; teacher of higher mathematics in Morehouse College and of English in the State College of South
Carolina; executive secretary of the Tampa, Florida, Urban League; national
student secretary of the Y.M.C.A.; director of a study of the Negro churches
in the United States under the auspices of the Institute of Social and Religious Research in New York, out of which study grew his book, The Negro
Church, written in collaboration with J. W. Nicholson.

His next position took him to Washington, D.C., where he became dean
of Howard University School of Religion from 1934 to 1940. He has represented the United States at various world conferences on the Church and
the Y.M.C.A. between 1937 and 1939: Mysore, India; Oxford, England;
Stockholm, Sweden; and Amsterdam, Holland.

Dr. Mays' many writings include articles in the Crisis, the Christian
Century, Christendom, Religion in Life, the Woman's Press, Journal of
Religious Thought, Journal of Negro Education and Missions. In 1939 his
second book, The Negro's God, was published. In December, 1944, Dr. Mays
was elected vice-president of the Federal Council of the Churches of Christ
in America. His sermon reveals his deep faith in Christ and all men's need
of him.

Sermon Five

TEXT: Pilate saith unto them, What then shall I do unto Jesus who is called Christ? They all say, Let him be crucified.

MATTHEW 27:22 (American Standard Revised Version)

FOR nineteen centuries Jesus has been a disturbing element in society. And for nineteen centuries the world has been trying to get rid of Jesus. We don't like him! We don't like him! We don't like him! Nineteen hundred years ago a man by the name of Pilate raised a baffling question, and what turned out to be in subsequent years an embarrassing question—"What then shall I do unto Jesus who is called Christ?" Almost two thousand years have passed by, yet the question is more pertinent in 1946 than it was then. What shall I do with Christ? What shall the nations of the world do with Christ? For nineteen hundred long years the world has been trying to answer the question, What shall I do with Christ?

Yielding to the demands of the crowd, Pilate thought he could save himself and get rid of Jesus by allowing him to be crucified, by washing his hands, saying, "I am innocent of the blood of this just man." But no man can get rid of Jesus by washing his hands and no man can get rid of Jesus by shirking the responsibility which God has placed upon him. We may not always rise to the demands of the hour; we may not always do that which we know we ought to do; we may even excuse ourselves as did Pilate saying, "I am innocent." But no man can ever get rid of Jesus that way. Nearly two thousand years have passed, but the world has not forgiven Pilate. It looks upon Pilate as a man in high office who had the mind to see what was good to do and who had the power to execute the right but who lacked the moral courage to do what he knew was right. And to see the light, to know the good, to perceive the true and not to be able to follow them—to see the high road and take the low road—that's a calamity, that's a lost soul.

And herein lies the tragedy of our time! We are confused and baffled today not because we do not know the right path, not because we are imbeciles in the mind or morons in the head, but because we are imbeciles in the heart and morons in the spirit. Never before in the history of the world have we developed so many brilliant minds, never before have we unearthed so many vital scientific facts, never before have we made so many physical improvements and brought so much material convenience to the world; yet we are more bewildered today than at any time in the history of the world— primarily because we lack the moral courage to do with our hearts and hands

[27]

that which we see with our minds. No! It isn't more light we need, important as light is. It isn't more truth we need, important as truth is. It isn't more scientific data, important as scientific data are. It is more Christ, more courage, more spiritual insight to act on the light we have. Pilate had plenty of light —so much light that he admitted that he found no fault in Jesus; but he lacked the moral courage to live up to the light he had. No! We cannot get rid of Christ by washing our hands nor by shirking our responsibility, nor by protesting that we are innocent. Jesus is real and he cannot be dismissed with a wave of the hand or a shrug of the shoulder.

Fearing the crowd, Pilate sacrificed an innocent man in order to save himself. Too often we sacrifice the right because we fear the immediate consequences of our actions. Right decisions frequently involve physical suffering and the temporary loss of position and prestige. Pilate, no doubt, would have exonerated Jesus if he could have believed that no harm would befall him.

How typical of our day and generation! We know enough about the physical and ethical implications of sin to live better and purer lives. We know enough about the cruelties and injuries in race relations to approximate the Kingdom of God in that area. We know enough about war, its cause and effects, to abolish it from the face of the earth. But we aren't willing to take the moral leadership and to run the risks involved in that leadership. Like Pilate of old, we fear the consequences to us if we do what we know is right. We may shirk our responsibility at these points, but we cannot get rid of Jesus that way.

There were others who sought to get rid of Jesus by crucifying him. Both the Romans and the Jews used this method. To the Romans Jesus was a traitor, unpatriotic, disloyal. To the Pharisees he was a heretic. To the Sadducees he was a menace to correct procedure. To the Zealots he was a coward and spineless. To the members of his own family he was out of his mind. When asked by Pilate, "What shall I do with Jesus which is called Christ?" they cried out, "Let him be crucified." They thought that they could get rid of Jesus by nailing him to a cross. But Jesus could not be so readily dismissed. Three days after the crucifixion the news got abroad that he was alive. The discouraged disciples who had gone back to their former occupations rallied around him again. A few days later Peter stood up at Pentecost and said that this same Jesus, "whom ye have crucified," had been lifted up and made both Lord and Christ. Out of this experience sprang the Christian Church to hold up the name of the Crucified Christ. And all the way from Stephen to the martyrs of the church in Germany, people by the millions have gone out to do battle for the Lord. We could not get rid of Jesus by nailing him to a cross. "Truth, crushed to earth, shall rise again."

Other devious methods have been used in our attempt to get rid of Jesus. Some have reduced him to the role of a man—a good man, probably better than the average—yea a prophet, but nevertheless a man. They would classify him along with the great prophets of Israel—Micah, Amos, Jeremiah and others; but beyond that they would not go. They would attribute to him no peculiar role of Saviour except the fact that he has indicated one of the ways that may lead to salvation. Therefore his way of salvation is to be taken no more seriously than the ways advocated by other great reformers. There is absolutely nothing divine about him. What he achieved in his life and person, you and I can achieve. But you cannot get rid of Jesus by making him a mere man. Any honest man who sets out to follow Jesus the man and goes with him through the Sermon on the Mount, goes with him through Gethsemane and the cross, with him at the Resurrection, will end up by saying: "My Lord and my God."

There are others who try to answer the question about Jesus by arguing that he is out-of-date, that his ethics and ideals were probably all right in days when a minority group found itself unable to resist with the sword the oppressive hands of Rome. The way of Jesus is the way of the weak and the coward, not of the strong and the militant. A weak people, unable to take what it wants, may find it advantageous to preach a gospel of love and to insist that nonresistance is the only way of life. But only the weakling would subscribe to the ethics and teachings of the Man of Galilee. The ethics of Jesus is the ethics of the underprivileged. Jesus was all right in his day, when life was simple and when civilization was far less complex than it is now. But he lived nearly two thousand years ago when social and political conditions differed widely from those that exist at present. How foolish it is to take the principles and teachings of Jesus enunciated over nineteen hundred years ago and try to make them applicable to modern problems when science has revealed to us a new world of which Jesus never dreamed! We might as well do as the humanists and the Communists do—try to lift ourselves by our own bootstraps and sing with Langston Hughes, *Good-by, Christ*. But we cannot get rid of Jesus by calling him out-of-date. It is true now and it will be true a million years from now that the hope for man lies in the direction which Jesus has indicated.

Some have tried to get rid of Jesus by denying his historicity. These argue that no such man as Jesus ever lived. The story of Jesus is a myth, a creation of the imagination. But we cannot get rid of Jesus by denying his historicity. Even if we could prove that Jesus never lived, experience testifies that the things attributed to him are real and inescapable.

But perhaps the most subtle and devastating answer to the question, "What shall I do with Christ?" comes from modern customs and practices. In 325, at Nicaea, we made Jesus a God, of one substance with the Father. At Nicaea, at Constantinople, at Ephesus, at Chalcedon, and in all subsequent creeds up to the dawn of the twentieth century, we dealt with Christ primarily on the basis of creeds, dogmas and rituals. And the ethical and moral teachings of Jesus were never written into the great creeds of Christendom. On the basis of the creeds, it seems possible to get into the Kingdom of God and hate your brother. We get rid of Jesus today by praising his holy name. We write scholarly books concerning him. We compose beautiful hymns to him; we sing inspiring songs about him. We paint beautiful pictures in adoration of him. We meet on Sunday and through the week to offer long prayers to him. We send missionaries to foreign lands to convert the heathen and teach them how to worship the God revealed through Jesus Christ. We defend his divinity and split hairs over what he did or did not teach. We magnify his name by erecting beautiful churches. We spend millions upon millions of dollars in the construction of cathedrals in order to make the house where God dwells beautiful, entire and clean. I have seen and worshiped in St. Paul's and Westminster Abbey; I have seen Westminster Cathedral and bowed my head in adoration in Notre Dame. I have seen the Cathedral of Cologne and I have seen some of the great churches and chapels of America. And when I see what is happening in the world today, I know we are trying to get rid of Jesus by building costly churches and by praising his holy name.

We talk glibly about the Prince of Peace. We sing fervently, "Joy to the World; the Lord is Come," "Silent Night," "Hark! the Herald Angels Sing," and "It Came Upon the Midnight Clear"—and yet, as we sing, we prepare for war. We go out to build the best army, the finest navy, the most durable airplanes, and each nation puts its chemists to work to discover the most deadly gases. The national debt may soar sky high, depressions may come and depressions may go, unemployment may mount on wings, and slow starvation wages may take thousands to their graves, but the preparation for war must go on. And when the war comes, we bless it in the name of Jesus. We call it a holy war, and we ask God to join us in our holy crusade to help kill other men who are his children and our brothers.

Let us hear the conclusion of the whole matter. We cannot get rid of Jesus. The only way to get rid of Jesus is to accept him in mind, in heart, and in soul. Jesus represents God and God is the absolute—not man, not race, not economic nor political systems—but God. And whenever man in his arrogance and pride sets himself up as the absolute, he will be beaten to the ground.

It was Napoleon who said: "The more I study the world, the more I am convinced of the inability of force to create anything durable. Alexander, Caesar, Charlemagne, and I have built empires. But upon what did they depend? They depended upon force. But Jesus Christ built his empire upon love and until this day millions will die for him."

Everywhere we turn we meet this man Jesus. When our anger gets out of control and we would enjoy inflicting the death blow upon another, we hear Jesus saying to us: "It is not enough not to kill; you must not get angry." "Love your enemies, bless them that curse you, do good to them that hate you, and pray for them which despitefully use you, and persecute you; that ye may be the children of your Father which is in heaven."

Jesus will not let my conscience be at ease. When we take advantage of the poor, the weak and the helpless just because they are poor, weak and helpless, we meet Jesus. He speaks softly but convincingly to us, telling us that when we take advantage of the helpless we take advantage of God, that when we hurt man we hurt God, that when we rob man we rob God, that when we kill man we kill God. Everywhere we turn, we meet this man, Jesus. He will not let my conscience be at ease. He haunts me in my dreams, he disturbs me in my business. When man lets his passion get the better of him and he lusts after a woman, he meets Jesus there, saying: "He who looks after a woman to lust after her has committed adultery already in his heart." Everywhere I turn, I meet him. He will not let my conscience be at ease. When we condemn and criticize others for their shortcomings, we hear Jesus saying to us: "He who is free from sin, let him cast the first stone." Everywhere I turn, I meet Jesus. When we are inclined to exercise our prejudice against a member of another race, we meet Jesus there. He tells us that a certain man went down from Jerusalem to Jericho and fell among thieves; and that it was a member of another race who came to his rescue, setting forth the eternal fact that he who responds helpfully to human need is your neighbor.

Everywhere I turn I meet this man, Jesus. He will not let my conscience be at ease. When we would build peace on war and an economic system on injustice, he whispers to us, "You can't do it that way." "Except the Lord build the house, they labor in vain that build it. Except the Lord keepeth the city the watchman waketh but in vain." Throughout the ages, man has tried to do it otherwise, and throughout the ages he has failed. There is something in the nature of the universe which says you can't do it that way and thrive.

God has decreed through the resurrected Lord that the world will never be what it ought to be until we develop an international ethics and learn that the fear of the Lord is the beginning of wisdom. As long as France distrusts Germany and Germany France; as long as Italy looks with suspecting eyes upon England and England cannot rely on Italy; as long as Japan has no confidence in China and China none in Japan—there is going to be war. And a billion armies will not be able to keep the peace. If all the world should turn communist tomorrow, fascist tomorrow; if all the world should develop democratic governments tomorrow—our social and economic problems would be essentially the same, if there were no radical change of heart.

Our trouble is not economic. It is not political. It is ethical and moral. The world is suffering today from spiritual and moral bankruptcy. And no political or economic system can permanently endure unless it is basically ethical and essentially moral. God has decreed that he is the absolute—not

[31]

man, not races, not nations, not political and economic systems—but God. As long as man moves contrary to these laws, God will beat him down. Kingdoms will rise and fall, races will degenerate, economic systems will collapse until we learn that the fear of the Lord is the beginning of wisdom.

Approximately nineteen hundred years ago, a Jew of Palestine hanged on a cross, dying between two thieves, because he dreamed a dream—that all men are sons of God, and when we hurt man we hurt God. Some blessed day a stupid world will rise to the divinity of God and acknowledge Jesus as Lord. Then the nations of the earth will know that armies and navies, battleships and machine guns, airplanes and submarines will never bring peace to a suffering world. And that the acquisitions of political, material and commercial powers are not permanent possessions, but are as "the vapors of night. They fade and die in the morning of reality."

"What shall I do then with Jesus which is called Christ?" The only answer is: Accept him—in our minds, in our hearts, in our wills, and in our souls.

The Robe

THE MOST REVEREND LOUIS F. KELLEHER, D.D.
*Titular Bishop of Thenae and Auxiliary
Roman Catholic Bishop of Boston*

Bishop Kelleher knows and loves the people of the parishes in the Archdiocese of Boston, and he is one of the popular Catholic preachers of New England. He was born fifty-five years ago in Cambridge, Massachusetts, and received his early education at old St. Mary's school. Later he distinguished himself at Boston College by his careful scholarship and unusual oratorical abilities, and his work has been recognized by that college with the Doctor of Laws degree. He attended North American College in Rome and received his degree from the University of the Propaganda with high honors.

Ordained to the priesthood in April, 1915, his three years as a curate in Jamaica Plain are remembered for his devotion to the sick during the influenza epidemic. Recognizing his genius of intellect the late Cardinal O'Connell appointed him to St. John's Seminary and later characterized him as its most brilliant teacher. During seventeen years as professor of dogmatic theology his superior abilities, priestly example and great personal charm endeared him to his students, one of whom is the present Archbishop of Boston.

In the pulpit and classroom, in public addresses and on the radio, His

Excellency's style is noted for a rugged simplicity, originality of thought and an abundance of ideas presented with an economy of phrase. An authority on St. Paul, the Bishop's purity of style and vigor of expression show the influence of the writings of this great saint. An expert in dramatics, he has produced and directed many outstanding plays. As pastor of St. John's, Canton, and St. Catherine's, Somerville, his scholarly nature and love of children, which draw him daily into the classrooms of the parish schools, have endeared him to all. Called to the episcopate by Pope Pius XII, he was consecrated Bishop on June 8, 1945. This sermon, in his usual simplicity of style, treats a very old question, what became of Christ's robe after his crucifixion? It was preached in St. Catherine's Church, Somerville, Massachusetts, on Good Friday, March 30, 1945.

Sermon Six

TEXT: And crucifying him, they divided his garments, casting lots upon them, what every man should take. MARK 15:24 (Douay Bible)

THE story of Good Friday is the story of Him Who hanged upon the cross looking down and of those who stood about the hill of Calvary looking up at the bleeding figure of the dying Jesus. Of these latter this sermon is concerned, particularly with the Roman soldiers who were there under orders to carry out the sentence of the crucifixion.

These soldiers were four in number. This was the fixed number of the guard in cases of capital punishment according to army regulations. The same Roman laws that determined the duties of the executioners of Jesus also established their rights. Did these soldiers have any rights? They did; it was written in Roman law that to them belonged the spoils of the one condemned.

What did Jesus possess that was worth their having? The Son of Man was so poor that He never had whereon to lay His head. And though He was dying the death of a criminal, yet He was no thief who might have concealed about His person a remnant of His ill-gotten goods.

All that He owned was His clothing. Of this he had been stripped before being nailed to the cross and there it lay in a heap on the ground, wet and soiled with His sweat and blood.

The garments of Jesus consisted of five articles: His cloak, His sandals, His headdress, His belt and His tunic. Five pieces of clothing, four soldiers among whom to divide them. Here was a difficulty—how to measure out an assorted lot of five so as to satisfy four claimants.

Soldiers in all times have a quick and effective way of settling arguments. They let the roll of the dice decide. By this resort to a game of chance, four pieces of Our Lord's apparel passed one by one to their new owners. Lastly there remained for disposal the tunic, and hardened though these rough soldiers were in their tastes, it did not take them long to see that the Robe of Christ of all His garments was the most desirable because of its material and workmanship. For this reason there arose a discussion among them. At first, they thought to divide it into four parts so that each would have an equal share. But seeing that it was without seam, they said: "Let us not cut it but let us cast lots for it, whose it shall be."

Again the dice were cast.

All the while the soldiers made His clothing the stakes of the game they played, Jesus was looking down upon them without remonstrance from the cross. What were His thoughts of this monstrous deed? Raising His eyes heavenward, He prayed: "Father forgive them, for they know not what they do."

It would be interesting to know which of the four soldiers won the seamless Robe of Christ? What was his name? What did he do with the Robe? Did he give it away or sell it to someone else? Did he keep it and wear it—for a curse or for a blessing? Wearing it, was he a jarring actor moving across the stage of this world, casting a shadow that did not match his figure, himself leading a wicked life, his frame draped in the coat of the Innocent One? Or wearing it, was his life consonant with his assumed habiliment; did virtue emanate from the Robe so that through a holy contact a miracle was worked, a convert made, and because a soul was gained, in that gain that began at the foot of the cross, Christ was the winner in the end?

The subject opens itself wide to speculation. The possibilities are well-nigh limitless. Only God knows what actually happened.

An American author of the present time felt himself intrigued by the question of what became of the garment of Christ for which the soldiers on Calvary gambled, and wrote a novel having for its title *The Robe*. Despite all the godlessness and ignorance of Christ of the present age, this book has had a sale of several hundred thousands of copies, a sign that religion is still capable of making a strong appeal to the hearts of many Americans, and a proof that whoever explores the path of a religious theme will have many to join him in an interested and sympathetic companionship.

Fiction aside, speaking now in accord with a holy tradition, light can be thrown on what became of the Robe by calling attention to the place where it is at present treasured. The Cathedral of Treves in Germany possesses this holy relic of Our Lord's passion, said to have been given to this ancient church by St. Helena in the fourth century. It was last exhibited for the veneration of the faithful in the year 1891 and attracted two million pilgrims.

Our Saviour from His cross was not the only one to behold with sorrow the spoliation and division of His garments. His mother who stood nearby also saw with wounded heart this woeful spectacle of man's barbarity. What mother would not stand aghast at the desecration of the personal belongings of her son! In these times of war with its bitter separations, many a mother in the home steals a tender glance during the day at the suit of clothes her boy left behind when from civilian life he was inducted into the armed forces of his country. The room he occupied, the bed he slept in, every object he owned are sacred souvenirs that it would be a profanation to approach and touch except with becoming reverence and affection.

Not the least among the many sorrows of the Mother of Christ was the pain she suffered when the rude soldiers with unfeeling manners appropriated to themselves the clothing of her dearly loved Son.

Her affliction was all the greater because, as Catholic tradition has it, her laborious hands had made this robe for her Son. The coat that Jesus wore was the work of His own Mother's love.

Mothers of young heroes in the military services—anxious for the safety of your sons on their distant, perilous stations, desirous for peace and your sons' return—listen. Let me show you a lesson contained in the seamless robe that the Blessed Virgin made for her Son. Seated at the loom she had fashioned it "woven from the top throughout," as St. John describes it in his gospel. Because it was the work of a mother's love, it was something perfect of its kind. One piece it was, without parts or divisions.

In this seamless garment of Our Saviour that His Mother's love had woven, I see and I present to you, Mothers of today, a pattern of a united world to be effected through the irresistible workings of the Love of Mothers.

A sanguinary war has divided this world against itself. One harmonious world—this is the strong desire of men of good will, shocked by this awful catastrophe that has darkened the lives of us all. ONE WORLD—how can it be achieved? Where is to be found a unifying force that can bring together antagonistic humanity in a lasting peace?

Can Knowledge accomplish world unity? Consider only the most modern product of Science—the airplane. It has shortened distances and contracted the dimensions of the earth. Although by its speed it has brought countries closer together, the truth is that it has divided, rather than united mankind. Its capacities for good have been surpassed by its powers for evil. As a vehicle and implement of warfare, it lets down death and destruction from the skies, and the more it kills and destroys, the more hatred it creates, and the more hatred it creates, the more it drives nations apart and widens the breach between man and man.

Scientific Knowledge can work evil as well as good, but Love is all for good. It contains no potentialities for evil. And the highest form of human love is mother love. What a force is here for world unity. It is a mighty force placed in human nature by God Himself—a multiplied force, not the endowment of one nation but of all peoples, as extensive as the human race itself, not the exclusive attributes of one class in the social order, but the equal possession of all, whether the rich or the poor, the learned or the unlettered. Tender and true, generous and unselfish, incapable of evil, directed only to the good—if this great moral power of mother love could be collected and marshaled to assert itself, divisions among men would be erased, enmities would vanish, and the world made over in peace and brotherly concord.

As her fingers worked the seamless garment of her Son, was Mary the Mother of Our Lord thinking of the divine plan of a world in a union of love to establish which Christ would die? Did she intend the Robe for something more than an article of clothing? In her mind was it a design of the mission of Christ among men, and a warning to men not to divide what the Son of God had come on earth to make one?

With the Mother of Jesus, there stood at the cross the beloved disciple St. John. When he saw the Robe of Christ left intact by the soldiers must He not have recalled the scene of the Last Supper of the preceding night when Jesus had prayed His sublime prayer for unity: "That all may be one, even as Thou, Father, in Me and I in Thee, that they also may be one in us"?

Although the prayer of Our Saviour has not as yet been fulfilled, although through the centuries that have elapsed since Calvary, Christ has been divided by reason of the dissensions in the family, by the heresies and schisms in the Church, by the wars among nations, yet we do not despair. The seamless Robe is a reproach to these sad divisions of humankind. At the same time, it affords us a strong motive of hope that these disunions will not always be.

For observe—when Our Lord died on Good Friday, the veil of the Temple was rent, the earth cracked, and the heavens were split by lightning. But although the former religious rite was taken away, and Nature itself shaken, in the midst of all these changes and convulsions, the Robe of Christ remained undamaged even as the Psalmist centuries before had predicted. When the soldiers on Calvary were confronted with this perfect texture, they refrained their rough hands and left it in its completeness. This would not have happened if it had not been for the will of God. In the preservation in its entirety of the seamless garment of the Divine Saviour, Faith will discern a sign that God's Providence holds and will yet reveal to us the One World which all lovers of Jesus desire.

Opportunity and Adversity

REVEREND WILLARD L. SPERRY, D.D.
*Congregational Minister and Dean of the Chapel, Harvard Divinity School,
Cambridge, Massachusetts*

*Dean Sperry is respected for his insight into the problems of men of our day,
for his spiritual guidance of Harvard students, and for the excellence of his
preaching. As dean of Harvard Divinity School and professor of practical
theology he has exercised a profound influence on the theological training of
hundreds of ministers in important churches all over the country. As chairman of the board of preachers to the University (college chaplain) he has
drawn to Harvard many of the world's outstanding ministers for special
sermons and courses of religious lectures for the last fifteen years.*

*The distinguished theologian was born in Peabody, Massachusetts, in
1882, was a Rhodes scholar at Oxford (first class honors in theology), studied
at Yale, and has received the doctorate from Yale, Amherst, Brown, Williams, Harvard, and Boston. He served in the pastorate in Fall River and
Boston, joined the faculty of Andover Theological Seminary, and has been
dean of Harvard Divinity School since 1922. For four years he was also
dean of the National Council on Religion in Higher Education (1927-31),
has given many famous lecture series, including the Upton Lectures at Manchester College, Oxford, the Hibbert Lectures, Essex Hall Lectures, London,
and the Lyman Beecher Lectures at Yale. He is a Fellow of the American
Academy of Arts and Sciences and is known for several significant books,
The Discipline of Liberty, Reality in Worship, The Paradox of Religion,
What You Owe Your Child, Wordsworth's Anti-Climax, What We Mean by
Religion, Summer Yesterdays in Maine and Rebuilding Our World.*

*Dean Sperry is accustomed to distinguish between words written to be
read and written to be spoken. His sermons deny themselves the leisure and
literary elaboration which is found in his books. They reveal a certain blunt-
ness and brevity in sentence style, which he thinks suited to the spoken word,
and to the school and college groups to which he habitually speaks. This
sermon was preached at Phillips Exeter Academy on September 30, 1945, for
the opening Sunday of the fall term. His discussion of religion, theology,
peace problems, his talk of books and of opportunity is fresh and stimulating.*

Sermon Seven

Text: A great door and effectual is opened unto me, and there are many adversaries. I Corinthians 16:9

IN THE previous verse St. Paul says that he is proposing to "tarry at Ephesus until Pentecost." Then he goes on, in our text, to give his friends in Corinth his reason for not coming to them as soon as they had hoped and as soon as he had intended. You might put his words into our vernacular by saying, "I have a great chance here just ahead of me, and it is going to be hard work."

It has been pointed out that the important word in the text is the word "and." Nine men out of ten would have said "but." They would have qualified the first half of the statement about their great opportunity, and in so doing would have disqualified themselves to that extent for making the most of their opportunity. You and I, unless we stopped to think twice, would instinctively say, "A great door and effectual is opened unto me, *but* there are many adversaries."

St. Paul, however, probably never stopped to argue the matter with himself, "Shall I say 'and' at this point, or shall I say 'but'?" He said instinctively what came into his mind. And what came into his mind was his native way of thinking about life and its problems.

He was like a track man looking down a cinder path where there is a succession of high hurdles. He did not say to himself, "This race that I am running (and he often spoke of the Christian life as a race) would be easier if it were a hundred yard straightaway dash; but, alas, it isn't. There are those hurdles in my way." He looked at his hurdles and made his mental peace with them in advance. He was already timing his stride to clear each one of them as he came to it.

One sometimes feels that religion is quite as much a matter of the way in which one thinks, as of what one thinks. Creeds and theologies are inevitable, they are even important. They are the religious man's sober second thought upon his experience. But before ever they come into being there is the experience itself and the way in which a man takes that experience. St. Paul himself tells us elsewhere, in what is probably his most famous saying, that what matters most of all in the Christian life is faith and hope and love. Faith and hope and love are attitudes of the mind and heart and will; they are ways of anticipating life.

Therefore St. Paul is true to himself in the words of our text. They represent his native, habitual way of meeting his experiences. If this attitude was a help to him in his day, it can be of equal help to us in our day. We are living through a hideously perplexing period of human history. We do not know just *what* to think about many, if not most, of the problems that are still ahead of us. But it is quite as important—personally I think it is more important—to decide *how* we are going to think. We need to recover and reaffirm the native mental habit of the Christian religion, when it is running true to form; "A great door and effectual is opened unto me, and there are many adversaries." St. Paul, for example, said that the pagan world in his day was "without hope." So today it is the man who has no religion who will say, "but there are many adversaries." Are you religious or irreligious? Are you going to say "and" or "but"?

Of the open door there is not the slightest doubt. We come here at the beginning of another fall term, when for the first time in four years the major and all absorbing business of mankind is no longer how to kill one another. In much of Europe that has been true for the past six years. Now the fighting and the killing are over for the present. No one knows what the future has in store in the farther, or even the nearer future. One of our generals recently told a Sunday school class of boys and girls in California that they would be the soldiers and nurses in the next war. An officer in our Army wrote an open letter to the general in the serviceman's own paper saying, in substance, "Can't you let that wait for just a bit? Give my kid brother a chance." Perhaps the general is right; for the moment we sympathize with his correspondent.

We are still a very long way off from any state of the world's affairs which we can call peace. "They make a desert," said Tacitus, "and call it peace." He knew even then that they were wrong. There are today more deserts in what were once relatively tranquil lands than there have ever been before, and we realize soberly that they are not peace. They are, at the best, a challenge to our hopes and plans for peace. The fact that so many of these deserts have had to be of our own making only throws the graver responsibility upon us. Every thoughtful and sensitive man knows this. But we have a chance, a sporting chance, if not a good chance, to set about the stern business of translating the dream of peace into the fact of peace. It is not a chance which will last indefinitely. And it is not a chance which can be renewed indefinitely. But for the moment we have a chance.

Now, in so far as any one of us can do anything, our chance of winning the praise rather than the blame of posterity is going to depend primarily upon the mental attitude with which we now look out over the problems which are ahead of us. So far as we are concerned, individually, the question is, do you see yourself taking life's difficulties in your stride, or are you beaten at the start by the dread that any one of the hurdles you see before you may trip you and throw you. Are you already saying to yourself, "*And* there are many adversaries," or "*But* there are many adversaries?"

A little earlier in this same letter to the Corinthians, from which the text comes, St. Paul says of himself, "So fight I, not as one that beateth the air." Moffatt translates the verse, "I do not plant my blows upon the empty air." We ought to know just who and what our adversaries are. These adversaries are, in the main, our own fears and our mistaken values. Our own worst enemy in the spiritual warfare is always the inner one. Let me try to identify two or three of the adversaries that stand in the door that is open before us, trying to block our passage through it.

The first is what might be called the materialistic view and valuation of life. According to this view money and what money will get are the most important things in life. There is nothing new about this view of life. The writer of the Wisdom of Solomon tells us that in his day the great majority of people said of themselves, "Our time here is a market for gain; we must be getting every way, though it be by evil means." That is a very old view of life, but it is also an equally popular modern view of life.

The things that money will get are in the first instance food and clothing and shelter. There is no good pretending that we are disembodied spirits and do not need these things. The only spirit we know is that which is embodied here and now in the flesh. Any attempt to live the life of a pure spirit, in contempt of the body, ends in disappointment, delusion, and even moral perversions. An English economist of the 1st century has said that the theory that poverty breeds religion and is good for the soul is not borne out by a study of the economic history of England. Revivals of religion took place and religion flourished best when people as a whole had the necessary food and clothing and shelter. He cites the fortunes of the English midlands in this connection.

Beyond these necessities there are those margins of comfort and even of luxury which most of us are human enough to want and to enjoy. But they begin to bring with them their own perils. They invite what a friend of mine once called "fatty degeneration of the moral sense." Comfort and luxuries of this sort are the boast of our American culture; they may also be one of its weaknesses. Someone said, paradoxically, the other day, "If we succeed in reducing Germany to the level of a self-supporting agricultural nation it may well turn out to be the happiest and most wholesome country in the world."

And further still, and still more sinister, is the conception of money as power. There is one school of psychiatrists who tell us that the will-to-power is the driving force and the secret spring of action in every man. One sometimes thinks that this is really so. Certainly, beyond food and clothing and shelter and comfort and luxury, there is the fascination which money has for men as a form of power. The struggle now going on between employers and workmen in this country is no longer a struggle for the bare decent necessities of life. It is a struggle for power as symbolized by money.

As a people we Americans are still left after the war economically powerful. It will be our shame if millions of people die of hunger and bitter cold this winter all over the world. How to get them fed and clothed and housed is a matter which calls for enlightened common sense, but for most of us it is something far more important than that, a matter of simple Christian charity. Meanwhile the fight for world markets is on and that warfare will be waged with all the skill our people can muster for it. It is the great game, and we love to play it. But if we allow ourselves to become absorbed in this game, to the neglect of other values, then this first sinister adversary will have slammed the open door in our face. As a people we are even now beginning to settle this matter already.

The second adversary that confronts us is the awareness that past history furnishes us few precedents or none to guide us into the future. You cannot pick up a road map to Utopia at a filling station. At the beginning of the First World War in August, 1914, John Morley resigned from Asquith's cabinet. He felt that the world in which he had believed and for which he had labored over a long lifetime was passing away, and that it was too late for him to try to remake himself to live in another world. In the preface to his *Recollections* which he wrote a few years later he said, "The world is travelling under formidable omens into a new era." He was one of the very few men who saw that plainly thirty years ago. It has taken most of us all the intervening years to realize what he meant and that he was right.

Have you ever been lost in the deep woods, say in northern Maine? Have you ever been lost sailing a yacht in a fog, having missed some buoy you should have picked up? A queer feeling of sudden panic comes over one at such a time.

Our generation is, in some such way, lost in history. A broadcaster in England said in the late summer of 1939, "It's not that we haven't any compass, it's that we doubt whether there is even any chart." We are half afraid to move, for fear we shall make a wrong move. One seems to sense this fear in some of the highest places in statecraft. The answer to this mood was given long ago, once again in the words of the Wisdom of Solomon, "Fear is nothing else but a betraying of the succours which reason offereth."

In his life of *The Admiral or the Sea*, Samuel Eliot Morison tells of the near mutiny of Columbus' crew on October 10, 1492.

> The enterprise [he writes], came nearest to failure through the stubborn conservatism of the men. Look back at the events of the voyage; think of the two first landfalls, the innumerable signs of land that failed to make good. They had long passed the position where Columbus predicted land would be found, and the men knew it. Can we fairly blame the men? Their issue with their commanders was the eternal one between imagination and doubt, between the spirit that creates and the spirit that denies. Oftentimes the doubters are right, for mankind has a hundred foolish notions for every sound one; it is at times of crisis, when unpredictable forces are dissolving society that the do-nothings are tragically wrong. There are tides in the affairs of men, and this was one of them.

And finally, there is a third adversary of which we are all aware, no matter how old we are. It is, at least on the part of those of us who have never seen battle action and have been civilians through all these years, a feeling of immaturity, almost of youthfulness. Centuries ago the Lord called Jeremiah to be a prophet, and he replied, "Ah, Lord God! behold, I cannot speak: for I am a child." Every man worth his salt knows the feeling which lies behind those words.

Four or five years after the First World War a Harvard college senior speaking for his fellows on Class Day told us, "The boys who were here before us and went to battle became men overnight. They have condemned us by contrast to perpetual childhood." It was precisely that mood which gave us the "lost generation of those years." We cannot afford it a second time and it need not be true.

A hundred and fifty years ago, Wordsworth, writing of the tremendous burst of enthusiasm wakened by the French Revolution, said,

> Bliss was it in that dawn to be alive,
> But to be young was very Heaven.

One wishes that the same might be said today. The sober fact is, however, that Dean Inge was much nearer the truth in his farewell sermon at the "other" Cambridge in England, "I do not suppose that the remainder of this century will be a very agreeable time for those who would like to be at ease in Zion, either physically or mentally. I do not think there has ever been a more perplexing age to live in. But let us not lose what Meredith calls 'the rapture of the forward view.'" That, perhaps, is the difference between living in a prose age rather than an age of poetry. But the prose periods of history, though less romantic, are not less real than its poetic periods, and in some ways are more important. To the adversary then, who would taunt us with our own immaturity and inexperience, there is the retort of the good counsel which long ago the Apostle gave to his son Timothy, "Let no man despise thy youth."

Such is our opportunity, and such are our adversaries. We may well remember the words of Christ to the churches, "I have set before thee an open door and no man can shut it." That is, no other man; only yourself.

A Very Present Help

REVEREND HAROLD V. JENSEN, D.D.
Pastor, First Baptist Church, Seattle, Washington

Dr. Jensen was born at St. Croix Falls, Wisconsin on March 31, 1901, of Danish parents. He grew up in the open country and small villages of Wisconsin and Iowa where his father, a Baptist minister, served in Danish-speaking churches. He worked his way through Des Moines University by doing odd jobs, and in his senior year, preached in two country churches on alternate weekends.

For two years he was principal of the high school and athletic coach at Bondurant, Iowa, and recalls as one of the greatest experiences of his life when his football team won the county championship in their class.

In 1924 he went to Newton Theological Seminary (now Andover-Newton). He has been the pastor of three churches: the Baptist church in Clinton, Massachusetts from 1927 to 1931; First Baptist Church of Melrose, Massachusetts from 1931 to 1938; and since 1938, the First Baptist Church of Seattle, the largest Baptist church in the Northwest.

Dr. Jensen is president of the Seattle Council of Churches and Christian Education which he previously served as chairman of its Civic Affairs Committee. He is a trustee of Berkeley Baptist Divinity School, of Linfield College and of Andover-Newton; a member of the Post-War Commission of the Northern Baptist Convention, and of the Board of Managers of the American Baptist Home Mission Society. He is a member of the Washington State Council of Social Work, of the Fellowship of Reconciliation and of the Knights of the Round Table. He is a frequent speaker at colleges and other youth groups. While he is especially interested in the problems of peace and race relationships, he believes deeply that the application of Christian principles to all of life is the only solution to the world's needs. He was given the degree of Doctor of Divinity by Linfield College in 1940. Dr. Jensen's sermon was preached on the Columbia Broadcasting System's Church of the Air, February 18, 1945, and it is given here through the courtesy of C.B.S. His discussion of the way Christians can meet and conquer trouble will be helpful to many in these days.

Sermon Eight

TEXT: God is our refuge and strength, a very present help in trouble.   PSALM 46:1

RELIGION is often represented as a city of refuge, to which we fly when our troubles are too great: when in the vernacular, "we can't take it." While that, by itself, is an utterly false view of religion, it would indeed be a false religion which did *not* provide help when trouble does come. It was on the basis of his own experience, that a vital relationship with God does provide such help, that the Psalmist declared "God is our refuge and strength, a very present help in trouble." If the untold suffering, the loss and disillusionment of this tragic day is not to plunge us into darkness and despair we also must discover a very present help in trouble.

Vital Christianity enables us to find help in time of trouble by refusing to run away. It accepts trouble as a part of life. And it ought to, for Christianity was born out of suffering and strengthened by it. It was a conquering dictator levying his impossible taxes that made it necessary for Christ to be born in a stable. It was the tragedy and cruelty of the cross which gave the heart of Christianity, the love of God, its clearest representation and irresistible appeal. Christianity even promises to its followers not delightful situations but "In the world ye shall have tribulation." "Blessed are ye when men shall persecute you." "I send you forth as sheep in the midst of wolves."

Out of this real experience of trouble, Christianity has learned that, although trouble is a part of life, it is *not* sent by God. Suffering and sorrow are the result of living contrary to God's laws; spiritual laws, natural laws, laws of health, laws of human relationship—God's laws every one. When we disobey, we take the consequences, because the laws are unbreakable. Therefore, present world-wide suffering does not indicate that God has abdicated; rather it shows, that He is still in control. The wages of sin are indeed death. God said they would be.

> This is my Father's world,
> O let me ne'er forget
> That, though the wrong seems oft so strong
> God is the Ruler yet.[1]

Christianity looks trouble full in the face; knows very well that we shall sail heavy dangerous seas, but it is made confident by the promise of God,

[1] "This Is My Father's World," from *Thoughts for Every Day Living*, by Maltbie D. Babcock. Copyright, 1901, by Charles Scribner's Sons.

"When thou passest through the waters, I will be with thee. . . ."—a very present help.

Far from being a way *around* trouble, Christianity is, in fact, a way *through* trouble. It provides two specific techniques for successfully dealing with trouble. The first of these is the yoke of Christ. That great invitation at the end of the eleventh chapter of Matthew is probably the most misunderstood passage of scripture. "Come unto me, all ye that labor and are heavy laden, and I will give you rest. Take my yoke upon you, and learn of me; for I am meek and lowly in heart: and ye shall find rest unto your souls." This is not, as so many think, an invitation to a rest cure with all troubles removed. It is Christ's invitation to "learn of me." Learn how to carry burdens successfully; then they will seem light; and you will find rest. The secret of the meaning of this passage lies in the yoke, a very common article in Jesus' day. It was a piece of wood, shaped to fit the shoulders; used, not for avoiding burdens, but for carrying them, one at each end. Its basic principle is balance. Jesus' meaning was very clear to his hearers, who had used the yoke so often. It was as though he were saying, in the language of our day, "Balance your own troubles with those of others and you will be able to carry both with far greater ease than if you struggled only with your own. When trouble descends upon you, reach out, help someone else and 'ye shall find rest unto your souls.'"

This is the same old law which Jesus everlastingly emphasized, "He that findeth his life shall lose it; and he that loseth his life for my sake shall find it." Be concerned, says Jesus, not primarily about your own needs, but first about helping to meet the needs of others. Now, after nineteen hundred years, modern psychology is discovering this same truth. It insists that the only way to have a happy co-ordinated life, in the midst of difficulties, is to become interested in and concerned about something outside oneself. This is the most effective, genuinely therapeutic method of dealing with difficulty. It is the *yoke* of Christ. Understood and applied, this yoke, this sincere effort to share the burdens of our fellow men, would go far toward eliminating the misunderstandings and conflicts between various cultures—and economic, racial, and national groups in our society. It would establish lasting peace on the basis of good will among men. It is God's way. It is the only way that will really work in this, God's world. "Take my yoke upon you . . . and ye shall find rest. . . ."—and peace.

Christianity's other technique for dealing with difficulties is to make them creative. When trouble comes, take hold of it; get something out of it; make it pay you dividends; make it a witness to the power of Christ. That's what Paul did in the prison in Rome which enabled him to write to the church at Philippi: "My bonds and suffering have really tended to advance the gospel." But, that did not just happen; Paul did it. That is what vast numbers of people are doing today, as they, from tragedy and difficulty, gain qualities and powers which enable them, more effectively, to minister to the needs of others. That is making trouble creative. That is what **Christ** did with the cross. That is Christian.

Seldom, if ever, are we free to determine what experiences come to us. We are, with Christ's help, free to determine how we use those experiences.

Vital Christianity also promises complete victory over trouble. Take away from any people all hope of victory and their power of effective conquest, of victorious living, is gone. The crippling of the Nazi war machine was probably due not so much to the superior numbers, strength and skill of their enemies, as to the loss of hope, the broken spirit of the Germans. Christianity, by giving the assurance of victory, gives hope that cannot die. It assures victory to the Christian's Cause—the Kingdom of God on earth, the supremacy of right and truth, of co-operation and brotherhood. We can delay that, but we cannot prevent it. "Truth, crushed to earth, shall rise again. The eternal years of God *are* hers." Knowing this, we can take trouble and setbacks of any sort and carry on, the eventual outcome never being in doubt. As Martin Luther put it in his great hymn:

> . . . though this world, with devils filled,
> Should threaten to undo us,
> We will not fear, for God hath willed
> His truth to triumph through us:

But Christianity makes victory certain not only for one's cause, but also assures one of personal victory: that is, of eternal life. Even though we get killed in the struggle we still live, and live better. Think of it. Think of people being equipped with the assurance of ultimate victory for their cause and of their own personal victory, too. What is the world going to do with people like that? It can never permanently discourage or defeat them. They dare to say:

> Let goods and kindred go,
> This mortal life also;
> The body they may kill,
> God's truth abideth still;
> His kingdom is for ever.

God does not send trouble, but stands by to see us through, and Christianity, far from evading difficulty, actually trains and equips one to deal with trouble. Therefore, since these things are true; when "the rains descend and the floods come, and the winds beat upon your house"—and they will—"Let not your heart be troubled, believe in God—a very present help in trouble."

> Keep heart, O Comrade! God may be delayed
> By evil, but He suffers no defeat;
> Even as a chance rock in an upland brook
> May change a river's course; and yet no rock—
> No, nor the baffling mountains of the world—
> Can hold it from its destiny, the sea.

So God is not foiled; the drift of the world will
Is stronger than all wrong. Earth and her years,
Down joy's bright way, or sorrow's longer road,
Are moving toward the purpose of the Skies.[2]

PRAYER: *Almighty God, our Father, in the midst of darkness and turmoil
we come to Thee. Forgive us that we have so often depended on our own
strength: help us now, so to open ourselves to Thee and Thy purposes
for our lives, that Thou mightest make clear to us the way of truth and
give us strength to walk in it victoriously, even unto the end; through
Jesus Christ our Lord. Amen.*

Put Off Thy Shoes

REVEREND FREDERICK J. SPRENKE
Rector, St. Ann's Roman Catholic Church, St. Louis, Missouri

*Father Sprenke was born in St. Louis, sometimes called the Rome of the
West, because of the comparatively large number of churches there. When
he was thirteen he was studying the humanities at St. Louis Preparatory
Seminary, when the death of his father forced him to devote as much time to
working to help support his family as he gave to his studies. For the next five
years he ran the gamut of jobs available for his time from drugstore soda
jerker to concrete mixer, truck driver, business manager of a parish magazine, manager of a school cafeteria, painter. The experience he gained from
these jobs has stood him in good stead.*

*He studied philosophy at Kendrick Seminary, after which he was sent by
Archbishop Glennon to the North American College at Rome, Italy, where
he spent four years in intensive study. He was ordained to the priesthood at
the Basilica of St. John Lateran on February 28, 1931, and said his first Mass
in what is probably the oldest Catacomb in Rome, Santa Priscilla, whose
Capella Greca contains one of the oldest known paintings of the Last Supper.
On his return to America, in July, 1931, Father Sprenke was appointed
assistant at St. Ann's Roman Catholic Church and professor at the Cathedral
Latin School in St. Louis, where he has been teaching Latin, Italian, English
Literature and Religion ever since. In 1940 he succeeded the late Father
Douglas as administrator of St. Ann's Shrine, which will celebrate its golden
jubilee as a parish in 1946.*

[2] E. W. Lyman, in 1,000 *Quotable Poems,* compiled by T. C. Clark.

He enjoys operas and paintings and can sing the baritone role of a number of the better known operas. The original title of this sermon was "Lost Ideals." It was preached to show that too many Americans have cast overboard the ideals which have been man's mainstay through the ages. He uses history effectively to illustrate his sermon and to prove his theses. It is a sermon which will stir a response in many hearts. It was preached on Columbia Broadcasting System's Church of the Air, on August 27, 1944.

Sermon Nine

TEXT: Put off the shoes from thy feet: for the place whereon thou standest is holy ground.   EXODUS 3:5 (Douay Bible)

I T'S a far cry from the green pastures around Mt. Horeb where a simple shepherd was privileged to receive the first direct revelation with regard to the nature of God. In response to the question as to what he should tell the captive children of Israel, were they to ask him the name of the god who had sent him to liberate them, he was told: "I AM WHO AM. Thou shalt say, 'HE WHO IS, hath sent me to you.'" Since that time, century after century has forged an aging link in the chain of civilization. Culture has given way to culture; man, to man; only truth has remained unchanged—truth which is identical with the Being Who said, "I AM WHO AM." The world saw emerge upon the horizon of time the seven wonders—the Hanging Gardens of Babylon, the Colossus of Rhodes, the Pyramids of Khufu and Khafra— thought in their time to be the acme of achievement. Today they exist with the exception of the pyramids only as reconstructed figments in the dreams of archaeologists. The world saw an Alexander the Great bewailing the fact that there were no more worlds to conquer. It saw a Caesar compel the then civilized world to bend the knee and grovel in the dust before the proud mistress of the world, Rome. And shortly after that it saw the scepter pass from Judah, saw God send His only Son into a world which hated Him. It wanted neither Him nor any part of His doctrine of love and repentance which was so diametrically opposed to the world's formula of might and lust. It saw that gentle, loving God-man, Who had merely wanted to gather sinners to Himself as a hen gathers her chickens under her wings, killed by a blasphemous, madding mob which He had many times challenged to convict Him of any sin. It saw His followers persecuted through the centuries by the same diabolical forces which had slain the Master—hunted down like so many poisonous fomenters of rebellion against an illegitimate state.

And what does it see today? It sees the bleeding hearts of fathers, mothers and wives—bleeding because their sons and husbands have been forced from their rightful homes to wreck other homes. It sees the mind of the youth of the world being filled with hate and fear—hatred and fear of the future when one generation has already seen two world wars—hatred and fear which have already liberally coated these young minds with a veneer of callousness, popularly known as juvenile delinquency. It sees the almost berserk, money-hungry production lines of the god of War, equally as morale-destroying as the ragged, drawn-out bread lines of a few years before, which had formed because of the "no help wanted" signs of the god of Greed. True, the one can win the war, but both can lose the peace. It sees the red cross on the great hospital transports, steaming in from all corners of the world, bringing back to their homelands for rehabilitation the mentally and physically disabled who have given their all.

These are the people—these suffering families—who can tell you what it means to have a personal God who so loved the world that He gave His only Son to save it. They recognize the value of those two great commandments of love which sum up all the obligations of life. They fully understand the words of the Prince of Peace, "Greater love than this no man hath, that he lay down his life for his friend." They realize that above all, in spite of its seeming complexities, life for man here holds only three loves—his God, his home, his country: his God first, because otherwise there would be no reason for man's existence, nor could he continue to exist, for we are here to know God, to love Him, to serve Him and thereby gain Heaven; his home, because the home is the nucleus of the State—and were it not for the home, the State would not exist; his country, because he recognizes in a properly constituted government the God-given protective authority under which he can the more easily love his neighbor, hold commerce with him in speech, in trade, in culture—under which he can the more easily educate his children and bring them to a sure knowledge of the God to Whom all beings are responsible.

After all, man is a being of ideals—ideals builded upon principles instilled into his breast by his God. And to see those ideals eventualize, he is ready to sacrifice everything, his dearest possessions, even life itself. In the pages of history we find that wars have existed throughout the ages ever since Cain slew Abel. But in those same pages of history we find that the majority of men were motivated by those same ideals of God, home and country. Man wasn't, and isn't today, the spineless creature misrepresented by the words, "theirs not to reason why, theirs but to do and die." The ancient Egyptians, misguided though they were in the means, enslaved peoples and took their land in order to rear the mighty temples of Luxor and Karnak to their mighty goddess the Immensa Ptha, so that she might be superior to all others in the universe. The Hebrews of the Old Testament slaughtered and pillaged and destroyed sometimes even defenseless towns with their women and children, at the command of Jahweh, in order to preserve themselves the free, unpolluted, chosen race of God. The Romans themselves, monstrous though they may seem to us for the terrible persecution of the Christians, were motivated by love for their gods and their country when they attempted to stamp out this, as they thought, venomous sect, so detrimental and traitorous to the life of the nation. The Middle Ages saw the Crusaders fling away their lives almost carelessly in the attempt to wrest the Holy Land from profanation at the hands of Mohammedan Saracens. Our own United States was cradled because the monstrous ape of religious bigotry tried to wrest from the flagpole of Justice in the mother-countries of France and England the flag of religious tolerance. The Incas of South America took captives in order to offer their living hearts to the great sun-god.

And then came the first world war! Our fathers and brothers marched away to that war. They, too, had ideals. They were told that this war was to end all wars, to make the world safe for democracy. They were told, that the future of civilization depended on them; that unless they won, they might consider themselves in the class of Bryant's "quarry slaves at night scourged to their dungeons"—slaves no longer free to worship their God nor to make laws for their country. Would they have called it a vain sacrifice twenty-five years later, had they been able to see? They would have seen the first of their cherished ideals—love of God—shattered in many parts of the world, because in many nations they would have seen the very existence of God challenged; they would have seen their God of Love and Justice, their Creator, supplanted by a man-made God—the State. They would have seen the second of their ideals—the home—tottering for various reasons: because the doctrine of birth control on a world scale had gotten in its nefarious work; rathskellers had supplanted the nursery in many homes; some governments were even offering bounties to large families. In those homes where children were welcomed, they would have found them so fettered by laws with regard to their up-bringing, their food, their education, their religious training, etc., that they would have seemed to belong not to the family but were to be considered as so much cannon fodder for the State. The dragon of divorce had not only reared its ugly head, but had dragged its entire slimy body over many homes, leaving in the wake of its lashing tail broken-hearted men, women and children. Their third ideal—love of country—would have been found almost entirely crushed. And why not? Where God and the home had been pushed far back into the hazy recesses of oblivion, country, in many places of the world, came simply to mean some so-called strong man, who treated men not as intelligent beings in accord with the moral law, but rather led them around by the nose like so many animals which neither knew whence they came nor whither they tended.

Now we have another world war. That should not be strange! It doesn't take a master mind to assign the cause. The experience of all history tells us! Time after time in the Old Testament, when the chosen people were led into idolatry by pagan allurements, the whiplash of God's anger descended upon them until, with chastened hearts and humble submission, they again found peace with Him. The history of the New Testament is the same old story. And, in each instance, man has discovered that there is but one way out—back to Christ! Remember the time when so many of the crowd were going away from CHRIST because they would not believe Him and He turned to His apostles with the words, "Will you also go away?" St. Peter's answer to that question should stand out like a blazing beacon in our memory because it has solved so many problems: "Lord, to whom shall we go? Thou hast the words of eternal life." You certainly recall that other instance when the young lawyer inquired about the means of salvation and Christ asked: "What readest thou in the Law?" The answer was: "Thou shalt love the Lord thy God with thy whole heart, mind and strength, and thy neighbor as thyself!" Our Lord's answer was brief but eternally true: "This do, and thou shalt live."

In our own great United States a kind, sorrowing man once said, "Our fathers brought forth upon this continent a new nation, conceived in liberty, and dedicated to the proposition that all men were created equal. Now we are . . . testing whether that nation, or any nation so conceived and so dedicated, can long endure." In this great country of freedom we still have our ideals of God, home and country; and we shall continue to have them if we keep ever before our minds the words of the Prince of Peace: "I am come to cast fire upon the earth, and what will I but that it be kindled?" He commands us to enkindle our hearts with flame of His divine love, to confess His name before men by wielding the sword of the Ten Commandments—the sword which cleaves good from evil, morality from immorality, right from wrong; wielding the sword to cut down the barriers erected by the Devil—the barriers of indecent speech, indecent plays, indecent literature, indecent living —in short, anything prejudicial to our ideals of God, Home and Country. In this way we shall assure ourselves of hearing not the awful curse: "Let this sceptre pass!," but instead: "Well done, thou good and faithful servant."

NIHIL OBSTAT: William Drumm, *Censor Librorum*
IMPRIMATUR: ✠ John J. Glennon, D.D., *Archbishop, St. Louis*

Mystery and Meaning

REVEREND REINHOLD NIEBUHR, D.D., LL.D.
*A Minister of the Evangelical and Reformed Church; Professor of
Applied Christianity, Union Theological Seminary, New York*

*Reinhold Niebuhr is one of the leading religious philosophers in the world
today. In his teaching at Union Theological Seminary in New York, he
moulds the thinking of many young ministers of our time. In his preaching
and addresses for churches and religious conventions, he brings a positive
message of faith and thought which in many ways is reminiscent of scholas-
ticism with its penetration and power.*

In his recent book, The Children of Light and the Children of Darkness,
*he has written a vindication of democracy that is different and original.
Democracy, he says, has certain inherent values that must be preserved for
man in the democracies and certain cardinal faults that must be eradicated
from the democratic tradition in modern civilization.*

His The Nature and Destiny of Man *is full of brilliantly penetrating
thinking; for once all philosophy is brought under the illuminating scrutiny
of Christian faith and logic.* Moral Man and Immoral Society, Reflections on
the End of an Era, Beyond Tragedy, *and* Christianity and Power Politics *all
show why the* Christian Century Pulpit *has said of him, "no thinker in the
American Church is exercising a wider influence today than Reinhold
Niebuhr." Dr. Niebuhr is farsighted, yet clear-sighted, and his work is important in the field of religious philosophy. It is a privilege to present this
distinguished sermon; in it he is at his best and has a message worthy of
reading and rereading with deliberation and care.*

Sermon Ten

TEXT: For now we see through a glass darkly; but then face to face: now I know in part, but then I shall know even as I am known. I CORINTHIANS 13:12

THE testimonies of religious faith are confused more greatly by those who claim to know too much about the mystery of life than by those who claim to know too little. Those who disavow all knowledge of the final mystery of life are so impressed by the fact that we see through a glass darkly, that they would make no claim of seeing at all. In the history of culture such a position is known as agnosticism. Agnosticism sees no practical value in seeking to solve the mystery of life. But there are not really many agnostics in any age or culture. A much larger number of people in any culture forget that they see through a glass darkly. They claim to know too much.

Those who claim to know too much may be divided into two groups, one ostensibly religious and the other irreligious. The irreligious resolve the problem of human existence and the mystery of the created world into systems of easily ascertained meaning. They deny that there is any mystery in life or the world. If they can find any previous cause for any subsequent effect in nature, they are certain that they have arrived at a full understanding of why such and such a thing exists. The natural cause is, for them, an adequate explanation of anything they may perceive.

The religious group on the other hand recognizes that the whole of the created world is not self-explanatory. They see that it points beyond itself to a mysterious ground of existence, to an enigmatic power beyond all known causes. But they usually claim to know too much about this eternal mystery. Sometimes they sharply define the limits of reason and the further limits of faith beyond reason and claim to know exactly how far reason penetrates into the eternal mystery and how much further faith reaches. Yet though they make a distinction between faith and reason, they straightway so mix and confuse reason and faith, that they pretend to be able to give a rational and sharply defined account of the character of God and of the eternal ground of existence. They define the power and knowledge of God precisely and explain the exact extent of His control and foreknowledge of the course of events. They dissect the mysterious relation between man's intellectual faculties and his vital capacities and claim to know the exact limits of *physis*, *psyche* and *nous*, of body, soul and spirit. They know that man is immortal and why; and just what portion and part of him is mortal and what part immortal. Thus they destroy the mystery of the unity of man's spiritual and

[53]

physical existence. They have no sense of mystery about the problem of immortality. They know the geography of heaven and of hell and the furniture of the one and the temperature of the other.

A genuine Christian faith must move between those who claim to know so much about the natural world that it ceases to point to any mystery beyond itself, and those who claim to know so much about the mystery of the "unseen" world that all reverence for its secret and hidden character is dissipated. A genuine faith must recognize the fact that it is through a dark glass that we see; though we do by faith penetrate sufficiently to the heart of the mystery not to be overwhelmed by it. A genuine faith resolves the mystery of life by the mystery of God. It recognizes that no aspect of life or existence explains itself, even after all known causes and consequences have been traced. All known existence points beyond itself. To realize that it points beyond itself to God is to assert that the mystery of life does not dissolve life into meaninglessness. Faith in God is faith in some ultimate unity of life, in some final comprehensive purpose which holds all the various, and frequently contradictory, realms of coherence and meaning together. A genuine faith does not mark this mysterious source and end of existence as merely an "X" or an unknown quantity. The Christian faith at least, is a faith in revelation. It believes that God has made himself known. It believes that He has spoken through the prophets and finally in His Son. It accepts the revelation in Christ as a final clue to the mystery of God's nature and purpose in the world, particularly the mystery of the relation of His justice to His mercy. But these clues to the mystery do not eliminate the periphery of mystery. God remains *deus absconditus*.

Of the prophets of the Old Testament the Second Isaiah is particularly conscious of the mystery which surrounds the eternal and the divine. He insists upon the distance between the divine wisdom and human counsels: "Who hath directed the spirit of the Lord, or being his counsellor hath taught him?"[1] He emphasizes the transcendence of God's power: "It is he that sitteth upon the circle of the earth, and the inhabitants thereof are as grasshoppers. . . . that bringeth the princes to nothing; he maketh the judges of the earth as vanity."[2] The question of the meaning of life must not be pressed too far, according to the prophet: "Woe unto him that striveth with his maker! . . . Shall the clay say to him that fashioneth it, What makest thou? . . . Woe unto him that saith unto his father, What begettest thou? or to the woman, What hast thou brought forth."[3] Faith, as the prophet conceives it, discerns the meaning of existence but must not seek to define it too carefully. The divine wisdom and purpose must always be partly hid from human understanding, "For my thoughts are not your thoughts, neither are your ways my

[1] Isa. 40:13.
[2] Isa. 40:22-23.
[3] Isa. 45:9-10.

ways, saith the Lord. For as the heavens are higher than the earth, so are my ways higher than your ways, and my thoughts than your thoughts."[4]

The sense of both mystery and meaning is perhaps most succinctly expressed in the forty-fifth chapter of Isaiah, where, practically in the same breath, the prophet declares on the one hand: "Verily thou art a God that hideth thyself, O God of Israel, the Saviour," and on the other, insists that God has made himself known: "I have not spoken in secret, in a dark place of the earth: I said not unto the seed of Jacob, Seek ye me in vain: I the Lord speak righteousness, I declare things that are right." This double emphasis is a perfect symbolic expression both of the meaning which faith discerns and of the penumbra of mystery which it recognizes around the core of meaning. The essential character of God, in His relations to the world, is known. He is the Creator, Judge and Saviour of men. Yet He does not fully disclose Himself and His thoughts are too high to be comprehended by human thought.

For some centuries the intellectual life of modern man has been dominated by rebellion against Medieval faith. The main outlines of modern culture are defined by modern man's faith in science and his defiance of the authority of religion. This conflict between the faith which flowered in the thirteenth century and that which flowered in the seventeenth and eighteenth century is a conflict between two forms of faith, which in their different way, obscured the depth of the mystery of life and made the core of meaning too large. Medieval Catholicism was not completely lacking in a reverent sense of mystery. The rites of the church frequently excel the more rationalized forms of the Protestant faith by their poetic expression of mystery. There is, for instance, an advantage in chanting rather than in saying a creed. The musical and poetical form of a creed emphasize the salient affirmation of faith which the creed contains; and slightly derogate the exact details of symbolism through which the basic affirmation is expressed. That is a virtue of the liturgical and sacramental church, which is hardened into a pitiless fundamentalism when every "I" is dotted and every "t" crossed in the soberly recited credo.

On the other hand the same Catholic faith combined a pretentious rationalism with its sense of poetry. Any careful reading of the works of Thomas Aquinas must impress the thoughtful student with the element of pretension which informs the flowering of the Catholic faith in the "golden" thirteenth century. There seems to be no mystery which is not carefully dissected; and no dark depth of evil which is not fully explained and no height of existence which is not scaled. The various attributes of God are all carefully defined and related to each other. The mysteries of the human soul and spirit are mastered and rationally defined in the most meticulous terms. The exact line which marks justice from injustice is known. Faith and reason are so intermingled that the characteristic certainty of each is compounded with the

[4] Isa. 55:8-9.

other. Thus a very imposing structure is created. Yet it ought to have been possible to anticipate the doubts which it would ultimately arouse. Granted its foundation of presuppositions every beam and joist in the intellectual structure is reared with perfect logical consistency. But the foundation is insecure. It is a foundation of faith in which the timeless affirmations of the Christian belief are compounded with detailed knowledge characteristic of a prescientific age. An age of science challenged this whole foundation of presuppositions and seemed to invalidate the whole structure.

The new age of science attempted an even more rigorous denial of mystery. The age of science traced the relations of the world of nature, studied the various causes which seemed to be at the root of various effects in every realm of natural coherence; and came to the conclusion that knowledge dissolved mystery. Mystery was simply the darkness of ignorance which the light of knowledge dispelled. Religious faith was, in its opinion, merely the fear of the unknown which could be dissipated by the knowledge of the known. In the one case the "spiritual," the "eternal" and the "supernatural," conceived as a separate and distinct realm of existence (instead of as the final ground and ultimate dimension of the unity of existence), is so exactly defined that the penumbra of mystery is destroyed. In the other case the "natural," the "temporal" and the "material" are supposedly comprehended so fully that they cease to point beyond themselves to a more ultimate mystery. There are significant differences between these two ways of apprehending the world about us and the depth of existence within us; but the differences are no greater than the similarity between them. Both ways contain an element of human pretension. Both fail to recognize that we see through a glass darkly.

We see through a glass darkly when we seek to understand the world about us; because no natural cause is ever a complete and adequate explanation of the subsequent event. The subsequent event is undoubtedly causally related to preceding events; but it is only one of many untold possibilities which might have been actualized. The Biblical idea of a divine creator moves on a different level from that on which move all scientific concepts of causation. The two become mutually exclusive, as they have done in the controversies of recent ages, only if on the one hand we deny the mysterious element in creation and regard it as an exact explanation of why things are as they are and become what they become; and if, on the other hand, we deny the mystery which overarches the process of causation in nature. Thus two dimensions of meaning each too exactly defined come in conflict with each other. More truly and justly conceived the realm of coherence which we call nature points to a realm of power beyond itself. This realm is discerned by faith but not fully known. It is a mystery which resolves the mystery of nature. But if mystery is denied in each realm, the meaning which men pretend to apprehend in each becomes too pat and calculated. The depth of meaning is destroyed in the process of charting it exactly. Thus the sense of meaning is deepened, and not annulled by the sense of mystery.

The understanding of ourselves is even more subject to seeing through a glass darkly than the understanding of the world about us. We "are fearfully and wonderfully made." Man is a creature of nature, subject to its necessities and bound by its limits. Yet he surveys the ages and touches the fringes of the eternal. Despite the limited character of his life, he is constantly under compulsions and responsibilities which reach to the very heart of the eternal.

> Thou hast beset me behind and before
> And laid Thine hand upon me
> Such knowledge is too wonderful for me
> I can not attain unto it

confesses the Psalmist, in recording the universal human experience of feeling related to a divine lawgiver and judge.

> Whither shall I go from Thy spirit?
> And whither shall I flee from thy presence?
> If I ascend into heaven Thou art there:
> If I make my bed in sheol behold Thou art there.
> If I take the wings of the morning
> And dwell in the uttermost parts of the sea;
> Even there shall Thy hand lead me and
> Thy right hand shall hold me.[5]

Thus the Psalmist continues in describing the boundless character of the human spirit, which rises above and beyond all finite limitations to confront and feel itself confronted by the divine.

The finiteness of human life contrasted with the limitless quality of the human spirit, presents us with a profound mystery. We are an enigma to ourselves.

There are many forms of modern thought which deny the mystery of our life by reducing the dimension of human existence to the level of nature. We are animals, we are told, with a slightly greater reach of reason and a slightly "more complex central nervous system," than the other brute creatures. But this is a palpable denial of the real stature of man's spirit. We may be only slightly more inventive than the most astute monkey. But there is, as far as we know, no *Weltschmerz* in the soul of any monkey, no anxiety about what he is and ought to be, and no visitation from a divine accuser who "besets us behind and before" and from whose spirit we cannot flee. There is among animals, as Walt Whitman observed, no lying awake at night fretting about their sins, no uneasy conscience and no ambition which tends to transgress all natural bounds and become the source of the highest nobility of spirit and of the most demonic madness.

We are a mystery to ourselves in our weakness and our greatness; and this mystery can be resolved in part only as we reach into the height of the

[5] Ps. 139.

mysterious dimension of the eternal into which the pinnacle of our spiritual freedom seems to rise. The mystery of God resolves the mystery of the self into meaning. By faith we find the source of our life: "It is he that hath made us and not we ourselves." Here too we find the author of our moral duties: "He that judges me is the Lord." And here is the certitude of our fulfillment: "But then I shall know even as also I am known," declares St. Paul. This is to say that, despite the height of our own vision no man can complete the structure of meaning in which he is involved except, as by faith he discerns that he "is known," though he himself only "knows in part." The human spirit reaches beyond the limit of nature and does not fully comprehend the level of reality into which it reaches. Any interpretation of life which denies this height of reality because it ends in mystery, gives a false picture of the stature of man. On the other hand, any interpretation which seeks to comprehend the ultimate dimension by the knowledge and the symbols of the known world also gives a false picture of man. Such theologies obscure the finiteness of human knowledge. We see through a glass darkly when we seek to discern the divine ground and end of human existence. We see only by faith but by faith we do see.

The source of the evil in us is almost as mysterious as the divine source and the end of our spiritual life. "O Lord," cried the prophet, "why hast thou made us to err from thy ways, and hardened our heart from thy fear?"[6] We desire the good and yet do evil. In the words of St. Paul, we "delight in the law of God after the inward man: But I see another law in my members which wars against the law that is in my mind."[7] The inclination to evil, which is primarily the inclination to inordinate self-love runs counter to our conscious desires. We seem to be betrayed into it. "Now if I do that I would not, it is no more I that do it, but sin that dwelleth in me,"[8] declares St. Paul, in trying to explain the powerful drift toward evil in us against our conscious purposes. There is a deep mystery here which has been simply resolved in modern culture. It has interpreted man as an essentially virtuous creature who is betrayed into evil by ignorance or by evil economic, political or religious institutions. These simple theories of historical evil do not explain how virtuous men of another generation created the evil in these inherited institutions, or how mere ignorance could give the evil in man the positive thrust and demonic energy in which it frequently expresses itself. Modern culture's understanding of the evil in man fails to do justice to the tragic and perplexing aspect of the problem.

Orthodox Christianity on the other hand has frequently given a dogmatic answer to the problem, which suggests mystery; but which immediately obscures the mystery by dogmatic formula. Men are evil, Christian orthodoxy declares, because of the "sin of Adam" which has been transmitted to all

6 Isa. 63:17.
7 Rom. 7:22-23.
8 Rom. 7:20.

[58]

men. Sometimes the mode of transmission is allowed to remain mysterious; but sometimes it is identified with the concupiscence in the act of procreation. This dogmatic explanation has prompted the justified protest and incredulity of modern man, particularly since it is generally couched in language and symbols, taken from a prescientific age.

Actually there is a great mystery in the fact that man, who is so created that he cannot fulfill his life except in his fellow men, and who has some consciousness of this law of love in his very nature, should nevertheless seek so persistently to make his fellow men the tools of his desires and the objects of his ambitions. If we try to explain this tendency toward self-love we can find various plausible explanations. We can say that it is due to the fact that man exists at the juncture of nature and spirit, of freedom and necessity. Being a weak creature he is anxious for his life; and being a resourceful creature, armed with the guile of spirit, he seeks to overcome his insecurity by the various instruments which are placed at his disposal by the resources of his freedom. But inevitably the security which he seeks for himself is bought at the price of other men's security. Being an insignificant creature with suggestions of great significance in the stature of his freedom, man uses his strength to hide his weakness and thus falls into the evil of the lust for power and self-idolatry.

These explanations of man's self-love are plausible enough, as far as they go. But they are wrong if they assume that the peculiar amphibious situation of man, being partly immersed in the time process and partly transcending it, must inevitably and necessarily tempt him to an inordinate self-love. The situation does not create evil, if it were not falsely interpreted. From whence comes the false interpretation? There is thus great profundity in the Biblical myth of the serpent who "tempted" Eve by suggesting that God was jealous of man's strength and sought to limit it. Man's situation tempts to evil provided man is unwilling to accept the peculiar weakness of his creaturely life, and is unable to find the ultimate source and end of his existence beyond himself. It is man's unbelief and pride which tempts to sin. And every such temptation presupposes a previous "tempter" (of which the serpent is the symbol). Thus before man fell into sin, there was, according to Biblical myth, a fall of the devil in heaven. The devil is a fallen angel, who refused to accept his rightful place in the scheme of things and sought a position equal to God.

This then is the real mystery of evil; that it presupposes itself. No matter how far back it is traced in the individual or the race, or even preceding the history of the race, a profound scrutiny of the nature of evil reveals that there is an element of sin in the temptation which leads to sin; and that without this presupposed evil the consequent sin would not necessarily arise from the situation in which man finds himself. This is what Kierkegaard means by saying that "sin posits itself." This is the mystery of "original sin" about which Pascal truly observes that "without this mystery man remains a mystery to himself."

Purely sociological and historical explanations of the rise of evil do not touch the depth of the mystery at all. Christian dogmatic explanations have some sense of it; but they obscure it as soon as they have revealed it by their pat dogmatic formulae. In dealing with the problem of sin the sense of meaning is inextricably interwoven with the sense of mystery. We see through a glass darkly when we seek to understand the cause and the nature of evil in our own souls. But we see more profoundly when we know that it is through a dark glass that we see than if we pretend to have a clear light upon this profound problem.

The final mystery about human life concerns the incompleteness of human life and the method of its completion. Here again modern culture has resolved all mystery into simple meaning. It believes that the historical process is such, that it guarantees the ultimate fulfillment of all legitimate human desires. It believes that history, as such, is redemptive. Men may be frustrated today, may live in poverty and in conflict and may feel that they "bring their years to an end like a tale that is told." But the modern man is certain that there will be a tomorrow in which poverty and war and all injustice will be abolished. Utopia is the simple answer which modern culture offers in various guises to the problem of man's ultimate frustration. History is, according to the most characteristic thought of modern life, a process which gradually closes the hiatus between what man is and what he would be. The difficulty with this answer is that there is no evidence that history has any such effect. In the collective enterprises of man, the progress of history arms the evil as well as the good with greater potency; and the mystery of how history is to be brought to completion therefore remains on every level of human achievement. It may in fact express itself more poignantly in the future than in the past.

Furthermore, there is no resolution of the problem of the individual in any collective achievement of mankind. The individual must continue to find the collective life of man his ultimate moral frustration as well as his fulfillment. For there is no human society and there can be none, the moral mediocrity of which must not be shocking to the individual's highest moral scruples. Furthermore, the individual dies before any of the promised collective completions of history.

But this is not all. The problem of death is deeply involved with the problem of sin. Men die with an uneasy conscience and must confess with the Psalmist, "for we are consumed by thine anger and by wrath are we troubled." Any honest self-analysis must persuade us that we end our life in frustration not only because "our reach is beyond our grasp," i.e., because we are finite creatures with more than finite conceptions of an ultimate consummation of life; but also because we are sinners who constantly introduce positive evil into the operations of divine providence.

The answer of Christian faith to this problem is belief in "the forgiveness of sin and life everlasting." We believe that only a power greater than our own can complete our incomplete life and only a divine mercy can heal us of our evil. Significantly St. Paul adds this expression of Christian hope immediately to his confession that we see through a glass darkly. We see through a glass darkly now, "but then" we shall "see face to face." Now we "know in part," but "then" we shall know even as we are known. This Christian hope makes it possible to look at all the complexities and mysteries of life without too much fear.

In another context St. Paul declares: "We are perplexed, but not unto despair." One might well divide the world into those who are not perplexed, those who are perplexed unto despair; and those who are perplexed, but not unto despair. Those who are not perplexed have dissolved all the mysteries and perplexities of life by some simple scheme of meaning. The scheme is always too simple to do justice to the whole depth of man's problem. When life reveals itself in its full terror, as well as its full beauty, these little schemes break down. Optimism gives way to despair. The Christian faith does not pretend to resolve all perplexities. It confesses the darkness of human sight and the perplexities of faith. It escapes despair nevertheless because it holds fast to the essential goodness of God as revealed in Christ and is therefore "persuaded that neither life nor death . . . are able to separate us from the love of God, which is in Christ Jesus our Lord."

It cannot be denied, however, that this same Christian faith is frequently vulgarized and cheapened to the point where all mystery is denied. The Christian faith in heaven is sometimes as cheap, and sometimes even more vulgar, than the modern faith in utopia. It may be even less capable of expressing the final perplexity and the final certainty of faith. On this issue, as on the others we have considered, a faith which measures the final dimension of existence but dissipates all mystery in that dimension, may be only a little better or worse than a shallow creed which reduces human existence to the level of nature.

Our situation is that by reason of the freedom of our spirit we have purposes and ends beyond the limits of the finiteness of our physical existence. Faith may discern the certainty of a final completion of life beyond our power; and a final purging of the evil which we introduce into life by our false efforts to complete it in our own strength. But faith cannot resolve the mystery of how this will be done. We see through a glass darkly when we look into the future. The important issue is whether we will be tempted by the incompleteness and frustration of life to be driven to despair; or whether we can, by faith, lay hold on the divine power and wisdom which completes what remains incomplete with us. A faith which resolves mystery too much denies the finiteness of all human knowledge, including the knowledge of faith. A faith which is overwhelmed by mystery denies the clues of divine meaning which shine through the perplexities of life. The proper combination of humility and trust is precisely defined when we affirm that we see, but admit that we see through a glass darkly.

Our primary concern in this exposition of the Pauline text has been to understand the fact that the Christian faith is conscious of the penumbra of mystery which surrounds its conception of meaning. Yet it must be emphasized in conclusion that our faith cannot be identified with poetic forms of religion which worship mystery without any conception of meaning. All such poetic forms of faith might well be placed in the category of the worship of the unknown Gods, typified in the religion which Paul found at Athens. In contrast to this religion Paul set the faith which is rooted in the certainty that the mysterious God has made Himself known and that the revelation of His nature and purpose, apprehended by faith must be proclaimed: "Whom therefore ye ignorantly worship," Paul declared, "him I declare unto you." This declaration of faith rests upon the belief that the divine is not pure mystery, the heart of it having been disclosed to those who are able to apprehend the divine disclosure in Christ. It is by the certainty of that faith, that St. Paul can confidently look toward a future completion of our imperfect knowledge: "Now I know in part, but *then* I shall know." The indication that faith regards the meaning which has been disclosed as essentially victorious over the mystery of existence is the expression of a certain hope that "then I shall know," of the expectation that ultimately all mystery will be resolved in the perfect knowledge of God.

Faith in a religion of revelation is thus distinguished on the one side from purely poetic appreciations of mystery, just as on the other side it is distinguished from philosophies of religion which find the idea of revelation meaningless. The idea is meaningless to all forms of rational religion which approach the mystery of life with the certainty that human reason can finally resolve the mystery into perfect meaning. The Christian faith is the right expression of the greatness and the weakness of man in his relation to the mystery and the meaning of life. It is an acknowledgment of human weakness, for unlike "natural religion" and "natural theology" it does not regard the human mind as capable of resolving the mystery of existence because it knows that human reason is itself involved in the mystery which it tries to comprehend. It is an acknowledgment of the greatness of the human spirit because it assumes that man is capable of apprehending clues to the divine mystery and accepting the disclosure of the purposes of God which He has made to us. It is a confession of both weakness and strength in one moment because it recognizes that the disclosures of the divine are given to man, who is capable of apprehending them, once made, but is not capable of anticipating them.

According to the Christian faith there is a light which shineth in darkness; and the darkness is not able to comprehend it. Reason does not light that light; but faith is able to pierce the darkness and apprehend it.

The Religion of the Incarnation

REVEREND LYNN HAROLD HOUGH, D.D.
Dean, Drew Theological Seminary, Madison, New Jersey

Lynn Harold Hough is a distinguished Methodist minister and teacher. As dean and professor of Homiletics and the Christian Criticism of Life at Drew Theological Seminary, Madison, New Jersey, he influences the future career of every man who attends the Seminary.

Beginning his pastorates in 1898 in a small church in New Jersey, he rose through his preaching ability to be the pastor of churches in Brooklyn. and Baltimore. Then from 1914 to 1919 he was professor of Historic Theology at Garrett Biblical Institute, Evanston, Illinois, and in 1919 he became president of Northwestern University.

In the following year he was called to be pastor of Central Methodist Church, Detroit, where his preaching attracted wide attention. In 1928 he was called to the American Presbyterian Church in Montreal. In 1930 he took the chair of Homiletics at Drew and has been dean since 1934. In the last thirty-eight years he has written thirty-eight books, including, In the Valley of Decision, The Significance of the Protestant Reformation, The Civilized Mind, The Christian Criticism of Life, *and* Patterns of the Mind.

He gave the Cole Lectures at Vanderbilt University (1919), the Merrick Lectures at Ohio Wesleyan University (1923), the Fernley Lecture, Lincoln, England (1925), the Fred J. Cato Lecture, General Conference of the Methodist Church in Australasia, Brisbane, Australia (1941), and half a dozen other famous courses.

In 1918 he was sent to England by the Lindgren Foundation of Northwestern University to interpret the moral and spiritual aims of the first World War. At the invitation of the British Ministry of Information, he spent eleven weeks in England during the summer of 1942 preaching to the congregation of The City Temple, London, and making addresses in army camps and to the general public.

This brilliant sermon is one of the finest Dr. Hough has preached in the last five years. It is filled with a deep and stimulating philosophy and with a spiritual message which will be helpful in these days when man has become so unlike God. In this sermon Dr. Hough shows how "man can again become like God . . . because God has already put eternity in his heart."

Sermon Eleven

Text: the Word became flesh. . . . John 1:14 (American Standard Revised Version)

ONE of the most fascinating paradoxes which comes to light in the study of the Greek New Testament has to do with the contrast in the use of the word σάρξ (flesh). The matter comes to a head in two famous sentences. Writing to the Galatians Paul says bluntly: "Now the works of the flesh are manifest, which are these: fornication, uncleanness, lasciviousness, idolatry, sorcery, enmities, strife, jealousies, wraths, factions, divisions, parties, envyings, drunkenness, revellings, and such like" (Galatians 5:19, 20, 21, American Standard Revised Version). On the other hand, the prologue of the fourth Gospel declares with equal directness "the Word became flesh, and dwelt among us." The contrast seems sharp enough. The flesh is so evil that it produces the ugliest and the worst things of which we can think. The flesh is so good that it can be inhabited by the Word of God. It is not too difficult, however, to resolve the problem. Paul is speaking of the flesh when it takes the bit in its teeth and runs away uncontrolled by any higher power. So it becomes evil and corrupts even the mind for it will be observed that some in this list of fleshly lusts such as jealousy and wrath are not physical at all but represent the action of an evil intelligence. On the other hand, in the fourth Gospel the flesh is seen in its true place as responsive to that which is higher than itself and indeed as completely dominated by it. It is the flesh misused which becomes the instrument of evil. It is the flesh rightly used which is the instrument of good and of God.

The sentence "the Word became flesh" is the most profound and far-reaching statement ever made about the Incarnation. It is the clearest declaration that God did indeed enter into human life and that he actually took upon himself the nature of man. It is the most tremendous conception which can take possession of the human mind. It is of its meaning and of some of its implications that we would now speak. We must see at once that if the Word did indeed become flesh, then it is the very true nature of the material to express the spiritual. Only when it goes contrary to its own nature does it become the servant of evil. The bad works of which Paul speaks are the fruits of a flesh corrupted and not of a flesh used according to its true purpose. If you want to find the real nature of the flesh, you will find it in Jesus Christ.

If we are to understand the religion of the Incarnation, the first thing we must do is to look backward. We must go back as far as creation. We shall

[64]

find a clew in the Genesis stories of the beginnings of things and people. We are told that God created man in his own image. And after the whole story of creation consummating in man the ruler and the controller has been told, we read: "And God saw everything that he had made, and, behold, it was very good" (Gen. 1:31). Clearly enough the creation stories see the nature of man as good and later the misuse of that nature turns everything to evil. And all this fits perfectly with the later belief that God became man, that the Word was made flesh. Because man was made in God's image, man could receive God into his own life. And when we come to the New Testament we can see that there was a relation between man's nature and God which the dark evil of the world had not corrupted. Otherwise the Incarnation would have been impossible. Not only was man originally made for God but after all the centuries of sinning man's very nature was always uttering an inarticulate cry for God. His essential nature was still capable of being responsive to the divine. Because the flesh was made for the Word, the Word could become flesh. We must not forget the note struck in the eighth Psalm: "For thou hast made him but little lower than God, and crownest him with glory and honor."

All this must be perpetually brought to the attention of men. It must be brought within the purview of the last and the lowest and the least. However low a man may sink, this higher life is that for which he was made. However he may misuse the flesh, until it seems to become the very symbol of all evil, not for this moral disaster was it made. The call to man is always a call back to his original dignity. It is always a call back to the true meaning of his nature. He was made in the image of God. And so when God would save men, he makes their true nature visible through his incarnate life. "This," in the days of his flesh Jesus is always saying, "This is what flesh dominated by the living God may become. See what you have made of it. And turn from your life in a corrupted flesh to the life of flesh dominated by the divine purpose and the divine will. Let me restore the image of God which was given to man at his creation."

If we are to understand the religion of the Incarnation, we must look upward to the nature of God as well as backward to the creation of man. We must think of the Word which was made flesh as well as of the flesh which submitted itself to the Word. Now it is the very quality of a true Word to express the actual mind of the one who speaks it. So it is the very quality of the perfect Word to express with complete finality the character of God. What God is in eternity, Jesus Christ made real to men in time. And he made it real in the very quality of a human life.

We may approach the matter in no better way than by thinking of what we may call the religious experience of Plato. That mighty Athenian turned from the transient, unstable and unsatisfactory life about him to find something deep and permanent and satisfying. This he found in the eternal ideas. He dared to believe in an invisible perfection in spite of the visible imper-

[65]

fection. And he saw the world of man and his experience as only a mirage unless it participated in the reality of the eternal ideas. This faith in indestructible goodness in the ultimate universe in spite of the evil in the world, in an indestructible beauty in spite of the ugliness in the world, in an indestructible truth in spite of the falsehood in the world is the very genius of Platonism. But at last, as we see in the tenth book of the Laws, Plato came to understand that this perfect truth and beauty and goodness must not be thought of as belonging to a world of glorious abstraction. The ideas must be alive in God. So they ceased to be abstractions and entered the very fabric of perfect being. And at every deepest place in his life man is related to this perfect being. Reality is in the perfect life of God and the shared life of men. In man at his best you get hints of what God is perfectly and forever. The ultimate life is a perfect reality of conscious being. And as he participates in that which comes from this perfect life man finds his own life based on truth and beauty and goodness.

When we have seen all this, we are not surprised to find that Plato was a schoolmaster leading many men to the Christ of the Incarnation. There has been a glorious stream of Platonism in all Christian thought.

The invisible perfection became real in human life in Jesus Christ. In just this sense he was the Word of God—the Word of God to men. And always we must go from the fact of the Incarnation up to the perfection of that divine life which became real in Jesus Christ. This ·upward look from the Incarnation sees the Christian religion soundly based on the character of God. It sees glimpses of that perfection in whose image man was made. To be sure, there are various ways of apprehending this perfection. That which is truth and goodness and beauty in the Platonic tradition becomes moral love in the Hebrew Christian witness. And so the Greek insights are deepened and sharpened and attain a magnificence of which the Greek mind was not capable. Perfection alive in God is the promise of perfection alive in man. That promise is realized in Jesus Christ. And it becomes the haunting, flying goal of human history.

If we are to understand the religion of the Incarnation, we must look inward as well as backward and upward. This inward look we may well take in the light of an insight provided by some deathless lines of Edmund Spenser. Given modern form they read:

> For of the soul the body form doth take:
> For soul is form, and doth the body make.

Here at once we are delivered from all the bleak and subtle materialisms which would insist that the body is fundamental and creates the soul—whatever we may mean by soul. Quite the opposite is true. It is the spirit which masters the flesh and when the flesh is evil, it is because it is dominated by an evil spirit. When the flesh is good, it is because it is dominated by a good spirit. And because it was created to be good and meant to be good, we may say that when it is good we see it according to its own true nature. So we see it in the Incarnation. When the Word became flesh, it revealed what flesh was meant to be. You get hints of this in the lives of men apart from the Incarnation as when Henry Vaughan

> felt through all this fleshy dress
> Bright shooes of everlastingness.

But the full and glorious revelation of the flesh as the expression of the divine purpose you find only in the Incarnation.

And in men you also find something quite different and something quite other. For if the body of the soul its form doth take, it is clear enough that an evil soul turns the body to evil purposes and in this sense it becomes evil. And so the flesh does the evil works castigated by Paul in the epistle to the Galatians. All about the world this has happened. In all centuries this has happened. In all men this has happened. Looking within, every man finds the tale of it in his own soul. There is a memorable sentence in the prayer of Solomon recorded in the Second Book of the Chronicles about every man knowing his own plague and his own sorrow (II Chronicles 6:29) which speaks straight to the experience of men over the centuries. And it is this which makes it necessary that the religion of the Incarnation shall also be the religion of the Cross. For the Word made flesh must rescue men by a mighty deed of personal agony if the flesh which they have desecrated is to become the flesh shot through by the glory of God. And by His grace the souls they have prostituted to evil thoughts and purposes must be transformed if they are not to corrupt the very bodies which they inhabit and control. But the very act of rescue is a saving of men from that which has no right to be to that whose right to be comes from the very nature of God and the very nature which in creation God gave to man. Redemption is restoring to man an image which he has in part—in all too great part—so tragically lost. And that restoration is possible because man was made for the highest and not for the lowest. The body was made to express a good soul and not a bad soul. The image of God expresses the true genius of man. When he has repudiated that image, he has despised his true self. Always by day and by night the Christ of the Incarnation reminds him of what flesh was meant to be and the same Christ from the Cross reminds him of what flesh can become in spite of the corroding evil to which men have subjected it. When he looks within, a man finds these truths in living biography. At his best he knows the glory of a good soul forming a good body. At his worst he knows the tragedy of a bad soul making the body evil. And now he is ready for that mighty "Come unto me" which the Christ of the Incarnation speaks from the Cross.

If you find evil in man's essential nature, you have all the materials for an unrelieved pessimism. If you find evil in man's will which corrupts a nature made in the image of God, you have still great hope within man's reach if

God is a God of redemption. If God made man evil in his nature, there is no hope for man. And there is no hope for God for in that case the God who condemned man to necessary evil by giving him a bad nature would be the chief sinner. The lines of Omar Khayyám would become relevant: "Man's forgiveness give . . . and take!" Only there would be no forgiveness. But if God truly made man in his own image and the Incarnation recalls man to a sense of what he has lost and the Cross opens the way to a great restoration, you have a truly glorious hope for man. You have this hope for the individual. And you have this hope for the company of men who allow the processes of regeneration to work at the very center of their lives. The transformed spirit is the promise of a transformed flesh. For now the soul which doth the body make does not corrupt the body but uses it for its true purposes. The Word made flesh becomes the revelation of what flesh may become.

That all this means a new society as well as a new man is surely clear enough. The Incarnation is the beginning of a new race as well as a revelation of the possibilities of men. The Word made flesh is a social being. In precisely this sense "As in Adam all die, so also in Christ shall all be made alive" (I Corinthians 15:22). In the place of the disintegrating society, you have the society of those in whom the divine image has been restored, those who reveal in actual institutions the invisible purposes of God, those who reveal that man's essential social nature is good even as his essential individual nature is good. The new society is the realization of the divine purpose in spite of the decadence and decay of the society of evil. There is the City of God and it is the city of men living according to their true nature. There is the City of Dreadful Night and it is the city in which each soul has betrayed the flesh which was meant to express the purposes of the Eternal. The perpetual social conflict is the battle between the City of God and the City of Dreadful Night.

It is the religion of the Incarnation which makes secure the faith and the victory of the City of God. Just as the Eternal can master the flesh and turn it to glorious purposes of the spirit, so the Eternal can master organization and institutions and societies. This Word made flesh is the promise of all that is human mastered by all that is divine.

The tragic note to be sure is not completely effaced. There is the misuse of freedom as well as its noble use. So there is the evil soul corrupting the human body. So there is the evil purpose creating an evil society. And the bending of the evil society as far as it is the company of those who have refused redemption, to the purposes of God always involves a force which now at last confronts a nature made evil by the bad will of man. The minor music cannot be entirely eliminated from the great sonata of life.

But the victory even in time is with the Eternal. And that victory expresses man's nature as God meant it to be. So man's nature becomes the servant of the deathless majesty of moral love. God could become man because God had put into man that which is capable of responding to the divine will. Man can become like God in character because God has already put eternity in his heart.

The Great Commandment

REVEREND BERNARD IDDINGS BELL, S.T.D., D.D., LITT.D., LL.D.
Canon of the Cathedral of SS. Peter and Paul, Chicago, Illinois

The Reverend Bernard Iddings Bell, who has just been appointed canon of the Protestant Episcopal Cathedral of SS. Peter and Paul in Chicago and Consultant to the Bishop of Chicago on Education, is fifty-nine years old. He was born in Dayton, Ohio and educated at the University of Chicago and Western Theological Seminary, Chicago. His interests have always been chiefly in religious education and in the relationship between religion and politics.

Before the first World War he was dean of the Episcopal Cathedral in Fond du Lac, Wisconsin, and during that war was aide to the senior chaplain at Great Lakes Naval Training Station. The war over, he became warden of St. Stephen's College, a country college of Columbia University, and professor of religion in Columbia University. In 1933 he retired from academic connections and since then has devoted his time to preaching, lecturing, research and writing.

A priest of the Episcopal church, he has written twenty-one books of which the best known are Beyond Agnosticism; The Church in Disrepute; The Altar and the World. *His most widely sold book is his latest one, published in 1945, entitled* God Is Not Dead. *He has written twenty-two articles for the* Atlantic Monthly *on religious topics and has contributed to* Harper's, *the* Criterion, *the* New York Times Magazine, *to many church papers. He has been in residence and lectured in six of the great English schools, including Rugby and Charterhouse, and has preached in thirteen English cathedrals. He has been Stated Preacher at various times at Harvard, Yale, Princeton, Chicago, Columbia, Williams, Amherst, Wellesley, Vassar, Smith, Mt. Holyoke and many other colleges.*

"The Great Commandment" was preached in Trinity Church, New York, in June, 1945.

Sermon Twelve

THE suggestion that a series of summer sermons be preached on *the Ten Commandments* comes from one who during most of these trying war years has been a member of the President's cabinet. This distinguished person has said to me: "It is impossible to sit in the high councils of a nation, where of necessity those who are guiding that nation find themselves turning from consideration of one problem incapable of solution to a half dozen other problems equally impossible to handle, without realizing that the whole world is sick, sick with a disease that goes deeper than the political or the economic, morally sick. Is it that man has forgotten the will of his Maker? We do not hear anything these days of *the Ten Commandments*. Children do not learn them, and those of us who once knew them are not reminded of them. They used to be painted on the walls of churches, up behind the Altar. They once were recited at every celebration of the Holy Communion. When I was young I heard sermons about them. Have they dropped out of Religion as well as out of secular life? Is that what is wrong with the world?"

Yes, I am afraid *the Ten Commandments* have for the most part dropped out. Neglect of them is what is the matter with modern life. It is also most of what is the matter with today's Religion.

In timid conformity with the world's evident desire, the churches have been too willing to forget that God is maker of man and judge of man quite as truly as He is creator and controller of things physical and organic. Modern man insists that man is an exception in the universe. Everything else must obey the God-given law of its being, but not man; man can do as he pleases, write his own rules, make his own morality. This is the veriest nonsense. For what is man? Whatever else is true of man, this at least is true of him, that man is a *creature—created*, he did not make himself—a creature who, if left unguided, lives a few short blundering years and perishes, usually with a broken heart. He cannot add one cubit to the measure of his life. He is like the flower of grass; today he blossoms, but tomorrow he is cast into the oven. He spends most of his days trying to learn how to avoid self-destruction, and he never learns it well. Man is a part of God's law-abiding universe, a confusedly rebellious part thereof. He cannot order himself aright. He needs to be taught the law of his own being, his natural destiny, the divine will for him and, when he has learned it, to obey. But modern man thinks otherwise. He is himself, so he supposes, a little god, master of his own fate, captain of his own soul. God, so modern man imagines if he thinks about God at all, is one who exists to serve man.

Contemporary religion, instead of opposing this mad conceit, for the greater part has gone along with modern man. It has reduced the God it preaches to the level of one who is man's dear, kind, doting servant. It has made God out to be a foolish grandfather, a bestower of spiritual sweetmeats and celestial circus tickets, a grandfather who lets the children do as their little hearts desire and laughs indulgently at their pranks. It has presented God as a giver of blessing to any sort of political folly, any sort of economic madness which the State devises and allows. It has in God's name uttered no commandments, made on His behalf no demands. To change the simile, contemporary Religion has presented God as a sort of permeating music, a sweet perfume, a gentle breeze, a fluffy meringue with which to supplement the human meal. It has dethroned the Almighty and bade modern man himself to occupy the throne of ultimate authority. It has, in short, helped men and women play the fool. God knows we have played the fool most ably; and now the enemies within cast a trench and lay us even with the ground, and our children. If only we had known the law of our being, God's intention for this age and day! If only we had known the things which belong to our peace; but now they are hidden from our eyes. *The Commandments* of God, known to our fathers at least as far back as Moses, the ethical basis of Religion, the law of life authenticated by history and endorsed by God-made-man—it is time, high time, to recall them, to proclaim them, to obey them.

Why do you suppose God cares whether or not we obey Him? He gazes, with all-seeing spiritual delight, upon an orderly universe. Therein unnumbered galaxies of stars move in celestial rhythm, utterly obedient to the natural law. Therein every physical creation of His, however large, however small, fits into the schematic picture. This is a universe of law, of a natural law which is the device of the divine Law-giver. Why, then, should it bother God if one of His creatures, the creature called man, make a fool of himself? The earth on which this creature lives out his little day is a small planet, once a part of that tenth-rate star called the Sun. Man is a speck—small organism which walks about upon the outer surface of that insignificant planet, an unreliable exception in a vast and obedient universe. Why should God take the trouble to instruct this willful absurdity who thinks the Heavens shine for his delectation, who seeks to make the universe a human tool? Why should God bother with man?

The answer lies in the fact that while man is a tiny creature, man is also a unique creature. The Bible puts this uniqueness in picturesque language when it says that man is made "in the image and likeness of God." This does not mean that man resembles God physically. God is not a physical being, with a face and a body that can be resembled; God is pure spirit. No, what is meant is that man can do the sort of thing that God does; man can *create*. His creative powers are very limited, of course, but man *can create*. Man can take material and manipulate it into something of what he wishes it to be. He can do things with it not by necessity but according to his dreams. He can think a tool and then devise it. He can think a symphony and then compose it. He can think a picture and then paint it. He can think a poem and then write it. He can think a cathedral and then erect it. This creative power in man is, as far as we know, unique in all the universe. That makes man important, important even to God, interesting to God as is nothing else which God has made. Man is exceedingly clever.

But man's very cleverness may well be man's undoing. It is easy for him, only too easy, when he has made some fascinating device, to use that device for self-destructive ends. He makes, for instance, an airplane. If used for God's purposes it can unite men as never before, result in their becoming friends and neighbors across land and sea. But it can also be used to drop block bombs and blow to pieces man's cities, to deal out death to innocent people. Man can learn to manipulate chemical elements and physical forces. Having done it, he may thereby harness nature, cure disease, spread happiness; but equally he may thereby make explosives, poison his fellows, even exterminate the human race. Man needs to be taught what is God's will for him to do with that creative cleverness of his.

This God has done for man. He has not done it merely by writing ten words on two tables of stone. *The Ten Commandments* of Moses are no unique performance, lightning out of the skies. They are an epitome of God's long, continuous message to man about human conduct—a brief of moral truths which man has had to learn by bitter trial and error through the centuries, of conclusions of able minds which have pondered the nature of the good life, of clear poetic visions seen by prophets and seers, of that which has been revealed when humble men and women have bowed in adoration before the Eternal and begged for guidance of the Holy Ghost who speaks within the heart. The reason *the Ten Commandments* have such authority is that they reduce all this to certain maxims which even the mind of a child can understand. They cannot with safety be ignored.

The Ten Commandments divide themselves into two groups. The first four deal with duty of man towards God; the last six, with duty of man towards man. Why does the duty towards God come first?

It comes first because, as has been said, it is man's conceit which ruins him, the pride which bids him regard himself as an end. He is not an end. We exist because God wills us to exist, because God thinks us into being. If men forget this and seek to serve themselves as end, they go mad and like all maniacs turn to contention with their fellows. Only if men remember whose they are will they live brotherly, co-operatively. "Man being in self-honor," says the Psalmist, "but who forgets God, becomes as the beasts that perish." As a matter of fact such sort of man becomes worse than the beasts and his fate is worse than theirs, for he not only perishes but perishes diabolically. Therefore it is that man must remember God, acknowledge that he belongs to God, adore God, seek to serve God's purposes. Only so can man hope to solve his problems of mutual living.

The first four Commandments are four variant, cumulative warnings that man must take God seriously, must put God first. This is the way these first four Commandments paraphrase themselves in modern speech:

I. Thou shalt have none other God (i.e. serve no other end) opposed to Me.
II. Thou shalt not make to thyself for worship the image of any created thing.
III. Thou shalt not regard the Name of the Lord thy God as though it were a common thing of small account.
IV. Thou shalt every seventh day remind thyself of Me by systematic adoration, give Me worship.

All of these first four Commandments unite to say: "Keep ever in mind whose you are, whose will it is that you, like all things else, must do or perish."

As my distinguished friend has said, modern people turn from one insoluble problem—economic, political, marital, educational, personal—from one insoluble problem to a dozen other equally insoluble problems. Why are they insoluble? Because we have lost our way in a tangled forest of pride. There will be no joy for man, no security for Society, no morals preservable or worth preserving, no ceasing of continued carnage until we lift our eyes beyond our small concerns, up toward the Heavens, toward the everlasting God; until we cry with a new humility: "When I consider the Heavens, the moon and the stars that thou hast ordained, what is Man that Thou art mindful of him? *It is Thou who hast made him.* O Lord our Governor, how excellent is Thy name in all the world." It is not our skill that will save us, not our technology, not a United Nations founded on national self-interests, existing by virtue of precarious assent, not our shrewd scheming, not even our benevolent desires. These, the erection of our dull-sighted blundering toward good, are flimsy shelter from the tempest of man's mad ambition, his soaring vainglory. "God of our fathers, God of all nature and beyond nature, God who art maker of Heaven and Earth, Thou canst save us. Thou alone."

"Lord Jesus, what is the great commandment in the Law?"

"Thou shalt love the Lord thy God. This is the first and great commandment."

The Purpose of Life

THE RIGHT REVEREND MONSIGNOR FULTON J. SHEEN, PH.D., D.D.
*Associate Professor of Philosophy, The Catholic University of America,
Washington, D.C.*

*Monsignor Sheen's is one of the important living voices of our day. His
forceful and convincing preaching makes every listener eager to catch each
word. To hear him is to realize that here is a man who believes what he says
and who has thought out his message calmly and prayerfully.*

*After graduate work at the Catholic University of America, the University
of Louvain, Belgium and Angelico University, Rome, he was ordained in
Peoria, Illinois, in 1919. Step by step he has risen from very modest places in
the Church to be one of the most honored Catholic preachers. He taught at
St. Edmund's College, Ware, and the Westminster (London) Diocesan Seminary in 1925-26; in 1926 the University of Louvain, recognizing his genius,
awarded him the Cardinal Mercier prize for International Philosophy, the
first time this honor was ever given an American.*

*Before the war, he was called to preach in Europe nearly every summer
from 1925 to 1939, speaking in London at Westminster Cathedral and St.
Patrick's Church, Soho Square; at the University of Cambridge Summer
School, at Glasgow; in Rome, and elsewhere on the continent. In 1934 he
was named a Papal Chamberlain of the late Pontiff, Pope Pius XI, with the
title of Very Reverend Monsignor, and the following year, Pius XI made
him a Domestic Prelate with the title of Right Reverend Monsignor.*

*During most of the year, he is busy teaching philosophy at the Catholic
University of America, but is in such demand as a speaker, that he gives
more than one hundred sermons and addresses each year, speaking in almost
every major city in the United States to secular and religious groups who
throng to hear him. For years he has been the regular Lenten preacher at
St. Patrick's Cathedral, New York, and is the special Advent preacher at the
Church of the Blessed Sacrament, New York, where his Advent messages
are enthusiastically received.*

*He has written some twenty books on philosophy, religion, morals and socio-
economic questions, including* Freedom Under God, Whence Come Wars
and Philosophies at War.

*In this sermon he discusses the age-old problem of freedom and its use
by men of free will.*

Sermon Thirteen

THERE is no word more often used in our modern world and more often misunderstood than the word *Freedom*. Almost everyone thinks of it as freedom *from* something, but rarely as freedom *for* something. Men think they are free only because they have no ball and chain on their feet, without ever adverting to why they want to be free. What I am trying to say is there are two kinds of freedom; an *external* freedom from restraints, and an *internal* freedom of perfection; a freedom to choose evil and a freedom to possess the good; a freedom outside law, and a freedom inside law; a freedom to do whatever you please, and a freedom to do whatever you ought.

This inner freedom the typical modern man does not want, because it implies responsibility and responsibility is a burden—the awful burden of answering: What is the purpose of your life? That is why theories which deny man's inner freedom are so popular today; for example, Marxism, which destroys freedom in terms of historical determinism; Freudianism, which dissolves freedom in the determinism of the subconscious and the erotic; Totalitarianism, which drowns individual freedom in the collectivity of race, nation, blood or clan.

The root of all our trouble is that freedom for God and in God has been interpreted as freedom from God. Fundamentally, freedom is ours to give away. Before we ask what you do with your freedom, let us turn to the life of Our Lord and Our Lady, for the supreme example of how they used their freedom. To whom did they surrender their freedom?

The first word Our Lord is recorded as speaking in the Scripture is at the age of twelve: "I must be about my Father's business" (Luke 2:49). During His public life, He reaffirmed this dedication to His Father's Will: "I do always the things that please him" (John 8:29). Now on the Cross, when He goes out to meet death by freely surrendering His Life, His last words are: "Father, into thy hands I commend my Spirit" (Luke 23:46).

The last words of other men are spoken in whispers, but He spoke these words in a loud voice. Death did not come to Him: He went to death. No one took His life away; He laid it down of Himself. He was strong enough to live, but He died by an act of will. The word was not an emphasis on dying, but an affirmation of uninterrupted Divine Life. It was the beginning of His return to the glory which He had with the Father before the foundations of the world were laid.

Father—Note the word of Eternal Parenthood. He did not say *Our Father* as we do, for the Father was not His and ours in the same way. He is the Natural Son of the Father; we are only the adopted sons.

Into thy hands—These were the hands the prophet called "good"; the

[75]

hands that guided Israel to its historical fulfillment of God's Providence; the hands that provided good things even for the birds of the air and the grass of the field.

I commend my spirit—Surrender! Consecration! Life is a cycle. We come from God and we go back again to God. Hence the purpose of living is to do God's will.

When Our Blessed Mother saw Hiw bow His head and deliver His Spirit, she remembered the last Word that she is recorded to have spoken in Scripture. It was to the wine steward at the marriage feast of Cana: "Whatsoever he shall say to you, do ye" (John 2:5).

What a beautiful valedictory! They are the most magnificent words that ever came from the lips of a woman: "Whatsoever he shall say to you, do ye." At the Transfiguration the Heavenly Father spoke from the Heavens and said: "This is my Beloved Son . . . hear ye him" (Matthew 17:5). Now Our Blessed Mother speaks and says, "Do His Will." The sweet relationship of three decades in Nazareth now draws to a close, as Mary is about to give Emmanuel to us all. She does it by pointing out to us the one and only way of salvation: complete consecration to her Divine Son. Nowhere in the Scripture is it ever said that Mary loved her Son. Words do not prove love. True love is surrender of the will and such is her final injunction to us: "Whatsoever he shall say to you, do ye" (John 2:5).

Both the last recorded words of Jesus and those of Mary were words about freedom: a freedom for something. For Jesus it was the will of the Father, for Mary the will of the Son. This is the law of the universe: Nature is for man, man is for Christ, and Christ is God's: "All are yours; and you are Christ's; and Christ is God's" (I Corinthians 3:22-23).

What do you do with your freedom? You can do three things with it:

(1) Keep it for your selfish desires.
(2) Break it up into tiny little areas of trivial allegiance or passing fancy.
(3) Surrender it to God.

If you keep freedom only for yourself, then, because it is arbitrary and without standards, you will find it deteriorating into a defiant self-affirmation. Once all things become allowable, simple because you desire them, you will become the slave of your choices. If your self-will decides to drink as much as you please, you soon find not only that you are no longer free not to drink, but that you belong to drink; it is your master, you are its slave. Boundless liberty is boundless tyranny. The abuse of freedom ends in the destruction of freedom, of which Lucifer is the supreme example. This is what Our Lord meant when He said: "Whosoever committeth sin, is the servant of sin" (John 8:34).

The second way to use freedom is to become like a hummingbird, hovering first over this flower, then over that, but living for none and dying without any. In that case, you desire nothing with all your heart, because your heart is broken into a thousand pieces. You thus become divided against yourself; a civil war rages within you, because you are striking out in contradictory directions. You change your likes and desires when dissatisfied, but you never change yourself. You become very much like the man who complained to the cook at breakfast that the egg was not fresh and asked her for another. She brought in an egg a minute later, but when he got to the bottom of it, he found it was the same old egg turned upside down. So it is with human nature; what has changed is the desire, not the soul.

As a result your interest in others is not real. In your more honest moments you discover that you have dealt with them on the basis of self-interest; you let them speak when they agree with you, but you silence them when they disagree. Your moments of love, if you looked into your soul, are nothing but barren exchanges of egotisms—you talk about yourself five minutes, and your neighbor talks about himself five minutes, but if he takes longer you call him a "bore."

No wonder such people often say: "I must pull myself together." Thus do they confess that they are like broken mirrors, each reflecting a different image. In essence this is debauchery, or the inability to choose one among many attractions; the soul is diffused, multiple, or "legion," as Satan called himself. And this is the sad state of millions in the world; they are free *from* something, but free *for* nothing.

Finally, you can use your freedom as Christ did on the Cross, by surrendering His Spirit to the Father, and as Mary bade us at Cana, by doing His Will in all things. This is perfect freedom: the displacement of self as the center of motivation and the fixation of our choices, decisions and actions on Divine Love. "Thy will be done on earth as it is in heaven." We are all like limpets that can live only when they cling to a rock. Our freedom forces us to cling to something. Freedom is ours to surrender; we are free to choose our servitudes. To give that freedom to anything less than the Perfect never brings ultimate peace. But to surrender to Perfect Love is to surrender to happiness and thereby be perfectly free. Thus to "serve Him is to reign."

But we are afraid to give away our will. Like St. Augustine in his early life we say: "I want to love you dear Lord, a little later on, but not now." Fearful of One who comes to us purple-robed and cypress-crowned, we ask: "Must Thy harvest fields be dunged with rotten death?" Must gold be purified by fire? Must hands that beckon bear the red livid marks of nails? Must I give up my candle, if I have the sun? Must I give up knocking if the door of love is opened? Do we not act toward God as a child who resents the affectionate embrace of his parents, because it is not our mood to love? Francis Thompson so reflected when he heard these words from the mouth of a child:

> "Why do you so clasp me,
> And draw me to your knee?
> Forsooth, you do but chafe me,
> I pray you let me be:

I will be loved but now and then
  When it liketh me!"
So I heard a young child,
  A thwart child, a young child
Rebellious against love's arms,
  Make its peevish cry.
To the tender God I turn:—
  "Pardon, Love most High!
For I think those arms were even Thine,
  And that child even I."

As Pascal said: "There are only two kinds of people we can call reasonable: either those who serve God with their whole heart because they know Him, or those who search after Him with all their heart because they do not know Him."

There is hope for you if you are dissatisfied with your present choices, and you want the Perfect: the very void you thus create makes it possible for God to fill it. I would rather hear you say, "I am a sinner," than to hear you say, "I have no need of religion." If you admit you are a sinner, you acknowledge the need of a Redeemer; but if you have no need of religion, then you are your own god. If you are empty, God can pour in His waters of Life; if you are self-intoxicated, there is no room for anything else.

No man who has ever shed a sincere tear before God for the way he abused his freedom was ever lost. Even in an earthly way, have you ever noticed how much more beautiful the hills look when there are tears in your eyes? You may even see rainbows of hope. It does not require much time to make us Saints; it requires only much Love. Our Lord took St. Augustine to Himself even though he lamented: "Too late, O ancient Beauty, have I loved Thee."

So He will take your freedom to choose the imperfect and make it a freedom in perfection, if you but surrender; and in the language of the poet, you will cry out in the ecstasy of the glorious liberty of the children of God:

O gain that lurk'st ungained in all gain
O love we just fall short of in all love!
O height that in all heights art still above!
O beauty that dost leave all beauty pain!
Thou unpossessed that mak'st possession vain.

I cannot tell you the secret of happiness so beautifully in my words, but I can tell you more simply: God love you!

PRAYER: *O Lord Jesus Christ, Who in Thy mercy hearest the prayers of sinners, pour forth, we beseech Thee, all grace and blessing upon our country and its citizens. We pray in particular for the President—for our Congress—for all our soldiers—for all who defend us in ships, whether on the seas or in the skies—for all who are suffering the hardships of war. We pray for all who are in peril or in danger. Bring us all after the troubles of this life into the haven of peace, and reunite us all together forever, O dear Lord, in Thy glorious heavenly kingdom. Amen.*

NIHIL OBSTAT: Rev. T. E. Dillon, *Censor Librorum*
IMPRIMATUR: ✠ John Francis Noll, D.D., *Bishop, Fort Wayne*

A Religion for the Atomic Age

REVEREND THEODORE FLOYD ADAMS, D.D.
Pastor, First Baptist Church, Richmond, Virginia

Dr. Adams is one of the leading Baptist preachers in the South.

He has held just three pastorates—Cleveland Heights Baptist Church, Cleveland, Ohio, from 1924 to 1927; Ashland Avenue Baptist Church, Toledo, Ohio, from 1927 to 1936; and First Baptist Church, Richmond, from 1936 to the present. The First Baptist Church—with a membership of over twenty-seven hundred—is one of the leading churches in the Southern Baptist Convention in missions and benevolences.

Dr. Adams discusses one of the most timely sermon topics of 1945, the atomic bomb. He shows quite clearly that only spiritual power can cope with atomic power to make of it a blessing rather than a curse. He preached this sermon twice, first in Richmond on September 9, 1945, and repeated it by request on Columbia Broadcasting System's Church of the Air on November 4, 1945.

Sermon Fourteen

A FEW days ago I saw a letter written by a young scientist who had shared in the long years of work that culminated in the first atomic bomb. In the course of the letter he said that to civilization the atomic bomb "will be as great a jolt as was the step from the Stone Age to the metal age." The young scientist is right. When the first news of the atomic bomb flashed on an amazed world, it brought more than the story of a shattered Hiroshima and the possibility of bringing the war to a dramatic and early end. It also made us realize anew how frightful war could be, and brought to America a new sense of power and of responsibility.

We do stand on the threshold of the atomic age, as we hold in trust for a time the secret that will usher in a new era in the life of the world—a secret that holds tremendous power for good or for ill. It can be either creative or destructive, the beginning either of new wonders of life or of chaos for civilization.

General MacArthur sensed this when he spoke at the close of the dramatic ceremony on the battleship "Missouri," and told the world that God has given us what may well be our last chance for peace. Those of you who heard that memorable message will remember that he went on to say that the solution of our problems is theological. Only with God's help shall we see the triumph of the spirit over the flesh.

Surely we must have a religion great enough for the atomic age, and we do have it in our Christian faith. It is good to know that ours is an adequate faith for today and tomorrow, whatever the new discoveries of science may be. Ours is a God who is both Creator and Father—the Creator who provides the physical forces for our use, and the Father who provides the spiritual power to use them aright. As we face the future with its challenging possibilities for good and for evil, we are led to say as did the disciples of old to Jesus, "Lord, to whom shall we go? thou hast the words of eternal life" (John 6:68).

Of necessity we turn to him who said, "All power is given unto me in heaven and in earth." In him we shall find the faith we need—a religion for the atomic age. Let us see then what that faith can give us.

First of all, we must have a faith adequate for our personal needs. Whatever may be the problems of the world, we all have our own personal problems and are constantly in need of help beyond ourselves. The bombshell experiences of life come to us all and we must have a faith that will make us ready and able to meet them. The Christian religion offers just that. How it works in life was well expressed in a letter I received early in the war from a young woman who had just found for the first time what Christ and the Church could mean to her. She wrote: "I can never tell you how happy I am to be a member of the Church. Ever since I first decided to join I have found a deep contentment—an engulfing comfort. I never realized before how much my life lacked this spiritual satisfaction. Now more than ever, I realize that I am never alone. God is always with me. His rod and his staff they comfort me. . . . The next time I am called upon to face a crisis, I shall slip my hand into God's hand and look ahead unafraid." Each one of us needs, and can have, just such a personal faith for the days ahead.

A religion for the atomic age must also provide adequate spiritual power to match the physical powers of nature. We are only beginning to see what atomic power can mean with its ability to destroy or to bless. We are told that if it can be properly released and controlled, there is enough atomic energy in five pounds of ordinary matter to drive an ocean liner ten times around the world. With such tremendous physical power in our hands, we need also adequate resources of mind and heart. Only spiritual power can cope with atomic power and make it a blessing rather than a curse. The atomic bomb will be no guarantee of peace any more than were the submarine or airplane. Its ultimate use and significance will be determined by the individuals who control it. Whatever may be the eventual solution of the problem of national or international control, Christians will need more spiritual power and grace than ever before. "To whom else shall we go?" Only Christ has the word of life our day demands.

A German prisoner of war summed it up in a sentence at a communion service conducted one Easter morning by an English chaplain in North Africa. The German prisoner was asked to lead in a prayer and he said, "Let us pray that Christ may rule the nations of tomorrow." If his spirit does rule in the use of this new physical power we shall find the way to peace. It is Christ or chaos.

A religion for the atomic age must also foster in our minds and hearts an attitude of brotherhood and love for all mankind—even for our enemies. This is not easy, but we must, in Christ's name, send help to the suffering, strengthen those who are weak, and feed and clothe those who rightly look to us for aid. The faith that is ours in Jesus Christ will lead us to do that. It can reunite us where we have been divided, enable us to rise above all man-made barriers, and develop in us a creative love that will bring out the best in others. Some time ago a leading Chinese Christian told how he traveled across Siberia in the same railroad compartment with a Japanese. For a time they were uncomfortable in each other's presence until one saw the other begin to read his Bible. That was the beginning of a new understanding between the two, "for," said the Chinese Christian, "we found that the faith that united us was greater than the nationalism that divided us."

What is our spirit to be? Is it to be a spirit of justice and good will, of Christian love and brotherhood, or are we to go again the old way of hate, vindictiveness and bitterness? Certainly those who have wronged their own people and the world must be punished and they will be, but only as we go further and in the spirit of the Lord Christ heal the wounds of the world can we foster an enduring peace. In a world that can be smashed overnight with the atomic bomb we dare not try any other way than his. How difficult and yet how essential this is, we find illustrated in the life of Robert E. Lee. When at the close of the Civil War General Lee was indicted for treason in violation of the surrender terms, a minister in the community came to see him and spoke very bitterly about it. General Lee replied: "It matters little what they may do to me. I am old, and have but a short time to live anyway. Doctor, there is a good old book I read and you preach from, which says, 'Love your enemies, bless them that curse you, and pray for them which despitefully use you and persecute you.' Do you think your remarks this evening were quite in the spirit of that teaching? I have fought the North, for I believed they were seeking to wrest from the South her dearest rights. I have never cherished bitter or vindictive feelings against them, nor seen the day when I did not pray for them." In the spirit of that great Christian is our hope for a future of peace and good will.

A religion for the atomic age must also make us world-minded. How good it is that we have a universal faith since we must live as citizens of "One World." Never again must we yield to isolationism. As our men have gone to fight in all the earth, so must we continue to send missionaries of peace to all the world. The united nations of war years must work together for years of peace. The Christian Church fosters such a world brotherhood and seeks with God's help, and in the spirit of Christ, to promote peace on earth and good will among men.

To whom else shall we go? Truly we can say of our Lord, "Thou only hast the words of life for our nation and for the world." We are beginning to realize the weakness of other false philosophies, of nationalism that puts one nation above all, of communism that puts one class above all, of fascism that puts one race above all. Thank God that America with her new world responsibilities has faith in Him who "Made of one blood all nations to dwell on the face of the earth." We long have said, "In God we trust." It is He who has given us the dream of a world of peace. It is because we believe in Him and are assured of His help that we continue to cherish the hope of the prophets of old, "They shall beat their swords into plowshares, and their spears into pruninghooks: nation shall not lift up sword against nation, neither shall they learn war any more." Now that we hold in trust the atomic power that can either help realize that dream or blast away our hopes, we need more than ever to turn to God and pray as Jesus taught, "Thy kingdom come, thy will be done on earth." To help answer that prayer, "God was in Christ reconciling the world unto himself." To whom else can we go, to whom else dare we turn, for guidance and hope? "There is none other name under heaven given among men whereby we must be saved."

Dr. E. Stanley Jones tells of a missionary lost in the jungles who finally found a native who agreed to lead him home. After they had gone through the trackless jungle for a long time, the missionary began to doubt and said to the native, "Are you sure this is the way?" The native said, "There is no way. I am the way." Just as truly there is One who says to us as we face the future, "I am the way." "Follow me."

He is our hope for today and tomorrow, but we must remember that hope exists, not in a nation, but in the individuals who constitute it. If the world is to be more Christian, we must be more Christlike ourselves. Only as this faith is personal can it be national. Only as Christ is given his rightful place in our individual lives can he shape and guide our national life. As you enter then, into the atomic age, claim for yourself this faith that is our only hope. How much such a faith can mean is beautifully illustrated in an incident that occurred in Texas a few years ago. One who had known her Lord for half a century and wanted to celebrate that fact, sent her friends an invitation printed in gold on paneled parchment. It read: "1890-1940.

You are cordially invited to rejoice with me, honoring the golden anniversary of my conversion at ten o'clock, Tuesday morning, the third of September, 1940. How sweet the time has been!" What a testimony that is of a religion that is adequate for every need in life. To sum up the faith of a half century of victorious living she added to the invitation the verse from the Psalms that we read at the beginning of our worship: "For the Lord God is a sun and shield: the Lord will give grace and glory: no good thing will he withhold from them that walk uprightly. O Lord of hosts, blessed is the man that trusteth in thee" (Psalm 84:11, 12). Hers was the faith the world needs, the faith you and I need as we face the future. "Lord, to whom shall we go? Thou—and thou alone—hast the words of eternal life." In thee we do have a religion for the atomic age.

> PRAYER: *Bless us, O Lord, in this faith that is ours. Help us to make America a truly Christian nation. To that end help us to be more Christlike ourselves. Trusting in Thee, we shall face our future unafraid. Grant that we may be, in spirit and in truth, workers together with Thee, for the advancing of thy kingdom in the hearts and lives of men. And now may the Lord bless you and keep you, the Lord make his face to shine upon you and be gracious unto you, the Lord lift up the light of his countenance upon you and give you peace. Through Jesus Christ our Lord, Amen.*

Does Christianity Have the Ghost of a Chance?

REVEREND PAUL E. SCHERER, D.D., LL.D.[1]
A Minister of the Evangelical Lutheran Church and Associate Professor of Practical Theology, Union Theological Seminary, New York

Those who know him best believe that Paul Scherer has a genius for preaching. He himself insists that it is mostly a matter of hard work in the preparation of each sermon. His sermons of the "Great Preacher Series" in Reading, Harrisburg, and other cities; his Lenten and Easter sermons in Detroit, and his sermon on the 400th Anniversary of Martin Luther have the elements of greatness.

Born in Mt. Holly Springs, Pennsylvania, in 1892, Dr. Scherer studied for his B.D. at the Lutheran Theological Seminary, Mt. Airy, Philadelphia, and

---

[1] Sermons by members of the Advisory Committee were contributed at the request of the editor and are included on his responsibility.

was ordained a minister of the Lutheran Church in 1916. He taught at the Mt. Airy Seminary for ten years—from 1919 to 1929—and was pastor of Holy Trinity Church, New York from 1920 to 1945. In addition he has preached frequently at colleges and universities along the eastern seaboard, in England during the summers of 1930 and 1931, and on N.B.C.'s Sunday Vespers program. At the August Conference in Northfield he has served as vice-chairman since 1937 and as dean since 1942.

This sermon is an excellent example of Dr. Scherer's style, which is timely, close to the New Testament, and deeply spiritual in its interpretation of life. It was preached on the Sunday Vespers of the American Broadcasting Company on August 12, 1945. His question, "Does Christianity Have a Ghost of a Chance?" is as pertinent as tomorrow.

Sermon Fifteen

PAUL spent a good deal of his time trying to persuade the people whom he had converted to Christianity that they didn't have to spend any of their time worrying about the outward observance of ritualistic procedures, rules and regulations. This new-found religion of theirs wasn't like that. It had to do with something else entirely. Yet he didn't want them on that account to think that it was nothing but a kind of mushroom growth either. It hadn't simply shot up overnight with no roots in the long past of human life. As a matter of fact, it ran back to Abraham and Isaac. It belonged to the eternal pattern of things. It was destined to occupy the center of the stage from that time on. The Almighty had designed it with that end in view. "Now we, brethren, as Isaac was," so writes this little apostle in the fourth chapter of his letter to the Galatians, "are the children of promise."

You will not find anything in the whole New Testament more, what shall I say?—momentous than that simple statement. Incidentally, it carried in its womb the seed of the Reformation, that great rebellion against the Middle Ages which brought along with it so much that's good about our modern world and so much that's almost indescribably bad: This brand of irresponsible freedom, for instance, which amounts to little more than ruinous license. But that isn't what concerns me here. I want you rather to think of the trouble Paul got himself into, and all his converts with him, by insisting that Christianity was something different from anything they had known. When the Roman authorities found that out, they were bound by imperial law to persecute it. Rome didn't take very kindly to any change. In the years that followed she tried to wipe this new religion off the map. For a long time it didn't seem to have the ghost of a chance. Yet strangely enough it came through simply because new as it seemed it was actually old. It was as old as Abraham. "Before Abraham was, I am." It was as old as God! "Now we, brethren, as Isaac was, are the children of promise." It was part of a project which ran as far back as Creation itself!

And this is what I wish we could be convinced of! As we stand here today on the threshold of peace. Nobody knows what we are going to do with our victory. A good many seem to believe that we shall have to rely on something else besides Christianity. That is pretty well played out. So they say. They shrug their shoulders and ask us, "How do you know it's going to last even? How can you tell what religion your great-grandchildren will have, if any? There have been quite a few in the history of the world!" And people have plenty of reason for shaking their heads. Let's be honest. The Christian religion runs counter to so much that's going on in front of our eyes! It's so thoroughly out of accord with so many of our habitual attitudes and reactions that we are always calling it impractical and insisting that it won't ever work. Men still grab and cheat and lie and steal and kill one another. Why keep worrying about such idealistic moonshine? It hasn't a chance. It hasn't the ghost of a chance!

But don't be in too big a hurry! Suppose it really were the way God Almighty had figured things out—not just that lovable Galilean Carpenter, whose name was Jesus, who dreamed such beautiful dreams. Suppose, in downright sober earnest, it were as much tied up with the very nature of our universe as the sun is, for example; or Jupiter, or Neptune; or the laws that hold them together, so that they won't fly off at a tangent into space like a foul ball. Then not only would Christianity have the ghost of a chance, but what other approach would have any?

And that's exactly how it looks! Because it fits the facts we've got to face as if it were made for them; and nothing else does. Take evil. That's a fact. And science has nothing much to say about it; except that we'll probably grow out of it. But we don't. We grow into it. Every day in every way, with its tanks and its airplanes, humanity is capable of getting nastier and nastier. Schools and colleges, when they mention this aspect of the human situation at all, keep saying how very bad it is to be bad. They go on talking about morals, and how very good it is to be good.

Only the Christian religion puts its finger on the fundamental fact. We can't! The gospel of Jesus Christ says it's absurd and suicidal for us to go on into this postwar world with nothing but a kind of superstitious reliance on knowledge and technique. They won't do for us the job we have to do now. No course of study, no well-thought-out program, no treaty, no new order, will get at it. No picking apart of economic systems to put them together again. No building up of political forms to tear them down. No amount of rummaging around among the textbooks on psychology.

It says that what we really need—think of it!—before we need anything else—even here in America—is just God's plain, everyday forgiveness. How realistic is that? You know how rotten you feel when you've been rotten, and get back among people that aren't? Nothing decent can happen to you until you get rid of that feeling. And you get rid of it not by covering it up and making believe it isn't there. You get rid of it by telling those others about it—those others you have wronged—and telling God about it and asking everybody's pardon! Why doesn't anyone mention that in our world, or think it important?

A very good article I came across recently in a periodical that wants very much to be called Christian suggested to young people that being religious had comparatively little to do with prayer or Bible reading or going to Church; but rather with helping others to be honest, making and keeping their athletics clean and their politics aboveboard; showing deep reverence for human personality. These are the things most of us are accustomed to say. But get your teeth into that last which of course is at the bottom of all the rest. Why show such deep reverence for human personality? Maybe man is nothing but the offspring of an ape that has learned how to shave! That's what they taught me. If it isn't for God's sake that we take off our hats to him, I suggest that we keep them on! And go on talking as we like about everybody who isn't our sort, calling them names to our heart's content: until God vomits us out of His mouth! May the day come soon! Reverence is born somewhere above us, or it isn't born! That's why we ought never to separate, even by implication, between honesty, for instance, on the one hand, and between Bible reading and athletics, between prayer and politics, and church attendance on the other. Primarily the Christian religion has to do with none of them and with all of them. It has to do with God and the human soul. Without Him everything else is nothing; and none of it will continue long. Without Him the whole of life is a ridiculous cage where human squirrels keep chasing themselves about in circles, gnawing on a few moral precepts for sustenance while they stop to catch their breath! Christianity is a friendship with God in Christ, where nothing stands between Him and any one of us any more. For that reason it has to begin in forgiveness. It grows through prayer and worship and the reading of the Bible. And it issues in as much honesty and uprightness at the center and all around the horizons of your life as you and He together can manage!

I submit that's facing the actual facts about human nature and human conduct as nothing else does. We aren't good enough of ourselves to be good. Can we remember that as we try to put this world together again? Why else did Christ come? It wasn't for nothing. No use taking him out of the middle and trying to fill it up with something else! We don't need him to teach us. There wasn't much about his teaching that was new. We don't need him as an example. We already have examples enough. We've had a number since. We need him as a Saviour: a God Who will be in it with us, and will provide us with everything it takes to keep the Sermon on the Mount after this from rating as pure nonsense. It is just that when you leave Him out. Nothing on earth but whistling in the dark!

Precisely because Christianity does fit those facts better than anything else, it has taken for itself the center of this stage which we call human history. Check what has happened through these twenty centuries as much as you like. Check it against what went before. Check it against conditions that still prevail over wide areas of the earth's surface. Why is it that the Christian nations have fashioned the modern world? I don't like what our Western civilization has done with the progress it has made any more than you do; but you do have to admit that its progress seems to have been bound up with its religion, while its failures have come at the very points where it has betrayed that religion! Christianity has at least set the standards of decency the world around, as if God's flag anyhow had been planted in the wind at the top of the future!

Now ask me your question: Does such a religion have the ghost of a chance? And I'll put it to you bluntly: Nothing else has any! It wasn't something added to history, a kind of afterthought when everything else had been tried and had failed and had been blown to bits. It wasn't just God's effort to pick up the pieces and put them together again. "Now we, brethren, as Isaac was, are the children of promise." It was part of the design! It was wrought into the fabric of life by the hands that did the weaving! To change the figure, it's the one solitary pivot around which history turns. There is no other.

And it's the only factor in our present situation that we can count on, which has muscle enough to bring all the other factors right. That's the second proposition I want to make you. Not only does it belong to the pattern of things; it's actually God's dynamite to change what's wrong! So says Paul in another place. He calls it the power of God unto salvation to every one that believeth. And in the original Greek that word power is our word dynamite. Maybe it does sound odd. You haven't been used to associate Christianity with power. You think of steam engines, driving pistons, huge guns, monstrous tanks, armies locked in the embrace of death: certainly you don't think of this Jesus who looked so weak; but he has proved stronger than all the violence that was done him! It looked as if you could despise him and leave him out of your calculation entirely; and he changed the course of human history! He seemed to be quite dead at the last; yet his cross has become not the symbol but the channel of new life! He seemed to go away; but how many millions since then would have answered with Paul, if you had asked them their secret, "I live; yet not I: Christ liveth in me!" Maybe we ought to revise some of our ideas about power.

Bertrand Russell wrote a whole book about it. He said you could set down the complete story of mankind in terms of what he called a mistaken and insane struggle for it. The men who have allowed their love of it to give them a distorted view of the world, he pointed out, are in every asylum: one will think he is governor of the Bank of England, another will think he is the King, another will think he's God. Highly educated people who express highly similar delusions and highly emotional people who express the same delusions in highly eloquent language become dictators. Only the certified lunatics are shut up because of their proneness to violence when their pretensions are questioned; the uncertified variety are given control of powerful armies, and can inflict death and disaster on all sane men within reach. The success of insanity, he concludes, in literature, in philosophy and in politics, is one of the peculiarities of our age. And the successful forms of it proceed almost entirely from impulses to power! Maybe we ought to revise some of our ideas!

In the New Testament, foolishly enough, power is associated with something called love. Perhaps we should at last remember that! Not force. That it is power is a proposition as capable of demonstration as anything else on this earth! Love is the source of all the decisive victories you've been able to win over yourself, for instance. You haven't won them because it was your duty to win them. You haven't won them in the name of reason. Nobody does anything much because it's reasonable. You've won them because some kind of love had done something to you! Not done a great deal perhaps, but all there was that was worth doing! You'll rule your home by love, if you do rule it. And whoever it is that will command the world, will command the world by it! Not by air bases in the Pacific! When we are done with that out there, we shall have to come back to it. You destroy a world that way; you don't build another that way on its ruins!

Nietzsche once called our Christian morality a morality fit only for slaves. He forgot that it was intended at least for conquerors. Triumph was always its goal. The Son of God went forth in this strange warfare "a kingly crown to gain"; and by the Almighty he gained it! What else did Bernard Shaw mean when he wrote to a fellow author, "How do you explain that you, George Moore, and I are now occupying ourselves with Jesus?" What else did Bertrand Russell himself mean when he wrote, again in his book on Power: "If I had to select the four men who have had more power than any others, I should mention Buddha and Christ, Pythagoras and Galileo." Which of them ruled by violence? When Jesus said, "Love your enemies," he wasn't indulging in bitter irony or bitter sarcasm. He wasn't leering at the world, making fun of it, ridiculing it with spiteful mockery: he was trying in his painful way to set life on its feet again! He never has succeeded. But don't be dismayed by that!

And don't ever dare to remind me either, as some tramp once reminded a street preacher, that Christianity has been here two thousand years; and just look at the world! The preacher came back with the only obvious answer: "Water has been here a great deal longer than that," he said, "and just look at your face!" The only thing that this religion of Jesus needs is somebody who will do something about it! We've got to understand from now on that nationalism of itself is a thoroughly stupid ideal. We've got to understand that race antagonism is plain suicide. We've got to understand some time that war is the final blasphemy, which makes it "necessary for men to change their ways or perish." The most desperate cry of human life at this moment of human history is a cry for human hearts that will show a little sympathy. One man on the Western Front twenty-five years ago put it this way: "How can you sleep while this goes on? Why did you let it come? Of what good are you? Have you learned nothing from your Christ? I'm not afraid of death: I'm afraid of life on terms like these!" He knew that the road we were traveling—and I haven't seen any fork in it recently!—was marked with a signpost: This way to Hell. And it wasn't far!

It isn't even that far now. Some people make me sick rubbing out the one glimmer of hope we had with their professional talk about nothing but justice, justice. "These things I command you," said Jesus, and solemnly repeated it as the night wore on which was to end for him in death. What things? punish the evildoer? Mete out justice to him? Hit him back? Teach him a lesson? All right, go on and try it! But don't come whimpering back to God in the end, and want to know what's wrong. Your skirts have been so clean! There must not be any God if this can happen to you! "These things I command you, that ye love one another." Maybe it's the prime junction of the Christian Church, and of the part you have in it, to keep that alive through these years to come! Maybe from the very beginning God set love to do this job; and for all the money we have been pouring out we can't pay anything else to do it!

Ask me your question then once more: Does Christianity have the ghost of a chance? It's a little like asking, has Truth the ghost of a chance? A good deal depends on what you yourself have decided to do about it. The rest depends on a holy God. I don't like the habit we have of setting ourselves defiantly in His way! Maybe I ought to ask you a question: Do you have the ghost of a chance—unless your hands are marked like His?

PRAYER: *Grant us, Thou God and Father of Mankind, of Whom the whole family in heaven and earth is named, to be willingly subject to this pattern of Thy mind, which was laid down before the foundation of the world; and through all our lives by Thy grace, in thought and word and deed, to make manifest the saving power of Thy great love: through Jesus Christ, our Lord and Saviour. Amen.*

The Christmas Story

REVEREND DAVID E. ROBERTS, PH.D., D.D.

A Minister of the Presbyterian Church; Union Theological Seminary, New York

Most of Dr. Roberts preaching is in colleges and universities; Princeton, Wesleyan, Hamilton, Sweetbriar, Connecticut College for Women, Smith, Union (Schenectady) and Wooster (Ohio).

As a member of the Joint Committee on Graduate Instruction of Columbia University and Union Theological Seminary, he influences the intellectual life of many of the graduates of Union.

He was educated at Occidental College, Union Theological Seminary, Edinburgh University, Marburg and Göttingen and Oxford. He is a member of the Presbytery of New York, and is associate professor of systematic theology and philosophy of religion in Union Theological Seminary, New York.

He is editor of the Union Seminary Quarterly Review *and wrote, in co-operation with H. P. Van Dusen, Liberal Theology.*

In this sermon he brings the age-old Christmas story and fills it with new meaning.

Sermon Sixteen

TEXT: There was no room for them in the inn.   LUKE 2:7

IT IS right that we should listen to the familiar words of the Christmas story as though we were hearing them for the first time. We can never cease to wonder at the new creation which God offers to us constantly. The Nativity can never become for us merely a precious bit of archaic lore, a cherished memory of a distant day. For it is the beginning of the story whereby we understand how God comes into the world for all times and for all men. Christmas is a recollection of something which *has* happened—yes; but it is also a recollection of something which is happening now.

Let us start the story afresh, then, seeing it as a contemporary event, like those painters who have depicted the Nativity in their own land and their own times—against the background of a New England winter or a Chinese landscape. Perhaps, for the moment, we should forget the outcome. Perhaps our gladness will be spoiled if we feel compelled to look ahead and see that our rejoicing is linked to a career which will culminate upon a Cross. Perhaps, for the moment, it would startle us to be told that we are rejoicing because of the birth of one who will suffer and die. We give ourselves undividedly to the wonderful fact that God is here among us. *Immanuel*. For the moment, that is enough; and we need a respite from the haunting foreknowledge of what the world will do to the Son of God.

Yet the very fact that we want this respite is significant. It shows the kind of world we are living in, the kind of people we know ourselves to be. Who has not tried to put aside solemn thoughts and misgivings when a child is born into the world? For the moment—in the sheer gladness of this new life —we do not want to look forward to the years of struggle and bitterness, sickness and sin, that lie ahead. Maybe it's because we are sentimental, maybe it's because we have a sound yearning for the recovery of lost peace and decency; but, in any event, we wish for the moment that babies didn't have to grow up. We want to give ourselves wholeheartedly to the unalloyed joy of a life which has come into the world—fresh, unspoiled, and surrounded by love.

But this is a flickering, nostalgic mood. When we think of Christ, we *do* know what's coming—the Baptism, the temptations, the calling of the twelve, the wonderful ministry of teaching and healing, the conflict with hardened Pharisaism, the acclaim of the mob, the Garden of Gethsemane, the Last Supper, the betrayal, the Crucifixion, the Resurrection—and then the long centuries when men should follow after, with their hearts burning within them as Jesus accompanies them along the road. And so, we cannot really forget what a fateful series of events God set going in Bethlehem on that morning; and when we reflect, we would not have them otherwise. We cannot rejoice at Christmastide unless we rejoice in the whole story; for the glory of God permeates it every step of the way. We cannot really affirm the beginning unless we affirm the culmination. If we feel joy, we must feel it through tears and mortification as we remember what the world did to the Son of God then, and what it does to him as he comes to us today.

Naturally St. Luke knew the end of the story when he wrote this Christmas narrative. And surely he must have recognized the dramatic appropriateness of the fact that Jesus began his life by being shut out. "There was no room for them in the inn." *Men tried to shut God out, but He was born in a manger just the same.*

Is it not the case that the saving powers are always the ones that we have tried to shut out? Whenever the light dawns, whenever a fresh access of hope lifts a man out of his sin and misery, whenever God's love breaks through and makes him a new creature—it always comes as something he has shut out. He has been willfully blind to it; he has allowed it to dry up inside; he has pressed it down, driven it out of mind, run away from it, disguised it, repudiated it, and tried to forget it. And when that man is rescued, despite himself, it is because although he has made no room for Christ in his heart, Christ has been born in him just the same. Like the birth of a new child in the world, the birth of the new man takes place in a way which we *cannot* prevent.

I hardly need dwell upon the fact that we are still shutting God out today. Jesus simply doesn't belong in this world. He doesn't belong where one has to make his living by competitive triumph over others. He doesn't belong where one maintains his own security by suspicion, ruthlessness, and a kind of foxy outguessing of his opponents. He doesn't belong where men are so caught in wholesale destruction that they have time to think of Heaven only in the last fleeting moment when death is crashing down upon them. He doesn't belong where communities are held together only by fear of external foes; where the comradeship of allies is based squarely upon calculation of each other's power and upon a hard-boiled exchange of conquered territory. He doesn't belong where millions are torn from their homes, where children are left without care, where enslaved peoples are tortured, and where decent young men die in the trenches, drown at sea and are shot down in the air. Oh, we *have* shut him out! There is no room for him here!

And we are tempted to cry out: "Oh gentle Son of God, don't come into such a world. It will destroy you. This is no place for sacrificial love. This is no place for someone who cares nothing for money, prestige and power. This is no place for someone who is ready to suffer agony and to confront hatred unflinchingly. This kind of a world will *break* you; it will work its utmost upon you and then cast you aside and forget you."

There is no room for him here. That's a fact. But the other fact is that God comes into the world, nevertheless. He is born in a manger. He belongs to the outcast, the downtrodden, the humble. He is destined to be a man of sorrows and acquainted with grief—wounded for our transgressions, by whose stripes we are healed. He belongs to everything in the heart of man which is still capable of contrition and mercy.

And for that reason, he baffles us. The touches of wonder with which the Christmas story is surrounded are an indispensable part of it. Some years ago I heard Dr. Moldenhawer tell of how, when he was a child, he knew so little that he believed the Christmas story, just as St. Luke tells it. Then came a time when he knew so much—after studying higher criticism, comparative religion and philosophy—that he couldn't believe the miraculous setting of the story. But now, once again, he knows so little, that he believes it just as St. Luke tells it.

What did he mean? I think he meant that if Christian faith is reached at all, it must be reached through wonder. If we reflect upon it in an ordinary way, we come to the conclusion that Christmas couldn't possibly happen. By all the rules of common sense, men should long ago have learned what to expect of themselves. They should have reconciled themselves to war, selfishness and hatred, and come to terms with these hard facts as best they could. Indeed, many of us have become such experts in predicting what to expect that we have lost hope in the postwar world already. We can easily see through the pretensions of the so-called "perfectionists." We know that the people who try to act from saintly motives are frequently self-assertive and bad tempered. We have learned by hard experience to be suspicious of those impractical individuals who try to live in terms of pure love. We know how easily self-deception can enter in. We know how smothering and how intolerant sweet Christians can be. We know the harm that well-intentioned visionaries can do.

We are like the natives of the African forest who were suspicious of Albert Schweitzer because they had never dealt with a white man before who did not want to exploit them. Like them, we are ready to protect ourselves against selfishness and tyranny as best we can; but we are not prepared for decency and generosity free from ulterior motives.

In fact, we are living in a world which wouldn't know what to make of the love of God if we saw it in the flesh. We say to ourselves: "If Christ were to come to earth today, would we not also fail to recognize him? Or might we not be like that army officer who admitted that if he were the military governor of Palestine today and Christ were to come again, he would have to execute him again?"

The very fact that we raise this as a hypothetical question shows how attenuated Christianity has become. We say: "If Christ were among us today." He *is* among us today. He is a living power in the world. We treat him as the world has always treated him; but he is born in us today, nevertheless. We say to ourselves that it can't possibly happen, but it has happened.

This is assuredly a firm foundation for our joy. For we desperately need this God who can do wonderful things. We desperately need to have our calculations upset. In many respects, human affairs are much the same today as they have always been. But there is one overwhelming difference. Since Christ is here, we cannot get rid of the haunting realization that *he* is the one who really belongs. He is the one who depicts for us human life as God means it to be. We are the strangers; we are the outcasts. He baffles and confuses us because we are the ones who are out of line, out of joint, out of focus. We are the distorted image of God; he is the clear picture. And since he has come, since he is here, men can never completely lose this recollection of what they are meant to be—this hope, despite all their misery and hopelessness—of what they may yet become. For Christmas has left indelibly upon the imagination of mankind the vision of a restored humanity and a restored creation. In it we see every level of existence brought into peace and harmony around the babe lying in a manger—the stars in their courses, the animal kingdom of the sheep and oxen, the work of mankind in the shepherds and the wisdom of mankind in the Magi.

But someone may well ask how this "mere memory" can heal us—how it can bring every one of us back to the point of a new birth, starting afresh, unspoiled, surrounded by love. What about the mark left by all the long miseries of human history? What about the mark left by all the searing agonies and failures in the lives of each one of us?

I reply by concluding as I began. If Christmas is merely a memory of things past, it cannot heal us. But if it is an awakening to things present, it can be the most healing event we have ever known. If we can believe that the impossible has happened, and that, though we have shut him out, God comes into our world just the same, a restored humanity and a restored creation may be born again in us today.

Perhaps you are familiar with the story of a French soldier who was found suffering from amnesia. When he was picked up at a railroad station, he looked at his questioners blankly, and all he could say was: "I don't know who I am. I don't know who I am." Because he had been disfigured by facial wounds, there were three different families who claimed him as belonging to them. So he was taken to one village after another, where these different families lived, and allowed to walk around by himself. Finally, when he entered the third village, a sudden light of recognition came into his eyes, he walked unerringly down a side street, in through a tidy gate, and up the steps of his father's home. Like the prodigal son, he had "come to himself." The old familiar surroundings had restored his mind. Once again, he knew who he was and where he belonged.

On Christmas morning we hear the old familiar story of Bethlehem, like amnesia victims in a shell-shocked world, who have forgotten who we are and where we belong. And as we make our way with unerring steps down that side street, where a star stands over a manger, we know that we have found the way home. We know that we have come to the only place where men can be restored in mind and heart. We know that this memory of what happened long ago is at the same time a fresh awakening to what is happening now, through the suffering love of God towards his children. We know that although we may shut Christ out, the door of the manger stands open for all the world!

PRAYER: *O holy child of Bethlehem*
Descend to us, we pray.
Cast out our sin and enter in;
Be born in us today.

Amen.

The Place of the Church of England

THE MOST REVEREND AND RIGHT HONORABLE
GEOFFREY FRANCIS FISHER, P.C., D.D.
Archbishop of Canterbury, The Church of England, Canterbury, England

His Grace, The Most Reverend and Right Honorable Geoffrey Francis Fisher, has spent his life as both an educator and a churchman, reminding us that once the Church and education went hand in hand, with education the child of the Church.

Born May 5, 1887, youngest son of the late Reverend H. Fisher, rector of Higham-on-the-Hill, Nuneaton, he was educated at Marlborough College; Exeter College, Oxford, where he was an open scholar; held a Liddon studentship in 1910; Wells Theological College. He taught at Marlborough College from 1911 to 1914, was headmaster of Repton School from 1914 to 1932, and was called to be Bishop of Chester in 1932.

He was Select Preacher at Oxford University, 1925-27, and at Cambridge University, 1937 and 1940. In 1939 he became dean of the Chapels Royal, Prelate of the Order of the British Empire, and Bishop of London. On the death of the late Dr. William Temple, he became Archbishop of Canterbury. In a certain sense, many Protestants look to him as in a certain special manner the leader of world Protestantism.

This sermon was preached at his enthronement on Thursday, April 19, 1945. His interpretation of the responsibility of the Church of England for leadership in bringing faith into the secular life of the people, for guidance in restoring peace and order, and his belief in the need for the love of God and man's place in God's plan, are all in his sermon. It is a sermon which may well come to have historic significance.

Sermon Seventeen

Text: Thine is the Kingdom, the power, and the glory.

Matthew 6:13

THE responsibility of the Catholic Church is always and altogether to our Lord Jesus Christ, in Whom the Church consists. From Him, as the very Word of God and Saviour of men, it draws its faith and its life, by Him it tests its doctrine, to Him it renders its worship and dutiful service. It is within and as part of that Catholic responsibility that the Church of England is also the national Church of England. All through our history, from its earliest beginnings, the Church has been in an organic relation to the nation, charged with the duty of the nation, charged with the duty of bringing into the secular life of our people the sanctities of the faith and fear of God, and of teaching them to fashion their character and policies by the obedience which Christians owe to our Lord. For long indeed Church and nation were different names for the same body of people, the one describing them on the side of their heavenly citizenship, and the other of their earthly citizenship. And though that is no longer so, this Church is still in a very real and profound sense the Church of England.

Its distinguishing characteristic is that in loyalty to Christ it endeavors to hold together in a due proportion truths which, though essential to the fullness of the Gospel of Christ, are through the frailty of man's spirit not easily combined—fidelity to the apostolic faith and freedom in its apprehension and application, liberty of the spirit and obedience to the disciplined life of the Church, the corporate unity of a divinely constituted people of God and the free response of each in his own person to the grace and guidance of the Holy Spirit. The stresses within the Church, so far as they are due to tensions between divine truths imperfectly integrated by men, are signs of truthfulness and of health. They may easily enough be allowed to cause a confusion of voices. But it is the conviction and the justification of this Church of England that Christ means us to essay this difficult comprehension, to hold together within our communion of the Catholic Church what may not be put asunder without grievous injury, and to present, as far as we may, the wholeness of the Gospel of Christ.

It is no accident that the Church in England should be of this kind. Church and people have grown up together, in intimate association, and we see God's providence at work in both. The stresses within the Church and the unifying loyalty which controls them have their counterpart in the secular history of our people. There, too, it has been the characteristic of our people to hold together in a due proportion freedom and order, faithfulness to our heritage from the past and adaptation to the opportunities and pressures of new conditions, a wholesome concern for social betterment and a wholesome liberty of enterprise and responsibility. There too, if the stresses have often been great and the balance unequal, the unifying forces of a free society have controlled and corrected them. It is that tried and tested unity in our people which in these last years has brought us by God's providence through great perils and great sacrifices to the verge of a great deliverance. And the unifying forces have their roots in that heritage of Christian faith which the Church has implanted and preserved among us through the centuries.

There is now a whole demon-ridden world to be reordered, and everything of stability and high purpose which man can find will be needed for the task. As through our long history, so now let Church and nation stand together under God to their interrelated duty. The Church has much to put in order if it is faithfully to serve the nation: the nation has much to learn and to unlearn if it is to heed what God says to it through His Church. For many years past the two have been drawing apart. There is the possibility, the fear that alienation may continue and increase. There is also before us a possibility, even a hope, certainly a challenge that they should look again to one another in a Christian faith which is not ashamed to be definite, explicit and binding, wherein Church and nation, each in its own sphere and function, may glorify God. And in speaking thus of the place within the nation of the Church of England, I thankfully associate with it the Free Churches of England which have borne their notable part in Christian witness and in the shaping of our national character, with a valiance for truth not to be neglected and with a zeal for righteousness not to be quenched. Once there was little but contention and strife and bitterness between us. By God's goodness, for distrust there is now goodwill: for conflict, co-operation: for controversy, quiet evaluation of those truths of Christ which we hold in common and of those which still divide us. The presence of their representatives here is the proof and the prayer that in God's good time we may stand wholly together in the one Body of Christ—to serve God and witness for Him to this people.

But the Church of England is more than the Church of this nation. As these islands have given birth to a commonwealth of nations over the world, so has this Church given birth to a commonwealth of Churches, the far-flung Anglican Communion which looks to Canterbury as its mother Church. And as this nation has been a strength to other nations and is bound in ties of comity with all who share her ideals of ordered liberty, so this Church has a close and growing fellowship in Christ with Churches of other communions which have a concern for us as we have for them that in the Ecumenical Church of Christ we may with one voice glorify God. This congregation, representative of this Church and people, contains also representatives honored and welcomed of the world-wide Anglican Communion, of the Orthodox

Churches of the East and of the reformed Churches of the West. It is profoundly moving, and a pregnant thing, that at this moment when the world begins to turn from the work of defense and destruction to the high and more exacting work of translating into reality its visions of righteousness and true peace, all these should gather in the fellowship of Christ, Lord and Saviour of men, to join in the act of enthroning in this Cathedral Church another Archbishop of Canterbury.

Another enthronement, barely three years ago, is in the minds of us all, and the sense of our impoverishment broods heavily upon us. William Temple, whose ardent spirit and creative mind ever joined truth to action, set the course for the Church and for many outside it and fired us with his own enthusiasm. Our primary need, he told us three years ago, is for minds nurtured by the truth of God, hearts open to the love of God, wills devoted to the purpose of God. That truth, that love, that purpose the Church is to proclaim: by them every member of it is to live; that the world which so needs them may find them.

The truth that God is and is the rewarder of them that seek Him—that first. Ignorance, indifference, doubtings, the seductions of the open and uncommitted mind have displaced God from the accepted beliefs and loyalties which govern, elevate and unite men. Frustration has come upon us and will come again unless men will return to the act of faith that God is the keeper of the cities and the souls of men. Let us faithfully recall men to the Sovereignty, the truth, the righteousness of God, to be known, to be reverenced, to be obeyed.

Then the love of God. In a sinful world love's highest work is that of reconciliation. It is the sorest need of men today in their own divided souls, in their divided homes and families, in divided and exhausted nations, in the moral wreckage of war and for the conquest of peace. Reconciliation, the making at one of the unruly hearts of men, can only be attempted or achieved by those who have the secret of it in their own hearts. It is God's secret, displayed in the crucified and risen Christ, whose love reconciles us first to God and so to one another. It must be learned from Him. When justice and duty have done their necessary work, it fails unless it be fulfilled by the more exacting and alone fruitful law of love. Christ has shown its working in His own self. Only by response to the love of God can we be reconciled to God and know how to be among men makers of the peace of God.

And then the purpose of God, that His righteousness and love shall be applied to personal life and social order and all human affairs. That needs power, a power of God to form our minds and bend our wills: a power of God by which we may bear patiently the obstinacy of things, combat resolutely the perversity, the poverty and self-pride of human hearts, and enlist in His service all the self-abnegation, comradeship and sacrifice of which those same human hearts are splendidly capable. That power God is ready to give us, gives us through the Holy Spirit. In that power it is for the Church and the nation to fashion a society nearer to the will of God, in which each is free to find himself in the service of God and of his neighbor.

To this work we dedicate ourselves. The world is ever prone to fashion its kingdoms after its own liking, to multiply and magnify its organs of material power, to ascribe glory to itself. The Church lives and bears witness after another fashion. All true citizenship is of the Kingdom of Christ, all true power is of the Holy Ghost, and all glory is to God, to glorify Whom is the true end of man.

To Whom Must We Look?

Reverend Douglas Horton, Ph.D., D.D.
Minister of the General Council of the Congregational-Christian Church in America, New York

Dr. Horton is an internationally known churchman, and an outstanding figure in the councils of the ecumenical church. He is as well known in other communions for his spiritual leadership as he is among the more than a million lay members and ministers of the Congregational-Christian Church.

As chairman of the American Committee for the World Council of Churches, a post of great importance at any time but peculiarly so now as the period of postwar reconstruction approaches, Dr. Horton is one of the central figures in the united efforts of Protestant Christendom. The World Council of Churches already links together churches in all the great nations of the world. Under its auspices a great work of reconstruction and relief has been organized for the places in Europe and the Orient that have been ravaged by war.

Dr. Horton's parish is indeed the world since he travels in Asia, Africa and the Near East to develop the overseas work of his denomination carried on by the American Board of Foreign Missions. He has been a delegate to many significant international conferences and councils, one of the largest being the great international Missionary Council at Madras, India in 1938.

He is an author, editor and translator. Among his books are Taking a City, The Art of Living Today and Out into Life. During the first World War, Dr. Horton served as a chaplain in the United States Navy. He is in constant demand as a speaker and preacher not only in the churches of many denominations but in schools, colleges and universities.

Born in New York, he was educated at Princeton University; New College, Edinburgh; Mansfield College, Oxford, England; the University of

Tubingen, Germany; and Hartford Seminary. He holds the honorary doctorate from Lawrence College, Chicago Theological Seminary and Princeton University. Ordained to the Congregational ministry in 1915, Dr. Horton served pastorates in Connecticut, Massachusetts and Illinois before he took his present post of denominational leadership. In this sermon he shows his belief in the importance of the laymen of the church in carrying out work of each local church in its spiritual and social program. It was preached on the Columbia Broadcasting System's Church of the Air April 15, 1945. Dr. Horton has just made a trip to Japan in the hope of enlisting Japanese Christians in the task of remaking right relations between men and nations.

Sermon Eighteen

TEXT: Paul, an Apostle of Jesus Christ by the will of God . . . unto . . . all the saints which are in all Achaia.

II CORINTHIANS 1:1

WHEN St. Paul wrote to the people of the churches in Corinth and the rest of Greece or Achaia, he began his letter, "Paul, an Apostle of Jesus Christ by the will of God . . . unto . . . all the saints which are in all Achaia." When he wrote to the Ephesians he began, "Paul, an Apostle of Jesus Christ by the will of God, to the saints which are at Ephesus" (Eph. 1:1). When he sent his letter to the Colossians, he addressed it "To the saints . . . which are at Colosse" (Col. 1:2). It is quite clear that if he had been writing to you he would have saluted you as "the saints who listen in on the Church of the Air," for a saint to him was an ordinary person like you and me who had committed himself to the love of God in Jesus Christ.

Generally speaking, we have a different meaning for the word "saint." To speak of them is usually to allude to the lovely delineation in glass of saints that have gone before, such as we see in the windows of Gothic churches, or to the statues in stone which unknown craftsmen have hewn out for the walls and towers of such churches, saving for generations to come the memory of famous men and godly. Saints dead to earth but living in heaven were a true concern of St. Paul; but most of all his heart was filled with the thought of the flesh-and-blood, breathing, speaking, yes and even sinning, saints who were the live core of the contemporary Church and on whom the future depended. You may squirm a little at the idea that you and the saints in the windows and on the walls of churches belong to the same company; but nonetheless St. Paul is right—there are saints departed and there are saints present, who are yourselves, and the strength of the Church Militant is always and forever the saints alive and active.

Dean Hodges of Cambridge used to say that the great days of the Church were those of the missionaries, the monks and the Methodists; and when you examine these eras, you will note that they were the times when the *lay membership* of the Church rose to its responsibilities.

When the Dean spoke of missionaries, he undoubtedly had in mind the first century of the Church in which the word of the Gospel, first spoken in an obscure province at the edge of the Roman Empire, was carried from city to city, being whispered by disfranchised groups in ghetto and slum until presently the whisper became a proclamation and the proclamation an exultant shout. So well did these lay missionaries do their work that they earned the admiration even of the secular historian Gibbon, who wrote his great work with the intention of discrediting Christianity.

Who were these missionaries? They were Matthew, a tax collector; Mark, a private secretary; Luke, a doctor; John, a member of the fishing industry. Though Paul the Apostle was trained to be a rabbi, he turned rather to his skill as a tent manufacturer for the earning of his living, and so far as we know never entered professionally into what today we might term the ministry. In a word, these men who revolutionized the world, who set the Roman Empire tottering on its base till it toppled and fell, were men precisely like you who are listening to me this morning.

When he spoke of the monks, the Dean undoubtedly had in mind St. Francis of Assisi and those that he gathered about him. To them more than to any others is due the new atmosphere that grew up in Europe in the thirteenth century. A new brotherhood was born when the young Francis leapt from his horse and saluted a leper, a man of a class which up to that time he had abhorred. That was the age in which the Gothic cathedrals, "the loveliest of man's attempts to imprison sublimity," rose into being. Europe found a new song on its lips and recaptured its soul. This with the Renaissance of new learning gave us the outlines of Europe for the next hundreds of years.

And who were these makers of the future? St. Francis himself was the son of a prosperous cloth merchant, one of the influential businessmen of his city. He was brought up to follow in his father's footsteps. One of his first friends was di Quintavalle, a member of the financial world of his city. Dei Cattanei was a lawyer. Brother Angelo was a landowner. These men came to the burning realization that one of the great needs of Europe was the renewal of the inner life of the Church—and to this end they devoted themselves, with the results that are now gloriously written on the pages of history. They were all men of Assisi and neighboring towns, as you are men and women of towns and cities in America.

When Dean Hodges spoke of the Methodists, he undoubtedly had in mind the Reformation of that England of the latter part of the eighteenth century which was as socially rotten as was France on the other side of the Channel. The French scene is probably more familiar to us because the dramatic change that took place in the French Revolution has called our attention to the conditions against which it constituted a revolt. The historian Lecky has pointed out that if it had not been for the Wesley brothers and the religious societies they formed, there would have been the same overturn in England that there was in France. Thanks to the Evangelical Revival, people in high places and low began to feel the need of mending their ways—and there followed reformation instead of revolution.

John Wesley himself was a minister, to be sure—but as long as he attempted his reforms on his own (witness the experiences of his younger maturity) he was very far from successful. When, however, he learned to surround himself with the laymen of the Class Meetings, he came into his destiny. Those Class Meetings are described in the following words:

> If good men of the Church will unite together in the several parts of the Kingdom, disposing themselves into friendly societies, and engaging each other . . . to be helpful . . . in all good Christian ways, it will be the most effectual means for restoring our decaying Christianity to its primitive life and vigor.

And it was! England was saved by men and women like you.

The days of laymen (and this means also, of course, lay women) have ever been the greatest days of the Church, since these have been times when God has had the greatest number of outlets for His power in the world. Some of you have stood in a power house of a great city and watched the dials at evening when the daylight fades. One dial shows the swift drainage of power as the housewives press the button on the kitchen wall to light the room where supper is to be prepared and a thousand thousand others for various reasons turn on the electric illumination to drive back the darkness. Another dial shows the mounting power available to supply the mighty demand, as the dynamos, one by one, are thrown in to take up their burden. Most eras in history are like a modern city which because of some accident or other finds itself with a limping battery of dynamos; there is not power enough available to fight back ignorance, superstition and sin. But now and then—in the days when laymen take hold—every wire in the great ecclesiastical dynamos throbs with power: and the vast city of God which is humanity glows with His spirit.

It would be bringing a most useless coal to Newcastle to hint to you that if ever the world needed all the light and power that God has in store for it, it is today, when mankind addresses itself to the ways of peace in a new world of technology which it has never seen before. It needs no torturing of an argument to make it clear that nothing will save us as a human society except saved men and women—that is, men and women saved from the selfishness into which they tend to drift without the Gospel, saved from taking their ideals from the cheap vulgarities of the day—saved and committed to decency and brotherly tolerance, to consulting and following those highest ideals which are the foe of the average and mediocre. You cannot have a "better world" without better nations, nor better nations without better citizens, nor better citizens in general without those little groups of citizens who are chiefly though not entirely to be found in the churches and who are the leaven of the whole lump. In a word, we need saints. We need you.

As I just said, the little groups of citizens upon whom the future depends are found largely though not wholly within the churches. They are all in the Church as God sees it, to be sure, but they are not all in the churches as men have organized them—and surely none of us is unrealistic enough not to realize that the Church of the past and the Church of today is at many points faulty and unworthy of its high calling. Nonetheless, it is undubitably true that with all its faults the Church is the best hope of mankind and may fairly be called the social instrument through which God intends to redeem humanity. The point at which the Church differs from every other organization under heaven is at its center. The Church is like a lodge in that it provides fellowship. The Church is like a school in that it furnishes instruction. The Church is like a social settlement in that it tends to reform its neighborhood. But it differs from all of these in that at its center one finds Jesus Christ. It is he who provides a standard against which the Church can constantly check its faith and practice. He supplies a principle of growth and regeneration—a veritable principle of life.

It is because of this that the Church is and must remain central in the attention of all those saints—I have in mind none but yourselves—who really mean to help their generation. It is the fountain of life to those who are ready to drink.

Most of all the Church can supply you with new life through the experience of worship. Coming into the presence of God is like no other experience in the whole of life, for in Him you have the source of all life. In coming to rest in Him, your soul is paradoxically snatched from its tranquility. You find yourself engulfed in a divine discontent—pushed, urged, pricked, lashed, prodded out of your routine into a dream of the destiny to which He has appointed you as one of His saints.

God is the life behind and beyond all life. Life as we know it is but a feeble symbol of Him. Consider the life of the vegetable, then go on to the fuller life of the animal, now on to that of the most vividly alive person you know—and out beyond, at the infinite end of the line thus indicated you have the living God. We dimly hint at the kind of life which is in Him when we use the word "eternal."

When a saint exposes his spirit to this kind of God, week after week, something happens to him. Inevitably he grows inwardly. One cannot even contemplate the thought of God, the highest thought the human mind can entertain, without being greatened by the experience. One cannot dream of the justice which is in God and continue to be at peace with the rude and compromised justice prevailing in our world. One cannot let his fancy play, as an artist might, with the picture of the world as it would be if God had a free hand in painting it, without discovering that new perfections are added in line and color to his own humble attempts. To worship a living God is to be drawn toward life in its fullness.

It is this contribution that the Church has to make to its saints: if they are willing, it can keep them alive spiritually. This generation does desperately need saints—more and better saints. My only fear is that we may come to believe that sainthood can be kept alive apart from its root—which is the Church. That cannot be.

The cut flowers in a vase often appear as beautiful as those growing in a garden. Do but let a few days pass, however, and the veins of the petals will grow brown, the ends of the petals curl back, the stalks will wither. They are marked for death because they are cut away from life. The flowers in the garden similarly wither, but before they do so, they develop the fruits which will result in other flowers. We shall not be here forever, but while we are here, is it not well for us to live deeply, grandly—to live at the height of our destiny, bearing fruit ere we join the saints beyond as red-blooded and creative saints today?

The Risen Christ

REVEREND ALAN P. TORY
Minister, St. Stephen's Presbyterian Church, Sydney, Australia

Reverend Tory has been minister of St. Stephen's Presbyterian Church, Sydney, Australia since 1939. Born in London on July 17, 1904, and educated first at Dame Alice Owen's school in London, then at St. John's and Mansfield College, Oxford, he worked as a journalist between 1923 and 1925, then lectured in psychology and philosophy at Rollins College, Winter Park, Florida in 1932-33.

Reverend Tory was minister of St. James' Presbyterian Church, Huddersfield, England from 1934 until he traveled to Australia in 1939 to become minister of St. Stephen's Presbyterian Church in Sydney.

His publications include Rain on Tin Roofs, a series of broadcast talks and essays, and a book of sketches and stories, Nod to Strangers.

In response to a request to lecture on the Earl Foundation at the Pacific School of Religion, Berkeley, California, he came to the United States in

August, 1945, and then proceeded to the East Coast to do a preaching and lecturing tour arranged through the Presbyterian Church.

This Easter sermon has a message good for any day in the year, the story of the voice in the garden and faith in immortality.

Sermon Nineteen

TEXT: Mary saw Jesus standing, and knew not that it was Jesus. Jesus saith unto her, Woman, why weepest thou? Whom seekest thou? She, supposing him to be the gardener, saith unto him, Sir, if thou have borne him hence, tell me where thou hast laid him, and I will take him away. Jesus saith unto her, Mary. She turned herself, and saith unto him, Master. JOHN 20:14-16

THE meeting of Mary with Jesus is one of the most appealing incidents of Easter day. It was in the dark and chill of early morning, and Mary was standing alone weeping. A terrible cry of desolation had fallen from her lips: "They have taken away my Lord, and I know not where they have laid him." What a scene of sorrow! It reflects the cry of many human hearts bereft of what they most prize and hold most dear. *"They."* How often do unfeeling hands or impersonal forces take away into some limbo of oblivion someone whose eye and voice bring understanding and light up the whole of life! *"They* have taken away my Lord."

It was after she had spoken those anguished words that Mary looked round and saw in the shadows dimly defined by the first struggling rays of light a figure whom she took to be the gardener. Distraught, she asked him a question which it would be natural to ask of the gardener. Instead of answering it, the voice which had already spoken, spoke just one word—Mary's name. Can you imagine what that meant? In her bleak despair and confusion the first words by which she was addressed had left her cold, and stirred no chord in her dead heart, but now that she heard her name uttered with an accent and inflexion known and loved, she recognized Jesus, and when she spoke the word "Master," her sorrow turned to joy. She knew in a flash when that dear familiar voice spoke her name that Jesus was alive—not some attenuated, ghostly Jesus, but Jesus himself, real and personal, a Jesus whom she could hail and recognize.

It was on that rock of conviction that the structure of Christian faith was raised. From that discovery of Mary, and of others came the possibility of a gallant facing up to life which saw beyond death and tragedy a mighty continuing comradeship. This Jesus who spoke to her in the shadows of early morning was in everything that mattered the same Jesus who had claimed her loyalty and understood her need and redeemed her life from muddle

[105]

and triviality, the same Jesus who had received her offering of precious spikenard in the home of Simon the Pharisee, who had not minded a bit when the other guests were shocked and had welcomed her desperate act of devotion.

Today we say: Christ is risen. "I have seen the Lord," reported Mary to the other disciples. To her it was given first to set eyes upon the risen Christ. There were other people much more reputable to whom we might think this special privilege would be given; but no, it is this deep-feeling lonely woman with her memories to whom the revelation first came. It is she who begins the chain of witnesses who declare that on the third day he was alive.

When you and I think back to that moment when Mary heard Jesus speak her name, don't we come to understand better what the risen Christ really means in human life? Christ risen and ascended is not Christ lifted so beyond and above us that his world and ours can never touch. Don't we too often think of the risen Christ as remote, having nothing to do with our dusty ways? Don't we misconceive the risen Christ? Quite without warrant we think of him apart, much less vivid and real than the Jesus who trod the hills of Galilee and walked the streets of Jerusalem. We substitute for the risen Christ who spoke to Mary an ecclesiastical Christ who keeps conveniently quiet in a stained glass window. But that's not the report which Mary handed on when she said: "I have seen the Lord." She talked about someone with whom she had to do who was real as she was, real and alive and filled with purpose and compassion and alert to human need.

I don't say that this claim isn't mysterious; but I do say it's true. This risen Christ is active, not passive. He prompts us to welcome change, as Jesus in his lifetime welcomed change when it meant true enrichment for mankind and the sloughing off of what was outworn. He invites us to take risks, for no seed is quickened except it fall into the ground and die. He asks us to put our ear to the ground and discover the needs of men. If we worship this risen Christ, not some pale, remote Being, but the Christ who spoke to Mary, we're saved from self-deceptions which blind us to the needs of others and the nature of the world we live in—we have to do with a living, personal Christ who reads our hearts, and touches with a friend's candour all that is specious and unreal in us.

If Christ's Church could recover the conviction that he is risen, that he is alive, that we have to do with this living Lord, do you imagine that any powers of evil could stop it? How would men rally to the standard of a faith inspired by this belief? I don't think there would be much chance any more for indifference and half-heartedness, for once men knew that indeed his touch has still its ancient power, they would be caught up in a great tide of hope and fervour. The lost radiance of the Christian religion would return, and the fruits of scientific discovery, the skill of engineers, the great potential of energy in our world might be directed to raising the level of human life above fears and squabbles and grasping to a new height of dignity and valour which is creative.

I don't know how you feel about it, but I'm much attracted by the thought that Mary mistook Jesus for a gardener in the half light of early morning. Gardeners have the delicate touch that makes things grow. You know the expression "green fingers" which conveys the notion of a magic power which spirits up green shoots from the earth. If Mary had to mistake Jesus for anybody, it was well that she should think he was the gardener, for gardeners are close friends of nature, and nature is forever creating and making new, nature is as Goethe said, "the living garment of God." Christ's kinship with God was unique. Christ knew the secrets of the dark earth, of the rain that falls on the just and on the unjust, of the winds and waves and sunsets, and in his magnanimity and charity I don't think he was offended when that distracted woman, first gazing upon him, thought that he was the gardener.

I think it's quite possible, indeed I dare to hope that our generation will recover the conviction that Christ is alive, and with that conviction the surge of energy, the will and purpose and faith which all men of good will recognize to be necessary if we are to prevent a third world war. But I think this revelation may come to the men and women of our time much as it came to Mary—in stages. Like Mary, our generation may first mistake Christ for the gardener. By that I mean that sensitive minds today are awaking to the fact that there are divine creative powers in the world, that man's dignity and peace are found through committing his life and fortunes to those divine creative powers which call forth the longing for justice, the passion for truth and liberty, and the hunger and thirst after righteousness. To put it another way, let me quote from Richard Hillary, the young airman who was a Spitfire pilot in the battle for Britain. This is the discovery he made: "It was impossible to look only to oneself, to take from life and not to give except by accident, deliberately to look at humanity and then pass by on the other side."

That is one voice speaking for our generation, and mistaking the risen Christ for the gardener, responding in the dim light of a new day for humanity to those creative forces in our world which make claims upon us, and link us up indissolubly with our fellow men. The divine revelation is much richer and fuller than that, but if the men of our day have not yet seen that fuller revelation, isn't it due in great part to our own poverty of devotion which has found it more convenient to filter God's light through a stained glass window to which we've relegated the risen Christ, instead of to bear the gaze of his eye and to hear the ring of his voice.

I want in closing to say a word to people who know what it is to love someone, and then to get a telegram or a message which means an end to companionship on this earth. When his favorite daughter Cordelia died, King Lear held her in his arms and said:

No, no, no life!
Why should a dog, a horse, a rat have life,
And thou no life at all? Thou'lt come no more,
Never, never . . . !

[107]

That depth of grief is known to many people. It is an echo of what Mary felt when she came in the early morning to the tomb of Jesus. This darkness is matched by the light of Christian belief which claims that as Mary recognized Christ, so all who suffer the pain of separation shall find sorrow turned to joy.

We don't think of some friend to whom we can no longer speak, nor hear his laugh, as just a "pulse in the Eternal Mind." We don't think of him whom we've known and recognized by endearing traits and qualities as just being absorbed back into the vast anonymous ocean of life. What a waste that would be, out of harmony with Christ's telling his disciples to gather up the fragments so that none might be lost! What a waste of stress and toil and shaping of destiny, if all that valor and tenacity is to be cast into nameless oblivion! No, we think of the real man, our friend recognizable as Christ was recognized, continuing all that was most worthwhile in the life he lived in the sun and wind of this earth.

A friend of mine was killed by a V-2 bomb in London. He was just doing his job, and this thing came from the sky. When you saw him in cities where his work lay, you knew instinctively that his ruddy complexion and his blue eyes meant for gazing across great distances belonged to the world of the mountaineer where there's more room to breathe, not to bricks and mortar and cramped streets. He took me once climbing mountains with him. He wore different clothes, naturally, from the clothes I'd been used to seeing him in. He used a different form of speech, the speech of mountaineers who have a freemasonry of their own, a way of communication different from what is used by town-bred people, a speech woven of silences and cryptic responses to natural splendor and strange deep candid intimacies. Now he who loved the smell of heather and the air of mountains is what we men call dead. But just as I who'd known him in the city found him in that more spacious world of Arran and the Isle of Skye in different garments and using new ways of expression, so faith claims that the resource of God which no man can measure provides beyond the range of our present understanding a way of continuing life for those who loved the sights and sounds and scents of earth, a way of life which heightens the relish of God's continuing revelation of Himself through His creation, a way which asks of those who tread it not that they cease to be themselves, but instead, that they fulfill themselves to the utmost.

I believe that, because I believe in the God Whom Christ revealed, the God by Whose power it was that Christ was seen alive by his disciples, first by Mary who thought him to be the gardener in the shadows of the early morning, and then, when he spoke her name, knew him for the risen Lord.

The American Postulates

REVEREND JOHN HUGH O'DONNELL, PH.D.
President, Notre Dame University (Roman Catholic), Notre Dame, Indiana

Father O'Donnell was born in Michigan in 1895 and was educated at the University of Notre Dame and Catholic University of America, receiving his Ph.D. in 1922. He entered the Congregation of the Holy Cross in 1917 and was ordained a priest in Grand Rapids, Michigan in 1921. He was assigned to the University of Notre Dame in 1922 and served there as prefect of discipline and director of student welfare from 1923 to 1930. In 1931 he was elected president of St. Edward's University, Austin, Texas, which position he gave up to become vice-president of Notre Dame and chairman of the faculty board in control of athletics in 1934. From January to July, 1940, he was Notre Dame's acting president and has been its president since July, 1940.

Father O'Donnell is vitally interested in young people and takes an active part in the Catholic Student's Mission Crusade, a predecessor of the Catholic Youth Movement. He is also an active member of the American Catholic History Association, was a member of the executive council for two terms, and is a contributor to the Catholic Historical Review.

In this sermon, delivered at commencement at Michigan State College, June 3, 1945, he discusses Christian education and insists that this is one of the vital issues before our country today.

Sermon Twenty

> ... let us strive on to finish the work we are in; ... to do all which may achieve and cherish a just and lasting peace among ourselves and with all nations.
> —ABRAHAM LINCOLN, Second Inaugural Address

COMING to this campus to take part in the ceremonies of Commencement gives me great pleasure. After all, I am a native of Michigan, and it is only natural that I should take a deep and justifiable pride in the institutions which maintain and enrich the State's cultural and spiritual heritage. Among such institutions, I believe, this school has a pre-eminent place. Michigan State College—the oldest of land-grant colleges in the country—was established primarily to serve the "agricultural and industrial classes of Michigan." But it has done more than that; it has developed into a great university devoted to the education of leaders of wisdom and vision without whom hope for the future is a vain hope.

Surely it would be strange if the people of Michigan did not have an unusually deep appreciation of the need of leaders who know and cherish the American heritage, because for us it is a double legacy. It was bequeathed to us first, as it was to all Americans, by the Founding Fathers, who believed that "all men are created equal, and that they are endowed by their Creator with certain unalienable rights." And it is ours again from another historic source, namely, the Northwest Ordinance of 1787, which set up the territory out of which the State of Michigan was to be carved fifty years later. That document contains these memorable words: "Religion, morality, and knowledge being necessary to good government and the happiness of mankind, schools and the means of education shall forever be encouraged."

Here is additional evidence, if such were needed, that the American tradition is a Christian tradition, a fact that we cannot emphasize too strongly or repeat too often. The Founding Fathers were men of principle; they were religious-minded stalwarts who firmly believed in the existence of God, the God-given rights of man, and the inherent dignity of the human personality. They voiced these beliefs in the Declaration of Independence, and then applied them practically in the Constitution of the United States, the two documents which give us, respectively, the substance and the form of our government. Together, they hold that there can be no basis for democracy unless it be in the divine origin of man. In the American credo these are basic truths, unchanging and unchangeable.

Four postulates give the United States the most unusual political philosophy the world has ever known. They are: first, a recognition of God the Creator; second, acknowledgment of the natural law, which has its source in God the Supreme Lawgiver; third, recognition of natural rights of persons flowing from that law; and, fourth, acknowledgment of the inherent dignity and integrity of the human person because of these God-given natural rights.

In the words of the Declaration of Independence, these truths are self-evident. Nothing that man can do can make them anything less than axiomatic. He may ignore them or defy them, but not for long, and never successfully. Man knows this, to his sorrow; yet with a doggedness worthy of a better purpose he has again and again tried to pervert the natural order. Even in the Garden of Eden his misguided spirit of research led him to prefer the apple to the Almighty.

Today these postulates are as immutable as ever. But how does man regard them? Perhaps I can illustrate by reminding you of a device found in amusement parks—a number of mirrors that produce distorted images for the hilarity of the beholder. As you stand before one, you seem to be at least twelve feet tall; stop before another, and you are no bigger than one of the seven dwarfs. A third makes you leaner than Cassius, and a fourth as rotund as Santa Claus. But you are still *you*, and the mirror can't change you. Well, there is abroad in the world a philosophy known as secularism that persists in holding nature up to its own faulty mirror. It tries to degrade man into an irresponsible automaton that comes into existence without God or basic morality, and eventually returns to the nothingness whence it came. Sometimes the philosophy has a different label—scientism, materialism, or agnosticism. Call it what you will, each secular funhouse has its own reflection, and each is a distortion of man created in the image of God.

Such distortions are not new. In fact, they recur all through history. The family tree of the present crop has some queerly twisted branches, one of which is the fallacy of scientism that disturbed England seventy-five or one hundred years ago. Scientism made its threat and then died, leaving behind it the seeds of other movements just as erroneous, such as pseudoscience. Despite pseudoscience's attempt to prove that man is just a glorified animal, differing in degree but not in kind from the lower animals, the human personality remained on the plane that God intended. As G. K. Chesterton once wrote: "In the days when Huxley and Herbert Spencer and the Victorian agnostics were trumpeting as a final truth the famous hypothesis of Darwin, it seemed to thousands of simple people almost impossible that Christianity should survive. It is all the more ironic that it has not only survived them all, but it is a perfect example, perhaps the only real example, of what they called the Survival of the Fittest."

Pseudoscience gave us the monkey-man, but true science has dissipated such a conception. Then came Karl Marx with his machine-man. Making a virtue of his own ideological necessities, Marx defined society by its economic character, and left God out of consideration altogether. Somewhat later, Sigmund Freud evolved a dream man, and I am not using that term as it is applied to cinema heroes of the moment. We are, mused Freud, such stuff as dreams are made of; and if our little lives are rounded with a sleep, the better the chance to explore the libido.

What happens to the American postulates in the light of such perversions? What happens to individuals and institutions? Ignore these basic truths, and you have effectively sapped the foundations of American law, medicine, business, government—yes, and even education. And why? Because man is dehumanized.

When man no longer believes in the spiritual, it is quixotic to accept absolute standards of good and evil. Natural rights and duties no longer exist because there is no absolute lawgiver. That reminds me that even now a little band of materialistic schemers is trying to secularize American law. Their watchword is expediency, and for them truth changes with time and circumstance. The effect of their theories is evident in those law schools that teach law, not in its God-related perspective, but by "statutes." Of course, as an old legal friend of mine once said, one danger of teaching law by statute is that some day an absent-minded legislature may repeal the lawyer's education. Unfortunately, many of our people are not even aware that this attack on American jurisprudence has been made. As evidence, consider the popular misconception of the juristic doctrines of the late Justice Holmes, so often called "the philosopher of the law." Examine his beliefs in the light of basic morality, and what do you find? That the essence of law is physical force, and that man is a cosmic ganglion. If this is true, as Monsignor Sheen so well says, why should we "go to war to prevent Hitler from making mince-meat of ganglia?"

The doctor who is no more than a biological materialist can do untold harm to society by assuming prerogatives that belong to God Himself. If justice is not absolute, then the phrase "unscrupulous businessman" is a contradiction in terms, for without objective standards there is nothing to be scrupulous about. Every kind of sharp practice may come under the head of "business is business"—another pagan phrase characteristic of our time.

Once secularism infects a people, it advances to a virulent stage, like a progressive disease. It takes the form of state-ism, or totalitarianism. That is, it denies that government is man's agent for the protection of God's gifts. It is a vicious philosophy which holds that man exists for the state, and not the state for man. One day we may find ourselves its victims if current movements so antagonistic to the American postulates are allowed to run their course. This is why I am opposed to the compulsory military service bill now before Congress. Personally, I favor military training. I believe that we must be a military nation, postwar, and we must defend our country. But I am unalterably opposed to a philosophy that means the regimentation of our youth—the very thing that we are fighting against in this global war. Such smacks too strongly of totalitarianism.

Underlying the American postulates is the natural law. In contrast to physical law, which can be verified experimentally, the natural law is impressed on every man and woman by the Creator. It is made known solely by reason. In each of us is a little spark of divine fire. It enables us to judge of certain acts as good or bad; it tells us to do good and avoid evil; and after acting we approve or reprove ourselves in accordance with these judgments. We call this divine spark "conscience"; it is the link between natural law and individual acts; it is the possession of every normal person. I mention this to show the rich heritage the Founding Fathers gave us when they defined our philosophy of government. Chancellor Hutchins of the University of Chicago put it well when he said:

> In order to believe in democracy we must believe that there is a differ-
> ence between truth and falsity, good and bad, right and wrong, and that
> truth, goodness and right are objective not subjective standards. . . . Are we
> prepared to defend these principles? Of course we are not. For forty years

and more our intellectual leaders have been telling us that they are not true. . . . In the whole realm of social thought there can be nothing but opinion. . . . If everything is a matter of opinion, force becomes the only way of settling differences of opinion. And, of course, if success is the test of rightness, right is on the side of the heavier battalions.

This is the totalitarian view. But you and I know that might does *not* make right, that

> Thrice is he arm'd that hath his quarrel just,
> And he but naked, though lock'd in steel,
> Whose conscience with injustice is corrupted.
> —*King Henry VI,*
> Part II, Act III, Scene 2

You have heard, as I have, solemn warnings against the effects of alien doctrines upon American traditions and institutions. These warnings are useful, but if I may revise the words of a popular song, they do not accentuate the positive. Here, it seems to me, is a danger. We must have a clear conception of the philosophy we believe in as an alternative to what we so vigorously oppose. We must be conscious of the American postulates and their nature. While we are fighting for them on foreign fields we must be alert to ward off attacks by enemies closer at hand who are just as dangerous because they are just as destructive of the dignity of the human person.

You, my dear graduates, are going into a war-weary world that is now trying to make a lasting peace. But no peace can last unless it is grounded on the American postulates. Peace on any other premises is an invitation to World War III, a prospect too terrible to be considered. Even now our physical scientists tell us that "scorched earth" will seem like a land of milk and honey as compared to the devastation that their discoveries will wreak if they are turned to destructive purposes. And I might add that our part in World War II will have been the most tragic blunder in our history if in making the peace we abandon the faith of our fathers, which is that God made man in His own image.

And this is concerned with the San Francisco Conference at which representatives of the United Nations met to clear the ground for a better peace than we have known in our time. That conference cannot be described as a love feast, but let us not be impatient, because while it is relatively easy to unite in time of war against a common enemy, it is difficult to have unity when the bonds of interest are being loosed.

Teheran seemed to be a step in the right direction, although the Balkans rumbled afterwards. Yalta showed signs of a conflict between expediency and principle, if we are to judge by the treatment of the Polish question. But as Hilaire Belloc, the distinguished English historian wrote in his classic essay six years ago, this war will have been won or lost so far as Poland is resurrected. The test of victory is Poland.

San Francisco may be the last chance to determine the basic structure for a world organization. But we have confidence in President Truman and our representatives. They know that the fate of Western civilization rests in large part with them, and in how they and the representatives of other nations lay the foundation for world security. It occurs to me that the foundation is in the American postulates, so that San Francisco will succeed or fail as the conference accepts or rejects the principles of the Declaration of Independence as they apply to the world.

In the words of the late President Roosevelt: "We are fighting for security and for progress and for peace. . . . We are inspired by a faith that goes back through the ages to the first chapter of the Book of Genesis—'God created man in His own image'! . . . We are fighting, as our fathers have fought, to uphold the doctrine that all men are created equal in the sight of God." If these truths were basic when we entered the war, they are no less basic now. Having clarified our position then, we cannot be accused of breaking faith now when we insist that they be respected as the American approach to a peace with charity and justice.

If the other powers will not subscribe to the American approach, then the United States must make known in unequivocal language that we have descended into the European shambles for the last time. Twice within a generation we have fought for an ideal, twice we have placed ourselves in jeopardy, have spent our wealth like water, almost stripped ourselves of our natural resources, and left the flower of American manhood dead on foreign fields. Isn't twice enough? Frankly, it hardly seems the part of wisdom to have other nations use the United States again and again for their own ends. This is the time for a *real apostrophe* to America in the light of the years that lie ahead.

You, my dear young men and women, are custodians of the American heritage. It is a heritage of principles as absolute as the general laws you learned in the so-called exact sciences—as absolute, and far more important, because they determine your relation to your fellow man and to your God. Hold fast, therefore, to the American tradition. Be wary of those who say that changing times should bring changing standards. Do what you can to help maintain our philosophy of government. The lackadaisical should be the last to complain if government is not shaped in accordance with our heritage, because eternal vigilance is still the price of liberty.

Furthermore, do not be victimized by the catch phrase that you are part of a lost generation—a phrase that is familiar to those who were about your age at the end of World War I. That expression is defeatist; it is pagan. As a matter of fact, it is complete nonsense. Regardless of what religion you profess, I ask you to remember that no generation has been lost since Christ redeemed man on Calvary—unless its members elected to be lost.

And now, this is the challenge that awaits you: As you look back on your years in college, you should be able to say that you have learned how to live, mindful of your own rights and respectful of the rights of others.

Excellent facilities were at your disposal as you prepared for your chosen work. But your means of livelihood is only part of a full life; and the primary purpose of any college should be to educate the whole man in the finest traditions of Christian culture, to help him mature his faculties of intellect and will, so that he may achieve his ultimate goal, set for him because he is a creature of God. With this in mind, you can, if you will, march on to a rebirth of Christian civilization, and then the dream of the Founding Fathers will remain a splendid reality. You will know how to live, and assuredly you will have something to live for. And through it all, don't lose your sense of humor based on the divine.

If the generations just before yours had accepted this challenge, would we not now be solving our problems more wisely? Would we, indeed, have so many vexing problems to solve? If the world had depended upon Almighty God for its truths—instead of upon Almighty Man—could we not look forward to tomorrow with greater confidence? Yet there is hope—great hope —for the future, and much of it lies in the fact that members of your generation should know the difference between shadow and substance. One of your generation, John Edward Spear, a lieutenant in the Army of the United States who gave his life for his country, wrote this:

> Professors, writers, learned men, what do
> You, faced with present circumstances, say
> About the things you taught us yesterday?
> For I remember clearly still how you,
> Enthroned upon the seats of wisdom, threw
> With pompous show and scholarly display
> The ancient laws God gave to man, away
> And introduced the lawlessness you knew.
>
> You taught us this in days before the war.
> What teach you now? There is no wrong or right?
> Truth is a myth? Man needs his God no more?
> You do not dare, for war has brought to light
> Your lies; so give us back the truths you swore
> Away, that we may honorably fight.[1]

As you young men and women leave this sanctuary of learning, my prayer for you is that you may fulfill your mission in life as crusaders for God and Country, remembering always that beautiful theme of the inimitable John Cardinal Newman: "Times come and go, and man will not believe that that is to be which is not yet, or that what now is continues for a season, and is not eternity. The world passes; it is but a pageant and a scene; the lofty palace crumbles; the busy city is mute; the ships of Tarshish have sped away. On heart and flesh death is coming; the end is the trial."

May God be with you as you walk the pathways of life. May He support and strengthen you until the lengthened shadows gather. Then, in His

[1] "The Guns Speak." *The Catholic World*, July, 1942, p. 468.

mercy, may He give you peace and contentment "in that undiscovered country from whose bourne no traveller returns."

IMPRIMATUR: ✠ John Francis Noll, D.D., *Bishop, Fort Wayne*

The Thessalonian Epistles

REVEREND HENRY ALLAN IRONSIDE, D.D., LITT.D.
Pastor, Moody Memorial Church, Chicago, Illinois

Never formally ordained, to many Dr. Harry Ironside is the "unofficial archbishop of American fundamentalism." He is considered one of the leading Biblical scholars of this generation, has been honored with the Doctor of Literature degree by the largest liberal arts college of Illinois and has written more than forty popular books and commentaries, yet had no classroom education beyond grammar school.

Dr. Ironside was born in Toronto, Canada in 1876, the son of a street preacher, known to all Toronto as "The Eternity Man." When he was ten his family moved to Los Angeles and there at the age of fourteen, having completed grammar school, he began to take part in the meetings of the Salvation Army, singing and testifying, until he became known as the "Boy Preacher of Los Angeles." At eighteen, he was made a captain in the Salvation Army and put in charge of a station. After four years, however, he resigned from the Army and began to fellowship with a group known as the Plymouth Brethren. For the next thirty-two years he associated with no organization, but traveled from place to place preaching wherever he had opportunity—on street corners, in churches, stores, missions and in desert taverns. Most summers he spent among the Indians of Arizona and New Mexico.

In 1930 Dr. Ironside was called to the pulpit of Moody Memorial Church, vacated by the resignation of Dr. P. W. Phillpot, and by accepting this, his first pastorate, he became the tenth pastor of this historic Chicago church.

The secret of the success of Dr. Ironside's ministry is that he knows how to preach on the level of the ordinary listener, and he finds present and practical value in every text he expounds.

Sermon Twenty=one

TEXT: For our gospel came not unto you in word only, but also in power, and in the Holy Ghost, and in much assurance; as ye know what manner of men we were among you for your sake. And ye became followers of us, and of the Lord, having received the word in much affliction, with joy of the Holy Ghost.

I THESSALONIANS 1:5, 6

THE Thessalonian Letters are the earliest of Paul's writings, under the guidance of the Holy Spirit, which the Lord in His grace has preserved for the edification of the Church. It is evident that they were written from Corinth after Paul had left Berea because of persecution. Timothy and Silas, at his request, had remained behind and gone on to Thessalonica and then came to him to report on the condition of the young church. According to Luke's account in the book of Acts, Paul had preached the gospel on three successive Sabbath days in the Jewish synagogue at Thessalonica. How much longer he remained in the city we are not told, but it could not have been very long. The results of his short visit were remarkable. Quite a group were brought to a saving knowledge of the Lord Jesus Christ. Some of these were Jews, but the majority were evidently Gentiles who had been brought to see the folly of idolatry and led to put their trust in the living God as manifested in His Son.

Paul was deeply concerned about these young converts, who seemed to be as sheep without a shepherd, though, of course, he realized the great Shepherd was ever watching over them; but he tells us he had no rest in his spirit while he waited for the coming of Timothy and Silas, because he feared lest Satan might take an advantage of those so recently brought to Christ. The word, however, that came to him was most encouraging and led to the writing of this letter.

It is an interesting fact that in this epistle the second coming of our Lord Jesus Christ is referred to in some way in every chapter. Although the letter was addressed to babes in Christ, the Apostle felt the importance of giving them clear instruction regarding this great theme. Often today we are told that the doctrine of the Second Advent is not something with which Christians generally are to be occupied. Many ministers never preach on it at all; many have no clear convictions regarding it. In the classroom of theological seminaries, this doctrine often just becomes a theme for an academic discussion, but to Paul it was a tremendously important and exceedingly practical truth that needed emphasis because of its bearing on the hearts and lives of God's beloved people.

[117]

The first chapter tells us how the gospel was received in Thessalonica and closes by picturing for us a group of happy believers earnestly serving God, while waiting expectantly for the return of Jesus Christ.

We have the apostolic salutation in the first verse: "Paul, and Silvanus, and Timotheus, unto the church of the Thessalonians which is in God the Father and in the Lord Jesus Christ: Grace be unto you, and peace, from God our Father, and the Lord Jesus Christ." Note that Paul's fellow laborers are linked with him in this greeting which he extends to these young converts. The expression "The church . . . which is in God the Father and in the Lord Jesus Christ," is peculiar to the Thessalonian Letters. Of course, it refers to the same church which elsewhere is spoken of as *the body of Christ*. But here the emphasis is upon the new relationship into which these young Christians had come. They were now linked up in infinite grace with God the Father: they were His children. They owed it all to the Lord Jesus Christ, who had given himself for them.

It is not the grace that saves from judgment of which he speaks, but grace that sustains from day to day. Neither is it peace with God that he has in view here. That was settled already. He refers to the peace *of* God, which is the abiding portion of all who trust in the loving Father and seek to walk in obedience to the Lord Jesus Christ.

Verses 2 and 4 are introductory. "We give thanks to God always for you all, making mention of you in our prayers; Remembering without ceasing your work of faith, and labour of love, and patience of hope in our Lord Jesus Christ, in the sight of God and our Father; Knowing, brethren beloved, your election of God."

It is remarkable how often the Apostle speaks of bearing up God's people in prayer. He was a man of intense activity, preaching publicly, visiting from house to house, often working at tentmaking for his daily bread, and yet he found time to intercede with God on behalf of all the churches which he was used of the Lord to found, as well as remembering in prayer those of whom he learned, though they had not seen his face, as in the case of the Colossians. He links together in verse 3 the three graces of which he was to write later in the Corinthian epistle: faith, hope and love, though here the order is different and he speaks not simply of these graces as such, but of the spiritual realities connected with them—the work of faith, the labor of love, the patience of hope. Faith, we are told elsewhere, worketh by love. James insists that faith without works is dead. These young converts manifested their faith by their work.

Love to be real must be self-sacrificing. Therefore we read here of the labor of love. It is one thing to talk about loving our brethren, loving Israel, loving poor, lost souls in general; but our love is not genuine unless we are willing to labor earnestly for the blessing of those for whom we profess to have this deep concern.

The hope of the believer is the coming of our Lord Jesus Christ, but here

[118]

the Apostle speaks of the patience of hope. Often we may well long for the day when trial and tribulation will be ended and Christ will take us to be with himself, but we are not to be impatient as we await that glad consummation. He himself is the Man of patience, seated upon the throne of God. "The husbandman waiteth for the precious fruit of the earth, and hath long patience for it, until he receive the early and latter rain." During all these centuries since he ascended to heaven, as we count time on earth, he has waited patiently until the Church's testimony is ended. Then he will descend to the air to call his own to be with himself. Thereupon that change the poet has expressed will be true for all believers:

> He and I in that bright glory
> One deep joy shall share:
> Mine to be forever with Him,
> His, that I am there.

Verse 4 is particularly interesting: "Knowing, brethren beloved, your election of God." How did he know this? Had he been permitted to look into the books of eternity and there behold their names written before the foundation of the world? Had God revealed to him His divine sovereign decrees? Not at all. But he saw in their lives such evidence of the new birth that he had no question concerning their election. He knew that the fruit of the Spirit which was manifest was not of nature, but was the outflowing of the new life in the power of the Holy Ghost. It is in this way that our election may be made manifest.

In verses 5 to 10, the Apostle epitomizes the effects of his ministry among these Thessalonians. "Our gospel," he says, "came not unto you in word only, but also in power, and in the Holy Ghost, and in much assurance; as ye know what manner of men we were among you for your sake." The gospel, of course, must come in word. It is the business of the servants of Christ to proclaim to a lost world the Word of the truth of the gospel. It has pleased God by the foolishness (that is, the simplicity) of preaching, to save them that believe. But the mere statement of gospel truth, apart from the power of the Holy Spirit, is not likely to produce such results as were seen in Thessalonica. It is true that God in His sovereignty may use His own Word, and often has done so, no matter who proclaims it, or even if it be found simply on the printed page. But His general method is to empower devoted men to set forth the Word with clearness and in the energy of the Holy Spirit. Then the results are assured. The Lord Jesus told his disciples, as recorded in Acts I, "Ye shall receive the power of the Holy Ghost coming upon you, and ye shall be witnesses unto me" (marginal reading). This is something that should never be ignored. To mistake human eloquence or oratory for preaching in the power of the Spirit of God is a great mistake. Someone has well said that "preaching is eloquence touched with fire." It was in this way that Paul and his companions proclaimed the gospel as they went from place to place; and the result of such a proclamation was not only that people were led to trust in Christ, but they received "much assurance." It is a lamentable fact that a great deal that passes for gospel preaching today would never give assurance of salvation to anyone. Sermons may be theologically correct that make no true application to the needs of the hearers and are, as someone has said, "clear as crystal, but cold as ice." When the Word is preached in simplicity and in the energy of the Holy Spirit, those who believe it receive the full assurance of faith.

The last part of verse 5 is exceedingly significant. "Ye know what manner of men we were among you for your sake." They were careful to walk before God in holiness of life and in righteousness toward their fellow men. A holy minister is a tremendous weapon in the hands of God for the pulling down of strongholds of sin. It was Emerson who said of one, "What you are speaks so loudly that I cannot hear what you say." What a pitiable thing if this should ever be true, as, alas, it has often been true, of ministers of Christ. Integrity of life, devotedness of heart, holiness of spirit should characterize the proclaimers of the gospel of grace.

The self-denying ways of Paul and his companions made a deep impression on these Thessalonians. He writes, "Ye became followers of us," that is, imitators of us, "and of the Lord, having received the word in much affliction, with joy of the Holy Ghost." It may seem strange that he here puts himself and his companions before he speaks of the Lord, but we need to remember that these Thessalonians had never heard of the Lord, probably never would have heard of him if Paul and the others had not gone to them. It was what they saw in them that led them to be interested in the things of the Lord and so, having trusted in Christ, they took his servants as their examples and in imitating them, they were really following the Lord.

They received the Word in much affliction and yet in joy. This sounds paradoxical and indeed it is, but the Christian may be sorrowful, yet always rejoicing. The affliction to which he refers may have been twofold. There was, of course, deep contrition as they recognized their sinfulness and mourned over their years of ungodliness and idolatry. Then, too, they knew that to decide for Christ would mean, in many instances, separation from loved ones, grievous misunderstandings and even bitter persecution. But they were prepared for them. They counted the cost and considered that Christ would mean far more to them than temporal comfort or worldly prosperity, and so they joyfully received the message which told them of sins forgiven and the hope of heaven.

So great was the change in their lives that others soon noticed it. They were ensamples, we are told, to all who believed in Macedonia and Achaia. Thessalonica was one of the chief cities of Macedonia; Achaia was the neighboring province. In place after place the word went forth of what had happened in this city, where Paul had labored so earnestly. They who had been converted through his preaching became in turn preachers themselves.

From them sounded out the word of the Lord. Not only in Macedonia but into other places too, the news of what had taken place was spread. It was not necessary for anyone to insist on the reality of their conversion. Their lives made it evident that they were in touch with God.

In the last two verses we have two words that cover the whole Christian life "serve" and "wait." Note the connection. "They themselves shew of us what manner of entering in we had unto you, and how ye turned to God from idols to serve the living and true God; And to wait for his Son from heaven, whom he raised from the dead, even Jesus, which delivered us from the wrath to come." This was real conversion. They turned to God and in turning to God they turned from idols. We have a different order in Acts 14:15. In speaking to the men of Iconium, Paul says, "We preach unto you that ye should turn from these vanities unto the living God." The two passages are not contradictory, both suggest true repentance, upon which conversion rests. To repent is to change the mind, that is, to reverse one's attitude, and so these, who had been idolaters, turned to the true and living God. They were through with idolatry. And so today, when men trust in Christ and bow before God in repentance, they turn from the things of a godless world and yield themselves to the one who died to redeem them. Following their conversion, as intimated above, two words set forth their new attitude. They now sought to serve the living and true God, while they waited for His Son from heaven. We are sometimes told that occupation with the second coming of the Lord has a tendency to throttle Christian activities. People become dreamers, become taken up with prophetic questions, and they are no longer interested in living for God or seeking to win others for Christ. Frankly, my own experience tells me that the contrary is true. The more this blessed truth grips the soul, the more one would be concerned not only about serving God himself, but winning others to Christ. It was so of these young believers. They lived day by day in the expectation of Christ's return; they looked for him, the risen and ascended One, to come back again as their deliverer from coming wrath. The wrath referred to here, I take it, is not eternal judgment. From that they have already been delivered, but wrath is coming upon the world. This wrath is still in the future, but the Lord has promised to take away his own before the trumpets of wrath begin to sound and the judgments of the Great Tribulation fall upon the world. It is evident that to some extent at least Paul had intimated that such a time of trouble was in the future, but that Jesus would come to snatch his own away ere that wrath is let loose. This is still the hope of his saints.

Religion and Life

THE VERY REVEREND VINCENT J. FLYNN, PH.D.
President, College of St. Thomas and St. Thomas Military Academy
(Roman Catholic), St. Paul, Minnesota

Father Flynn is one of the younger priests and college presidents of the Catholic Church, who has three great passions, the literature of the Renaissance, the education of young men and religion. He was born in Avoca, Minnesota, September 11, 1901, studied at the College of St. Thomas, St. Paul Seminary, the University of Minnesota and the University of Chicago. He spent 1934 and 1935 abroad for research and discovered a manuscript giving new light on Anglo-Italian relations during the Renaissance, was awarded a Guggenheim Fellowship to pursue further research during the summer of 1942, and published a new edition of William Lily's Short Introduction to Grammar (1567) in 1945.

He was ordained to the priesthood of the Catholic Church in 1927 and has spent most of his mature years teaching English at St. Thomas College. Since January, 1944, he has been president of the college. During the summers, 1939-41, he was visiting lecturer at the Catholic University of America, is Catholic co-chairman of the North Central region of the National Conference of Christians and Jews, a member of the Modern Language Association, and a member of the Catholic Historical Association. In 1942 he edited Prose Readings, an anthology for Catholic colleges. His travels abroad have taken him to England, France, Italy, Germany and Belgium.

This sermon was preached at the Commencement of the University of Minnesota in the spring of 1945. In it he discusses the importance of knowledge, shows the fallacies of materialism, the limitations of science, the dilemma of the unbeliever and the need for faith in the life of our day.

Sermon Twenty=two

TEXT: Now I know in part, but then I shall know even as I have been known. So there abide faith, hope and charity. . . .
I CORINTHIANS 13:12, 13 (Catholic New Testament, 1941)

KNOWLEDGE is important, but wisdom is more important. It is important to know who discovered America, what water is made of, and why apples fall from trees. But, I submit, it is more important to know the essential nature of man and the universe—to know what man is, his origin and destiny; to know where he fits in the vast scale of being; to know whether man and the universe are responsible to a Supreme Being or not; to know what constitutes proper conduct for man.

At this point someone will say: "Yes, of course; what you say is true; the questions you put are the vital ones; but by their nature they are unanswerable, insoluble, by this poor creature, man." This, I venture to say, leaves us with a pretty bleak outlook. It is a defeatist view; it robs life of any real significance. The quest for the essential truth about the universe is admittedly hard; but I should think that any serious man would search all his life before giving up on such an important matter. Perhaps he cannot possess the whole truth; but a fragment of that truth, a partial view, a fleeting glimpse, even, would seem to be worth any amount of trouble. It is a well known fact, however, that many have given up the search for ultimate religious truth and called themselves agnostics or atheists. This is particularly true of our own day, coincident with, and perhaps owing partly to, the widespread interest in the physical and biological sciences, and the great advances made in these fields. The consequent absorption in the natural has tended to turn man's attention from the supernatural. The chief cause, however, of the recent spread of agnosticism is, to all appearances, the breakup in the unity of Western thought.

As far back as history goes, we find examples of agnosticism, if not of atheism. But the number of nonbelievers was never very large. Even today, the number of nonbelievers is only a tiny fraction of the great mass of humanity. But it is a fact, nevertheless, that in our Western world religion has been losing its hold on people in the last two or three generations.

In giving up religion, men have, for the most part, adopted a philosophy of materialism; that is, a belief that there is no such thing as the spiritual— that everything in material. Men have likewise given up their belief in the moral law—in an absolute standard of right and wrong. They have said that what we call right and wrong is not a matter of principle, but a matter of utility, of expedience, or of custom. In taking their stand on this ground, men have paid a terrible price; for it is becoming increasingly clear that in giving up religion we give up any right to talk about such things as the dignity of a human being, right and wrong, democracy, freedom, toleration, war guilt, war criminals. I do not say that every agnostic is a foe to the dignity of human beings, to democracy, to freedom, to toleration; that he has no conception of right and wrong or of guilt and of innocence; but I do say that when he has thrown away his religion, he has thrown away his only real ground for having an opinion on these subjects.

If there is no absolute lawgiver, what becomes of law? If you say that the ultimate basis of right and wrong is custom, or utility, or expedience, you do not necessarily make *your* utility, or *your* expediency, or *your* notion of what a custom should be the basis of all your action. But you will be perfectly logical if you do so. Most human beings are too fundamentally decent or are still so thoroughly under the spell of the believing atmosphere of their childhood—or of the world's childhood—ever to carry into practice the conclusions of these premises. But when men like Hitler and Mussolini and Stalin come along, and, acting on these same principles, form totalitarian states, making those states supreme over individuals, exterminating individuals and nations, the person who does not believe in God or in right and wrong has no grounds for objecting. Why should not Hitler, spurning toleration, deprive peoples of their freedom and even of their lives if it will be to his advantage? Similarly, why should not a business man lie and steal, coerce and murder, if it will help him to amass a fortune?

If man has any dignity, it is because he is a child of God. If man has any rights, it is because he is a child of God. If there is such a thing as guilt, it is because some things are right and some things are wrong. If the concept of democracy has any validity, the concept that peoples should rule themselves, it is because—in the words to which we so often pay lip service—men were created free and equal.

You see the terrible confusion that has resulted because a few ruthlessly logical nonbelievers were able to put their ideas into effect; we have the whole world in turmoil today. For thousands of years the world got along, for the most part, on the theory that there was a Supreme Being, all just, all good, all powerful; that man was created to live forever; that he will be rewarded for his good deeds and punished for his bad ones. This view of life was held alike by Jews and Christians and Mohammedans. Even the pagans believed in some kind of god or gods, and in some sort of future life; and they believed in a moral law. But it was left for this enlightened era to produce a generation of bright young men who emancipated themselves from superstition, who overthrew timeworn formulas, who discarded outworn dogmas. These bright young men—brighter than Plato and Aristotle, brighter than Paul and Augustine, brighter than Thomas Aquinas and Abelard, brighter than Thomas More and Erasmus and John Colet, brighter even than

Martin Luther and John Calvin, brighter than Samuel Johnson and Alexander Pope, brighter than John Ruskin and John Henry Newman—these bright young men, who saw their way clear where others had stumbled darkly, gave us first totalitarianism and then total war.

There is no good in our saying that science has advanced so far since the days of Plato and Erasmus, and even of Newman, that it has taught us the unreasonableness of belief. No matter how far the natural sciences advance, they can never teach that belief is either reasonable or unreasonable. The two are in quite separate fields. Science works by observation and experiment. The scientist says: "I mixed mud and molasses, let it boil, and observed such and such a result." He never says: "This proves that mud and molasses came into being at the command of a creator." He hardly ever says: "This proves that there is no God." No matter how much science learns about the universe, it can never attempt to answer such questions as, Where did it come from? Was it always there? Is there an activating Intelligence behind it or not?

The point is that such questions are answered by hard study and thinking. This method requires no laboratories, no apparatus except intelligence. Aristotle, therefore, and Augustine, if they had comparable intellectual equipment, were as well able to investigate these problems as are any of us today. No doubt the world is at present full of intellectual giants, but most of us have still some lingering respect for the mental capacities of the great pagans, the great prophets of the Old Testament, and the great Christian Fathers.

In the light of our present miserable state, I wonder whether the time has not come for us to re-examine the grounds of belief. You will sometimes hear it said that theism is a beautiful dream; that it is a pity that it cannot be true. Well, if it cannot be true, it is indeed a pity, if you wish to make any sense out of reality at all; if the reality is simply the wretched condition of mankind that we have today, or even a condition which is a shade less miserable, why continue to propagate the race? If this life is the be-all and end-all, for the most part of humanity it is very questionable whether the game is worth the candle. Even in the so-called "normal times" the amount of misery in the world is appalling. If you doubt it, talk to your doctor; talk to a clergyman; talk to a judge in the law courts; talk to any man or woman who has passed his middle age. Is it, after all, antecedently improbable that there is more to man than his body and mind; that there is more to existence than the present life; that there is more to reality than what we see?

It is true of course that no argument is as weak as the argument from authority, but it is likewise true that a humble respect for the opinions of others is the beginning of wisdom. There is no folly like the folly of the proud man, who summarily rejects the opinions of others; there is no folly like that of the modern who despises the ancients simply because they are ancients. Everybody recognizes the great advances in matters technological made by our age. But few would have the effrontery to maintain that we are a nobler race today than were our forebears. Is not the matter of sufficient importance that we ought once more to ask ourselves whether we have not been hasty in rejecting the view of life held by Shakespeare and Milton, by Newton, and Pasteur, by Washington, Jefferson and Lincoln? Is it not possible that a swollen pride has blinded our eyes to the truth?

There are many arguments for the existence of God, for the existence of the human soul, for the immortality of that soul, for the moral law. Time does not permit me to enter into even a mere recital of these arguments. If you are serious, if you wish to endeavor to weigh these arguments once more, any priest, any minister or any rabbi can show you where to find them set forth. There is one argument, however, for the existence of God which presents the nonbeliever with a dreadful dilemma. He either believes in God or stops believing in the validity of human thought. The argument is presented in laymen's language by a recent convert from atheism to Anglicanism, Mr. C. S. Lewis, fellow and tutor of Magdalen College, Oxford.

In his recent book, *The Case for Christianity*, Mr. Lewis says:

> There are all sorts of different reasons for believing in God, and here I'll mention only one. It is this. Supposing there were no intelligence behind the universe, no creative mind. In that case nobody designed my brain for the purpose of thinking. It is merely that when the atoms inside my skull happen for physical or chemical reasons to arrange themselves in a certain way, this gives me, as a by-product, the sensation I call thought. But if so, how can I trust my own thinking to be true? It's like upsetting a milk-jug and hoping that the way the splash arranges itself will give you a map of London. But if I can't trust my own thinking, of course I can't trust the arguments leading to atheism, and therefore have no reason to be an atheist, or anything else. Unless I believe in God, I can't believe in thought: so I can never use thought to disbelieve in God.

This is a sample of the arguments that you must examine if you wish to give the case for the supernatural a hearing. By its very nature, this case cannot be decided upon the evidence of one's senses. Nobody ever claimed that God could be seen with human eyes, or weighed or measured by human instruments. But if you have faith in reason, you may be willing to set your reason to work upon a problem of such utter significance as this one. Your reason will not tell you as much about the nature of God as scientific analysis will tell you about the nature of the potato. But in view of the importance of this question of God and of man, it is difficult, I make bold to assert, to justify a lack of concern in the answer.

IMPRIMATUR: ✠ John Gregory Murray, D.D., *Archbishop, St. Paul*

Worshiping the Net

REVEREND ISRAEL BETTAN, D.D.
Rabbi and Professor of Homiletics, Hebrew Union College, Cincinnati, Ohio

Rabbi Bettan is one of the preachers who molds the young rabbis of Reform Judaism and in his own preaching has force, intellectual power and spiritual perception. Born in Lithuania in 1889, his studies were done at the University of Cincinnati and Hebrew Union College. He was rabbi of B'nai Israel Congregation, Charleston, West Virginia, from 1912 to 1922, was president of the Charleston Federated Charities, chairman of the City Survey Commission, member of the West Virginia Child Welfare Commission, and member of the West Virginia School Code Commission. In 1915 Hebrew Union College conferred the D.D. upon him.

During the first World War, he was chaplain in the United States Army. He has been professor of homiletics and Midrash at Hebrew Union College since 1922, is chairman of the Committee on Responsa, Central Conference American Rabbis; member Committee on Liturgy C.C.A.R.; member Tract Commission; member Committee on Ceremonies. He is the author of a number of monographs on homiletical and historical subjects; chief work: Studies in Jewish Preaching, 1939.

He gave a series of lectures at Garrett Biblical Institute, the Divinity School of the University of Chicago and Duke Divinity School. In "Worshiping the Net" Dr. Bettan shows his ability to make full homiletic use of his material and to keep his message as the important matter.

Sermon Twenty=three

TEXT: Therefore they sacrifice unto their net, and offer unto their drag; because by them their portion is fat, and their food plenteous. HABAKKUK 1:16.

IN THE opening chapter of the Book of Habakkuk, the prophet draws a somber picture of the grave social disorders of his day. Injustice and violence reign supreme in the land. Tyranny and wrong triumph everywhere. The wicked inflict merciless cruelty upon the innocent. Men have become

[127]

like the fishes of the sea, only to be gathered into the dragnet of their de-spoilers. And these oppressors of the people, the prophet observes ironically, not only rejoice in their successes and exult in their triumphs, but pay homage to their net and their drag, worshiping the very means by which they have come into the possession of their spoils. "Therefore they sacrifice unto their net, and offer unto their drag; because by them their portion is fat, and their food plenteous."

This graphic picture of the prophet, in which the figure of the fisherman worshiping his net stands out prominently, cannot but capture the attention and kindle the imagination. There he stands, the prosperous fisherman, elated by the good fortune that has come to him, and deluded, by an exuberant fancy, into thinking that, if his portion is fat and his food plenteous, it must be that the tool of his trade, the dragnet bulging with his catch, has favored his enterprise. And so, he proceeds forthwith to worship his net.

The pathetic figure of the fisherman sacrificing unto his net, the bare in-strumentality by which his prosperity has been achieved, is no solitary individual on the human scene. Ironical as the situation may appear at first glance, it arises frequently in the serious affairs of men, and in forms that are more grievous than ludicrous. It is a common failing of the human mind, to lose sight of the main objective in any weighty undertaking and fall to wor-shiping the means by which some partial triumph has been won. How often, and after only the slightest advance, is the pursuit after a cherished goal abandoned, and the way that may lead to it glorified? How often is the essen-tial forgotten, and the incidental exalted? How often is the substance neg-lected, and the shell sanctified?

This tendency to worship the net, however grotesque the scene it presents, is quite prevalent in our modern life. Many are the forms in which the spirit of net-worship finds clear and startling expression. We need but examine some of the more notable of these forms, to realize the menacing nature of this strange phenomenon.

And, first, let us consider the distressing attitude of so many of the trained and enlightened minds of our day toward that prodigy of man's searching spirit which goes by the name of modern science. It is surely unnecessary at this late date to rehearse the matchless exploits of the physical sciences. What distinguishes our century as one of the greatest epochs in the history of the race is the amazing growth in scientific knowledge. The great progress of the age, we owe to the researches and discoveries of modern science. Like a huge dragnet, it spreads over the vast reaches of the universe and gathers from the secret recesses of nature ever new facts and wondrous sights. It has not originated these facts and phenomena. What it has brought to light is and always has been. Out of the immensity of time and space, it has gathered the rich spoils of knowledge; it has not created them. The most profound revelations of science: the power of electricity, the miracle of the air wave, the boundless energy of the atom—what are they but disclosures of existing forces, of laws and methods in operation since time began?

To the reverent mind, the world of nature appears all the more glorious and faith-inspiring because of its vastness and mysterious depths. Looking out upon the stupendous panorama unfolded before his gaze by the researches of science, he perceives all the more clearly the pulsating life of the universe, the creative power of God. His faith is strengthened and purified by the very knowledge revealed to him. For behind the visible phenomena he discerns unmistakable evidences of a planning and ruling eternal Spirit.

But what vain chatter assails our ears from laboratory and lecture hall, about the supremacy of scientific truth, the self-sufficiency of the senses, the eternity of matter, the tyranny of natural law? Must we burrow beneath a mound of secondary causes and banish from our minds the First Cause? Is the world to be stripped of divinity, that science may be deified? Surely, nothing but an uncontrolled passion for net-worship could impel the human mind to sacrifice unto the dragnet of scientific discovery. Nothing but a blind devotion to the external could cloud our vision of the "stupendous whole, whose body nature is and God the soul."

If we focus our attention on another characteristic feature of our age, which bears the proud name of social service, we shall encounter there, too, the same tendency at work, making for the patent ineffectiveness of so much of our social effort.

This is an age not only of great material expansion and scientific progress but also one of unprecedented social change. A new vision of social obligation has come to us. The insistent cry of the age is for social reform. The man of the hour is the man of social consecration. The New Deal, with its elaborate legislative program for the common good, is perhaps the most convincing expression of the social idealism of our time.

Fundamentally, the social ideal is rooted in the conviction that the individual is not an isolated entity; that his life is influenced by the environment in which he is placed; and that, to attain the inner development of which he is capable, he must not be denied the outer opportunity. Circumstance will influence character. External conditions will affect moral progress. Poverty, frustration, discontent, will drain the soul of its strength. The social ideal is thus chiefly concerned with the health of the human spirit. It cherishes, above all else, the imperishable worth of man's soul. It demands, therefore, that our social structure be rebuilt, that our political and economic life be regenerated, so that our world may become a place that is fit for the full unfoldment of the human personality.

Such is the essential faith, the challenging spirit, of the social idealism of our day. What, then, with such a lofty principle to direct its policies and such a noble enthusiasm to inform its actions, what shall we say then of the organized social service of our time, with its cramped outlook and uninspired projects, with its kindly patronage and pretended philanthropy, its elaborate mechanical devices and commercial methods, unmotivated by a controlling spiritual purpose, unimpelled by the moral force of religious inspiration? Are we to suppose that the soul of man is the candle of conditions, quenched by want and relit by relief? Doth man live by bread alone? Can human life be redeemed by the transference of the slums from the back alley to the broad avenue? Shall the end be crowded out by the mechanical devotion to the means? Shall we sacrifice unto the net, and offer unto the drag?

It is a general, deep-rooted tendency that we are tracing, whose manifestation can perhaps be best observed from the vantage ground of Jewish life and thought. In the midst of present-day Jewish conditions, we are indeed occupying a most advantageous position for the minute observation of this puzzling phenomenon. When we turn to consider the New Nationalism, which in recent years has become a dominant issue in Jewish life, we behold a form of net-worship that is particularly grievous and alarming.

The exponents of the New Nationalism can see no future hope for Israel save in the rebirth of the national ideal and in the restoration of his ancient Palestinian home. Caught in the maelstrom of modern nationalism, from which a despairing world is sending up its cry of distress, they would reinterpret our function in the economy of the world. Israel is henceforth to retreat from his historic position as the champion of the living God, and take his place in the scheme of national grouping as a separate political unit, exercising his powers within restricted area and limited scope, beating out his soul in self-imposed retirement.

The issue is clear and definite. That we constitute a separate group in the world, only the captious spirit of a narrow partisanship will venture to deny. We are more than a religious sect, more than a denominational church. We are a people; we are a nation, if you will; but a "peculiar people," a "holy nation": a people bound together by the unbreakable ties of a common past and a common religious heritage; a nation rooted in the spiritual soil of an immortal ideal.

This conception of Jewish nationhood the Hebrew prophets never wearied of proclaiming when the community of Israel still dwelt in its own land. They solemnly and ceaselessly asserted that Israel was projected into the world not by accident but by design; that he has lived through the centuries not by his own power and for his own aggrandizement but by the will of God and for the dissemination of His truth; and that he must continue to live, if live he shall, as the "servant of the Lord," holding aloft the banner of religious idealism until the Jewish conception of God and man, which was cradled in Palestine and fostered in Jerusalem, shall have conquered the hearts of all men.

Not only as a land, then, not only as a territory, has Palestine been precious to the Jewish heart, but chiefly as the birthplace of Judaism, the home of the great molders of his faith; the land from which issued forth God's law and

God's truth. To secularize this fundamentally spiritual idea of the Jew, to seek to substitute an outward national fabric for this inward reality, to glorify Palestine apart from the spiritual riches it has conferred upon the life of the human race—is not this to sacrifice unto the net, and offer unto the drag?

Religion, true religion, spurns the worship of the net. It values the aid that can come to the spirit from the proper use of external means, but it will not magnify the importance of the machinery of life. The chief concern of religion is not with the outward and the transitory, but with the inward and the permanent. Religion directs our gaze to the splendors of the sky, that they may declare unto us the glory of God. Religion dreads the curse of poverty, for the moral disintegration wrought by it; even as it discredits riches, for the peril to the spirit lurking in them. Religion exalts devotion to past, to land, to people, if it be centered on the living spirit that pulsates within them. Everywhere, in all external phenomena and in all regions of activity, religion discovers a deeper meaning, a higher purpose, and seeks to read the outer life in the light of the inner experience.

Religion denies the efficacy of external means in shaping the destiny of the human soul. A Bill of Rights may compel obedience to the letter of the law; it cannot engrave that law upon the tablet of the human heart. A United Nations Charter, with all the machinery it may devise, is but calculated to hold in check the forces of evil; it cannot cultivate in us those qualities of the spirit from which mutual understanding and kindly relationships must ultimately flow. Political parties may, by enlightened legislation, alter the conditions of life, making them more ample and equitable; they cannot endow the individual soul with the moral strength to use well the new resources and opportunities. Science may extend the boundaries of knowledge; it cannot furnish men and nations with the needed vision and self-control to profit by the new and perilous power. Art may portray the grandeur of nature's forms and colors; it cannot attune our life to the life of the all-pervading Spirit, of which shapes and forms and colors are but modes of manifestation. Literature and philosophy may reveal to us the enchanting beauty of lovely thought; they cannot stamp upon the soul the radiant loveliness of a transfiguring faith.

We shall not realize to the full the wondrous possibilities of our nature, we shall not rise to the height of life's great argument, unless we learn to reserve our deepest devotion for what is most profound in nature and in man. We would have, not fainter appreciation of the power and glory of nature, but more marked responsiveness to the Spirit that animates it; not less knowledge, but more faith. We do not depreciate the conspicuous undertakings of our time to solve the pressing problems of society; we only urge that our vision of the deeper purposes of life shall be kept clear and sharp. We plead, not for feebler attachment to the past, but for greater concern with the current of life that runs through it; not for lessened interest in Israel's future, but for increased devotion to the sacred cause Israel represents in the world. We would eradicate from human life the worship of the external, that we might fix our gaze all the more intently on the permanent and commanding issues of life.

Getting Along With Adolescents

REVEREND JAMES GORDON GILKEY, D.D., LL.D.
Pastor, South Congregational Church, Springfield, Massachusetts

Men and women find comfort and help in the sermons of Dr. James Gordon Gilkey. He combines religion, psychology and personal living, into messages which assist those who are emotionally upset.

In 1916 he was ordained as a Presbyterian minister and served as assistant pastor of Bryn Mawr (Pennsylvania) Church in 1916 and 1917. Since that time he has been minister of South Congregational Church, Springfield, Massachusetts. This church has a membership of nearly eighteen hundred and he has one of the largest Sunday morning congregations in New England. Dr. Gilkey was one of the first ministers to preach on the radio, broadcasting his morning service regularly as far back as 1923.

Since 1927, he has published fourteen books dealing with problems in religious thought and everyday living. Among them are Solving Life's Everyday Problems, *which has been transcribed into Braille for the use of blind readers,* How to Be Your Best, God Will Help You, *and* When Life Gets Hard.

During the summers preceding World War II he traveled widely, visiting places as remote as Australia and Russia.

"Getting Along With Adolescents" was preached in South Church on Father's Day, June 17, 1945. In it Dr. Gilkey shows his ability to apply religion and psychology to the training, raising and understanding of children, which is probably the biggest job mankind faces. It is distinctly a sermon for parents. The best place to prevent juvenile delinquency is in the home.

Sermon Twenty=four

TEXT: The younger son said to his father: Give me the share of your property that is coming to me! Then he got everything together, and went off to a far country. LUKE 15:12

NUMBERLESS sermons have been written about the prodigal son. Many sermons have been written about his elder brother. Only a few sermons have been written about the third character in the story—the prodigal son's father. Yet the father, presumably a man in the forties or fifties, is a very appealing figure. He is appealing because he faced a problem which is painfully familiar to virtually all parents. It is the problem of getting along with adolescents. Evidently this father had two of them to handle—a boy in the teens who set out for parts unknown, and a somewhat older boy who when the prodigal returned home made a disgraceful scene. Getting along with the two boys when they were young was probably easy. Getting along with them when they became mature would probably not be hard. But getting along with them when they were in the late teens and early twenties—what a job that was! Adolescents are human beings in the most awkward, unreasonable, cantankerous stage of their development. No one knows what they will suddenly propose to do, or what will happen to them when they actually do it.

Now let me say at once that some youngsters get through the adolescent years without becoming a problem. There are a few boys, and probably a somewhat larger number of girls, who are *always* a joy to their parents. But when most youngsters reach the middle teens they begin to be difficult. They continue being difficult till they reach the early twenties. If their obstreperous stage is delayed in starting it may continue till the late twenties. Now why are most adolescents a problem? Why are they a problem no matter how intelligent and hardworking their parents may be? The answer is, I think, this.

As human beings develop, they disclose four successive needs. The first, of course, is the need for a vast amount of physical care. That need appears, as we all realize, as soon as children are born. Fortunately babies are attractive, and fortunately adults are so constituted that they will do virtually anything in return for an occasional toothless grin. Were the pattern of life different, babies would not get the care they require, and then the human race would presently die out. The second need which emerges in a child's life is the need for security. The child must have a home in which he feels safe, older people on whose loyalty and protecting care he can rely. Otherwise normal development is impossible. I am much interested in a small girl of three who recently became involved in her first fist fight with a contemporary. When the youngsters were finally separated, my young friend yelled at her opponent, "When my Daddy comes home he'll knock your block off!" Like all children my granddaughter needs a sense of security, and apparently my son-in-law is providing it. The third need in a youngster's life? It is the need for love, affection, interest, concern. Of course this need is always present within a child, but when the child reaches the years between five and ten it becomes acute. The child *must* have someone who cares, cares deeply. Otherwise a dangerous sense of isolation develops, and then queer personality traits may take shape. This is why a child who loses both parents, or whose parents are cold and indifferent, is apt to become a conduct problem. This is why a child who is ignored while the family's interest is focused on a more gifted brother or sister tends to acquire unnatural attitudes. The love and affection, the interest and concern, which the child needs and craves are denied him.

The fourth need in a youngster's life makes its appearance soon after the teen age begins. It is the need for ever-increasing amounts of independence. Why does this need take shape? Because Nature is trying to prepare the child for the next stage in his career—the stage in which he will live his own life and build his own home. The child's increasingly vigorous demands for independence, his insistent attempts to establish his own identity, are evidences that Nature is trying to fit him for maturity. To realize this—to realize that it is quite as natural for a sixteen-year old to disagree violently with his parents as it is for a two-year-old to cling affectionately to them—is to understand the growing-up process and gain the ability to manage adolescents.

Of course the difficulty is that many of these early ventures in independence take distressing forms. This was the case with the prodigal son. It was highly annoying for him to demand when he was in the teens the portion of the family's wealth which would normally come to him only when he reached middle life. It was stupid for him to take that wealth and start jauntily for parts unknown. There, almost inevitably, he would lose his patrimony! No one can justify such demonstrations of independence, yet they took place in the first century and they have taken place in every century since. They take place century after century because youngsters need independence and demand independence, and then show presently that they are not yet old enough to use independence wisely. The distressing actions which characterize adolescents today? How often we find modern youngsters contradicting everything their parents say, deliberately violating their family's codes of speech and conduct, seeking ways by which to shock the elderly people in the vicinity! Let me give an illustration which—unfortunately—contains violent language. You realize of course that the violent language is someone else's, not mine. In 1849 James Fenimore Cooper, our American novelist, visited a certain Mr. and Mrs. Culver. At that time Mr. Cooper was sixty years old, and the conduct and speech of the two Culver girls—aged sixteen and nineteen—greatly distressed him. He wrote indignantly to his wife, "The girls smoke large, strong cigars. They also drink brandy and water. When their father sent them word they had shut their dog in a room which was not theirs, the fairy of sixteen shouted, 'Tell father to go to hell!' And she said it in the presence of her mother." There is typical adolescent conduct in modern times. Distressing but not actually dangerous.

Recently our difficulties with adolescents have been greatly accentuated by a prolonged war. Most boys in the later adolescent years have entered some branch of the service, and this means they have been suddenly emancipated from direct parental influence and control. In some instances the results have proved disastrous. Meantime most girls in the later adolescent years have become secretly apprehensive about their chances of marriage, and dangerously willing to consider any offer of marriage that came along. Many hasty and unfortunate weddings have been the result. And the younger adolescents, the so-called "high school crowd"? Their predicament has been quite as difficult. The boys have not been able to make plans for a long future, and this means that an important steadying influence has been removed from their lives. Meantime the girls have been thrust into a state of emotional turmoil which, as far as I can learn, defies analysis. Some months ago one hundred high school boys and girls in this city met at our local Y.M.C.A. to discuss themselves, their parents and the unsatisfactory state of things in general. As I read the newspaper account of their gathering I did not know whether to laugh or cry. How hard life today is for youngsters!

> The boys said that getting the use of the family car is now their main problem. In addition to the familiar parental objection "You'll smash the car if we let you take it," and the equally old statement, "If we give you the car we don't know where you and your friends will finally go," there are now the new difficulties created by a shortage of tires and gas. One boy at the meeting declared that a fellow can't get a date unless he has a car, but the moment he made that statement a girl rose to contradict him. She said this may have been the case before Pearl Harbor, but now a girl is so anxious to get dates that a car no longer matters. Another boy said that his father had had the nerve to offer to drive him and his girl friend to their graduation dance, and then call for them afterward and take them home. What a swell idea! Going home after the dance with the girl *and also Dad* was not his notion of a party.

Suppose now all this is true. What should we older people do when we must deal with adolescents? Obviously I cannot lay down rules for each of the hundred and one difficult situations which emerge in hitherto-happy homes. All I can do (I think) is state four facts we older people should remember as we try to get on with youngsters in the late teens and early twenties.

First: we should remember that we tend to picture our children as much younger than they really are. At my Alma Mater there is a classic story of a mother who wrote President Eliot asking if she could count on him to see that her son—a Harvard freshman—was tucked under the bedclothes every night. The boy had developed the habit of kicking off the covers, and this meant he was likely to catch cold. If he caught cold he would not do well in his work, and then his college career would be a disappointment. Therefore would President Eliot see to it that . . . You and I smile at this persistence of a child-image in the mother's mind, and then we permit equally inaccurate images to persist in our minds. To make a personal confession, I find myself picturing my son as an immature boy: it is only with the greatest difficulty that I can realize he is now older than I was when I became minister of South Church. The mental picture we have of our children is the appealing one which took shape when the children were young, dependent on us, unable to care for themselves. That picture has persisted and still persists, but meantime the children have grown up. Now they no longer fit the picture. You say this theory does not apply in your case? That your boys and girls would be helpless if you ceased making their decisions for them? I wonder. There was a time in American history when girls, still in the teens, had homes of their own. There was a time when boys, still in the early twenties, were masters of sailing vessels that circumnavigated the globe. Maybe you are wrong in thinking your youngsters are not yet old enough to start living their own lives.

Second: we older people should *expect* collisions with our adolescent children. We should expect these collisions because they are the attempts of maturing youngsters to assert their own independence, and establish (at least in their own eyes) their own identity. When these collisions—necessary and inevitable—take place, we older people should be neither surprised nor alarmed. Certainly we should not conclude that the collisions prove we have failed in the job of child training. We should view our situation in perspective, meet it with good humor, and then stubbornly refuse to take either our children's hasty remarks or our own wounded feelings too seriously.

Third: if our collisions with our children become serious, we should remember that our most important task is to preserve family unity—preserve it at any cost. No matter what happens, no matter how many adjustments have to be made, the family *must* be kept united. My guess is that these were the considerations which led the father of the prodigal son to do the surprising things he did. Of course it was outrageous for his younger son to demand, at that early date, his share of the family's wealth. Of course it was stupid for an adolescent boy to take that money and go to a far country. But if yielding to the boy's insistent demand, permitting the boy to learn the hard way rather than the easy way, was the price of holding the family together—then the boy's father was probably wise to pay the price. At least one significant result followed. When the boy had learned the hard way, and when he then undertook the long and embarrassing journey home, he felt he still had a home to come to. Thus there was a possibility that the family's life could be rebuilt.

Should parents today yield when a youngster insists on marrying someone whom the parents do not like? The parents certainly have the right to oppose the marriage as long as the marriage can be opposed. They certainly have the right to say all that can be said as long as saying it does any good. But when the marriage actually takes place, when opposition and argument finally become useless because the bewildering in-law is now a member of the family, then the parents should do what numberless parents in the past have done. They should yield. They should accept with as good a grace as they can a situation which is now—obviously—beyond their control. Preserving friendly relationships within the family, preserving them at any cost—this is the parents' primary task.

I have saved for the end the most important point of all. In dealing with adolescents we older people must remember that youngsters finally make their way through the adolescent stage, and then become reasonable, sensible, practical, maybe affectionate adults. You realize of course what the great words in the parable of the prodigal son are. "When he came to himself . . ." Finally that headstrong, defiant, troublesome boy passed his difficult stage. Finally he realized that he had made a fool of himself, finally he realized that his father was a decent person after all, finally he realized that his home was a better place than the one in which he had been trying to find happiness. "When he came to himself . . ." How long did it take him to come to himself? How old was he when he finally grew up? I do not know. Neither do I know how long it will take your children to pass the adolescent stage. But some day your children *will* pass that stage. They will grow up, they will learn how to use independence, they will acquire the qualities and abilities of adults. Then your life and theirs will merge again. "When he came to himself . . ." Ultimately and inevitably the life process brings that happy moment. We older people can wait for it—wait with unwavering confidence and hope.

A person is not mature until he or she is able to say, "I am wrong and you are right," and really, humbly, mean it. Witness — the Prodigal Son.

I. Teach children that they do not live by bread alone. See Jowett, "The Eagle Tip," p. 33.

Human Fellowship

REVEREND LOUIS FINKELSTEIN, PH.D., S.T.D.
Rabbi and President, The Jewish Theological Seminary of America, New York

Dr. Finkelstein is one of the truly great Jewish leaders of today. Since his appointment as president in 1940 his leadership has been the most important force in the development of the Jewish Theological Seminary and the Institute for Religious Studies. To meet the needs of the nation at war, he instituted the accelerated program of the Rabbinical School which made it possible for the Seminary to give one hundred of its graduates to the chaplaincy of the Army, Navy and Maritime Services of the United States and Canada. He is also the directing genius behind the annual Conference on Science, Philosophy and Religion.

Educated at the College of the City of New York, he took his Ph.D. at Columbia in 1918, and the degree of Rabbi from the Jewish Theological Seminary of America in 1919. He has been the Solomon Schechter professor of theology at the Seminary since 1931, a lecturer at Johns Hopkins, Oberlin, Duke and Harvard, and is adviser to the committee on Judaica research at Yale University. Dr. Finkelstein was elected an alumnus member of Phi Beta Kappa, and in 1944, at a special convocation, Columbia University conferred upon him the degree of Doctor of Sacred Theology "in recognition of many years of work as religious teacher, scholar and author."

Among the many organizations with which he is affiliated are the Rabbinical Assembly of America; United Synagogue of America; the Executive Committee of the Jewish Publication Society; the Executive Committee of the Joint Distribution Committee; National Conference of Christians and Jews; the Board of Directors of the American Friends of Hebrew University; the National Council of the League for Religious Labor in Palestine; fellow and member of Executive Committee of the American Academy for Jewish Research; member of the Religious Book Commission of American Library Association; and the New York Committee of the National War Fund.

He is the author of Jewish Self-government in the Middle Ages, The Pharisees, Akiba, and other books and articles. He is co-author of The Religions of Democracy and Faith for Today, and the co-editor of the second, third and fourth symposia of the Conference on Science, Philosophy and Religion. In 1940 he was awarded the Townsend Harris Medal, and was appointed by President Roosevelt to succeed Dr. Cyrus Adler as the Representative of Judaism advising the President on steps toward world peace.

Sermon Twenty=five

TEXT: Let there be no strife, I pray thee, between me and thee, and between my herdmen and thy herdmen; for we be brethren.

GENESIS 13:8

THIRTY-SEVEN centuries ago, men throughout the world, built their lives about their families, their clans and their tribes. Their worship was family or clan worship; their wars were family or clan wars; they regarded themselves as but insignificant instruments of their families or their clans. Each group commanded its members to protect one another, to help one another, to love one another; but they regarded it as equally necessary to struggle against all outsiders, to fight them, and to hate them.

Into this warlike world, there came first Abraham, the founder of our faith, and then, some centuries later, Moses, in whom Abraham's doctrines took clearer form and implementation. They differed from all their contemporaries and even, it must be admitted, from most men of later times, in holding that there is but one human family, embracing the whole species; that all of us are the children of One God, who loves us all, and who has created us in His image. They regarded it as sinful to hate anyone; to worship any clan or tribal or family god; to seek to dominate any group. However one might differ from them in form, in speech, in pigmentation, he was their brother, because he was the child and creature of their God.

The thirty-seven centuries which have passed since the time of Abraham, and more particularly the thirty-three centuries which have passed since the time of Moses, have been the witnesses to a singular enterprise: the effort to persuade mankind to recognize its own brotherhood.

We are living in an age when this doctrine of human brotherhood is being challenged more vigorously and brazenly than in any generation since the time of Abraham. Nimrod, in whom the Bible personifies the power-hungry rulers who were Abraham's contemporaries, sought to destroy him; but their effort only led to his thinking more deeply about his faith, and his taking the first steps toward its permanent establishment. The Pharaoh, under whom Moses lived in Egypt, flouted this principle beyond all other men, and this extreme rejection of the Abrahamitic doctrine, led to Moses' energetic espousal of it, and the further development of a people devoted to it. Some centuries later, Sennacherib, the ruler of Assyria, once more tried to crush this Abrahamitic and Mosaic faith, but his struggles only led to the emergence of Isaiah, who translated the concept of universal love into the concept of universal peace and a united human society. A few centuries later,

Nebuchadnezzar, king of Babylonia, made another attempt to extirpate this faith, but his effort, too, was the means of furthering it, for it led to the emergence of other interpreters, Jeremiah and Ezekiel, who recognized beyond all their predecessors that the principle of human brotherhood, and the Fatherhood of God, is the cornerstone of Judaism, and insisted that the Jewish people make itself the vehicle for the transmission of this principle to all men.

We can, at this day, begin to see how the attack on this ancient doctrine in our time may become the means for an understanding and implementation of it, far deeper than any we had only a decade ago. Throughout the world, men are beginning to see the deep, universalistic meaning of their religious traditions; and perhaps more than any other, we in whom the Mosaic faith has survived without change, and on whom the wrath of the enemies of this faith was poured in all its fury, are beginning to understand better than we did the meaning of our lives, of our work, of our struggles, of the sacrifices demanded of us in the past, and those which we are called upon to make in the present.

This curious development itself gives us a new insight into the realities of the world. Nimrod was the unwilling instrument for the emergence of Abraham; Pharaoh the unwilling instrument for the emergence of Moses; Sennacherib the unwilling instrument for the emergence of Isaiah; Nebuchadnezzar the unwilling instrument for the emergence of Jeremiah and Ezekiel.

Who knows whether there are not among us who are gathered here those who owe their insights into Divine truth to the very war waged upon it by the enemies of God and man? The Nazis, who wrought so much evil in the world, were themselves the means of extirpating the evil they intended, and giving the human species a new immunity to the spiritual disease which produced Nazism.

The increased generosity and eagerness to serve which is pervading the whole community, the new hunger for the spiritual truths and for God, everywhere obvious—everything testifies to the fact that like tyrants who preceded him, the tyrant of our time becomes the means for making the truth, discovered by Abraham and by Moses, everywhere better recognized and respected.

There is a Rabbinic legend that in his last day, the veil of mortality was lifted from the eyes of Moses, the foremost of all Prophets, and that he could see the whole future of the effort which he had so much advanced, uncovered. The Rabbinic Sages, pondering over this picture, tried to reconstruct the thoughts which passed through the mind of the Father of Prophecy, as he saw the suffering of his disciples of distant times, and their ultimate triumph, as each obstacle became a means for the advancement of their teaching. When he saw Rabbi Akiba, for example, he rejoiced at his learning, but he wept at his martyrdom.

i cannot but think that the merciful Prophet, watching us, his spiritual children, from a distant land, and a distant time, was deeply moved when he thought of Lublin, of Dachau, of New Guinea, of the Anzio Beachhead, or Normandy. Everywhere, he must have seen men dying, for the sake of the word he was leaving for men's unity; and yet perhaps in the midst of his grief, he also found a moment to glance at us, here, gathered in peace and quiet, trying in the midst of thundering cannon, each with his heart aching for some beloved one in the ranks or in suffering, to help keep his tradition. Perhaps he could even smile through his tears, as he smiled through the tears he shed for Rabbi Akiba's martyrdom, because he was so much moved by Rabbi Akiba's piety and permanent greatness.

In our time the pathos and the grandeur of human life have reached new climaxes. Never before has there been so much suffering, and never before has there been so much heroism, such widespread martyrdom, such determination to free the world from the horrors of hatred. Destiny itself is beating upon the heart and mind of mankind, driving us to accept the formula of human brotherhood, proclaimed those many centuries ago, or perish. The vision of Abraham and Moses must be fulfilled in our day, because without that there is no hope at all. As a new chapter opens for the human race, a chapter giving so much promise of a better world of better men, let us think of the lowly shepherds of Ur of Chaldees and of the Wilderness of Sinai, who initiated man's trek upwards, and to whom we owe the glories we have achieved, and the glories still in store for us.

The Hands of God

REVEREND ANSLEY C. MOORE, D.D.
Minister, Government Street Presbyterian Church, Mobile, Alabama

Dr. Moore's entrance into his pulpit has the effect upon his congregation of an "on the alert" signal. The congregation comes alive—they are eager; they are expectant. There emanates from him a verve which stimulates those present. This is evidenced in his energetic step, his accurate and graceful movements and his purposeful expression. He never leaves a congregation passive or apathetic. Even a casual visitor would conclude that Dr. Moore is a successful minister.

Two of his most striking assets are his spirituality and his versatility.

His spirituality is seen in his own consecration, his inspiring sermons, the beauty and adequacy of his worship service and in personal counseling. Through these things he is constantly leading people to Christ.

Dr. Moore appeals to all age groups. He speaks their language, understands their problems, and has an awareness of their needs. He has the art of making a person of any age feel that he is his contemporary.

Dr. Moore holds the interest of his entire congregation by varying his sermons. His messages range from those which strengthen one's devotional life to those which challenge one to social action.

His activities are broad in scope. He is chairman of Student Work for the Synod of Alabama, is associate editor of the Presbyterian Outlook, is a member of the Board of Trustees for Agnes Scott College, is active in the Mobile Council of Churches and is deeply interested in all the activites of his church.

Dr. Moore is a minister who makes his congregation proud of him and proud of their church.

Sermon Twenty=six

TEXT: Even there shall thy hand lead me, and thy right hand shall hold me. PSALM 139:10

THERE are all sorts of hands. Sometimes, as I stand at one of the five exits of our church, shaking hands with the people on a Sunday morning, I am offered a stiff hand which does not fold around my hand, or my heart—it is like shaking hands with a fish; again the hand is limp—it is like shaking hands with a dishrag! Often the hand is soft and warm and speaks of indoor life, books, music and antique furniture. Occasionally the hand is broad and hard, the grip like a vise, a hand that puts me for a fleeting moment in the atmosphere of the great out-of-doors, the forest, the camp, the sea. Indeed there *are* all sorts of hands. All of us can appreciate that line in "Toward a More Picturesque Speech" in the *Reader's Digest* which ran, "She offered me an assortment of rings and knuckles."

Hands have their story to tell. In the handclasp I always feel the heartthrob of my people. Salesmen who study the matter of approaching people effectively say that the man who offers you his hand with his palm down is the domineering type who will "do" you if you don't watch out, the man who turns his palm up places himself beneath you, and you don't like that. But the man who offers his hand with his own palm parallel to his body, meets you as an equal, as a friend, and we all respond to that. Hands *certainly* have their story to tell.

Alexis Carrel in *Man the Unknown*, speaking simply as a man of science, has this to say of the hand:

The hand is a masterpiece. Simultaneously it feels and it acts. It acts as if endowed with sight. . . . It has wielded with equal skill the flint knife of the primitive hunter, the blacksmith's hammer, the woodcutter's axe, the

[142]

farmer's plow, the sword of the medieval knight, the controls of the modern aviator, the artist's brush, the journalist's pen, the threads of the silk weaver. It is able to kill and to bless, to steal and to give, to sow grain . . . and to throw grenades.

Hands have always fascinated me. Dr. G. Campbell Morgan, the London preacher, has the most expressive hands I've ever seen. When he points up your thoughts go up, and when he makes a gesture depicting a man sowing seed, you smell the fresh-turned earth.

It is little wonder then that hands play so large a part in the writing of Scripture because hands are simply thoughts in action. Abraham stretched forth his *hand* and took the knife to slay his son. Isaac in his blindness would distinguish his sons by feeling their *hands.* Nehemiah prayed, "O God, strengthen my *hands.*" Through Isaiah, God calls Israel "the work of my *hands.*" "I will uphold thee with the right *hand* of my righteousness," said Jehovah to Israel. "If thy right *hand* offend thee, cut it off," said Jesus. The man with the withered *hand* comes to Christ and is cured. In the great Assize, the sheep were on the right *hand* and the goats on the left. And in the end of it all, the Son of Man is pictured as "seated on the right *hand* of Power." Thomas said, "Unless I see in his *hands* the print of the nails, I will not believe." "Jesus showed them his *hands*, and then were the disciples glad when they saw the Lord."

John Richard Moreland has spoken of Christ's hands in these moving words:

> The hands of Christ
> Seem very frail
> For they were broken
> By a nail.
>
> But only they reach
> Heaven at last
> Whom these frail, broken
> Hands hold fast.[1]

The brilliant Professor Horton somewhere has said this about the hands of God:

> God has two hands: with one hand He offers us grace, forgiveness, reconciliation; but if we refuse that hand, He has another, with which He offers penalty, result, consequence. But both of those hands are redemptive, one by appeal and the other by restraint.

My soul, what a thought for our sermon! Let us look first of all at the right hand of God.

God, with His right hand, offers us grace, forgiveness, reconciliation.

Here is the very crux of the Gospel. Do you know what it means? It means simply that you need not face another hour defeated. You need not groan and struggle and stumble and fall beneath the weight of sin and temptation.

[1] "His Hands," by John Richard Moreland.

Indeed, you need not live another moment as you are. God, with His right hand—the friendly hand—offers each of us: grace, forgiveness, reconciliation. This is another way of saying that you can surrender all to Christ and begin life now as a new creature in Him.

I was interested in a recent account of the cutting down of a giant sequoia tree in California. The scientists were called in to make a study of this tree's life cycle, and they published its biography.

> This sequoia was a seedling [they wrote], in 271 B.C. Just 516 years later, in 245 A.D., it was severely damaged by a forest fire. Nature immediately set to work to repair the damage, and began to fold successive layers of living tissue over the gigantic scar left by the flames. By 350 A.D. the wounds had been completely healed. In later centuries two other fires damaged the tree badly. But when the tree was finally cut down, the scar left by the first of these fires had been completely obliterated, and the scar left by the second was in process of being covered. That last scar was a tremendous wound 18 feet wide and 30 feet high, but had nature been given a chance, even that would have been entirely healed.

Here is one of nature's truths: The God of nature heals the wounds of trees! A basic truth of the Gospel is that the God and Father of our Lord Jesus Christ also heals the wounds left in the lives of men by sin. With His right hand God offers us: grace, forgiveness, reconciliation. But if we refuse God's right hand—and many men do refuse this redeeming grace, this healing power, this forgiving love—He offers us His left hand.

God's left hand, according to Professor Horton's novel way of putting it, offers us: penalty, result, consequence.

I do not know much about God, but I think I know this for sure; God *wants* every man to accept the offer of His right hand—the friendly hand—but when we refuse that, only the left remains. Robert Louis Stevenson put his finger on a basic moral truth when he said, "Sooner or later we all sit down to the banquet of consequences." This means simply that every man and every woman faces every day a judgment day. As we sit at the banquet of consequences, the dishes served us—whether they be bitter or sweet—depend entirely upon us. The ancient Scripture has it that we reap what we sow. In the physical universe this means that if I plant cotton seed, I will reap a harvest not of cabbages, but of cotton. If I mate elephants, I will get not kittens, but elephants. In the moral realm it means that if I sow immorality, I will reap immorality. If I sow purity, I will reap a harvest of purity. Here is one of God's immutable laws and it cannot be changed, even for you!

All of us know beforehand what the penalty, the result, the consequence is. Frequently when I rush to some parishioner who has crashed the moral barriers, he cries in his desolation, "If I had only known . . ." Don't ever say that! You do know, now, the consequences of morality and of immorality. God's law works as irreparably in this realm as in any other.

[144]

If I refuse the offer of God's right hand—grace, forgiveness, reconciliation —I automatically take God's left hand—penalty, result, consequence. If I accept the offer of God's left hand, then I go blundering back to God, and what a pity for any of us to go blundering into His holy presence when we could accept the offer of His right hand and be enfolded immediately in His fellowship. You see, whether God is a loving Father or an austere Judge is entirely up to us. There are the two sides of His character and the side we see and meet is determined by which hand of His we choose.

We have considered briefly God's right and God's left hand. Let us think of God's two hands.

The two hands of God—and sovereign hands are they—offer us guidance, security, peace.

It is easy to see the hands of God in history. It is comparatively easy to see the impelling hands of the Almighty as they shape up the nations for the coming of Christ. See how His hands influenced the Greek, the Roman and the Jew. The Greek contributed the spirit of inquiry and a universal language which immeasurably helped the early evangelists. The Roman brought all the world under the Roman eagle and thus the world was at peace when the first Christian preachers set out to tell the glad tidings, and they could travel over military roads made by the Romans, which led in all directions. The Jew contributed an expectancy of a coming One, belief in monotheism, a religious literature and faith and prayer. It is not difficult to see the hands of God—those sovereign hands—as they prepared the way and made crooked paths straight for the coming of the Son of Man. The sovereign hands of God here give new meaning to that little sentence tucked in the midst of the New Testament, "In the *fullness of time* God sent forth his Son into the world."

It is easy to see the hands of God—and, mind you, they are sovereign hands—in the shaping of the life of the great Apostle to the Gentiles. He grew up, not amid the narrow prejudices of the Palestinian Jews, but over in Tarsus, capital city of Cilicia, a great heathen city but one noted for its commercial and intellectual prowess. So that while one little Jewish boy who was to come first of all to the House of Israel was growing up on the streets of Nazareth, far over the ridges of Lebanon, another little Jewish boy who was to go to the Gentile world was growing up on the streets of Tarsus, a great cosmopolitan center. And their two lives, like water falling on opposite sides of a watershed, as James Stalker has put it, were destined one day to run down the course of history as one mighty stream. One can easily see the hands of God in faraway times.

It is much more difficult to see the hands of God in our own times. I think, however, that I can see His hands—those sovereign hands—leading us in the matter of world peace. There was the Malvern Conference, the Delaware Conference, the Princeton Conference and the one day conferences all over America on the Christian Bases of World Order. John R. Mott says that this is one of the brightest spots in the world today, the fact that more people than ever in the history of the world are thinking about the problems of peace.

Again, I think that I can see the hands of God leading us in the matter of drawing the Christians of the world together. There was the Oxford Ecumenical Conference on Life and Work in 1937; the Edinburgh Conference on Faith and Order; the Madras Missionary Conference; the Amsterdam Youth Conference; and there is the Federal Council of the Churches of Christ in America which ought to receive our sympathetic and intelligent support, for it is one of the greatest movements of our time. And there is the embryonic World Council of Churches. I say I think I see the hands of God leading us in drawing the Christians of the world closer together.

But I am especially concerned at the moment with a more personal matter. I think that I see the hands of God—those strong sovereign hands which have held nations in other days by the might of His power—leading many of us in a personal experience of religion in spite of the tragedy of the years of war through which we have passed. Many men and women have received from the blackness of this night some deep and abiding spiritual experience which has changed the course of their lives. The grandest thing I have heard in recent years was said to me by a father who had just lost a son in Europe. We were discussing the matter of prejudice. As he went down the steps he made the remark, "I don't have any real racial prejudice. I am not even prejudiced against the German boy who killed my boy." Then as he went away, he turned and said over his shoulder, "But I *would* like to tell that German boy what a fine boy he killed." That is the biggest thing I heard in World War II. The natural man does not talk like that. It is only when the hands of God—those sovereign hands—hands which do not coerce but rather persuade, are laid upon our lives. Many of us are feeling the hands of God upon us as we grope into the darkness of the night, giving us guidance, security, peace.

In one of the great art museums of our country there is a famous piece of sculpture by Auguste Rodin called "The Hand of God." Out of a rough-hewn block there rises a strong right hand. Lying in that hand there are some human figures which are just taking shape. In a very real sense those who have struck hands with Christ in these dark days have been conscious of being held in the sovereign hands of the Father of us all. It is only in His hands that we find guidance, security and peace. E. Louise Haskins has a fine word for us when she said, "And I said to the man who stood at the gate of the years, 'Give me a light, that I may tread safely into the unknown,' and he replied, 'Go out into the darkness and put your hand into the hand of God. That shall be to you better than a light and safer than a known way.'" This brings us to our text which is Psalm 139:10:

> Even there shall thy hand lead me,
> and thy right hand shall hold me.

Is Life Finally Just?

REVEREND LESLIE D. WEATHERHEAD, D.D.
Minister, City Temple (Congregational), London, England

Dr. Weatherhead is one of the great preachers of England today. He is minister of the famous City Temple of London, where he has served since 1936. He is also Honorary Chaplain to His Majesty's Forces.

Born in London in 1893, he was educated at Richmond Theological College, London University and Manchester University. He took an active part in World War I as second lieutenant of the Indian Army Reserve of Officers, as staff lieutenant during the Mesopotamian Campaign, living for a time with the Arab Tribes, and after the Armistice with Turkey, as chaplain of Devon Regiments where his work took him to units in Kurdistan and Persia.

In 1919 he returned to India and took charge of the English Methodist Church in Madras, where he remained until 1922. The next three years he spent at Manchester, England, and from then until 1936 he was minister of the Brunswick Methodist Church in Leeds. He is greatly interested in psychology and has specialized in that field. He is a teacher of psychology under the Board of Education, a lecturer in psychology for the Worker's Educational Association, and was formerly an examiner in psychology for Ordination Candidates in the Wesleyan Methodist Church.

The long list of Dr. Weatherhead's books reflects his varied interests: After Death, The Afterworld of the Poets, Psychology and Life, The Mastery of Sex Through Psychology and Religion, Jesus and Ourselves, How Can I Find God? Why Do Men Suffer? It Happened in Palestine, A Shepherd Remembers, Thinking Aloud in Wartime, This Is the Victory and Personalities of the Passion.

In the following sermon his discussion of human and divine justice opens new worlds of thought to the disillusioned and to the man of faith.

Sermon Twenty=seven

PRAYER: O Thou, Who art the Way, the Truth and the Life, make Thy way plain before our face. Suffer us not to stray from Thee Who art the Way, nor to distrust Thee Who art the Truth, nor to rest in any other than Thee Who art the Life. Teach us what we should think, what we should do, and wherein to take our rest, that in Thy light we may see light, and in Thy straight path may not stumble. Through Jesus Christ our Lord. Amen.
—A PRAYER OF ERASMUS

O God of many voices, all language is thine and all music, all lovely shapes and colours, and every word of friendship, every touch of love; all thoughts of holiness, all pure and noble feeling; use these and such as these to speak to us and we shall hear. Speak in the ancient wisdom of Thy saints, and in the poetry of Thy prophets; speak in the history of the past, and in the history that is made to-day; speak in the life that surges round us now; speak in the silence of our solitudes; speak in the joyous eagerness of youth, and in the calm maturity of age; speak in our sorrows and our joys, our triumphs and our failures, our expectations and our disillusionments; speak to our hearts, speak to our consciences, that, listening and heeding, our souls shall live. Through Jesus Christ our Lord. Amen.
—PRAYERS OF WORLD FELLOWSHIP

Father, we thank Thee that, just as in the drabness and dust of the town, we may remember the freshness and cleanness, the silence and peace, of the country which lieth all around us unseen, with its birds and flowers, woods and streams—so, in the turmoil of our hurrying lives, in the midst even of pain and failure, we may remember that beyond and all around, is Thyself, quiet and cool, trusty, beautiful and brave, in Whom is our Hope and our Stay for ever.
—"PRAYERS FOR USE IN AN INDIAN COLLEGE," BY JOHN HOYLAND

THE problem of the seeming injustice and unfairness of life is one which, again and again, troubles the minds of thoughtful people. How often we hear people say, "It isn't fair," and, as we listen to the story of their lives, we cannot but agree with them. One man at fifty is in full health, the owner of his own business, with plenty of money, a happy home and growing sons and daughters to delight him. Another, at the same age, who deserves just as well of the community, is ill, perhaps without any job at all or with a job he hates doing, and ill-paid at that, without any happiness in his home, living a life that is lonely and sad. One woman at fifty has had twenty-five years of happy, married life with a good husband. She has sons and daughters growing up around her. She has no economic needs, is healthy and happy and prosperous. Another woman at fifty is unmarried, toils all day at an uncongenial job, dare not think about the future, suffers from all kinds of nervous fears and emotional instabilities, and is barred from the supreme happiness one feels God meant all women to enjoy. Here is a young fellow who goes to the university, follows the career he chooses, has a fit body and a fit mind. Here is another without any of these privileges; without any prospects at all. This woman had a baby and did not want one; that woman would give anything, save her self-respect, to have a child and cannot or must not. She must witness the happiness of others and cope with frustration herself. This girl is popular everywhere, goes to everything, has seen the world and does not know the meaning of financial stringency; that girl, a loyal daughter, hardly ever leaves the four walls in which she looks after difficult, old folk, and is getting old and angular, cynical and resentful herself.

So we could go on. The war has emphasized that sense of injustice. There are members of this church who expressed conscientious objection and certainly met with a degree of criticism, but they are alive and well. Some of them are married with their little families, and life stretches out brightly before them for the years that almost certainly lie ahead. Some young men, who went out to fight for all our liberties, will never come back again, and some have come back maimed in body or mind or soul, or all three. It is hard for the parents of the latter to think that life is fair. There are members of this congregation who have lost sons and home and livelihood. There are members of this congregation who, at the beginning of the war, evacuated themselves to safe areas where people hardly knew a war was on, and, apart from the trifling inconveniences which even people in distant country places have had to suffer, they have not felt any serious disadvantage and have now come back to the city, unshattered in nerve and unaffected in body or mind. Their bank manager has assured them that their dividends will be regularly paid, and they are settling back on the cushions on which they were reclining six years ago.

I do not imply a criticism in any of these cases. It would be presumptuous to do so. But we must not be surprised if those who seem victimized through following the light they saw, cry out sometimes that life is not fair, that it is unjust, that it is cruel. This is a problem we ought to try to think through together, for if we can face it and find a clue to its solution, we shall be able to help one another guard against that cynicism and resentment and bitterness which do us more real harm than the original sense of injustice.

We must begin, I think, with the nature of God. If there is a God at all He must be just. I read the passage from the book of Job[1] to save time at this point of the sermon. "Shall mortal man be more just than God?" There

[1] Job 4:1-17.

can only be one answer to that question. We cannot suppose that God is less just than man, or that God can fall below the demand for justice in the heart of man. We can say that briefly by saying that justice is an eternal value or a final standard. It is a quality which must belong to the Being we call God and Whom we worship, for if it were not, then, in the matter of justice, man at his best would be greater than God.

Try, if you can, to realize just all that is implied there. When we cry out and say, "It is not fair," it is the God within us crying out. "Every virtue we possess," every idea man has of goodness and truth and beauty and kindness and justice and so on, comes to him from God. As Professor Emil Brunner says:[2] "Whoever says with serious intent, 'That is just,' or 'That is unjust,' has, even though unwittingly, appealed to a superhuman, supreme or ultimate tribunal, to a standard which transcends all human laws, contracts, customs and usages, a standard by which all these human standards are measured." And really, I think, when men rise up against God and say, "It is not fair," they do not mean to accuse God of injustice, for a very little thought would show them how impossible it is to suppose God unjust if our very ideas of justice come from Him. They really mean that they cannot see how and when and where God is going to vindicate the justice of His own nature in a way that satisfies the human mind, for, if justice is an eternal value, then it must be vindicated. However justice may be obscured by our false standards of what justice is and by our shortened perspective of the plans of God, yet it is intolerable to suppose that finally life for a single soul in the universe remains unjust and unfair. To call a thing an "eternal value" means that it has an ultimate worth and stability and can never be overthrown or defeated.

It is because justice lies as an eternal value behind our minds that, to be true people at all, we must always obtain justice for others wherever that is possible. Whether as individuals or as a community responsible for the social order, we must, as far as in us lies, determine that in every relationship of life, justice shall be done. And it hardly needs saying that no one must argue, "God will see that justice is vindicated at last, therefore I need do nothing about it," for it is sin to see something wrong that we could put right, without endeavoring to put it right. Passively to acquiesce in an injustice that could be remedied is treachery to the kingdom of God.

But the difficulty does not lie there. The center of the problem, as I see it, is that, as far as human eyes can see, there are some people who never get a fair deal. For years I have pondered over the lives of two girls I knew in another city, and, since their cases illustrate my theme, I shall give them in some detail. I will call one Joan and the other Betty, because these are not their names.

Joan was the daughter of wealthy people and she lived in a lovely home. Her childhood was guarded, but she was not unwisely coddled. Her parents

[2] *Justice and the Social Order* (Harper & Brothers, 1946), p. 46.

were people who set her a Christian example and who had magnificent ideals for the bringing up of their daughter. Joan went to the right school, took all the right examinations, went to a "finishing school" in Switzerland, took up some social work, married the right man, had the right number of children, lives still, as far as I know, in a beautiful house. Her husband has prospered. Joan is surrounded by cars and books and lovely pictures. She has a house at the seaside. I cannot think of anything, physical, mental or spiritual, which is lacking to make her life complete and happy. Save for the passing of her parents when they had completed the full three score years and ten, Joan has never known a moment's sorrow or pain or frustration in the thirty odd years of her life. Nor do I mean that there is anything wrong about that. She did not merit all that happiness and joy and success, but neither did she merit pain or poverty or failure. Things came her way and she took them, and I do not see how she merits any blame. She is not without social sympathies, is generous in every way, and she and her husband have done many gracious and unselfish acts for the poor and unprivileged.

Now turn from her to Betty. Betty lived in the slum of a great city. She was the only child. Her father was unemployed and died when Betty was very young. Her mother was so crippled that I have seen her wait upon Betty by going from the little scullery to the one living room on her knees. Betty has to be waited upon because she is a complete invalid. In childhood she was physically fit enough, but something went wrong at an operation, and Betty has been in bed ever since and is very often in great pain. I remember going to see Betty on a hot afternoon, and finding her tossing on a bed in a slum room that looks out on to a slum street, with nothing in sight that God made except a strip of sky, and that is usually obscured by the smoke of the city. Nor must you imagine that Betty provides a splendid pulpit illustration of one who, though greatly handicapped, is a benediction to all who come near her because of her radiant faith in God. No, poor Betty is not like that! She curses God. She swears at those who visit her. If they expostulate with her about her tempers and tantrums and tears and language, she tells them that they would talk a "damned sight different" if they were where she is. Adequate medical opinion has been consulted, of course, but no one holds out any hope for Betty. As far as can be seen, she will stay in that slum bed until merciful death intervenes. Indeed, she provides a strong argument for euthanasia; an argument quickened when pain is upon her, for poor Betty writhes and screams and bites her fingers. No one would be allowed to keep a dog in that condition. Day after hopeless day passed by and still Betty lingered. I have lost touch with both girls now but I should be relieved to hear that Betty was dead.

Well, God is a God of justice. Even if you argue that Betty's pain is the result of the world's ignorance or folly or sin; not God's fault and certainly not His will, I find little comfort there. God is responsible for the *possibility* of things going so terribly wrong. He has made a universe in which ignorance and folly and sin—admittedly not His Will—are capable of bringing to the innocent an anguish out of all proportion to any observed or demonstrable value here on earth. If Betty reacted with courage and faith, so that pain was the occasion of the growth of the soul, the problem would not be so hard to solve. But Betty makes the opposite reaction. The pain has made her hard and cynical and bitter.

How do you suppose the God of justice is going to put things right? Surely He will not, in another world, scale down the happiness of Joan and make her suffer just because she has been happy, so that Betty will feel that things have been leveled up. We can dismiss that. Even Betty would not wish it.

Do you think then that God will make it up to Betty in the next world; that because she has been so unhappy in this, spiritual gifts will be given her so lavishly that she will feel it is made up to her? Frankly, I can see no solution there either. Is there anything in heaven that can "make up" for thirty years' unhappiness on earth? If you take a little boy to the zoo to try to "make up" to him for, shall we say, a couple of days' toothache, he is, no doubt, glad enough to go, but he may not forget that Willie Jones across the road went to the zoo and yet had no toothache, and he may wonder whether a visit to the zoo cancels out the pain he has had to bear. I do not think things can be balanced up in this way at all.

Whether I can carry you with me in my own solution of this problem, I do not know, but light came to me in contemplating the phrase used by a business friend when he talked about a "frozen asset." He explained that by a frozen asset is meant something that at the moment cannot be turned into cash gain, but something which ultimately can be turned into cash. If someone leaves you a thousand pounds in his will, only to be paid to you when you are twenty-one, then in the years before you come of age the thousand pounds is a "frozen asset." It is not capable of enriching you now, but it is capable, if you go through a few simple formalities, of bringing you a thousand pounds on your twenty-first birthday. When we come to look at the case of Betty, we realize that IF she had made the right reaction to pain, she could have won something from it. She did not do so, and, as far as we can see, will not do so. But I can see sense and justice in regarding Betty's pain as a frozen asset. It is part of her experience and in a sense always will be part of her. I believe that in another world she may make a magnificent reaction to something that in terms of time is over and done with, but which in a timeless world is still part of her experience. Life would be finally unjust if the fact that undeserved pain to which a wrong reaction was made, was left as a permanent liability in the ledger of the soul. If it is "never too late to mend," it is never too late to react spiritually to pain, or other suffering, to which a false reaction was originally made. So that, in a sense, Betty's suffering is a "frozen asset." As long as she makes the wrong reaction it remains frozen, but when she makes the right reaction, she will convert that frozen asset into a wealth which can enrich her character to such an extent that I can even imagine Joan wishing that she had had more to bear, if the right reaction to great trouble so enriches the character, for, of course, in the next world, spirituality of character is the only wealth there is.

It is intriguing to think that Joan, having had all the good things of life, might even feel that it was she who had been treated unjustly, since Betty had had so much more material for spiritual gain than she herself had had. If ever she should feel like that, I think God will say to her, "If you feel like that, come and help Me share the pain of the world." For I have a very strong feeling that, in the life after this, those who really love God will be invited to do something which will be an immense privilege, but a heavy burden; an immense source of spiritual wealth and development, but also a fearsome discipline of the spirit; nothing less than helping God to bear the burden of His world. Wherever there is love there is no desire to escape pain, but a longing to share it with the beloved, and if the pain of God (not a pain of body, of course, but the more dreadful pain of the spirit) is the cost He meets in order to redeem the world, then, those who love Him and who would fain have the world redeemed, cannot live the carefree life of escape from the burden of earth's sorrow.

There will be some who say, "Ah! that's the old solution the parsons always give us. If they can't solve a problem in this world they talk about everything being put right in the next. It's the old story of 'pie in the sky when you die.'" Well, I cannot see that there is any weight in that objection. Quite frankly, this life taken by itself, simply does not make sense. There are wrongs which are never put right. There are people who never have a chance. There are possibilities in every man which only a very few ever realize in the earth life at all. If there is no life beyond this, then we are certainly miserable sinners, doomed to the despair of a hopeless night. I regard this life as the lowest form of the infant class in the school in which God is educating us, and He alone knows how many forms we shall have to pass through before we graduate as beings fit for unclouded communion with Him. In this matter of justice, even on earth the condemned person has to *await* justice, and he has to wait so that all the factors which are relevant that justice may be done, have a chance to be brought into play. In the earth life this is impossible in many cases: in the other life it can be achieved.

But now I want to pass on to an equally important part of our meditation. The concept of justice is always evolving and developing. In last Sunday morning's sermon we noted that in Old Testament days it was considered quite just for a whole tribe to be put to death for the wrong done by an individual. Nobody in those far-off days thought that unjust. Even here in England, a hundred years ago, a little child was hanged for stealing 1s. 10d., and tiny toddlers toiled for ten and twelve hours in the coal mines, opening the gates for the pit ponies. Indeed, so far from regarding that as unjust, there was an outcry in Parliament when someone suggested a reduction in the hours of labor of these children. Now we boil with a sense of injustice that such a crime was ever permitted. Note, therefore, that the more the human mind expands and the charity of the heart enlarges, in a word, the nearer we move towards God, the more our sense of justice alters.

Therefore, what we now regard as justice is probably far indeed from that eternal concept in the mind of God, for even we revolt at what men, who were as earnest as ourselves, regarded as justice a hundred years ago. I wonder what would happen if God answered our prayers for justice. What would be the response of a just and holy God to the demand for justice from men who have made the whole world a shambles, industrially crushed their brethren, engaged in cutthroat competition in business, ridden rough shod over the rights of others, and treated their subordinates with a greater injustice than life has dealt out to them?

We have passed a long way from our fathers who were not afraid to call themselves "hell-deserving sinners" and I think we must conclude our meditation on justice by saying this: God is a God of justice. In the end, no one will be able to accuse Him of injustice.

I was very interested in reading that fine novel by Elizabeth Goudge called *Green Dolphin Street* to note how those who play the chief parts in a seemingly inextricable muddle feel that in the end, justice is done. "It seemed to William that whatever else the mystery might do or not do *it did not cheat*." And again:

"Has it been worth while?" he asked Marguerite in a hoarse whisper. (Marguerite was the girl who became a nun when William married her sister.)

"Yes," she answered, "I doubt if we nuns are as self-sacrificing as we must seem to be to you who live in the world. We don't give everything for nothing, you know. *The mystery plays fair*."

Life is finally just to every man, and, unless man finally turns his back on God and will not realize his frozen assets, then no pain is wasted, no suffering or frustration or loneliness or unhappiness can *for ever* be on the wrong side of the ledger. Nor are those things now entered on the liability side of our account against God, merely met by assets on the other side. In the end liabilities will become assets, if we will have it so. For mercy is greater than justice, and we might do well, when we cry out to God for justice, to realize that we should be better engaged crying out for mercy.

> Depth of mercy! can there be
> Mercy still reserved for me?
> Can my God His wrath forbear?
> Me, the chief of sinners, spare?
>
> I have long withstood His grace,
> Long provoked Him to His face,
> Would not hearken to His calls,
> Grieved Him by a thousand falls.

> Whence to me this waste of love?
> Ask my Advocate above!
> See the cause in Jesu's face,
> Now before the throne of grace.
>
> There for me the Saviour stands;
> Shows His wounds and spreads His hands.
> God is love; I know, I feel;
> Jesus lives, and loves me still.

If you leave this church by the eastern end, you can see at one and the same time the symbol on the top of the Old Bailey Courts of Law and the symbol above the dome of St. Paul's Cathedral. As Dr. Farmer has noted, both buildings deal with sin and sinners. On the top of the Old Bailey is the famous gilded figure of Justice, with the sword in her right hand and the balances perfectly steady and level in the left. Above St. Paul's you will see another golden symbol against the sky—the Cross. The first symbol says, "Sinners justice will receive." The second symbol says, "Sinners Jesus will receive." In the Law Courts you may be saved by the oratory of an advocate. In St. Paul's you may hear these words: "We have an Advocate with the Father, Jesus Christ the righteous, and He is the propitiation for our sins."

The more I think about the nature of God, the more I ponder the nature of justice and my own faulty way of thinking about it; the more I think about the nature of sin, the more ready I am to try to do justly to others but to leave the problem of seeming injustice in the hands of God; to realize that no accusation of injustice can stand against Him at last, and that for myself I shall be glad enough to cry not for justice, but for mercy, and that at the last I shall be confronted not with a relentless figure with sword in one hand and scales in the other. I shall be humbly glad that, seated on the Great White Throne, is Jesus, the Saviour.

The Silence of Christ: A Lenten Sermon

THE RIGHT REVEREND MONSIGNOR AMBROSE J. BURKE, PH.D.
President, St. Ambrose College (Roman Catholic), Davenport, Iowa

Father Burke believes in education which reaches the heart as well as the mind. To him any learning is empty which does not enrich character as well as the intellect. He took his studies at St. Ambrose College, St. Mary's in Baltimore, Catholic University, the University of Iowa, and received his Ph.D. in course at Yale in 1927.

He was ordained a priest in May, 1921, and in recognition of his work was appointed a domestic prelate by Pope Pius XII on April 17, 1941. He was professor of English at St. Ambrose College from 1921 to 1928, principal of St. Ambrose High School, Davenport, from 1928 to 1929, and chairman of the department of English at Ambrose College from 1936 to 1940. Since February, 1940, he has been its president.

Father Burke is a director of the Tri-City Symphony Orchestra, a member of the Modern Language Association of Iowa College, Presidents' Association, and the Davenport Chamber of Commerce. In this Lenten sermon, given on Mutual's Radio Chapel, February 25, 1945, he presents the Catholic views on Lent, but his message is universal enough to be helpful to people of many religious faiths as they attempt "to imitate the sacred silence of Christ."

Sermon Twenty=eight

TEXT: If any man will follow me, let him deny himself and take up his cross and follow me.   MARK 8:34 (Douay Bible)

THE Holy season of Lent, which is now upon us, has always been for Christians a time of self-denial. Once converted to Christ, a Christian is bound to accept all that Christ has taught and to practice in his daily life all that Christ has commanded to be observed. There is no recess, no vacation, from Christian living, yet there are certain times of the year when Christians endeavor to follow Christ more closely. Lent is such a time. We respond more willingly to the invitation of Christ, "If any man will follow me, let him deny himself, and take up his cross, and follow me."

Before the war, the generally accepted means of self-denial were fasting and abstinence. Among Christian people, Catholics were limited by the law of fasting as to the amount of food they could eat, and were required by the law of abstinence to avoid the use of meat on certain days in the week. Today, because of rigors of wartime living, these laws are no longer in force. Yet a dispensation from fasting and abstinence does not excuse us from doing penance. "Except you do penance, you shall . . . perish" (Luke 13:5). In wartime Lent it is evident that we must seek the means of self-denial elsewhere.

Besides fasting and abstinence the life of Christ abounds in other types of penance. The most striking of these were His remarkable silence before His accusers and His patient, wordless acceptance of the suffering thrust upon Him. Does not the example of Christ in this regard offer to Christians in wartime an excellent means of penance?

If one reads the account of the Passion as related by the Evangelists with

[156]

the express purpose of noting the absence of speech, the silent behavior of Christ is astounding. When the false witnesses had borne testimony against Christ before the chief priests and the council, the High Priest asked, "answerest thou nothing to the things that are laid to thy charge by these men?" (Mark 14:60). "But he held his peace, and answered nothing" (Mark 14:61). Later when the Jewish leaders had turned Christ over to the Roman authorities to stand trial, Pilate, the Governor, said to Him, "Dost not thou hear how great testimonies they allege against thee?" "And he answered him never a word; so that the governor wondered exceedingly" (Matthew 27:13-14). In his perplexity Pilate took advantage of a legal technicality. Since this man was a Galilean, why not let him stand trial before Herod, who was then in Jerusalem? "And Herod seeing Jesus, was very glad for he was desirous of a long time to see him, because he had heard many things of him; and hoped to see some sign wrought by him. And he questioned him in many words. But he answered him nothing" (Luke 24:8-9).

Silently, too, Christ bore all the indignities of the "third degree" methods tried alike by the unfeeling mob and by the professional soldiers. Some spat in His face and buffeted Him; others struck His face with the palms of their hands and jeeringly asked, "Prophesy unto us, O Christ, who is he that struck thee?" (Matthew 26:67-68). Their cruelty reached its climax in the scourging at the pillar. This was a torture so cruel and so degrading that it was reserved for slaves. The poor victim often died under it, and it was in itself far worse than death Trembling with fear, for He was truly man, our Lord was fastened by His wrists to a pillar. Then the executioners standing on a step to deliver their blows more surely, struck Him unmercifully with their horrible iron-spiked lashes, tearing the flesh to the very bone. The Sacred Body was soon one wound. "From the sole of the foot unto the top of the head there is no soundness therein, wounds and bruises and swelling sores," as the prophet had foretold (Isaiah 1:6). Yet not a single word of protest escaped His lips. Gasping for breath, He sank to the ground, only to be dragged off to a fresh torment.

He had called Himself a King—well, the soldiers would have a coronation in their barracks. They threw over His shoulders an old scarlet cloak, and put a reed in His hand for a scepter. Then they plaited a crown of hard sharp thorns and beat it down upon His head and forehead, so that streams of blood trickled through His hair and ran down His face. They formed a line and marched before Him, bending the knee as they passed and crying out in derision, "Hail, King of the Jews." "And spitting upon Him, they took the reed, and struck His head" (Matthew 27:30). Again, Jesus bore all this in silence.

Accustomed as He was to cruel sights, Pilate was struck with horror and compassion as our Lord appeared again before him. Surely the people would be satisfied now. Pilate had Christ brought to the balcony that He might be seen by all. "Behold the man," he cried. "I bring him forth unto you, that

[157]

you may know that I find no cause in him." But his words were lost in the savage cry that came up from the mob below, "Crucify Him, Crucify Him . . . he ought to die because he made himself the Son of God" (John 19:4-7).

"Son of God!" Pilate was filled with a new and terrible fear. Innocent the man certainly was. But what if He were something more? What if He were a God? Never had a man borne himself like this Man, with such calm dignity, such invincible patience in the midst of torments and shame. He dared not leave this question unsolved. He must see Him again in private. "Whence art thou?" he asked. "But Jesus gave him no answer" (John 19:9).

How frequently, like a refrain, that phrase repeats itself in the account of Christ's passion. Silence is the most striking and the most characteristic trait of the suffering Jesus. He carried His cross in silence, speaking only a word of comfort to the weeping daughters of Jerusalem. In the three hours that He hanged upon the cross all that He uttered can be repeated in twenty-two seconds. There was silence before the falsifying witnesses, silence before the high priest, silence before Pilate, silence before Herod, silence at the scourging, silence at the crowning of thorns, silence on being nailed to the cross, silence on the cross itself!

How closely do the followers of Christ imitate His example of silence? Despite the time-tested truth of the adage, "Silence is golden," restraint of the tongue has never been a popular virtue. The confusion resulting from speaking different languages was not the only evil that befell mankind at the Tower of Babel. Men's tongues were set in perpetual motion with the result of more speech and less thought. There is no silence today unless it be observed in the houses of men and women in religious orders. Everywhere else words tumble over one another in a constant flow of speech and print. The presses of the world deluge the newsstands, the magazine racks, the mail boxes and our library tables. As far as the printed word is concerned the present paper shortage is a blessed restraint holding back the engulfing flood. But for every word written there are a thousand spoken. Even when men have nothing to say they speak anyway, as though silence were too painful an experience to be endured. When the emotions are stirred, words come forth in a positive torrent of speech.

Speech is so characteristic of mankind that we use such epithets as "chattering schoolgirls," "gossipy women," and "garrulous old men." Such phrases are not spoken in approval. Yet it is seldom that the descriptive term "silent" is used in a complimentary sense. The word must be supported by another flattering adjective before we are willing to accept it. We do not, it is true, object to hearing ourselves described as "the strong, silent type." How do we classify ourselves? Are we incessant chatterers, or do we pride ourselves on knowing when to speak and when to refrain from speaking?

Some years ago a boy in his early teens was practicing his typing at home. In the adjoining room his older sister was entertaining the young man of her choice. The boy, naturally curious in the progress of his sister, decided to kill two birds with one stone. The rather deliberately paced dialogue of the young couple made excellent dictation for a beginner. As they spoke, he typed. All was going well until the couple finally noticed that the clicking of the keys followed too closely their own speech. Rushing to the next room, they seized the paper from the roll and retired to the davenport to read the record of their conversation. Needless to say, the copy was destroyed, for the sweet nothings that were so delightful to the ears of the lovers, lost something of their character when transcribed on paper.

Suppose that someone was able to hide a dictaphone on our person so that, unknown to us, every word that we uttered for a whole week was recorded, and at the end of that time the transcriptions were played back to us. What percentage of our speech would we find completely inane? What percentage would be idle, time-consuming chitchat? How much would there be of purposeless faultfinding? What proportion would be malicious slander and calumny? What percentage could be classified as coarse, suggestive or obscene? And how much would there be of the good, the generous, the charitable? The very thought of such an experiment is sufficient to make us pause. What kind of reading would the complete record of our speech make to our own eyes?

Alexander Pope, who regarded himself as the greatest English poet of all time, endeavored to recall all his letters that he might rewrite them and so appear in a better light to posterity. Unfortunately for him, the deceit was discovered. While condemning the fraud, we cannot help regard his attempt with sympathy. For how much of our own spoken or written word would we like to blot out, or at least amend? We can do little to correct the mistakes of the past but for the present and the future we can learn to control our tongues.

The task is not easy. It will be a test of any man's will power. If, however, we want to accomplish something really worth-while this Lent, we can assign ourselves no better and no greater penance than to practice silence. The reward is worth the striving. The man who can keep quiet when he wants to talk has gone a long way towards conquering all of his bad habits. He has gained a fundamental control of himself that will make it easier to force other impulses to obey his will. "If any man offend not in word, the same is a perfect man" (James 3:2).

It was the example of Christ that taught St. James the truth of this statement. It is from the behavior of Christ during His trial and passion that we can likewise learn the necessity of keeping a close guard upon our tongues. Placing ourselves at the foot of the cross, where we belong in time of Lent, we may study a perfect object lesson in silence. The mute patience of Christ was not a stolid acceptance of an inevitable fate. Nor was He silent because He was incapable of speech. His behavior was a voluntary self-control over a faculty that demanded frequent and full expression, yet "Jesus held his peace" (Matthew 26:63). What Christ has done for us, that we should do for Him. In proportion as we learn to imitate the sacred silence of Christ, in the same proportion do we become true followers of Him, who is the "way and the truth and the life" (John 14:6).

Nihil obstat: A. J. Burke, *Censor Librorum*
Imprimatur: ✠ Ralph L. Hayes, D.D., *Bishop, Davenport*

Christ or Chaos?

Reverend Russell V. Delong, Ph.D., D.D.
A Minister of the Nazarene Church; Professor of Philosophy and Evangelism,
Nazarene Theological Seminary, Kansas City, Missouri

Dr. Delong has been especially active in evangelistic work in the Churches of the Nazarene. He was born in Dover, New Hampshire, on August 24, 1901, the son of a minister, and was educated at Northwest Nazarene College, Eastern Nazarene College, at Harvard, and took his Ph.D. at Boston University and received the D.D. from Northwest Nazarene College.

He was pastor at Waltham, Massachusetts, professor of philosophy and theology, Northwest Nazarene College, Nampa, Idaho, 1926-32, 1935-42; President, Northwest Nazarene College, 1927-32, 1935-42; district superintendent, Northwest Indiana District, Church of the Nazarene, 1942-45, and professor of philosophy and evangelism at the Nazarene Theological Seminary, Kansas City, Missouri, since 1945. He is a member of the General Board of the Church of the Nazarene, of the Board of Foreign Missions, the General Board of Publication, and is on the board of trustees of Olivet College and of Nazarene Theological Seminary.

His sermon is simple and moving and represents an effective type of evangelistic preaching. His plea for missions and missionaries is timely when we realize that only where the Christian Church has taken its message among the Oriental peoples do we have loyal friends.

Sermon Twenty=nine

TEXT: Choose you this day . . . JOSHUA 24:15
Go ye into all the world, and preach the gospel to every
creature. MARK 16:15

ISRAEL faced a crisis. A choice had to be made. The prophet cried out for immediate decision. "Choose you this day," he exhorted.

History does repeat itself. America is at the crossroads. Our nation will either make a definite, clear-cut decision to return to the principles which have made us great or continue to drop to lower levels of debauchery, sin and corruption. And, what is true of the United States is also true of the world. With actual war over and peace upon us, two roads bid for postwar travel. Shall it be up or down?

We have to a great extent forgotten God. Church attendance is at an all-time low, while gambling is at all-time high. The consumption of distilled liquors is making new records. Divorce is increasing at an alarming rate. Rape, murder, suicide, burglary and sex offenses are increasing rapidly. Juvenile delinquency is the Number One problem of our educators, criminologists and public officials. Governor Dewey said recently, "Juvenile delinquency today means a crime wave tomorrow." And it might be added, behind every juvenile delinquent is a delinquent parent. Appalling conditions demand a change.

We face a decision. The crisis is upon us. The choice is ours. "Choose you this day."

Our present crisis is not the work of Hitler. He did not precipitate it. Dr. E. Stanley Jones is right when he says, "Hitler is a symptom—not the disease." World War II was only the by-product of the real war between righteousness and unrighteousness, between the forces of right and those of evil.

Twenty-five years ago we had a similar conflagration—World War I. The Kaiser was then the personification of the Evil One. We won that war. Peace and calm came. We set up the League of Nations and the World Court. Countless sermons were preached on world peace. All seemed serene and complacent. And yet—in less than a quarter of a century we have witnessed a worse eruption than before.

Have you ever visited Yellowstone National Park and seen the geyser, Old Faithful, erupt? All appears calm; you watch with expectancy. Soon you hear a rumbling, gurgling noise—and then—hot, molten liquid shoots up into the air hundreds of feet, plays a few seconds and slowly dies down. The sound and turbulent outburst passes. All is quiet and peaceful. But—fifty-

[161]

three minutes later it all happens again. Why? Because down beneath the quiet surface is a sea of hot, molten substance awaiting the right chemical condition to erupt. So it is with our world—a geyser every twenty-five years, more or less. Our education, culture, civilization and social service beautifully landscape the environmental surface. We delude ourselves into quiet complacency, dreaming that all is well until another kaiser or a Hitler appears, creating the right formula for a sinful putrefaction to erupt in war. We fight —and win—and then proceed to clean up the landscape and beautify it. We create the San Francisco Charter. We try to control humanity effectively. We treat *symptoms* and *effects*. We don't deal primarily with *diseases* and *causes*.

We need every good organization that is working for peace. The San Francisco Charter is without doubt the best man-made agreement between nations in history. Let us forestall war as long as possible. Our need is not for less social activity, but more. Yet—there is need for something in addition.

It is the human heart that must be changed. Someone has aptly said, "No rearrangement of bad eggs can make a satisfactory omelet." We might have a perfect agreement or an ideal organization between nations, but if we lack good will or have such organization administered by bad men, we will never have a world with enduring peace or where the welfare of the majority is truly sought. We built magnificent new palaces to house the League of Nations, then proceeded to disobey its decisions and to violate its mandates.

The heart of man must be transformed. Herein lies the task of the Church. Not a salve to mollify the outward manifestation, but a serum to change the inward ill; not an organization, but an organic purging; not an environmental change, but an inner transformation; these are the things man dreadfully needs. It is not a question of external reorganization, but internal regeneration; not a clean environment, but clean hearts; not a just society, but just persons. Let us not delude ourselves by thinking that an orderly hospital room with clean sheets and a pleasant nurse can rid a patient of smallpox. There is need of medicine to cope with the disease that festers in man and society. It is not a system that man needs, but a Saviour.

Our paramount need is not so much more education, better laws or increased culture. These all help, but what we need is a concentrated, powerful, spiritual-moral penicillin-sulfanilamide-radium treatment that will transform men. Is there such? There is. That is why Christ came. His power can result in newborn men. New creatures. Old desires—old habits—can pass away. "Behold, all things become new," the Apostle Paul declares.

The American stage is set for a revival of soul-transforming religion. Conditions now parallel those that preceded the Great Awakening of 1840 and the Great Revival of 1860. Homrighausen, Campbell, Cartwright, Leavell, Muncy, Jones, Hughes and others have written books recently proclaiming this possibility. Will we actualize it? "Choose you this day."

[162]

A moral choice is, however, not a collective, corporate matter. *It is individual.* Our greatest need in America is:

Not for better legislation but for better legislators
Not for better business but for better businessmen
Not for better banking but for better bankers
Not for better farming but for betters farmers
Not for better teaching but for better teachers
Not for better laws but for better lawyers
Not for better preaching but for better preachers.

A revival of religion that would transform millions of individuals would result in increased justice, goodness, righteousness and spirituality.

What America needs, the world needs. A great Christian leader some years ago said in 1904, "Send 1,000 Missionaries to Japan now or 1,000,000 soldiers later." Prophetic? Yes. What did America do? Very little. Then it cost $600 to convert a Japanese. It has cost since then $50,000 to kill one. If we had heeded the plea of Dr. Mott forty years ago, we might have avoided the recent war with Japan. If we had heeded the command of Jesus, "Go ye," we might have assured eternal peace. We now face the crisis. It is Christ for the nations or the atomic bomb with annihilation for all of us.

The program of world evangelization began in the heart of God. He made the first gift—his Son (John 3:16). Jesus became the first missionary to begin the process of world conquest. He gave his life. For the first century the disciples of Christ carried out the Great Commission with intense effectiveness. But soon the dynamic "Go" gave way to "Stay." A new evangelistic fire took hold of the Church with Luther, Zwingli, Calvin and later the Wesleys and John Knox; and in America, Jonathan Edwards, Whitefield, Finney and many other renowned religious leaders.

It is a striking fact that only in the past century and a half has the world witnessed anything comparable to the missionary urge of the early Church. William Carey began his work in India in 1782; Robert Morrison in China in 1807; Adoniram Judson in Calcutta in 1812; Robert Moffat in Africa in 1818; David Livingstone in Africa in 1841; J. Hudson Taylor founded the China Inland Mission in 1853; John G. Paton in the New Hebrides in 1859 and Bishop William Taylor in Africa in 1884. Most of the great names of Christian missions have appeared quite recently—within the past one hundred and fifty years.

Reiterating the words of young Mills, uttered back in 1806 at the famous haystack prayer meeting at Williams College, we cry out afresh, *"We can if we will."* We can do what? Evangelize the world in our generation if we will make up our minds and formulate plans to do so.

By "evangelize" we do not mean "save." In the Great Commission, Jesus didn't promise that all would be saved. He did say, "He that believeth . . . shall be saved; but he that believeth not shall be damned." Our task is to take the gospel. The work of the Holy Spirit is to apply it, and it is the responsibility of the hearer to accept or reject it. By "evangelize" we mean: to give every man, woman and child an adequate knowledge of the gospel so that each may believe and be saved, if he will.

We can do this in our own generation if we will. The fields are open. This was not true a century ago. Early missionaries had to fight their way in and die as martyrs. Their blood has become the seed of the Church. We are about to reap. They opened the fields. We should enter them now. Not only are the fields open but they are calling for us to come. They are not merely passive, but are pressing us to come with ministers, teachers, nurses and doctors.

Hundreds of mission stations are now established. This was not so a century ago. Practically none was open then. But today through the sacrifice of our missionaries hundreds of stations are established. We should respond now.

Bible schools, with thousands of native students, are organized. There were none a century ago. Native preachers are especially successful in reaching their own people. Now, with native evangelists, we are ready to launch a most effective crusade. The Bible, or portions of it, has now been translated and printed in more than a thousand languages or dialects. We could place a portion of the New Testament in the hands of every man, woman and child in the world. We should do this now.

Modern inventions will expedite the spread of the gospel. Machines which have brought destruction can now bring hope and new life through Christ. The airplane, printing press, radio, automobile, television and other recent inventions can speed the evangelization of the world. Last spring Franklin Delano Roosevelt, our great war president, suddenly passed away. Within twenty-four hours after his death the entire world knew of his passing. Every newspaper in the world carried the story and his picture. This news was made available rapidly through radio, airplane, telephone and modern inventions. The following thought seized my mind: If we, with modern inventions could let the whole world know of the death of President Roosevelt within twenty-four hours, why cannot the Christian Church let the entire world know of the death of the Saviour within the next twenty-five years? WE CAN IF WE WILL.

The Church has the money to do the task. If church members would contribute one-tenth of their income to the spread of the gospel, as commanded by Jesus, we could evangelize the world in our generation.

Young people are ready to enlist in such a Christian crusade. The challenge of Christ has always appealed to youth. It demands the heroic. It offers a worth-while objective to living. It is romantic. It grips the heart. If the Church would outline a comprehensive, world-wide crusade, there would be volunteers by the thousands who would say with Isaiah, "Here am I; send me."

When Madame Chiang Kai-shek visited Chicago, I experienced the most inspiring hour of my life. Something happened to me that I trust will make me a better minister. It was a momentous occasion. Flags of all the Allied Nations were draped about the Stadium. On the platform were seated city, state and national celebrities. In the auditorium was a cosmopolitan group of all nationalities, all races, rich and poor alike, to do homage to a great woman. To the right of the platform the Metropolitan Church Choir was seated. Just in back of the rostrum the Women's Symphony Orchestra of Chicago was placed, and to the right of the platform in the mezzanine was the Great Lakes Naval Training School Choir of three hundred selected voices. It was a glorious setting. The program started as the organ and bands played and the WAVES in uniform came from one corner of the Stadium and the WACS from the other side, each carrying a flag of one of the United Nations. They met in the center aisle and marched together, placing the flags in sockets just in front of the platform. Soon Madame Chiang came onto the platform, and thirty thousand persons stood waving American and Chinese flags, cheering for many minutes, until she finally motioned the audience to their seats. Before the address, which was to be broadcast to the world, the Great Lakes Naval Training Choir sang "Anchors Aweigh" and the "Marines Song," and then was encored back. They stood as the great organ began playing, and the choir began to sing:

> We've a story to tell to the nations,
>   That shall turn their hearts to the right,
> A story of truth and mercy,
>   A story of peace and light.

And then the chorus:

> For the darkness shall turn to dawning,
>   And the dawning to noon-day bright,
> And Christ's great Kingdom shall come to earth,
>   The Kingdom of love and light.

Something seemed to be happening within my heart; a new room in my soul appeared to open. The choir continued: the second and third stanzas were sung; and as the fourth was reached the audience was very tense and deeply stirred.

> We've a Saviour to show to the nations,
>   Who the path of sorrow hath trod,
> That all the world's great peoples,
>   Might come to the truth of God.

I looked around and the people were wiping their eyes. Tears were shed unashamedly. A common desire had been touched deep within the hearts of all of us. It was a thrilling moment sufficient to lift one out of himself as the choir reached its great crescendo with power and feeling:

> For the darkness shall turn to dawning,
>   And the dawning to noon-day bright,

> And Christ's great Kingdom shall come to earth,
> The Kingdom of love and light.

What a moment! And what a challenge! And then—the chairman was about to present Madame Chiang Kai-shek, but before he did so he made a request, coming from her, that at the close of the address all remain seated and join in singing her favorite song. She was then presented. What an address, spirited, clear in thought, perfect in diction.

> There must be no bitterness in the reconstructed world. No matter what we have undergone and suffered, *we must try and forgive* those who injured us and remember only the lesson gained thereby.

Like Christ speaking! When Madame Chiang concluded that address, thirty thousand persons stood waving flags and cheering minute after minute. No one left. Everyone was held spellbound by the power of it all. Finally we took our seats to comply with her request to join in singing her favorite song. What was it? We did not know. But soon the magnificent organ began to peal out the first measures and in a flash we knew what was going to happen. Led by the Great Lakes Naval Choir and that great organ, thirty thousand persons of all colors, nations and stations began to sing Madame Chiang Kai-shek's favorite song:

> Onward, Christian soldiers,
> Marching as to war,
> With the cross of Jesus
> Going on before:
> Christ the royal Master
> Leads against the foe;
> Forward into battle
> See His banners go.

What a mighty chorus! I looked about me. Persons of all classes were moved, tears filled many eyes. The personality of a great Christian woman moved by the spirit of Christ had prevailed. As we left that auditorium and walked down the long ramps, the pipe organ pealing out the strains of "Onward Christian Soldiers," I said to myself, "God help us that the Christian Church of America does not let that woman down, but that we arise and send an army of Christian soldiers to China to bring the light of Christ, that truly

> the darkness shall turn to dawning,
> And the dawning to noon-day bright,
> And Christ's great Kingdom shall come to earth,
> The Kingdom of love and light."

The war is over. The forces of right have prevailed. The world is wide open. China with 450,000,000 souls is in the hands of Christian leadership. India, with her 350,000,000, is ready for a Christian revolution. Africa is set for a great Christian advance. South America is closer to us than ever before.

Europe is crying for a revival of religion. Japan is ready for a change. Toyo-hiko Kagawa, that outstanding Japanese Christian evangelist, has been asked by Premier Higashi-Kuni to lead in a crusade for the moral regeneration and rebirth of the nation.[1]

The hour has struck. Why don't we try Christ and his principles? If we do not, another world war will confront us within our generation. BUT—we can *evangelize* the world in our generation *if we will*.

It is apparent that Christ again stands before his followers saying, "Go ye." The opportunity of the centuries is ours. Will we grasp it and save civilization and the world? Or will we continue in our sin until the atomic bomb in the hands of wicked men, or some other worse calamity, destroys us from the face of the earth?

The crisis is upon us. We face the decision. It is literally, Christ or Chaos.

Religion and Power

REVEREND ROBERT W. SEARLE, D.D.
A Minister of the Reformed Church; General Secretary of the Greater New York Federation of Churches

The first passion of Robert Searle's life is finding and applying a solution to the problems of race which mar our contemporary American civilization in many places and threaten more serious physical difficulties unless a spiritual answer is found.

Dr. Searle took pre-law training at Rutgers University, in 1915, was phys-ical director at Kingsley School from 1915 to 1916 and entered New Bruns-wick Theological Seminary in the fall of 1916. In April, 1917, he resigned to enter the Army Y.M.C.A., but in October enlisted in the Army Ambulance Corps and later transferred and served overseas with the 303rd Field Artillery as battalion sergeant major. After the war he served on the staff of the Americanism Commission of the American Legion under Colonel Arthur Woods from 1919 to 1920, then returned to the Theological Seminary, graduating in 1921. He began his ministry as Youth Director of Fort Wash-ington Collegiate Church, New York, in 1921, then spent seven years as minister of First Reformed Church, Albany, from 1923 to 1930. For five years of this time he served as chaplain of the Fort Orange Post, American Legion, and it was while in Albany that Rutgers honored him with the D.D.

[1] Associated Press, Tokyo, September 15, 1945.

He was called to be associate minister of Madison Avenue Presbyterian Church, New York, in 1930.

In 1934 he became general secretary of the Greater New York Federation of Churches, directing the co-operative program of the Protestant Churches of Manhattan, Bronx and Richmond. His work here has made him chairman of the Board of the Social Service Bureau, Magistrates Court; vice-president, City Wide Citizens Committee on Harlem; member of the Board of directors of Citizens Housing Council; Organization Committee of Boy Scouts of America; American Committee for Christian Refugees; New York Defense Recreation Committee; Board of Directors, Wiltwyck School; Advisory Committee, National Youth Administration. He is active on several commissions of the Federal Council of Churches, International Justice and Goodwill, Interracial Relations, Industrial Relations, and Religion and Health. He was a delegate to the World Conference of Churches at Oxford, England, 1937; to the North American Conference of Churches, Toronto, Canada, 1941; to the National Church Conference on the Bases of a Just and Durable Peace at Delaware, Ohio, in 1942.

As an author three books are significant of his thinking, City Shadows, Author of Liberty and Tell It to the Padre. During World War II he spoke to approximately 400,000 service men and women in Army camps and Navy stations in co-operation with a Roman Catholic Priest and a Jewish Rabbi. This sermon shows his thinking and feeling about the problems of power and of race and suggests the spirit needed to solve these great issues.

Sermon Thirty

TEXT: Therefore all things whatsoever ye would that men should do to you, do ye even so to them: for this is the law and the prophets. MATTHEW 7:12

OUR times have been characterized by an ominous paradox. That paradox was precisely defined by the late Professor A. A. Bowman when he said: "The age in which we live is notable for two things: Man's progressive triumph over nature in the sphere of theoretical and applied science, and his tragic inability to order his own life." Since those words were written, a few years ago, two events have raised them to critical and imperative importance: The first was World War II with its unprecedented slaughter, its incalculable misery and its boundless agony. That alone should have focused the best energy of man upon self-mastery.

But, if that should be the effect of the war, what are we to say of man's grasp of atomic energy?

Our paradox is no longer the subject of leisurely argument; it is an issue of life and death, not just for some men, but for all men and the means for you and for me.

The most profound—the transcendent, the ever-present fact of this day is that man holds in his hands the means of sudden racial annihilation. And the terrible sequence to that fact is its inescapable corollary—that unless man gains a vastly larger "ability to master his own life," unless he suddenly and profoundly changes his attitudes and patterns of life, he will destroy himself.

Not long ago I sat in the study of a distinguished scientist. After a conversation which briefly reviewed the human scene and over against it man's new and awful means of self-destruction, the learned man remarked: "I am convinced that it is merely touch-and-go, whether in the next few generations we will not so completely have destroyed ourselves that any survivors will be forced to live in a new and primitive and perhaps prehistoric age."

Those words are staggering. The first inclination is to thrust them from the mind as unthinkable. But, thrust them from the mind as we will in the blindest of folly, the fact of atomic energy remains. It is there—always there —no mere bogy of the mind, but a grim reality which cannot be avoided. It must be met.

Consider what we know!

On August 5, 1945, a B-29 dropped a single bomb which exploded over Hiroshima. That bomb killed tens of thousands of human beings and devastated four square miles of the city.

Now, note this: That bomb was a first—a primitive—effort. We are told that it utilized but one-one-thousandth of the potential destructive energy. Without a doubt a bomb now exists that is many times as effective.

How shall we measure the capability of this vast new power? Albert Einstein has shown us that if 2.2 pounds of matter were converted entirely into energy it would match the entire output of electric power generated in the United States during a period of two months.

There is no use in our attempting to comprehend this; our minds are not sufficiently elastic, but this one fact we must comprehend: Humanity will be obliterated unless we learn to order our human life.

A responsibility is before us, a responsibility so great that it dwarfs every unrelated purpose into insignificance.

The all-important question is simply this: How shall we order our human life? How shall we master human nature? It is obvious that the threat is not in atomic energy, itself; the threat is in our disordered society. It is in the human heart.

Man can make of atomic energy a source of immeasurable material benefit or he can make of it Race Suicide. Toward one of those goals we will progress —not driven by fate, not borne along by irresistible powers, but—and mark this—of our own volition.

Before us today is literally set Life or Death and we must choose—Now. How, then, shall we choose life?

I ask you to turn back again to Professor Bowman's paradox: Man's increasing mastery of nature, side by side with the increasing evidence of his inability to master human nature.

Since this is one world—and God said it before Mr. Willkie did—there is in it, not only an intention of unity for all humanity, but there must be a unity that pervades all creation.

Consequently, when we say that man lives on three levels—the inorganic, the organic and the human—we are not saying that he lives in three separate and distinct realms, but rather three interrelated areas. The preacher who falls down stairs, bumping his head and developing a terrific headache, while on his way to preach a sermon, knows full well the relationship between the inorganic, the organic, and the spiritual.

Professor Bowman points to "our progressive triumph over nature"; that is, over the inorganic and the organic realms—the first two levels of life. And he designates theoretical and applied science as the means of that progressive triumph or mastery.

What is theoretical science? In the largest sense of the word theoretical science is the search of nature to discover the way it works, to find its laws. And, by the same token, applied science is the attempt to find out how to work with nature, how to obey its laws. Behind those two quests lies a great presupposition, namely, that nature is a realm of law, of indigenous law which man cannot alter or evade, but can only discover and—if he will have the blessedness of material benefit and bodily health—obey.

There have been three steps in every scientific achievement: First, there has been the recognition that nature is a realm of law; second, there has been the search for that law; third, there has been adaptation to obedience to those laws as discovered.

This is true for chemistry and physics. It is true for biology and medicine. It is true for every division and for every subdivision of science. There, in three stages, is the formula for our increasing mastery of the inorganic level of life, the most marvelous accomplishment of which is the release of atomic energy.

There is the formula of our increasing mastery of the organic level in which penicillin and streptomycin are but two of our latest "miracles."

Mastery "over nature," but not over human nature: Here, where the issue of all things lies, there are war and racial hatred; there are industrial strife and crime; there are broken homes and mental breakdowns; and there are religious conflicts. And here, mark this, to all intents and purposes there is not only anarchy, but an anarchy so strident as to deny the existence of law.

If man is a law unto himself, if nations and races and classes are not subject to an objective law—a natural law, if you please—a law of creation, then there is no escape from chaos, there is no chance for order, and we should logically turn loose the atomic energy and get it over with at once.

But, just as the rasping of gears in a car shows disorder or the violation of patterns which the laws of physics demand, and just as sickness shows a bodily maladjustment and the violation of laws of health, so the very chaos, on our human level, is compelling evidence of the existence of laws unrecognized and violated.

Our way to the mastery of human nature, to the ordering of our own lives —in order that we may have heaven and not hell—that we may reap the benefits of atomic energy and not be destroyed by it, is, first, to recognize that there are in life itself immutable laws, inexorable laws, to which every man and nation and race are subject.

Second, we must discover those laws.

Third, no matter what it means to pride and prejudice and to privilege of any kind, we must conform to the very best of our ability with the demands of those laws.

Now, at this point I face a dilemma: Were I speaking to men and women who ignored religion, I would endeavor to show them the fact that religion is intended to be to the mastery of human nature what its companion, science, is to the mastery of nature. I would beg them to re-examine the validity of religion, to discover the values which, unfortunately, all too often religious organization has obscured and I would plead with them to bring their strength and devotion to the service of religion.

But it is seldom that a minister gets a chance to speak to those who ignore religion. Your very presence here is witness, to an extent at least, that you consider yourselves Christians. I speak to you then as to the Christian Church.

Can't you see that when you say "God," you are saying: "I believe in a created world. I believe that there exists a creator's purpose for personal being. I believe that even as there are laws for the relationship of atom to atom, of living cell to living cell, so there are laws—the creator's laws—for the relationship of man to man and of men to men."

Can't you see that the recognition of "God," the great presupposition of religion, is the recognition of the existence of laws of human life—the first step in our mastery of life, the first step in our salvation from atomic destruction.

And can't you see that to call Jesus the Son of God, the unique Son of God, to ascribe to him divinity, to call him the Lord of Life or the Master of Life, is, if it means anything, if it is not pure superstition and mumbo-jumbo, to accept the fact that he has announced to us and he has exemplified before us the basic immutable and inexorable laws of personal and of human fulfillment. Call it the way of salvation, if you will, or any other great historic Christian phrase; the minute you call Jesus, Lord, and mean it, that minute you profess your conviction that he is, if you please, the theoretical scientist of human nature, the revealer of the laws with which creation surrounds us.

If to learn to say God is the first step in salvation, in mastery over human nature; then, to learn to say Jesus, is the second step, for it means the discovery of the fundamental laws of life.

But there is the third and the all important step, in which we must be the active agents:

If science accepted the existence of law in nature and followed acceptance with discovery, but went no further, we would have no mastery over nature. It is the applied scientist, the man who obeys and teaches us what obedience means for us, it is we ourselves when we conform to the laws of nature, who are responsible for "Man's progressive triumph."

And just so with human nature: Theoretical religion alone is meaningless. It is applied religion, it is obedience to Jesus' law, it is conformity to God's rules of life announced through him, which are the end and aim of all.

How clearly Jesus, himself, said that; listen: "Why call ye me Lord and do not the things I say?" Listen again: "Not every one who saith unto me 'Lord, Lord' shall enter into the Kingdom, but he that doeth the will of my Father."

And, listen—this time with the reverberations of the atomic bomb ringing in your ears—"Whosoever heareth these sayings of mine and *doeth them not* shall be likened unto a foolish man who built his house upon the sand." You know the rest.

There is no message in the Gospel which organized religion—Protestant, Roman Catholic or Jewish—needs to ponder more than that contained in these words in a dire, dark day of terrible responsibility, like the present.

It is not enough to say: "I believe in God, the Father Almighty."

It is not enough to add: "I believe in Jesus Christ, His only Son."

Those are mere words; words are but formula; only how we live gives them sincerity, truth and meaning.

As a matter of fact, if we really believed, we would be constrained to obey.

But let us—for salvation depends on it—see our tragic error. Let us single out one elemental law which Jesus announced and let us apply that law in relation to one aspect of human relations.

Shortly before that terrible warning to the builder of a house on the sand, of hearing but not doing, Jesus said: "All things whatsoever ye would that men should do to you, do ye even so to them: for this is the law and the prophets"; in other words, this is the very essence of religion.

Now here is not only a specific law of Jesus, but one which he defines as fundamental.

May I, as an aside, remark that I was told recently by a prominent psychiatrist that he considered this the fundamental law of personality integration. That psychiatrist actually believed in Jesus more than do many ecclesiastics who have asserted Jesus' authority and ignored his teachings.

Well, here is the law we call the Golden Rule; we might better call it the iron law of life. Gold is trimming; iron is framework. Now, for the area of life, that demonstrates our failure. We might speak of crime or the family, of industrial or of international relations, but let us consider what is probably the most grievous fault in our national life.

Alongside this law of Jesus, this demand of creation upon us, stand the white man and the Negro, stand the professing Christian and the Negro.

Do we believe in Jesus? Do we believe in God? Or are we parts of that anarchy which means death?

The Negro was kidnaped by the white man in his native Africa. With a brutality matched only by a modern Hitler, families were torn asunder, transported on slave ships comparable only to Axis prison camps and sold into absolute slavery to work God's soil that the white man might enjoy the benefits.

The people who stole the Negro, who transported him, who sold him, who bought him, who worked him and reaped the fruits of his labor, were white men and women, most of whom professed to be Christians.

Hitler, let us remind ourselves, at least repudiated Christianity.

But what was yesterday. What of today? How stands the Negro in our midst? Do we treat him as we would be treated? To ask that question is to invite a thundering "No." We segregate him; we discriminate against him; we indignify him; we call him and treat him "inferior."

What are we doing thereby? In God's name, can't we see?

We are not defying the Negro. We are defying—and blatantly denying—Jesus Christ. We are defying and denying the inexorable laws of the universe. We are active agents of the anarchy which ends in death.

We are inviting misery and anguish for our children. We are treading the path toward atomic destruction.

Oh, Christian Church, you have the answer; you have the specific; you have the secret of the mastery of human nature; you have the means of turning the threat of atomic death to the blessing, to more abundant life.

Speak that answer now. Apply that specific. Reveal that secret. Demonstrate in your own life that means of salvation. If you don't live it, the world may be turned from it—turned to the path of destruction.

If you proclaim it and practice it and teach it, you will indeed be the Church of Christ, the Saviour of the world.

Life's Deeper Meanings

REVEREND PRESTON BRADLEY, LL.D., D.D.
Pastor, The People's Church of Chicago, Chicago, Illinois

Dr. Preston Bradley is definitely a part of the life of Chicago. For thirty-three years he has been pastor of the great People's Church of Chicago, where the morning service of his church has been broadcast every Sunday for twenty-two years and is the second oldest continuous broadcast of its kind in the United States. During the season, Dr. Bradley speaks to more than five thousand people a week in his own church, besides his daily radio activities over WGN, Chicago.

He is a life member of the Chicago Art Institute, the Adventurers Club, the Authors Club, the Chicago Historical Society and many other organizations. He is an honorary life member of Lions International, is a member of the Board of Directors of the Chicago Public Library and a member of the State Normal School Board of Illinois. He was elected national president of the Izaak Walton League of America for three consecutive terms. He is chairman of the Chicago Council Against Racial Discrimination and a member of the Mayor's Commission on Race Relations.

He is the author of six books, two of which, Courage for Today and Mastering Fear are best sellers. He has traveled extensively in Europe, Central and South America, having crossed the Atlantic Ocean twenty-two times. He has preached in London, Belfast, Paris, Berlin and Prague. He was a delegate to the International Congress of Religions meeting in Czechoslovakia and knew Dr. Masaryk, its founder and president.

Dr. Bradley is a Chicago institution and no man in the city has impressed his personality more upon the life of Chicago. His Sunday evening church audience averages more than two thousand people, with many turned away, and his Wednesday evening book lectures, which are famous throughout the Middle West, are always crowded. To hear Dr. Bradley is an unforgettable experience. He had more than three hundred men and women in the services of this country during the war and kept in contact with each of them. He attended, on the invitation of Secretary of State Stettinius, the San Francisco Conference, the United Nations Conference on International Organization. "Life's Deeper Meanings" was given on March 18, 1945, and is representative of the sermons he preaches to the great crowds at the People's Church.

Sermon Thirty-one

TEXT: Finally, brethren, whatsoever things are true, whatsoever things are honest, whatsoever things are just, whatsoever things are pure, whatsoever things are lovely, whatsoever things are of good report; if there be any virtue, and if there be any praise, think on these things. PHILIPPIANS 4:8

THE great tendency of many people in the development and rationalization of religious truth, is that they advance so speedily in their effort to encompass all of the mysteries of life, that they lose, in their anxiety, many of the deeper meanings as they go along. It is some of these deeper meanings which I am concerned with, meanings which are vital to every life. Life never had deeper meaning than it has today, although human life is cheaper than it has ever been. We have taken more human life out of the world in the past four years through the instrumentality of war than in any similar period in the life of man. Human life is spoken of, at times, rather carelessly; "so many dead, so many losses," two thousand here, four thousand there, until I am a little fearful that some of us may become accustomed to the loss of life—not those who lose loved ones, but the people in general for whom those who die, die; until if we are not a little careful we are very apt to lose our whole sense of the mystery of certain deeper values of life.

The usual idea has been that the more we know, and the more science opens up to us vistas and areas of reality and knowledge—the farther out beyond the lens of the telescope we go, into interstellar space that John Burroughs talks about, and the more minute the universe that opens up with the microscope, the less will be the mystery; yet in truth, the enlargement of man's knowledge of the cosmos only deepens the mystery. We are just beginning to know about electronic energy. We have merely penetrated the outer shell of this energy of the cosmos, for all is vibrant with potential energy; nothing rests; we have gone beyond molecules; we have gone beyond atoms. When I was a little lad studying physics in school, they taught me that an atom was the smallest indivisible particle of matter. How ridiculous that sounds today! And they had another law that I recall, called "the indestructibility of matter," and then we used to debate, in our childish adventuresomeness, on what would happen if indestructible force met an immovable object; and how we debated it and argued it! And now we are reaching out into the vistas of the unknown and conquering them, and within five years I predict that a boat of 100,000 tons will leave New York harbor for any port in the world and will go to that port safely and directly without a human

[175]

being on board the ship. It will be directed through electronic energy from the land. Man has available a potentiality that will bring a complete and perfect revolution to every area of his life. It will change the world, and in the changing bring a new culture, an entirely different emphasis to religion, an entirely new concept to civilization. Sometimes it makes me almost breathless when I think of what the lad ten years old today will see and hear and know before he is of the age of my dear friend, F. Marion Smith, who at the age of 98 sits in my church every Sunday morning! I marvel at the possibilities for the ten-year-old boy who lives through the next eighty years of life. Oh, how I wish I could live with him through it! I never want to die and leave this world; I wish I could live here a hundred lifetimes. I have had as much sorrow, as much disappointment, as much trouble as the average person has in this world. I have carried many wounds in my heart; but in spite of the weight of the heaviest burden in life, I have never seen a moment yet when I wanted to run away from life and leave it—never!

I have tried to anchor my hopes in the deeper things of life. The people who want to run away from life are the people who are living life in shallow waters. The people who want to run away from life are the victims of pride and loss and selfishness and grief—victims, not masters! People who cannot stand life are the people who have not implemented their roots in the subsoil, a soil that is never washed away by the storms, and never blown away by the winds, no matter how heavy the rain or how powerful the hurricane. Those who stand are those who have deeply implemented their roots beneath the superficials of life so they can stand in the tempest; and the more man knows about his universe, paradoxically one can say the less he knows, for instead of decreasing man's area of ignorance, there has never been an invention or a discovery which did not at the same time make man realize the inexhaustibility of the universe of ideas.

The world went along pretty well with the old mythological idea that the world rested on the back of a turtle, and that idea was being generally accepted, until some person finally asked: "But what does the turtle stand on?" and then the trouble started. That was the beginning of man's conception that the sun had movement, and it rose and set, and then into the arena of man's widening consciousness came Galileo and Copernicus and Hippocrates, and later on down to the gigantic intellects, who were not afraid to venture out into the realm of the unknown, and man has been discovering, revealing, inventing, widening, opening a universe until the petty limitations of prescientific creeds no longer, to the intellectual, have any power at all; they are meaningless. But remember that man does not create the laws, he discovers them. Remember that the principle of electronics was in the world when man was scratching his record crudely on rocks. Remember that the law of gravitation was in the world before man knew that his own blood circulated. Remember that back of everything that man has accomplished in the realm of science and invention, are those basic laws of the cosmos, which man did not create. All man is doing is bringing to light that which already had existence. Man learned that if he fell from a tree he would be hurt, and the whole principle of the law of gravitation was suggested to the questing mind of Sir Isaac Newton in the fall of an apple. Sir Isaac Newton did not create the law of gravitation; that law was operating and co-existent with every other cosmic law. From the first blush of the first dawn of space that law existed.

One would naturally assume that in this continuing evolution of man's quest of the unknown and his mastery of the hidden, he is solving the mystery of life, but he is not at all, for every time man reaches out into the hidden world of God's law, man, with that achievement and that effort, suddenly awakens to the fact that there is something beyond the last discovery; that every discovery means another one; every invention means another one; every conception of cosmic law means another discovery; and man will go on, and on, and on, penetrating to the mystery of God and the creative cosmos of which the creative Spirit of divine Intelligence is the operating force, until man will have such a clear conception of the fundamental law of the cosmos, which is the law of God, that man will say to himself: "How silly and absurd and ridiculous it is that man, the whole microcosm of God, the only thing in all the cosmos that thinks—you, you, you, the only creation with mind, in a universe like this with its great diseases, where I die fifty years before my time, in a universe like this, how absurd that I organize to kill my fellow men and murder them, and the more atrociously I can do it the better."

Man is the only principle of life in the whole cosmic universe that organizes instruments of destruction to kill his own species! Only man does that —no other species of life organizes to destroy its own species except man; and man is going to reach the height of sensitiveness some day where the deeper significance of the cosmos will be revealed to him through his own science and inventions, and some day he is going to rise in the true dignity and power of his own personality and he is going to say to this cosmos: "How cheap and shoddy of me, man, to destroy myself, to hurt myself physically, to scar myself by wrong habits and bad living, to violate the established laws of physical harmony! How shoddy of me to permit myself to get into an emotional reflex against my own experience so that the only way out is a revolver, or a sleeping potion! How silly and absurd of me, man, to develop myself into such a sense of possessiveness of land, and boundary lines, and distinctive identities of racial emphasis, and a thousand other things that are the compelling imperative of man's own operations of life! How silly to get myself maneuvered into a blind alley—man, whose intellect has wrested the secrets from the darkest caves of oblivion itself, until he can use every agency, force and power, and can make a parking space of the clouds with the airplane, and chart the bottom of the sea with the submarine, and whisper and be heard around the world! Man! Man!" Man is going to take this electronic energy, direct it, control it, and shoot it through space, just as this microphone here is taking these words through this telephone wire down to WJJD, out from there to the radio towers in the country, so that a person six hundred miles away from this broadcast or from this church can hear me before the last person sitting in the top balcony can hear me. Man directing energy! And he is going to take electronic energy and develop with it such a sense of mastery and such a control that if man would strike the depths of his own being and spiritualize his own personality through complete obedience to the harmonic law of God, does it not make you breathless what man could do? Why, it makes me almost limp when I envisage what man could do if he got out of the shallows; if he found life's deeper meanings instead of dissipating his energy and killing himself, and condemning himself! Man has sufficient creative energy in his own physical construction, in the capacity of the heart itself to re-create its own cells and body, that this body of man should live for 250 years—and we die at sixty!

Man out of the shallows into the depths of life, finding its deeper meanings, not dissipating his energies; that's the meaning in my heart for you at this moment. I would like each one of you now, to stop immediately whatever thoughts are going through your minds and hearts, whatever experiences you are in, for I would like to miraculously, if I could, project to the very depths of your souls this thought: God and you are one. You need not be ill; you need not hate; you need not fail; you need not despair; life is to be masterly for you! You have all this energy in your hearts, in your souls; if you will get into the depths of life and away from its surface, you will not be tyrannized by tradition! If you will let your minds go free, and let your spirit soar and not let anything, or anyone, own you, you will liberate your whole beings with the truth that makes men free! That was the meaning of the Teacher when he said: "Ye shall know the truth and the truth shall make you free." Free to give these blessed bodies and souls and minds of ours an opportunity to grow and blossom and deepen and bloom in the great garden of humanity! Free, free, because we know the truth. No tyranny of a creed, nothing, nothing to coerce, to pinch, to hurt, nothing to limit. Let the soul go; let the mind go; the bigger the universe, the more we know of science, of the cosmos, of the sweep of a great God activity in the universe, the more there is to know, and the greater can be our personal victory over life. Don't think there is a conflict between true religion and true science; there is none. Don't let the illiterates, those who attempt to speak of profound truths, who can hardly speak the English language correctly or utter one sentence with the dignity of the importance of good speech, don't let them befog your minds and spirits in an illiterate conception of religion, but sweep the cobwebs from the mind, the barriers from the soul, and go on to the heights, knowing that nothing can harm you because your foundation is in the depths that cannot be disturbed!

What are you, a thermometer or a thermostat? What is a thermometer? It tells the temperature. What is a thermostat? It regulates the temperature. Most people are thermometers. They are just going through life registering the temperature, and when it goes up with trouble and down with hate, we stand in front of our little thermometer of life, victims, reflecting all the time and reacting to life, looking at the thermometer and saying: "What's the temperature?" I would rather be a thermostat than a thermometer, for a thermostat regulates life and a thermostat is in control of the temperature. The thermostat directs the temperature; the power of the thermometer cannot do anything but register it. Be a thermostat and you will change the temperature of life.

I Have a Glory

REVEREND PAUL MINNICH ROBINSON
Minister, Church of the Brethren, Hagerstown, Maryland

Paul Minnich Robinson was born in Denver, Colorado in 1914, the son of a prominent Church of the Brethren clergyman. After spending his early years in southern Ohio, he attended Juniata College, Princeton Theological Seminary and the Lutheran Theological Seminary, at Mount Airy, Philadelphia.

He began his ministry as pastor of the Church of the Brethren in Ambler, Pennsylvania, where he served for three and one-half years. In 1940 he was called to the influential pulpit of the First Church of the Brethren, Hagerstown, Maryland, the largest church of his denomination, where he still ministers.

Mr. Robinson is a leader of youth, serving for several years as Youth Director for the Southeastern Region in his denomination. The Church of the Brethren, although small in numbers, came into prominence during the war years with a unique and practical program of world-wide relief, known as "Heifers for Relief" project of the Brethren Service Committee, which caught the imagination of Christians everywhere. Historically inclined to remain aloof from co-operation with other church bodies, in recent years the Church of the Brethren, formerly known as "Dunkers," has begun to take an active place in American Protestantism. He has been one of the moving spirits among the younger men of his communion in urging full participation in interdenominational enterprises. For many years he has been a member of the Board of Directors of the Maryland-Delaware Council of Churches and is now vice-president of the State Council.

[179]

In his local community, he has found time to take an active part in many civic projects, is a member of the Municipal Recreation Commission, the Board of Directors of the Y.M.C.A. and the Board of Directors of the Kiwanis Club. Each year hundreds of persons come to his study for counsel and advice. He has been an active member of the Commissions on Religion and Health of the Federal Council of the Churches of Christ in America. Through his psychological approach to religion, or his "down-to-earth preaching," as it is known in his community, he has maintained an eminently successful Sunday evening Vesper Hour. It is in relation to the central problem of the nature of man that "I Have a Glory" was written.

Sermon Thirty=two

TEXT: What is man, that thou are mindful of him. . . . for thou hast made him a little lower than the angels, and hast crowned him with glory and honour. PSALM 8:4-5

IN HIS delightful little book, *My Colonel and His Lady*, Archibald Rutledge tells of an experience he had as a lad down on the Santee River, where there was a Negro who piloted the old ferry boat, "Foam." The boat was dirty and so odorous that the arrival on the other side was always a "consummation devoutly to be wished for." But one day, when he went down to the river boat, Dr. Rutledge found her completely transformed. She was cleaned from bow to stern. She fairly gleamed in the sunlight, with her brass polished into mirrors. The bilge water was gone from behind the seats and her deck was scoured to the raw wood. No less miraculous was the transformation in the Negro captain himself. Shining and immaculate, he sat at the wheel with an open Bible on his lap. When asked the meaning of this sudden transformation, he replied, "Well, you see, sir, I have a glory." Religion had changed his life. He was still a river boat captain, but he resolved to make the glory of his life the keeping of that boat spotlessly clean.

That story haunts my mind in these tremendous days which have been called a time between the times, for never has the mind of man been so confused and perplexed. A minister friend who has seen four decades of pastoral service said to me recently, "I have never been so out of heart, nor so discouraged in my ministry." We can easily understand that mood which borders on despair when we look out upon the contemporary scene.

Man himself is certainly the greatest problem of our time. We have mastered to a marvelous degree the world of science with the promise of new and greater miracles to come. We are learning more and more how to control the forces of nature. But the realm of human relations is still unconquered.

With all of our material and mechanical progress, we have not learned to live together. We are learning to understand and master everything but ourselves.

And, I am convinced that man is the greatest problem in our theology today. Our ideas of God are rather clearly fixed. But what can we believe about man? Pascal, in his unique way, expresses something of this perplexity when he says, "What a chimera then is man! What a novelty! What a monster, what a chaos, what a contradiction, what a prodigy. Judge of all things, imbecile worm of the earth; depository of truth, a sink of uncertainty and error; the pride and refuse of the universe. Know then, proud man, what a paradox you are to yourself."

We can better understand the human problem when we remember that we are emerging from an era which believed that man was everything. He was idealized because of his limitless possibilities. If only we could educate him properly, he could by his own genius bring in the golden age. Then came depression and the clouds of war. How completely was the dream shattered. How utterly man had failed, and how tragically did he discover the emptiness of this humanism which had depended upon man to deliver himself from the wilderness into the promised land. It was a futile faith and a false theology, in which, as Dr. Richard Niebuhr has said, "A God without wrath called a man without sin, to a Kingdom without judgment, through a Christ without a cross."

Then came the inevitable swing of the pendulum of thought to a "neo-orthodoxy," which has said to the popular mind, man of himself is incapable of any good. It is God by His own cataclysmic force who will bring about His Kingdom. Now in the midst of all of this confusion about what we call, "the human problem," I think the answer, strangely enough, lies in those simple words of the river boat captain, "I have a glory." And, as always, we must turn to the Book of Eternal Wisdom for light. There are three verses of scripture, in widely separated places, which I believe can lead us to the Biblical conception of man.

The first word comes from Psalm 8, probably from the pen of David. "When I consider thy heavens, the work of thy fingers, the moon and the stars, which thou hast ordained; *what is* man that thou art mindful of *him*. . . . for thou hast made him a little lower than the angels, and hast crowned him with glory and honour." The original Hebrew says, "Thou hast made him a little lower than God," which is a perfectly proper and preferable translation. Says the Psalmist, when compared with the vastness of the universe, man according to his size seems insignificant. And yet it is upon man that God has bestowed his greatest glory. Man is the crowning effort of all creation, for he is made in God's own image. Let us never forget that. Whatever he has become, man was created in honor and dignity. He was made for God. God breathed into him the breath of life, and he became a living soul. Thus inspired by God, man has risen to great heights of achievement. He has written sonnets of infinite beauty. He has composed magnificent anthems of praise which have drawn men nearer God. He has captured the sublime upon his painted canvas and transformed into the beautiful the ugly and the sordid, as did the Negro on the river boat. Think of the genius of which man has shown himself capable. No wonder the Psalmist could say, "Thou hast made him a little lower than God." We are made for God, inspired by God. There is a glory in that.

But here reality brings a note of tragedy. What has man done with this glory in which he was created? Has it brought him closer to God or made him more fit to bear the divine image in which he was created? We need only to look at our world for the answer. He has prostituted his God-given power and used his consummate skill for his own destruction. He has turned his mind, which has been able to unlock the secrets of nature, not to good, but to evil.

Dr. Frederick Norwood tells that on D-Day when the Allied forces were invading the coast of Normandy, he was sitting by his radio listening to the description of the invasion by a British announcer. As he painted the vivid picture of the stupendous military operation, he exclaimed in a sudden burst of emotion, "This is the most amazing demonstration of human power the world has ever seen." And Dr. Norwood said he bowed his head and said, "Power? It is the most awful demonstration of human weakness the world has ever seen, that man should muster all the resources which his genius has produced to destroy his fellowmen."

The mastery of the natural world through science which might have brought the blessings of peace and brotherhood has been used by man to enslave and destroy his brother. As we look at what man has made of himself, we wonder if he is the same being

> . . . so eminently raised
> Amid the vast creation, . . . ordained
> Through life and death to dart his piercing eye,
> With thoughts beyond the limits of his frame,
> That the Omnipotent might send him forth
> In sight of mortal and Immortal powers,
> As on a boundless theater, to run
> The great career of justice; to exalt
> His generous aim to all diviner deeds;
> To chase each partial purpose from his breast,
> And through the mists of Passion and of Sense,
> And through the tossing tides of Chance and Pain,
> To hold his course unfaltering, while the voice
> Of Truth and Virtue, up the steep ascent
> Of Nature, calls him to his high reward,
> The applauding smile of heaven.[1]

No wonder there is confusion in our minds. How shall we reconcile the noble words, "Thou hast made him a little lower than God and hast crowned

[1] "The Mind of Man," by Mark Akenside (c. 1770).

him with glory and honor," with the bestial, hating caricature that has brought the world into such bloodshed and chaos?

There can be no understanding until we turn to the second word about man in the scriptures. It comes from St. Paul, that matchless soldier of the cross, who says in Galatians 6:14, "God forbid that I should glory, save in the cross of our Lord Jesus Christ." This devout exclamation was born out of the absolute realism in which the great Apostle lived. The New Testament never for a moment minimizes the failure of man. "All have sinned and come short of the glory of God." And yet the Christian faith never gives man up in despair, no matter how desperate his plight may become. God has not forsaken man. This is the note that must be sounded again and again around the world. It is the ray of hope in the darkness. Though man has lost the glory with which he was created through his perfidy and sin, God's redemptive love can restore him to his rightful place.

Why did God sacrifice His only begotten Son to redeem man? Was it because of what man was? No, it was rather because of what man could become by God's grace. This is the only basis for any moral optimism today. Whatever kind of a monster man has made of himself, by the grace of God through Jesus Christ, he can again become God's man. Here is the imperative of Christian evangelism.

During my seminary days, I preached in a water front mission in Trenton, New Jersey. Night after night, human derelicts, outcasts of society, would find their way into the chapel where they heard of a Christ who loves them and who gave himself for them. There was certainly not much in the appearance of any one of them to make him a likely candidate for the Kingdom of God. But each of them was a man, with infinite possibilities, a man for whom Christ died. Time after time we saw miracles in lives that had known nothing but unspeakable shame. Drunkards became Christian teachers; outcasts of society became respected Christian citizens. Why? Because the power of Christ restored them to the glory in which they were created. No wonder the apostle said, "God forbid that I should glory, save in the cross of our Lord Jesus Christ." In the mission one night, a man who had been converted only a few weeks before gave his testimony, "I praise the Lord because he took me, as I was, vile and sinful and made me fit for him to live in me." That was a marvelous testimony, one which any humble Christian might well give. I have a glory because Christ is my Saviour, and can take me at my worst, and transform me into a creature fit to share his best.

That leads us to the third word about man, which comes from what is, I suppose, the most neglected book in the Bible, the Revelation of Christ, through St. John. It is a book within whose cryptic pages is written a tremendous message for our times. I am well aware that it has become the favorite camping ground for those who try to write history before it happens, and because it is so often abused, we tend to relegate it to the cults and neglect it in our preaching. And yet it might well have been written for these days, so timely is its message. It is a vivid picture of the inevitable struggle of good and evil, Christ and anti-Christ. And its glory lies in the full assurances that Christ and his Kingdom must ultimately triumph over the Prince of this world. Out of the ecstasy of his vision, John bursts into praise, in the first chapter and the fifth and sixth verses, "Unto him that loved us, and washed us from our sins in his own blood, and hath made us kings and priests unto God and his Father; to him be glory and dominion for ever and ever. Amen." Here is the final consummation of man—man who was created in glory, but who lost his favored place through sin, redeemed by Jesus Christ through his death upon the cross, restored to his place of glory, a king and priest before God, to reign with Him forever. This is the Biblical picture of man.

God does not force His will upon the world. Rather has he chosen to work through the weakness of man to accomplish his purposes. "We are workers together with God," says St. Paul. This is the exalted place to which God has again raised man. We are a part of an everlasting Kingdom. "For we know that the sufferings of this present time are not worthy to be compared with the glory that shall be revealed in us."

It is rather difficult for us to see the glory of that Kingdom in these days. Instead of a Kingdom of love, we can see only a world divided by hatred and prejudice. Instead of palaces of peace, we see our cities in shambles and battlefields bathed in blood. The song of the angels, "Peace on earth, and good will toward men," is lost in the drone of air armadas of destruction, and the sickening whine of falling bombs and the terrified cries of little children.

And yet we know that the future belongs to Christ. His is the Kingdom, the power and the glory. Those precious words of Maltbie Babcock were never truer than today, "Though the wrong seems oft so strong, God is the Ruler yet." Again and again my mind recalls those courageous lines of James Russell Lowell:

> Though the cause of evil prosper,
> Yet 'tis truth alone 'tis strong;
> Truth, forever on the scaffold,
> Wrong, forever on the throne.
> Yet that scaffold sways the future,
> And behind the dim unknown
> Standeth God, within the shadows,
> Keeping watch above his own.

It is not easy to live with a glory in these days, nor is it a simple matter to keep alive either faith or courage. And yet, there is no Biblical ground for ultimate pessimism. In spite of the tragic failure of man we know that God is depending upon redeemed mankind to establish His Kingdom. So we cannot despair. "We are troubled on every side, yet not distressed; we are perplexed, but not in despair, persecuted, but not forsaken, cast down, but not destroyed."

These days call for great souls—men who will not give in to the temper of the times—men who find their highest joy in their service of their King, who glory in the glory he has given them—men of faith and courage who believe in the Kingdom of our Lord and of His Christ—men who can say when the world is at its worst, "I have a glory!"

The Crack in the Bell

REVEREND EUGENE CARSON BLAKE, D.D.
Minister, Pasadena Presbyterian Church, Pasadena, California

Dr. Blake is one of the younger ministers of force and power. He was born in St. Louis, Missouri, in 1906, attended Princeton University, then studied for two years at New College, Edinburgh, Scotland. He entered Princeton Theological Seminary in 1932, and received the D.D. from Occidental College in 1941.

He was a teacher at Forman Christian College, Lahore, India, in 1928 and 1929, and became assistant pastor of the Collegiate Church of St. Nicholas, New York, in 1932, where he remained until 1935. Then he went to Albany as pastor of First Presbyterian Church. In 1940 he was called to the Pasadena Presbyterian Church.

From 1938 to 1940 Dr. Blake was visiting lecturer on religion at Williams College. He is a trustee of Occidental College, a member of the Board of Monte Vista Grove Homes, a member of the Board of Christian Education of the Presbyterian Church in the United States of America, and pastor of radio station KPPC. His religious views have been influenced by Professor Theodore Meyer Green, the late Hugh R. MacIntosh, and by Reinhold Niebuhr. He is in favor of Church union to strengthen the Protestant churches.

In this sermon Dr. Blake discusses true liberty and the things that threaten it. He fittingly points out the place of religion in real liberty. The sermon was preached on Sunday, May 28, 1944.

Sermon Thirty=three

MY TEXT may be found in two places: First, in the Book of Leviticus, the 25th chapter and the tenth verse, these words: "And proclaim liberty throughout all the land unto all the inhabitants thereof." And second, if you will go to Philadelphia and look at the Liberty Bell in Independence Hall, you will find inscribed upon that symbol of our national beginnings these same words: "Proclaim liberty throughout all the land."

Now as every schoolboy knows, there is a crack in the Liberty Bell. It apparently was not easy at the time when the bell was made, to cast it so that it could peal the majestic tones of liberty and not have a flaw in it somewhere which would break under the pounding of the weighty clapper. And to me that old bell stands symbolic of the difficulty of establishing in this or any land a pattern and fabric of liberty which will not crack under the pressures of life and experience. So just as the guardians of the bell recast it at least once and have watched it since it cracked again, taking extreme care that it shall not be broken more, so we the citizen guardians of our nation must stand watch on the liberty inherited from our fathers, recasting it and protecting it that the proclamation shall continue to be heard of "Liberty throughout all the land unto all the inhabitants thereof."

It seems especially fitting that one should speak of liberty on this Sunday that falls before Memorial Day. For this holiday was established scores of years ago in memory of soldiers who fought and died for the union of a free people on the bloody battlefields of the Civil War. Those of you, who are at least as old as I, can remember when Memorial Day was almost entirely the day of the Grand Army of the Republic. (For the Spanish War did not touch the nation comparably.) It was only after the first World War that we began to think of this day as a memorial not only to those old veterans in blue but also to all our country's gallant dead, whether they had fought for union and freedom at home or perhaps vainly to make the world safe for democracy across the seas.

So now as we approach this third Memorial Day of World War II, we all are thinking of the new straight rows of white crosses that it shall be ours to decorate not only with the flowers of our memory but also with the devoted determination of our souls that these new dead shall not have died in vain. For however confused the issues of this war, they are no more confused than were the issues of those earlier wars of our embattled nation. Through deep emotion, once it was even brother against brother, the great war efforts of our country have been in each case for liberty, to win it or preserve it. And that this latest and greatest army the Republic has ever known, poised on the eve of its invasion at the margin of the grim Nazi fortress of tyranny, that these young men shall not make that effort and sacrifice in vain must be the deep concern of all of us who in relative ease and peace watch breathlessly for the decisive hour to strike. And we need to remind ourselves that we are about to make an effort as a nation that may cost our country more of the lives of its young men than any war so far known.

How then stands our liberty at this crucial hour? What are the prospects that these dead shall not die in vain? What is the condition of liberty in our land?

Well, without blinking, let us note that there *is* a crack in the liberty bell. And by this I mean to say that liberty is always threatened, that it might split into fragments under too heavy a blow from within or without. Like the bell, it is sound at the center, I believe, but at the edge, on the periphery, it has its fault that could easily destroy it without our vigilance. We need to remember that there has never been perfect liberty for all men in any society though we may have cast and recast in the attempt to get it. I do not want to be counted one of those who forget this most obvious fact of history and experience, so becoming a danger by glossing over the liberty we have because they are so much concerned at its imperfections.

There are some Americans, of good intentions, so much agitated over the repressions and injustices that exist among us that they fail to appreciate the freedom that we have. They note that even eighty years after the Civil War, Negroes are not yet free of the bondage of economic serfdom due to the chance of their black birth. They mark that in some states they are not even free of political serfdom, lacking the opportunity to vote, so remaining dependent on the good will of their rulers even in this land so proud of its democracy. And others call attention to the mockery of the right to vote of the poorest of our land unless we as a nation remove the fear and want that mass unemployment ever threatens. Others are much concerned that certain American citizens are in concentration camps due not to any overt act of theirs proved against them in a court of justice, but rather due to the fact that they were born of Japanese parents.

That I share this concern about these flaws in the liberty of our nation, I believe you all already know (and later in this sermon it will become more clear). But just now let me emphasize my faith that the heart of our liberty is sound. The crack doesn't reach to the center yet! And though there is a constant threat to liberty in these and other flaws, we must cherish and protect what we have. Even the cracked bell is well worth fighting for. We need not feel ashamed of the idealism nor suppose that it is hypocrisy that we Americans ask men to fight and die for freedom.

There is a difference between the Stars and Stripes and the swastika, between Old Glory and the pennant of the rising sun; and the essence of that difference is the liberty for all the inhabitants of the land over which our flag waves in sovereignty. What I have said seems so obvious as not to need to be mentioned, let alone argued. And yet there is a danger that any who are conscious of its crack should be thought not to cherish the bell.

With then, this statement of the obvious, that our free country is well worth living and dying for, let us proceed to examine the crack in the bell. What are the major threats to our liberty? I mention briefly three.

There is a grave tendency towards forgetting the God who is the only ground of liberty. Stây with me now even though this may sound like a preacher's pious phrase. ("After all *he* must get God into the sermon somewhere!") No, it is not a pious word; it is a fact. The gravest danger to our liberty is that for a long time now many Americans have forgotten, neglected, or rejected the God who was the source and the safeguard of the kind of liberty we have here enjoyed. It was not by chance that my text of the morning was found in two places: on the rim of the Liberty Bell and in the Bible. There was no place else for the molders of our liberty to find it except in the Bible. The conception of liberty for all the people of a land (even of a world) came from God through the Bible. And not only from the New Testament where Christ taught of the universal Fatherhood of God. The roots of the conception start away back in the Old Testament. Moses in the Book of Leviticus is pictured as speaking to the people for Jehovah, (whom some would belittle as a tribal deity) and saying to them: "Ye shall have one manner of law, as well for the stranger as for one of your own country, for I am Jehovah your God."

It was a brand new idea then. The law that was given, an eye for an eye and a tooth for a tooth, is apt to strike us as harsh and cruel even though it was clearly an advance over the desert custom of unrestrained vendetta. But that the law should apply equally to all the inhabitants of the land, the stranger and foreigner as well as to the native son, was an even greater advance and became the foundation for the American conception of liberty.

And if you will note the reason given for having this one and equal law, you will see why it is dangerous to our liberty to forget God. The only reason given is: "for I am Jehovah your God." That is, God doesn't like it when you treat men differently because they are different from you. Therefore, treat all alike with one even law. "Proclaim liberty throughout all the land unto *all* the inhabitants thereof." And that is about the only cogent fundamental reason for our kind of liberty today. Why not brush aside the rights and desires of the Negro, or the Jew, or the Nisei if you can get away with it and so provide a much simpler problem of government and of liberty? Why not? There is only one reason. God doesn't like it! And God won't have it!

And just as faith in this God was the source of the idea in the first place, this faith held by a majority of determined Americans today will be its only safeguard. Yes, the first and major threat to our liberty is the tendency towards forgetting (and neglecting and rejecting) the God who is the only ground of such liberty as we have enjoyed and shared.

The other two threats to our liberty which I shall mention are both somewhat dependent on this first.

There is a growing tendency to be concerned only with our own liberty or that of our own group, kind, or interest. It is true that by national inheritance all Americans love freedom. No king or dictator would have an easy time taking away the rights of the sons of Western pioneers or of the Dodger fans in the Brooklyn bleachers for that matter who have never been west of the Gowanus Canal. But the same was true and is of France. For a period almost as long as our American history of liberty it seemed unthinkable to the whole civilized world that the French peasant on his bit of land, the Parisian shopkeeper with his wife at the cashdrawer, or the laborer on the streets of Paris, let alone the intellectuals to whom the world looked for light and inspiration, could succumb to any tyrant rule. But losing his God, the Frenchman began to lose his interest in liberty and equality for anybody but himself. Fraternity was left out. The Chamber of Deputies became a corrupt house made up of blocs of special interests. They still talked of liberty, but it was their own rights only with which they were concerned. And that leads not to liberty confirmed in law, but leads to anarchy.

Unless you who are white are equally concerned with the liberty of the black man and the rights of the Nisei, your own liberty is threatened. Unless you who are employers are equally concerned about the freedom of labor and its rights, free enterprise will surely be lost. Unless you who are labor are equally concerned about the freedom of the manager to run his business and make it profitable and productive, your own rights are in sharp jeopardy. Don't, my friends, be so foolish as to suppose that anything better than anarchy or tyranny can come in a society in which men and groups are solely concerned with their own liberty.

And we must remember this: Liberty for other people requires you to take the risk that you may be imposed upon. Have you ever become impatient, when reading of a criminal trial at great public expense, at the hedging about protections that seem sometimes almost to have been drawn up so that a criminal can't be convicted? Sometimes the police department or the district attorney's office seems to be on trial rather than the accused. No wire tapping, no hearsay evidence, no background of former criminal record allowed to be introduced into the record! Why did our fathers allow this tangled mass of protection to grow up seemingly designed to save the criminal from well due justice? For one reason only, to assure as far as possible that no man shall be punished for a crime *he* did not commit. If we have believed it necessary to go to these extremes to protect under our law a known gangster from specific injustice, how much more important that you and I should by law and social custom and business practice protect all those in our land whose only "crime" is the color of their skin or the accident of their birth?

I do not know the solution of the so-called Negro problem, the Japanese-American problem, or the labor problem, or the management problem, but I know this: unless we all concern ourselves about the rights of all our citizens and groups, the fabric of our liberty, which men are dying for, will crack as with the sound of doom!

Finally, there are forces loose among us which are the deadly enemies of liberty and which must be fought against and beaten. All of us agree that fascism is the enemy of democracy. But some appear to think that fascism is dangerous only in Germany and Japan.

There was a story told not long ago in *Life* magazine that should dispel such an illusion. A Mr. Yamamoto was hired by a farmer in New Jersey to work on his shorthanded farm. He had been investigated by those in our government charged with the responsibility of seeing that any Japanese disloyal to this country are kept in custody. Mr. Yamamoto was found to be a loyal American, anxious to work. According to the law of this free land, he was released to take the job in New Jersey. There is no charge by anybody that Mr. Yamamoto did not behave himself. But the good people of that district in New Jersey took the law into their own hands and Mr. Yamamoto had to leave for his own safety and that of his employer. Such an episode is a disgrace to any free community. I was glad to see that the weight of *Life*'s correspondence from service men as well as ordinary citizens was on the side of the harmless Japanese farmer and against those fascist citizens of New Jersey.

But I do not criticize New Jersey. To the shame of us, citizens of California, it is generally predicted that worse would happen here if the government and war department decided it was now safe to allow the return of *any* Japanese to this state. I am told by some that this is too touchy a subject to mention now; that the natural emotions of the war against the Japanese would make it wise to wait until the war is over; that then all will be forgotten and the law and tradition of liberty of our land will see that justice is done. I wish I could be sure. I hope that it may be true.

But today I sound the call for good citizens and good Christians (I would not have *Life* magazine be the only voice that dares to speak). "Stand up for liberty under equal law for all the inhabitants of the land." Perfect liberty is hard to mold, dear friends. It won't come by miracle nor by neglect. Every crack in it must be guarded by vigilant citizens who believe that God doesn't like injustice (and won't have it), who are selfless enough to be concerned for others' liberty; and who are militant against tyranny wherever found either in others or in ourselves.

Wild Grapes

REVEREND SAMUEL M. GOLDENSON, PH.D., D.H.L.
Rabbi, Congregation Emanu-El of the City of New York

Dr. Goldenson is known to leaders of the religious world as a scholarly and spiritual rabbi, whose preaching reflects the outlook of the ancient prophets. He is convinced that personal goodness is the first step in solving the many problems that trouble society today. He believes in the democratic tradition and is often referred to as "a rabbi's rabbi." Much of his time is given to counseling laymen who come to him with their problems.

One of the most stimulating rabbis in Reform Judaism, he was born in Rochester, New York, studied at the University of Cincinnati and at the same time attended Hebrew Union College. After seven years of study in preparation for the pulpit, he was called to a congregation in Lexington, Kentucky, while he was yet in his senior year at college. Two years later Temple Beth Emeth of Albany, New York, called him to its pulpit, and from 1906 until he assumed his ministry in Pittsburgh in 1918, Dr. Goldenson remained in Albany, where he was one of its active civic as well as spiritual leaders.

Meanwhile, he pursued advanced studies in the field of Philosophy at Columbia University, where he earned in course the Doctorate in Philosophy. In 1925 Hebrew Union College conferred upon him the degree of Doctor of Hebrew Law. On February 1 of that year he became the spiritual leader of Temple Emanu-El, New York, which is one of the most beautiful Jewish Temples in America. He served as president of the Central Conference of American Rabbis during the years 1933 to 1935. He is known as a scholar, thinker and preacher of great ability.

"Wild Grapes" was given on March 18, 1945, as one of Dr. Goldenson's series on "Moral and Spiritual Foundations for the World of Tomorrow." In it he emphasizes "elementary morals and the better world." Here Dr. Goldenson's rare spiritual and poetic mind can be seen brooding over the life of his people and the whole world.

Sermon Thirty-four

Text: Wherefore, when I looked that it should bring forth grapes, brought it forth wild grapes?   Isaiah 5:4

IN A few days the eagerly awaited spring months will be upon us. How welcome they will be, after the bleakest and dreariest of winters! Yet, in recent years I have not been able to think of springtime without recalling the somber poem by Wordsworth, in which he voices the melancholy thoughts that spring stirs within him.

In the "Lines Written in Early Spring" that great lover of nature broods over a contrast that haunts him. It is the contrast between the "sweet mood" induced by a "thousand blended notes" heard in the grove, and the "sad thoughts" brought to his mind when he recalls

> What man has made of man.

Confident as Wordsworth is "that every flower enjoys the air it breathes," that the least motion of every bird "thrills with pleasure," and believing "that such be Nature's holy plan," he is moved to ask sadly:

> Have I not reason to lament
> What man has made of man?

As I think of this lamentation about human life I cannot but couple with it another pensive and plaintive utterance. It was made thousands of years earlier and is recorded in the Book of Isaiah. In the parable of the vineyard that prophet represents God speaking of his people thus:

> Let me sing of my well-beloved,
> A song of my beloved touching his vineyard.
> My well-beloved had a vineyard
> In a very fruitful hill;
> And he digged it, and cleared it of stones,
> And planted it with the choicest vine,
>
> And he looked that it should bring forth grapes,
> And it brought forth wild grapes.

Then the Infinite Giver goes on to ask:

> What could have been done more to my vineyard,
> That I have not done in it?
> Wherefore, when I looked that it should bring
>   forth grapes,
> Brought it forth wild grapes?

[192]

Wild grapes, indeed! When have the grapes been wilder than now? Never has the contrast been as great between the beneficence of Nature, and of Nature's God on the one hand, and man's wild and bitter malevolence on the other. Since Wordsworth's time, not to speak of the time going back to Isaiah, Nature, through man's digging with the aid of his many new sciences and arts, has yielded her increase beyond the hopes and dreams of the most imaginative intellect. So lavish has Nature become in recent years that its very abundance has become embarrassing to commerce, and its surplus a problem to industry. Only a few years ago the produce of Nature was actually and deliberately destroyed by man for fear that it would glut the market and upset the supposedly correct balance between supply and demand. The important thing, however, to note in all this is that Nature has not failed man. What has failed man is man himself. It is his discontent and ingratitude, his covetousness and greed, his arrogance and conceit that have brought dislocations in his own world and finally led to the burst of global destructiveness and homicidal mania.

To realize the full meaning of this fact and to personalize it is the first step toward moral and social recovery. To be willing to see in man's inhumanity an arraignment of one's own self is the first prerequisite for the creation of the Better World. Every moral attitude to any of the evils of society, particularly when such have become prevalent, requires first of all that a man shall search his own heart to see whether by acts of omission or commission he does not bear some responsibility for these very evils.

There is always the temptation to put the blame upon others. This temptation is especially great when the evils perpetrated are so outrageous and shocking as to overshadow all the habitual misdeeds and offenses of men. By the side of the heinous and indescribable crimes of Hitler and Himmler and the brutalities and atrocities of Nazi Germany and of the Japanese, the inhumanities of other men and other peoples are but trivial and mild misdemeanors, mere peccadilloes. But we must not forget that all extremes are terms of degree. They only show to what lengths certain tendencies will go. They but demonstrate the final ends to which propensities will lead, when unchecked.

Behind the hounds of war let loose by Nazi Germany which afflicted and horrified the world as never before, is the war system, sanctioned, developed and even glorified and glamourized by human society. The Nazis were simply the chief exponents of that system. They were of a people who have been the most convinced believers in war as an instrument of national policy and advancement. Believing in war so utterly, it was inevitable that they should bring out the very worst features of it. This they certainly did as was abundantly evident in such diabolical devices as the robot bomb and the many new contrivances developed for hideous and fiendish mass murders.

Sometimes it seems as if destiny did indeed assign to the German people a special role in human history. Not to rule and dominate the rest of mankind.

That every child now knows, even in Germany. Their part was rather to demonstrate once and for all the utter folly, futility and inhumanity of war. Verily, the Nazis have shown what man can make of man, of their own selves as well as of their fellow men. Under the delusive spell of the false notions of racial and national superiority, of confidence in their technological mastery, and of their will to power and their belief in it, Nazi Germany finally brought down upon its own head and upon countless others the pillars of the whole social structure, and plunged mankind into a raging sea of human carnage, the dire effects of which will be felt for generations and generations.

Yet, if the world is to be made better, the guilt for this war will have to be joined with the guilt for all other wars as well. Men of all other peoples will have to confess: "We have sinned. We, too, have sinned. We have transgressed. We have done perversely." Moreover, when all men everywhere learn to see war as an evil, as an unmitigated evil and not be misled by some of its useful by-products, then will they be in the mood to repent. If men would keep the evil of war in mind as steadily as does a mother who loses a beloved son on the battlefield, then would they search their own hearts to make certain that the blood of their fellow men is not on their own hands as well.

But contrition, however genuine it may appear to be, will remain empty and vain piety, unless it issues in searching inquiries into the situations in life that are distressing, and unless these lead to truly remedial action. The situations requiring correction are for the most part, if not entirely, social. Hence they are man-made.

It appears that the self-preservative instinct develops in some persons predatory propensities. These propensities, in turn, express themselves in devices and contrivances, sometimes crude, sometimes cunning, by which such men become masters of the food supply and of other goods of life. Alas, such are the tiger and wolf qualities in some human beings!

Those that suffer from the predatory possessiveness of their fellow men naturally yearn for relief, and the cry for the remedial condition is always the same. It is for freedom. They yearn for freedom to earn and enjoy their daily bread and freedom to speak their own minds and hearts.

The primary freedoms relative to man's basic needs were proclaimed by President Roosevelt as the general goals of the new and better world. Millions and millions of human beings have been heartened by such a proclamation, for the sad fact is that heretofore only a fraction of mankind have enjoyed these freedoms.

Here in this blessed land, these freedoms have happily been built into the very structure of our commonwealth. Every American child knows that the Declaration of Independence and the Bill of Rights either directly, or by implication, guarantee these freedoms to him. The recent enactment of a law by the State of New York which aims to remove stumbling blocks to means of livelihood by penalizing discrimination in employment, is the natural and altogether logical application of the belief in the inalienable rights of men.

The enunciation of the Four Freedoms—freedom of speech, freedom of worship, freedom from want, and freedom from fear—is itself an event of far-reaching social and political promise. Especially is it significant when emanating from a source so influential and when the freedoms are conceived as goals for all men and all nations.

But a goal is what the term indicates. It is something to be reached. Hence it requires effort and change, change in the environment, and also change in oneself. A social goal is the most difficult to reach because of the radical demands it often makes upon the pursuers. The cry for freedom, to be heard and heeded, requires that men shall identify themselves with those who are deprived of the very things that they themselves enjoy. Unless men imaginatively suffer with those crying for relief, there is no real possibility of making a genuine effort to improve the lot of one's fellow men.

Whether one states the Golden Rule in the positive or the negative form it comes to the same rule of personal and self-searching conduct. As thou enjoyest essential freedoms and believest in them for thyself, thou must believe in them for others as well and thou must will that they, too, shall enjoy them. As thou wouldst not suffer from hindrances to life, liberty and the pursuit of happiness, so shalt thou not stand idly by when these hindrances are placed in the path of thy neighbors.

These very goals, as rational and as self-appealing as they are, will by themselves not change the society in which we live. It sometimes seems as if the more rational a human cause is, the less men feel called upon to do anything about it. Men appear to feel that the very rationality should secure ready and unaided acceptance. But, alas, every cause, however good and commendable it is, has to win its way gradually and laboriously. Only by the aid of guiding concepts and through the medium of well-constructed instrumentalities can social purposes hope to be realized.

Both the usefulness and the risk of enunciating principles is becoming evident in the controversy about Poland. Already there is very grave doubt as to whether the principle that no territorial changes be made without the consent of the peoples concerned, is being carried out with reference to that country. If it is not, it is certainly not because that principle has not been well formulated or not sufficiently well understood. But rather because other considerations have entered into the application of it—considerations which may have their roots in economic or political interests, but which, I fear, may not pass the bar of moral judgment.

It is obvious, therefore, that principles alone, no matter how well conceived and precisely expressed, are not sufficient to bring us to our final objectives. If they had been, the human family would have begun to live in Utopia from the very first day when men became wise enough to discern the difference between good and evil, and intelligent enough to generalize that difference in terms of prescriptions for right conduct. But, alas, it seems as if the human family is afflicted with some kind of allergy to principles. That allergy may be explained by the strange notion that has developed with reference to them, the notion that as ideals these principles belong only in the transcendental world. Men always pay ideals the doubtful compliment that they are too fine for this mundane world.

But the real reason for the tardy use made of principles in fashioning human conduct is that they are, after all, the costliest things in the world. As ideals they stand over the individual and demand of him complete and unswerving loyalty. There is no private property in them. There is no privileged status with reference to them. Hence it is always so difficult to find men who will take them seriously enough to make them effectual in the conduct of daily affairs.

It is at this point, however, that we find the most hopeful sign in present-day society, for never before has a more earnest effort been made to translate principles into means, ideals into methods and techniques for devising a better world structure. The most comprehensive attempt thus far made is along the lines indicated at the Dumbarton Oaks Conference. At that Conference serious men, representing most of the nations of the world, undertook to devise machinery, both of a political and economic nature, through whose operation the peoples will be able to live together more securely and in greater freedom than heretofore.

Yet once more we are obliged to utter a word of warning. Put not your trust in machinery. No device by itself, no matter how well constructed, and no instrumentality, no matter how finely made, will bring us to the millennium. This does not mean that every effort should not be made to develop the most efficient devices and most smoothly operating techniques for the building of the better society. But the warning must be given, nonetheless, and men must be made to understand that in the last analysis the solutions of the problems of human relationship cannot be ground out by mechanical processes. The world of machinery is the world of things. Every machine is a complex thing of which every part is a thing, and through its operation things, and only things, are produced.

And if the machine operates with reference to man, or upon man, it does so only by handling him precisely as if he were a thing like every other thing.

Systems of human relationship, therefore, cannot be left to mechanical devices in the hope that through automatic operations cherished results will be achieved. For in enterprises of human welfare and betterment, values and satisfactions can only be realized when the individuals participating regard themselves as moral agents and when they regard their fellow men, like themselves, not as things, but as persons who are ends in their own right. What every person as a person requires from his neighbors is that he and his interests shall be consulted, not only in the goals set for him, but also in the determination of the processes through which these very goals are to be realized.

In the end all social ventures depend upon the individual's willingness to do his part. Hence the ultimate problem in connection with every effort to create a Better World is not an intellectual one, or a mechanical one, or even a political or economic one. It is searchingly and profoundly personal and moral. Every social problem is a challenge to the will of individuals as persons. In this connection we cannot but recall the prayer of John Drinkwater:

> Grant us the will to fashion as we feel,
> Grant us the strength to labor as we know,
> Grant us the purpose, ribbed and edged with steel,
> To strike the blow.
>
> Knowledge we ask not—knowledge Thou hast lent;
> But Lord, the will—there lies our bitter need.
> Give us to build above the deep intent
> The deed, the deed.[1]

The central moral question is, Can we have a world of men with wills good enough and strong enough to bear the strain of the Better World? When we think how much human beings can bear in time of adversity and how much agony they have suffered during these warring years, it would seem as if they would be capable of bearing the cost and pain of social betterment. But, alas, it is one thing to suffer under the pressure of force from without, and it is another to accept burdens and yokes freely and willingly. In the one instance men have no alternative. In the other they can choose. Therein lies the significance of the most momentous decisions in life. Said the ancient Lawgiver in the Name of God: "I call heaven and earth to witness against you this day, that I have set before thee life and death, the blessing and the curse. Therefore choose life that thou mayest live, thou and thy seed."

It will be seen that the Scriptural writer issued the call for decision to each person singly and separately, even as the Commandments are addressed to the second person singular: "Thou shalt not murder. Thou shalt not steal. Thou shalt not bear false witness against thy neighbor. Thou shalt not covet."

In the attempt to create a more humane and just society the eternal choice will present itself at many points. To some at the very threshold. Some men, as is well known, are not willing to enter any new structure for world betterment. To them the world as it is, is good enough. Good enough only for them and others of their kind. For surely the world in which the vast majority of human beings live in want and fear is not good enough. To be unwilling, therefore, to participate in making the world better is sheer isolationism. Isolationism is the high-sounding word for plain and ordinary selfishness.

But such utterly self-sufficient persons are not the only ones that may retard the progress toward the finer world. There are others who may be willing to enter the new world structure, but only warily and cautiously. Such persons hesitate because they are not ready to pay the full price for

[1] "Grant Us the Will," by John Drinkwater (Boston: Houghton Mifflin Company).

membership in the new society. They sense beforehand that changes will have to be made in their own habits and interests. But in seeking to win the support of such men it is important not to gloss over the necessary changes or to make light of them, but rather to treat them frankly and courageously. For changes will have to be made, and basic ones, in every department of life. Some in the social and religious attitudes of men; some in their political theories and affiliations; and some in their economic interests and fortunes.

In the world of social relations men will have to become broad enough and understanding enough to overcome their silly and supercilious notions about racial differences. Such invidious notions are only forms of self-flattery. They satisfy personal or group vanity. To make distinctions on such grounds and to classify some as inferiors and others as superiors (and we ourselves are always the superiors) is to perpetrate an initial wrong upon one's fellow men. From the moment a man regards another as inferior he tends to treat him as a menial and serf, as a bearer of burdens from which he himself is, of course, to be exempt. This is the inner meaning of the universal revolt against the philosophy of the master race. The Nazis could not have promulgated a doctrine that was as sure to arouse suspicion of and hostility to German people as the claim that they are the destined master folk of mankind. For in that boast men and nations saw immediately the threat of their own enslavement.

In the religious world, too, some cherished concepts will have to be revised, and the one most certainly is the monopolistic conception of spiritual truth and value. He who holds that his belief in God and in God's governance of the universe is the only one, is a man who cannot enter into any genuine and inward fellowship with those who do not share the same religious ideas.

By exclusive and arrogant theological concepts men set boundaries to God's infinitude, fix limits to God's love, and lay special claims to God's grace.

How the tragic history of mankind has been made still more sorrowful by such theological fence building! All the acrimonious disputations, the heated polemics, the heresy hunting, the persecutions, inquisitions, and religious wars bear sad testimony to such mental and moral obsessions and fixations! The cure for this strange malady is simple humility—humility before God. If theologians would only pause to ask the question whether God's thoughts may really not be higher than theirs, and God's ways higher than their own! An ancient Rabbi once pictured God as saying: "If my people forget me, but obey my law, they will yet be acceptable to me." What counts most with the Infinitely Compassionate Father in Heaven is personal goodness and genuine obedience to the moral law.

It is obvious that in the political world especially men will have to be ready and willing to alter their views if men and nations are henceforth to live in security and peace. One cannot believe in the doctrine of exclusive nationalism or in absolute state sovereignty and yet be entirely free to join in the promotion of political ends common to all. For every common end is a shared end, and every shared end is one in which one's own part cannot be considered the whole. A person living in a dwelling with others can never hope to enjoy the security of his own room therein, unless the whole household is kept from harm. It is strange that such obvious things are not realized in connection with men's living together in larger groupings, as in the same neighborhood, the same hemisphere, or in the same world, their earthly home. It is as if logical and moral laws apply only to small units and not to large ones.

Alas, for ages and ages men have set up arbitrary and differing standards of moral conduct—some for individuals and others for nations—some for the poor, others for the rich—some for the powerful, others for the weak—some for the strangers, others for the homeborn. With reference to all this the ancient Lawgiver enjoined: "Thou shalt not have in thy house diverse measures, a great and a small. A perfect and just weight shalt thou have, a perfect and just measure shalt thou have."

Another moral problem within the political sphere arises from the unavoidable circumstance that among the peoples that are now undertaking the creation of the Better World there are some who are so much more powerful than others. How much more powerful some countries are, has certainly been demonstrated in recent years. The result of this circumstance has been that the leadership and the responsibility for the creation of the Better World has naturally been taken by those nations that are described as the Big Powers. Promising as this seems to be, for big jobs can only be done by powerful agencies, yet there lurks within this situation a real danger. That danger is suggested by the very description of these outstanding nations as Big Powers. The term "Powers" is frightening. It brings to mind the whole sad story of mankind, the story written by the innumerable persons and nations who have yielded to the seductions and temptations of power. "The test of virtue," said Addison, "is to have power and not abuse it." Alas, too many have not been able to bear this test, to the great sorrow of myriads and myriads of human beings.

It is because the problem of power is so real and so difficult of solution that wise and good men are now scrutinizing with so much care the provisions dealing with the relationship of the Big Powers to the smaller ones in the administration of the world security system. The problem of power also explains the difficulty that was experienced in arriving at a satisfactory voting procedure at the Yalta Conference. That difficulty arose from the inveterate temptation of power to act unilaterally, and thus arbitrarily to veto the plans and frustrate the purposes of those less powerful.

At this point one cannot but express the hope that the day will soon come when Russia, one of the greatest of the great powers, will become more democratic. For one of democracy's keenest convictions is that power must be put under restraint and made more and more responsive to the common will. The regulating way by which power is thus socialized and moralized is in accordance with the democratic principle that the just powers of government are derived from the consent of the governed.

One does not need to subscribe to the theory of the economic interpretation of history to realize how profoundly the material needs and interests of persons affect their thinking and behavior. If the world is, therefore, to be made better, most certainly revisions will have to be made in economic views and practices. Here, if anywhere, men will be confronted with moral challenges and choices. One cannot believe in free and unrestrained competition and yet enter wholeheartedly into co-operative ventures to serve the common good.

Nor can one derive profits from war without having one's sensibilities to its horrors dulled and deadened. The profits of war and the blessings of peace do not go well together. Profits cushion men's conscientious scruples. They make them quiescent and complacent. But if men really mean to live in a peaceful world, they will have to awaken to every evil of war and be ever ready to forego any and all its profits and benefits.

Moreover, not only in changing from a war to a peace economy will men be obliged to make sacrifices. They will be called upon to relinquish special advantages and privileges whenever men endeavor to change the social order from a less to a more equitable society. For some to have more, others will have to be willing to take less.

It should be obvious, now, that the responsibility for the creation of the Better World rests upon every man and in every walk of life. That responsibility is at bottom altogether personal and moral. Scientists, philosophers, artists, poets, statesmen, men in capital and in labor—all must do their share. But since the problem of bettering the human structure is essentially a moral one, the major obligation rests upon the teachers of religion. To declare this at a time when the unhappy human world has just passed through the most destructive and murderous orgy in human history, is at once to indict and to challenge the spiritual leaders of mankind. The indictment is as great as the combined suffering of all those who have become broken and bereft by war. How much of this suffering could have been prevented if the spiritual teachers had taught real religion, the religion suffused by God-conscientiousness—if they had only taught such a religion more earnestly and exemplified it more truly!

Of all the spiritual teachers of mankind none has such a great stake and none should be under such great inner compulsion to build the Better World as we of the Children of Israel. Our stake in the World of Tomorrow derives from the tragic circumstance that our people have almost always been the first victims of the dislocations of society and of the passions, lusts and hatreds of men. What has befallen the Jews in recent years is simply the latest and worst instance of this sad historic fact. Thousands and millions of others have suffered too, but we were the first to feel the evil days.

But there is another reason why a special obligation rests upon us of Israel to give ourselves wholly to the task of bringing the World of Tomorrow a little nearer. For it was our prophets and lawgivers who saw earlier and more clearly than others the universal and eternal truths by which man should live. And they were the ones who advocated and championed these truths with the deepest earnestness and with unwearying persistence. One of them enunciated the spiritual philosophy of human history:

Not by might, nor by power, but by my spirit, saith the Lord of Hosts.

Another defined the moral basis of a peaceful society:

The work of righteousness shall be peace, and the effect thereof quietness and rest forever.

Still another, and at the very threshold of our history, insisted upon the inward immediacy of the moral law:

This commandment which I give thee this day is not in the heavens above, nor over the seas beyond, but it is very nigh unto thee; in thy mouth and in thy heart—that thou mayest do it.

May we, together with men of all other creeds, take these truths to heart, renew our faith in them, and go forward to the supreme task of the ages— that of building the Better World.

Uplifted Desires

REVEREND WILLIAM ORLANDO CARRINGTON, D.D.
Minister, First A. M. E. Zion Church, Brooklyn, N. Y.

Dr. Carrington was born in Georgetown, British Guiana, but came to the United States in 1905. He has held pastorates in Charlotte, North Carolina, Washington, D.C., New Rochelle, New York, and Hartford, Connecticut. Dr. Carrington was dean of Hood Theological Seminary, Salisbury, North Carolina from 1910 to 1920, instructor in the School of Religion, Howard University, Washington, D.C., from 1920 to 1924, and 1932 to 1936. He was editor of the A. M. E. Zion Quarterly Review from 1924 to 1932. He has been pastor of the First African Methodist Episcopal Zion Church, Brooklyn, New York since 1936. In 1936 and 1937 he was a member of the National Preaching Mission, and was also a member of the National Christian Mission from 1940 to 1943. Livingstone College conferred the D.D. in recognition of his work for his people.

In 1916 Dr. Carrington was the winner of the Homiletic Review Sermon *Contest and a contributor to* Prize Sermons *published by the Macmillan Company in 1932. He was the winner of the* Church Management Sermon Contest *in 1934. He is one of sixty-four representative American preachers whose sermons comprise* The American Pulpit Series *published by the Abingdon-Cokesbury Press, and the author of* Carry a Little Honey. *For the past ten years he has been instructor and lecturer at institutes for ministers. He is interested in literature, especially in Scott, Shakespeare and Dickens. His membership is over three thousand, "good, bad and indifferent," and he has been gradually developing a seven day church program. The church is meeting its challenging opportunity with educational, recreational and nursery work.*

Sermon Thirty=five

TEXT: Unto thee, O Lord, do I lift up my desire. PSALM 25:1
(An American Translation)

THESE desires of ours and what to do with them constitute a real problem and a perennial one. What is their function? How shall we regard them? To what extent should they be permitted to influence thought and action? Within what category should they be placed—good or evil, blessing or curse? The teachers of the ancient East, for the most part, regarded them as essentially evil, something to be repressed, eliminated, annihilated. And it has been said: "It was this tradition of the 'immemorial East' which, flowing into the early Church, produced there the asceticism of the anchorites and hermits of the Libyan desert, and which has been present sporadically throughout Catholicism ever since." Whatever fascination it has had for certain select and heroic souls, and whatever response it has won from them, this view of the East has never gained any general following in the West. Here, indeed, at times and in certain quarters, there has been a swing to the other extreme, that is, flinging away all restraint and yielding to the unqualified gratification and exploitation of desire.

It seems to me that the truth is this: desire is part of the life inheritance of the race; it is an integral part of the human constitution, neither good nor evil in itself but possessing vast potentialities of good and evil. Elemental, eruptive, dynamic, it needs to be harnessed to the nobler powers of life. Left to itself it will drag us down to the level of the brute. Controlled and sublimated it will ennoble and glorify life, lifting it to heights that seemed too high for our aspiring. Mismanaged it may become "procuress to the lords of hell"; wisely directed it can allure to brighter worlds and lead the way.

In the text we see how one man long ago dealt most effectively with his desires. They had evidently given him grave concern, had been a sore trouble to him. Perhaps he had tried suppressing them, but that had proved a rather ineffectual way of handling them. He might hold them in partial subjection so long as he kept them under his eyes and under his feet, but as soon as the vigilance was relaxed and the pressure relieved they were snarling and clamoring and insisting on doing as they would. To remove all restraint and let them have their way would never do. That was the way of folly and madness and tragedy; and it would avail nothing in the hour of betrayal and undoing to cry, as did Robert Burns at a later date:

> But yet the light that led astray
> Was light from Heaven.

No, he finds a better way. He will bring his desires into the open and submit them to God for His approval. "Unto Thee, O Lord, do I lift up my desire." We may be safe in concluding that he soon came to the end of his troubles in this matter, and if we are wise we shall learn the secret of his success and profit from his experience.

First, then, *these uplifted desires will bear the marks of discipline.* If we take seriously this business of living we are bound to give more than passing consideration to our desires, for they constitute one of our most difficult and disturbing problems. They ought to be subjected to examination, appraisal, criticism; brought before the Supreme Court of our highest and best judgment; they should be so ordered and organized that the lowest might not usurp the place of the highest, and the basest might not crowd the best out of the foreground. And if in the final analysis we purpose to submit them to God we can hardly afford to neglect at the outset some such procedure. There are certain desires that we wouldn't dare bring before God at all, that we wouldn't want Him to know we cherished even for one brief moment. They are so base, so utterly unworthy, that we are ashamed of them in our better moments; and there are other desires which can only be classified as "miserable aims which end with self." Of course there are people who want what they want when they want it, at any cost, even at the tragic cost of "blacking out" God from their thought and from their little world. They frequently resort to a mental trick comparable to the act of the little girl who wanted to help herself to some forbidden sweets. As she reached for the coveted thing, she looked around to make sure no one was watching and there on the wall was a portrait, the eyes of which were fixed on her. She changed her position repeatedly in her effort to evade them, but wherever she turned those unescapable, reproving eyes were looking at her. Finally she climbed up on a chair and punched them out and proceeded to help herself to what she wanted.

There are those who think they dispose of God by simply ignoring Him and then go on to gratify their desires however and whenever they please

Jane Addams used to tell of a working girl in Chicago who, for her health's sake, was put on a very strict diet, but who utterly disregarded the rigid dietetic requirements of her physician. When she was taken to task for her failure to follow his prescription, she dismissed the matter by remarking that she'd "druther eat what she'd druther." Human nature is always being tempted to do what it would "druther," but if it is to escape disaster and come to its highest and best it would better discipline its "druthers" by lifting them up to God.

In the very act of bringing our desires before God we shall find ourselves appraising them, judging them, looking at them in the light not only of what we are but of what we should like to be; seeing them not only in relation to our present satisfaction but setting them in the context of life's total meaning and ultimate good; considering them from the standpoint not merely of personal gratification and benefit but of their social value and influence. And, what is more, we shall find ourselves submitting them to the final arbitrament of God's mind and will and purpose. To be sure, many of these desires could not survive such summary treatment; they would shrivel and die in the fierce light of such a judgment; many of them we ourselves should be forced to cast as rubbish to the void; while those that remained would have earned their right to survival by being cleansed, chastened, sublimated. Dr. W. C. Bower sums up the matter admirably for us:

> It is impossible to share with God desires that under the criticism of one's best intellectual, social or moral judgment are felt to be unworthy. Much less is it possible to seek divine assistance in the pursuit of such ends. On the other hand, ends that are so approved are enhanced by sharing them with God and by seeking the enlistment of extra-human resources in their attainment.

This has been an open secret with the saints, and wherever life has blossomed into the miracle and glory of distinctive goodness or yielded the rich, ripe fruit of noble character; achieved the distinction of spiritual charm and power, or reached unwonted levels of service and sacrifice, we may be sure there has been this discipline of desire. So Daniel early purposed in his heart that he would not defile himself and kept the window of his chamber open toward Jerusalem and his heart open toward God. So Paul could say, "I buffet my body, and bring it into bondage." So General Charles George Gordon, better known as "Chinese" Gordon, personified some of his own desires and told of his merciless handling of them: "I had a terrible half-hour this morning, hewing Agag in pieces before the Lord." "I had a terrible struggle this morning with Agag." And all of us might well make William Sharp's little poem, "The Mystic's Prayer," our own:

Lay me to sleep in sheltering flame,
O Master of the Hidden Fire!
Wash pure my heart, and cleanse for me
My soul's desire.

In flame of sunrise bathe my mind,
O Master of the Hidden Fire,
That, when I wake, clear-eyed may be
My soul's desire.[1]

But there is another stage beyond discipline. Having gone that far we should take the next step. *These uplifted desires should bear the touch of consecration.* Discipline can go far toward resolving the conflict of desires which goes on in the interior places of one's life, by crushing those that are evil, subordinating the lower to the higher, and helping him to bring them finally into conformity with the moral and spiritual realities of the universe. But it is the touch of consecration which will enable him to achieve complete mastery over his wayward impulses and absolute dominion over his clamorous desires, for that involves the surrender of his will to the Highest. Apart from such consecration the time might come when, weary of discipline, one might cry out in the words of Lew Sarett:

> God, let me flower as I will
> For I am weary of the chill
> Companionship of waxen vines
> And hothouse nurtured columbines;
> O, weary of the pruning knife
> That shapes my prim decorous life;
> Of clambering trellises that hold me;
> Of flawless patterned forms that mold me.
> God, let me flower as I will!
> A shaggy rambler on the hill![2]

As might be expected, Jesus the Master of life and of life's situations brought his profound insight to bear on this problem. In the Model Prayer which he gave us he includes the petition: "Thy will be done, as in heaven, so on earth." Without anything like emotional excitement or appeal, but rather with calm and deliberate purpose, he challenges us to this audacious and glorious commitment to God's will. But someone might complain that this suppresses our personality, takes away from us the freedom of self-expression. Far from it. This is in reality the surest path to the highest self-realization and the finest self-expression.

> Make me a captive, Lord,
> And then I shall be free,

is a prayer in which deep religious insight gets to the root of the matter. Too often we are disposed to interpret the petition in terms of resignation and submission. Of course they are involved in it, but unless we make room for consecration and put the

[1] From *Poems and Dramas*, by William Sharp (New York: Dodd, Mead & Company), p. 291.
[2] "Let Me Flower As I Will," from *The Box of God*, by Lew Sarett (New York: Henry Holt and Company, Inc.), p. 38.

emphasis there, we shall miss the main point. The will of God is more than something to be suffered or endured with as good grace as possible; it is something to be done, to be adventured upon in the brave mood of glad acceptance, in the fine spirit of high consecration.

Jesus exemplified in his own life just what he seeks to commit us to in this petition. "My meat," he said, "is to do the will of him that sent me and to finish his work." "I am come, not to do mine own will, but the will of him that sent me." "I seek not mine own will, but the will of him that sent me." What is here reiterated in his words received perfect fulfillment in his life. Thinking of all this Paul, trying to win the Christians in Rome—and, for that matter, Christians everywhere in all ages—from self-pleasing, cries out: "Wait, wait! Think of this: even Christ pleased not himself." And somebody has remarked: "With such a self to please, would not self-pleasing for once have become a beautiful and godlike thing?" Jesus did not think so, however, for he pleased not himself. For him the will of God was so sovereign as to be unchallenged by any rivalry. He hammered his own impulses and desires into the perfect pattern of his Father's design.

This is not to imply that Jesus took this matter of doing God's will in his stride, found it easy, went rollicking through it. No one will think so who recalls the statement in the Epistle to the Hebrews about his having "offered up prayers and supplications, with strong crying and tears"; or his Gethsemane prayer, that agonizing supplication of a breaking heart striving to reconcile its passionate desire with the Father's will: "O, my Father, if it be possible, let this cup pass from me; nevertheless, not as I will, but as thou wilt." And if we sincerely lift up our desires to God we may come upon an experience like this, when the thing we so desperately want—perhaps not bad or wrong in itself, not mean or in any sense unworthy—will have to be given up because it is not in harmony with God's will, does not gear into His plan. How sorely and urgently it will need the touch of consecration then! That is, if we are to go beyond submission and resignation and come at last to glad acceptance of, and active co-operation with, the Divine will and purpose.

With the touch of consecration on them, *these uplifted desires will leave no bitterness of disappointment*. In a single stanza of the *Rubáiyát*, the astronomer poet of Persia summarizes the drama of desire for any number of people:

> The Worldly Hope men set their Hearts upon
> Turns Ashes—or it prospers; and anon,
>   Like Snow upon the Desert's dusty Face,
> Lighting a little hour or two—is gone.

Behind those words we can discern the pain of the unfulfilled, the bitterness of disappointment, the emptiness of satisfied desire. Life sometimes seems to grant our desires with one hand and take them away with the other; or we get what we clamor for so insistently only to find that we should have been better off without them. A Psalmist expressed this in an unforgettable sentence which is instinct with tragedy: "He gave them their request; but sent leanness into their souls."

In *Beggars' Horses* by P. C. Wren we have a story which illustrates and emphasizes the fearful penalty we sometimes pay for getting what we want, even though it may not be essentially bad. Some British officers are visiting a holy man in India, and before they leave he asks each of them what one thing he would desire if he were sure it could be attained. Never dreaming that any seriousness could be attached to it, each expressed his deepest desire. One wanted to be the richest man, and another the strongest man, in the world. One whose immediate paternal forebears had all died early requested for himself long life; another, haunted by forebodings of personal tragedy longed for happiness; the fifth wanted perfect health, and the last desired the gift of courage. The holy man then surprised them by promising that each of them should have what he desired, and so it turned out ultimately. But in each case it developed that the desire attained was the worst thing that could have happened, for it was charged with tragic consequences.

Sometimes it is the withheld desire, the frustrated longing, the thwarted ambition, which embitters life and produces the gnawing discontents that undermine its serenity and destroy its happiness. There is a medieval legend which tells that sometime during the twelfth century Henry II of England laid siege to the French city of Le Mans, but failed to take it, and had to retire enraged and baffled. According to the legend he deliberately blasphemed against God in order to ensure his own damnation. "Since Thou hast taken from me the thing I most delight in—Le Mans—I will deprive Thee of the thing Thou hast most delight in—my soul." Perhaps nobody would go to that extreme, but some people just simply can't take it when their desires are denied. They go to pieces, become sullen and embittered; they whine and complain and charge God foolishly. We have known a few poor souls who could not survive such disappointment. If they did not curse God, they nevertheless died because of it. Much of the tragedy connected with our desires springs out of the fact that we rarely know what we really need, or what is best for us, and we can hardly forecast all the consequences of our choices.

But if our desires have been disciplined to the point of consecration we should be saved from all that. Whatever may happen to them they will leave no bitterness or sting of disappointment; and in the end they may turn out not only none the worse, but all the better, for us. So Rabindranath Tagore came to feel: "My desires are many and my cry is pitiful, but ever didst thou save me by hard refusals; and this strong mercy has been wrought into my life through and through."

I do not mean to suggest that it is always easy for us to adjust ourselves to our unfulfilled desires, to be reconciled to the denial of our most cherished longings, especially when these represent our finest idealism and our worthiest aspirations. It does not appear that it was easy for Paul to accept his thorn in the flesh for the removal of which he prayed repeatedly but unavailingly. I can hardly imagine that it was easy for David to abandon the great dream of his life and become resigned to the revelation that the temple which he carried in his heart should never, in his time and under his direction, be translated into a shining reality on Zion's hill. And shall we think it was easy for Moses to say "Amen" to the Divine decree which denied his entrance into the land of promise? For this he had lived and labored, suffered and sacrificed, hoped and prayed. For this he had turned his back on the power and the glory of the mightiest empire of his day, spurned the diadem and scepter of the Pharaohs, counted the treasures of Egypt as nothing worth, and given his life to what appeared a wild dream, or at best a thankless, if not a hopeless, task. For this, according to a fine old story in the Book, he had stood in the gap between the wrath of God and his sinful people. "Let me alone," protested God, "that I may destroy them." "You can't! You can't!" cried Moses. "Your name, your honor, your promise are all at stake." "Let me destroy them," urged God, "and I will make of thee a great nation." "No, no, not that! Remember Abraham, Isaac, and Jacob, thy servants, to whom thou swarest by thine own self. . . . Oh, this people have sinned a great sin, . . . Yet now, if thou wilt forgive their sin—; and if not, blot me, I pray thee, out of thy book which thou hast written." After all this, when at last they reach the borders of the Promised Land, he is denied the privilege of entering it. "Let me go over, I pray thee," passionately pleads the great lawgiver. But the Divine prohibition remains irrevocable and immutable: "Thou shalt not go over thither. . . . Go up, and die." No, it was not easy to say "Amen" to that. And in our own case we may come to it only after much pleading, and searching of heart, and anguish of spirit, and fierce struggles within the citadel of the soul. But the touch of consecration will enable us to win through.

And now we have come by these successive steps to this last word. *These uplifted desires hold the secret of peace.* When we have come to the place where we can sincerely say: "Have Thine own way, Lord; have Thine own way"; "not my will, but thine, be done"—and say it not as the plaintive wail of those who have been subdued by superior force, but as the response of a consecration which lifts our wills into high and satisfying harmony with the Divine will so essential to our well-being—we may be sure that we are already initiated into the secret of peace for, in the noble words of Dante, "In His will is our peace." If people would only learn that as one of the primary lessons of life instead of missing it altogether, or making it one of the last which life eventually forces upon them, what a lot of pain and trouble and heartbreaking experiences they could avoid. How many of us batter and bruise and sometimes break ourselves against the will of God, simply because we do not understand that its sovereignty, as Principal Whale of Cheshunt College puts it, "is not the sovereignty of arbitrariness, but of love"; that it has, as Henry Calderwood once said about another matter, "absolute right to command, not force to constrain"; or better still, that this will, as Jesus teaches, is the will of our Heavenly Father. George Herbert knew something of this conflict of desires, of the pain of renunciation, of restiveness under restraint, and was all but carried away by insurgent moods. He expresses it very strikingly in his fine poem, "The Collar." Just when he decides to throw off restraint, to get from under the yoke, something happened which resulted in acceptance and peace:

> But as I raved, and grew more fierce and wild
>   At every word,
> Methought I heard one calling, "Child!"
>   And I replied, "My Lord!"

God is our Father and is actuated by holy love in all His dealings with us. He means only our highest good, means it intensely, passionately, unswervingly. Back of all His silences, behind all His denials of our desires and frustrations of our plans, through all the severity of His discipline, underlying the bewilderments of His providence and perplexities of His ways, there is His loving purpose from which He never turns aside, even though it involves Him in participation in the experience of our suffering and the tragedy of our sin. Whatever else the Incarnation and Calvary may mean, they mean that. "God was in Christ reconciling the world unto himself." Surely Lynn Harold Hough is right when he says, "Back of the pierced hands of Jesus is the pierced heart of God." We can trust a God like that, and where there is that trust there will be nothing like resentment or rebellion or even stolid submission, but rather complete acquiescence in His will, and the experience of peace such as he must have known who sang: "Thy statutes have been my song in the house of my pilgrimage"; or that other who cried: "I delight to do thy will, O my God." Let us then lift up our desires unto the Lord. "So shall God's peace, that surpasses all our dreams, keep guard over our hearts and minds in Christ Jesus." And life shall be

"Touched to a sudden glory round the edge."

Reaping With Joy

REVEREND W. A. VISSER 'T HOOFT, PH.D.
General Secretary, World Council of Churches, Geneva, Switzerland

Dr. Visser 't Hooft was born in Haarlem, Holland in 1900. He took his major education in Holland and received his Doctorate from the University of Leiden in 1928.

After special studies in America, during which he wrote the book entitled The Background of the Social Gospel in America, he served as a staff member of the World's Committee of the Y.M.C.A., and later general secretary of the World's Student Christian Federation. From that post he was called to the general secretaryship of the Provisional Committee of the World Council of Churches in 1938, and in the same year was elected president of the World's Student Christian Federation.

He is the author of many books; among his more recent works are None Other Gods (1937); The Church and Its Function in Society (1937); The Struggle of the Dutch Church (1944); The Wretchedness and Greatness of the Church (1944).

Dr. Visser 't Hooft was a prominent member of the World Conference at Oxford and Edinburgh in 1937; Madras, 1938; Amsterdam, 1938. His work is known by Christian leaders around the world and his influence has rapidly increased through his prominent connection with the World Council head office which he administers in Geneva. He recently visited Holland, France and Germany for consultations with leaders of the churches, in connection with the World Council's co-operative program of inter-church aid, reconstruction and material relief.

HENRY SMITH LEIPER

Sermon Thirty=six

TEXT: They that sow in tears shall reap in joy. PSALM 126:5

ON THIS very first Sunday after the day of victory in Europe, we have come together before the face of God to ask, not of men, but of Him what is the lesson that we have to learn, what is the message that we have to receive, what is the hidden word that through these terrible and great events, He wishes to speak to us? The history of God is not so easy to discover. It is only those who have the ears of faith who can hear that hidden message; and it is only when we take our guidance from His word that we have any chance of hearing it.

So we turn to His word and read in Psalm 126, the fifth verse: "They that sow in tears shall reap in joy."

God is the great Sower. Man can only sow in His name. God sows the seed of life, of the abundant life, of the real life in this world where, without God's seed, everything would die; nothing would have any permanence.

But sowing, the sowing of God, is a work that implies tears. Why? Because the soil is so hard; because the soil needs breaking up; because you and I belong to a stiff-necked people; because our hearts are closed against the word of God until we let them be broken open. That is why the history of God's plan in this world, the history of God's action in this world, is a history full of suffering and full of tears and full of judgment. Unless the grain of wheat dies, it will not bring forth fruit.

The way of God is the way of the cross. When we say the Apostles' Creed, do we not remark that movement from high up above: "conceived by the Holy Spirit," and then downward to the cross; the burial, "descended into hell," and then upward again to the Resurrection and to the Ascension. Those who try to by-pass the cross miss the center of the Christian evangel. Only those who are willing to pay the full price for partnership with God, who are not afraid of the cross—only those can be soil for God. Only those can help in sowing the seed of life.

Is that a very pessimistic view of life? No. It would be pessimistic if we remained obsessed by the suffering and the tears and saw nothing through the tears. But, thank God, the Christian message is that right through the tears one already sees from afar, and sometimes from quite near, the joy of harvest time. The reaping is with joy. The reaping is the victory of God. That, of course, refers to the ultimate future, to the definite victory of the Kingdom, to the great harvest which one day God will have in this world.

But if you read that 126th Psalm and, in fact, if you read your whole

Bible, you will find again and again that that last victory already throws its rays of light into the present, into our actual life, into the here and now. There are signs, marvelous signs, of the last victory. There are harvest times in the history of man that announce the great harvest time of God at the end of history.

What has all that to do with the days in which we are living? This, that seen from the perspective of God these last years, these terrible years, have been sowing time, time in which the seed of life came to the earth from God —a time, therefore, in which there was a great breaking open of the hard soil of our modern life; a time of judgment; a time, therefore, in which there was much suffering, in which many tears were shed.

Oh, how deep the plough has gone through the soil of some countries in our time! But, thank God, it has not been wholly in vain. You see, the worst thing is not to suffer. The worst thing is to suffer *in vain*. There are those in our world today who have suffered in vain, and we must pity them. But there are also those who have suffered meaningfully, who have understood that something absolutely unusual was happening in the world, that in and through the events of our time God visited His world—and those we must not pity. On the contrary, those are the ones who have a message for us all; those are the ones to whom we must listen.

It has been quite clear in these last years that, where there was much breaking up of human soil, there the life of God and the word of God was received in a new, in an eager way, in which it had not been received for a long time. I think of some of the prisoner of war camps. Prisoners of war are generally not sentimental or pious people. Yet here in many of these camps, we have suddenly seen a spontaneous uprising of Christian life, such as some of us had never dared to believe would be possible. At first one wondered whether it was not just a psychological reaction of fatigue, of loneliness. Would it last? Well, it has lasted, and I do not know of any more alive parishes of these last years than those that existed behind the barbed wire in the lonely camps of Germany.

Perhaps more amazing still is what happened in these places of misery where the refugees were herded together from all over Europe, refugees of all sorts of faiths, but principally of the Jewish faith. In those camps just a few young Christians who could not tolerate the thought that these men and women and children would be left all alone in a purely hostile world, simply went to live with them. They were not very effective preachers. They hardly knew the language of these refugees. But around them there has grown up a living Christian community. I have seen men come out of these refugee camps, saying, "After this kind of thing has happened to me, and this message of God had come to me when it seemed that absolutely everything was lost, I am willing to give all the rest of my life to this Saviour God who does not leave alone those who are in deepest misery."

I think of the men who have paid the price for their partnership with their Lord in sowing. I think especially of a pastor who was put in a concentration camp because of the all too clear and frank Christian sermons he preached. Since he was a minister of the word of God, he said to himself: "In this camp I must go on preaching." But how do you do that when you are in a little cell? Well, if the cell is of wood and you can reach with your voice the other cells, you can at least shout from one cell to another a message of God. And that is what he did. As a result the S.S. men would come in and beat him day after day, but he continued his ministry. Finally the camp commander said, "This cannot go on. This man is undermining the whole discipline in my camp." He had the pastor appear before him, and said, "I am going to make you a very generous offer. You will have to choose. I am willing to let you go if you promise that you will never again preach. But you can live freely as a private individual."

"What is the alternative?" asked the preacher.

"The alternative is to be shot."

"In that case," said the preacher, "you can shoot me right away."

"No," said the commander. "I will give you three days to think it over, for I know that after three days you will change your mind."

After three days, the commander came and said, "What is your decision?"

"The same as it was three days ago," said the preacher. And he was shot.

Or one thinks of the ploughing, of the sowing with tears, that has gone on in some of the fighting Churches. You can almost take the map of Europe and ask yourself, Where were the Churches really willing to suffer? And in those places you will find that sowing has gone on during this war, such as never before. Those Churches have not waited till they were attacked but have said, "Now, if ever, is the time to attack with the word of God, to use this period of questioning and breaking up and opening of closed doors, to sow, and to sow with the undiluted word of God. And there has been sowing, as we had not seen for many and many a year. And that is why they are now entering into harvest time.

Some of us may be inclined to pity the fighting Churches when we hear of what happened to them, and of men sent to concentration camps and to prisons, of exhausted pastors, and of Churches that lack nearly everything in the way of material and other means of existence. But you must not pity them, because they know now the joy of harvest time that comes after the tears of sowing time. It is a very great—perhaps the greatest—joy for a Christian community to have discovered that God is as good as His word and that precisely when no earthly power can help you out, indeed, when all earthly powers seem to be against you and to want to destroy you, that even then you can live—and live more abundantly—because God gives you new force, new energy.

A few days ago I spent an unforgettable evening with Bishop Fjellbu— at that time the only liberated Bishop of the Church of Norway, who had escaped from Norway and was now working in the north of that country; and

[213]

with a leader of the Greek Orthodox Church in Greece. We spent a whole evening comparing notes as to what had happened in our three Churches—those of Norway, Greece and Holland. Yes, we had a lot to tell each other about suffering, about the tears of those years. But the whole undertone of that conversation, especially when we came to look at the present and the future, was one of deep gratitude for here we saw before us a new era for the Church, open doors for the Church in the nation such as we had not dreamed of in the routine days before the war. So we could feel that the fields were really white and ripe for the harvest.

Only—how shall these Churches take this wonderful opportunity unless the whole Christian community in the world stands by them? How shall these exhausted pastors and priests do this job of harvesting unless they are given help to increase their ranks? How shall they preach the word of God unless someone helps them to put some simple buildings in the place of the thousands and thousands of destroyed churches all over Europe? How shall they reconstruct the life of their country unless the whole Christian world rises up and says, "We are going to be in on this harvest time. We want to be part of this"?

For that must be my last word. Some of you may say, "Yes, that is all right for those far-away Churches that have gone through the suffering. But what about us who have not suffered to the same extent?" To them I would say: The point is not whether you have suffered or whether you have not suffered. That is God's secret and if God needs for His plan your suffering, you will discover it in time.

No, the real question asked of you is whether you are willing to enter in communion, first of all, with the Cross, with the Crucified, and through Him with those who have suffered and are now reaping with joy. I think we all ought to ask God to permit us to enter into a very real, a spiritual but also a very practical, communion with them so that it may become clear, that we know what the Body of Christ is and that when one member suffers, all of the other members suffer with it. In view of the joy of harvesting time, let us pray:

Our Father, we thank Thee from the bottom of our hearts that when Thy judgments come upon the earth, they do not come only to punish us but, above all, to purify us and to save us from the hardness of our own hearts, to break us open for Thy word and Thy salvation. And we ask Thee to be permitted to enter into communion with all those whose suffering has not been in vain but whose suffering has been the preparation of the soil for the great harvesting time. Help us, O Lord, to remember the way of the Cross; for Jesus Christ's sake. Amen.

The Armor of God

THE MOST REVEREND ROBERT E. LUCEY, D.D., S.T.D.
Roman Catholic Archbishop of San Antonio, Texas

Archbishop Lucey is a fearless preacher, known and respected for the forcefulness of his sermons, especially those on labor and the rights of the workingman. Born in Los Angeles, California, he recognized the call to the priesthood and studied at St. Vincent's College and St. Patrick's Seminary. Then he took a four-year course in theology in the North American College in Rome, where he was graduated with an S.T.D. He was ordained to the priesthood on May 14, 1916.

In 1921, after serving as assistant pastor in several churches, he was appointed director of the Catholic Welfare Bureau of Los Angeles. In 1925 he was appointed pastor of St. Kevins Church, Los Angeles, and in 1929 he became pastor of St. Anthony's Church, Long Beach, California. His leadership led to his consecration as Bishop of Amarillo, Texas, on May 1, 1934; and seven years later he became Archbishop of San Antonio where he has won an enviable place in the community.

He is vice-president of the Catholic Conference on Industrial Problems, of the Catholic Association for International Peace, and is a member of the Texas State Committee on Postwar Planning. At present he is executive chairman of the Bishops' Committee for the Spanish Speaking. This committee is composed of the archbishops and bishops of the Southwest and was organized for the spiritual and social welfare of our Latin-American people.

This sermon was preached on Cap and Gown Day at Our Lady of the Lake, San Antonio, on November 5, 1944. In it his ability as a preacher can be seen in his discussion of the seeming paradoxes in Christianity in our modern world. He connects education, religion and life in a realistic and idealistic manner.

Sermon Thirty=seven

TEXT: Therefore take up the armor of God, that you may be able to resist in the evil day. EPHESIANS 6:13 (Confraternity Edition of the New Testament)

CHRISTIANITY is a religion of seeming paradoxes because it offers to its followers joy and gladness while demanding of them self-sacrifice and self-denial. Christianity involves strong purpose and peaceful certitude; it requires the highest personal energy and continual action. It promises tranquility and calls for the greatest heroism; for "the Kingdom of heaven suffereth violence and the violent bear it away." The Psalmist tells us that the life of man on earth is a warfare; we must therefore see in Christianity the religion of a soldier.

If the qualities of a good soldier were analyzed I think we might put in the first place that virtue which is known as a sense of responsibility. It seems fair to say that if a soldier is deeply conscious of his obligations to God and country he may be expected courageously to perform his allotted task and even to go beyond the call of duty. And if we apply this test to the soldiers of the cross, to the Christians of our time, we are constrained to declare that many of them are woefully lacking in a sense of responsibility.

I would not be understood as saying that many followers of Christ have no appreciation whatever of natural or revealed law. The truth is that an astonishing number of Christians have elected to practice certain virtues and to ignore others. The moral standards of our time seem to indicate that we may pick out from the full category of Christian virtues those that please our fancy and disregard the rest. In fact, we have wandered so far from the good life that some virtues seem to have no binding power whatever.

The average Christian will readily admit that the virtue of humility requires us to avoid vanity and pride; the virtue of chastity demands that we be pure; temperance calls upon us to use moderately our material goods, particularly food and drink. But there are social virtues whose binding power in the field of civic, political and economic welfare are scarcely recognized. One of the great tragedies of our time is the utter lack of social responsibility on the part of otherwise reputable Christians. These unfortunate men and women are unworthy of the name of soldiers. They have not fought for the things of Christ; they have not defended Christian principles in human relations; and many have not troubled themselves to discover what those principles are.

If there be those among us who would cast stones of accusation against

[216]

other nations let them call to mind our own blunders and crimes of the recent past. It was less than five years ago that we as a nation lacked the wisdom and the courage to defend, even in theory, the moral order of the world. Our concept of public morality was so low that we waved the white rag of neutrality in the face of unjust aggression. We declared publicly that we would treat with fine impartiality the ruthless aggressor and the innocent nation defending its homeland. Publicly we recognized no difference between black and white, between world morality and international crime. Fortunately our people have now come to realize that if the world moral order is not supported it will disintegrate.

In this country we are slowly moving toward a knowledge and practice of social justice. We have chosen justice as our ideal but in several departments of human relations we have not made it a reality. Much less have we as a people climbed the heights of heroism in the practice of justice and good will.

But we should not belittle our own progress. One of the most delicate, and one of the most perverted, departments of human life is that of race relations. To our great honor be it said that here in this lovely southland there are not lacking men and women of heroic stature who are determined to make Christianity operative among the people in the field of race relations even at the cost of personal sacrifice. They believe that Jesus Christ proclaimed a universal mandate when He said: "Love your neighbor as yourself." They believe that St. John the Apostle was terribly in earnest when he declared: "Everyone who hates his brother is a murderer" (I John 3:15).

Those of us who are members of the ancient Church should ponder the words of St. Paul: "And the bread that we break, is it not the partaking of the body of the Lord? Because the bread is one, we though many, are one body, all of us who partake of the one bread" (I Corinthians 10:16). Therefore, when people whose skin is dark receive Holy Communion they become one body with us in Christ. And shall we despise the body of the Lord, of which they and we are members? Too long have we bowed before a hollow and perverse tradition. Too long have we forgotten the charity of Christ. It must be pleasing to the heart of God that unhallowed manners are beginning to depart.

In the field of civic and political virtue apathy has been our scourge. This is the more regrettable because in a republic such as ours the people are responsible for their government. That unworthy representatives can repeatedly obtain public office emphasizes the lethargy of the people. This is a particularly hazardous situation in view of the enlarged function of government in our time. That the decrees of the civil power should vitally affect the lives of all citizens is not to be wondered at, much less condemned. It is the proper function of government to safeguard natural rights and to promote the common good with special solicitude for the poor and the weak. In our day the civil power is unjustly condemned for class legislation in favor of working people and farmers. The principle of such legislation is to be commended; in a specific case its value is to be judged by its wisdom.

The point which we wish to emphasize is that civil government is today more active and more powerful than ever before in the national and international life of the citizen. As a result there is no place for apathy in the political life of our people. Either we shall give anxious thought to problems of government or endure the consequences.

To give intelligent thought to problems of government is not easy. The qualifications of candidates for public office must be considered and the needs of the community or nation must be studied. The conduct of candidates who have never held public office is to some extent unpredictable but the voting record of those who have previously served is available to all and should be studied in the light of the common good. If such a candidate asks to be returned to office not because of his achievements but because he is a demagogue and rabble rouser; because he hates racial minorities and has established white supremacy to his own satisfaction—such a man should be consigned to political oblivion.

So far as the constituent elements of the common good are concerned judgment is not easy. In many countries of the world, including our own, there is a new awareness of the needs of the common people, but many citizens, some of them college graduates, do not know what types of legislation are actually conducive to justice and the common good. In our own country during the past ten years much social legislation has been enacted. Many civic leaders who understand the problems of public welfare have warmly welcomed these laws; other leaders have just as warmly condemned them. It is for this reason that we have recently established discussion clubs among a group of men so that at least some of our people will understand what we mean by social justice and the common good.

In Christian Europe an unwholesome situation has existed among the working classes for many years. The number of workers enrolled in socialist and communist labor unions was far greater than the membership of Christian labor unions. Perhaps now our brethren in Europe will pay the price of apathy. The lengthening shadow of Communism is cast upon the land.

Many thoughtful people are hoping that out of this tragedy of war, with all its sin and suffering, there may come to the leaders of the people the conviction that moral integrity is necessary for individuals and nations. While it is true that this conflict is causing a sad loss of spiritual values it must be remembered that the war is itself an effect rather than a cause. It was brought about by a general decline of morals; it was caused by crimes of selfishness, dishonesty, hatred, greed of gain and lust of power. These are moral considerations and the fact that these crimes were committed collectively by governments as well as by individuals only makes them worse.

Opposed to these crimes are the virtues of honesty and good will, fair dealing and social justice. The question logically arises, who can teach charity and justice to men? What institution deals in morality and the good life as its prime objective? Shall we find in government, in business, in the professions, in industry, in the natural sciences the message of sin and grace, of virtue and high heroism, of white integrity and a blessed immortality? Can any institution speak with authority of God and the human spirit? Unless there is a teacher with a divine mandate to interpret God's will to men there is no hope for the human race.

You who are students in this Church-related college know the answer. Only the science of religion gives any adequate knowledge of man's origin, nature and destiny. The Church is the teacher of religion and the custodian of the grace of God.

When we think of the two strong weapons of Christ's followers—religious truth and divine grace, we feel a sense of loss and frustration. Looking back through recent centuries we note that the enemies of God have made considerable progress toward their dark objective—the elimination of God from human life. By successive stages, intelligent creatures have shunted their Creator, to an alarming extent, from government, public life, education and the home. The movement culminated last year when Christian civilization stood on the brink of disaster. It was saved very largely by our own beloved country.

But the mystery of it all demands some explanation. A tremendous conflict has been waged by the enemies of God against His friends. The unbelievers were armed with falsehood and a denial of the supernatural; the friends of God were endowed with every weapon needed for the battle—the power of truth, the breastplate of justice, the gospel of peace, the shield of faith, the helmet of salvation and the sword of the spirit. Why could they not conquer with all of these?

One single answer would oversimplify the problem of the centuries. Certainly truth and grace should have conquered but we who carried the gospel in our hands have retreated before the powers of darkness. The enemies of God have been active, restless, dynamic; we, His friends, have been complacent.

The damage has been done. We have a world to reconstruct. It is a time for high heroism and deep devotion. You who wear the cap and gown today for the first time must play your part in the great adventure now unfolding. The College of Our Lady of the Lake has tried to make you good citizens and good soldiers. Beneath your cap and gown—unseen but very real, you carry the weapons of conquest; the shield of faith, the resistless power of truth, the breastplate of justice, the sword of the spirit. This is the armor of God. Wear it for Victory. And continue to wear it for peace.

Pearl Harbor—Feast of Our Lady's Assumption, 1945

His Eminence, Francis Cardinal Spellman, D.D.
Roman Catholic Archbishop of New York

Cardinal Spellman succeeded the late Cardinal Hayes in the great arch-diocese of New York and has given brilliant guidance to his people in their churches, their hospitals, their homes, their schools, and their personal lives. Born in Whitman, Massachusetts, May 4, 1889, he took his A.B. at Fordham University, his S.T.D. at the University of the Propaganda, Rome, in 1916, and was ordained at St. John Lateran, Rome, May 14, 1916. He celebrated his first Mass at the tomb of St. Peter in the Basilica of St. Peter in Vatican City, May 15, 1916.

He returned to Boston, served on the editorial staff of the Boston Pilot and as Assistant Chancellor of the Archdiocese of Boston, then returned to Rome as Attaché to the Secretary of State's Office at the Vatican from 1925 to 1932. In September of 1932 he was consecrated Titular Bishop of Sila by His Eminence Eugenio Cardinal Pacelli and was Auxiliary Bishop of Boston from 1932 to 1939. Pope Pius XII appointed him as Archbishop of New York on April 15, 1939, and he was installed at St. Patrick's Cathedral on May 23. Sequere Deum ("Follow God") was the motto he chose then. On December 11 of that year he was appointed Military Vicar for the Armed Forces of the United States and made two journeys overseas to minister to the religious needs of the men in the army, navy and air corps. In 1945 he traveled around the world on a 32,000 mile journey to visit the men in service, the chaplains and the wounded in many hospitals. He has frequently taken an entire day to go from bed to bed to visit every one of the fifteen hundred wounded in a military or naval hospital. He was created a Cardinal by His Holiness, Pope Pius XII at Christmas, 1945, in recognition of his world-wide service to the Catholics of the United States, and received the red hat in Rome in February, 1946.

His books are making a place for themselves, especially those in blank verse. He is the author of The Word of God, In the Footsteps of the Master, The Road to Victory, Action This Day, The Risen Soldier *and* No Greater Love *(1945).*

The sermon given here was preached at Pearl Harbor, Honolulu, Hawaii, on his famous round-the-world visitation, on August 15, 1945. In it he reminds us that there are lessons to be learned from Pearl Harbor and from the war and from God's grace. It is a historic sermon with a spiritual message.

Sermon Thirty=eight

THE morning of Sunday, December 7, 1941, brought the unnatural night of war to naturally beautiful Pearl Harbor. The next day was the feast of Our Lady's Immaculate Conception, the title under which the Blessed Virgin is represented in art as rising above the earth with her eyes set toward the vision of God in the peace of paradise. On that December 8, 1941, the world learned that through the unspeakable agonies and indescribable anguish of total war, the United States would, with its military might, defend its own liberties and embark on the task of purchasing liberty and security for other peoples. The destroyed and damaged ships in this harbor, the hundreds of planes wrecked, the smashed hangars, barracks and other military installations, the thousands of dead and wounded on this heavenly island, made Our Lady's feast in 1941 a day of terrible tears, a day of pitiful, prayerful pleading to Mary Immaculate, the patroness of all the Americas, a day of heroically courageous confidence in the might of the righteous.

But darkness covered the earth and in a few months the enemy overran an immense land and water area in southeastern Asia and the southwestern Pacific enslaving 125 million people. The invaders broke into the Indian Ocean and threatened the sea routes to India. They were at the northern portals of Australia. They had gained space, raw materials and manpower with which to form an empire that was self-sufficient. The serpent that artists depict as crushed to earth through the power of Mary our intercessor seemed to have escaped, and war with its hateful, death-dealing venom was spreading its poison throughout the world.

Today is August 15, 1945 at Pearl Harbor, less than four years after the unforgettable day of treachery and tragedy that shocked the civilized world. Again it is Our Lady's Day, a feast commemorating Mary's victory and triumph over sin and Satan, death and destruction, hate and horror. And thanks to God, and thanks to the valor of the men in our armed services, thanks to the support of the people at home, thanks to America's great natural resources and her inventive genius, industry and integrity, the scene and the situation is totally different today. How changed the mood of all of us on these islands! The war is over! America has triumphed and in the truth of her triumph mankind will once again find freedom and peace. In the light of this glorious day of grace and of victory, we may be joyful and grateful that our ships again can safely sail these waters; that our planes may wing their ways through friendly spaces on their missions of mercy and of commerce. Hangars, barracks and other installations have been repaired. Our dead have been reverently buried and our prayers for them carry our love to them in a better world. With our wounded hearts healing and with exultant spirit we chant the Introit of this day's holy Mass: "Let us all rejoice in the Lord, celebrating this feast in honor of the Blessed Virgin."

For the world in 1945, the Feast of Our Lady's Assumption gives us a firmer hope that we too may share in the Victory of Mary's Son over sin and the wages of sin that is death. Our sad experiences should give us also a keener appreciation of war's sin against man and nature, and make, or should make all of us, the more determined to destroy the diabolical tyranny that causes war. War is inhuman and unnatural, and this, the second world war in our generation, has been the most inhuman and unnatural of wars. Our scientific age has devised weapons of war undreamed of in ages past. We have unearthed secrets of nature and powers of nature and have in many ways overcome nature, but all this is fruitless and senseless if we cannot control our own human nature. Millions of dead and wounded men whose blood has crimsoned every land and every sea, proclaim to our shame the perversity of human nature in its wanton disregard and disrespect of human dignity. Add to this "the tears of nature" caused by the unnatural wounds inflicted on the beauties of nature and of art, as hundreds of thousands of tons of deadly explosives leave them in utter ruin! Man has divorced life from the divine until he is not only inhuman toward his fellow man, he is even unnatural in his attitude toward material things. But in God's Providence we pray that the wounds of war will one day be healed, the tears of men will be dried, and for all eternity spirit and matter will show forth the glory of God in man's relationship with his fellow man, that man's planning will be in accordance with God's law. And on this, Mary's day at Pearl Harbor, as we fervently hope and devoutly pray there will dawn a new era of peace, we speak our gratitude to God through Mary. But we must not forget that this cessation of hostilities does not mean peace, for when the guns of battle are silenced, political, social and moral wars must be fought and won. With heroic courage we must conquer our fear and lift our souls in prayer to Our Lady in her heavenly glory, to bless our country, to bless mankind with a peace that man by himself cannot gain by warfare, but can gain only through God's grace and man's good will!

The End of the Old Year

REVEREND ROBERT I. GANNON, S.J., D.D.

President, Fordham University (Roman Catholic), New York

The Reverend Robert I. Gannon, S.J., was born in New York in 1893. He was educated at Loyola School, New York, and Georgetown University, Washington, D.C. In 1913 he entered the Society of Jesus. From 1919 to 1923, he was instructor of English and philosophy at Fordham College. Soon he founded the "Play Shop" and in 1925 wrote The Technique of the One-Act Play.

After leaving Fordham, he made his theological studies at Woodstock and was ordained in 1926. After his ordination he was sent abroad for special studies, taking his S.T.D. from Gregorian University in Rome in 1927, and his M.A. from Cambridge (Christ's College), in 1930. Since then a shower of doctor's degrees has rained upon him, seven doctorates in five years—from Georgetown University, Manhattan College, Holy Cross College, Boston College, Columbia University, Bowdoin College and New York University.

In 1930, Father Gannon reopened St. Peter's College, Jersey City, which had been closed during the war, and became its dean. He opened Hudson College of Commerce and Finance, of which he was the first dean from 1933 to 1935. He remained as dean of St. Peter's until his appointment as President of Fordham University in June, 1936.

In 1937 he went to Venezuela on the invitation of President Lopez Contreras for consultation on school problems, and in 1942, received the Award of the New York Academy of Public Education for distinguished service in the field of Education. He is a trustee of Town Hall, an elective manager of the New York Botanical Garden, a trustee of the New York Zoölogical Society, a director of the Netherland-American Foundation, and a member of the Committee for International Economic Reconstruction.

Father Gannon's most interesting pulpit assignment was in air-raided London, where he preached the Lent in 1943 at Westminster Cathedral as the guest of the late Cardinal Hinsley.

"The End of the Old Year" was delivered over the Mutual Broadcasting System's Radio Chapel Catholic Program on Sunday, December 31, 1944. In it Father Gannon makes a significance of the new year a matter of faith and hope. It has the simplicity of a truly great preacher.

Sermon Thirty=nine

TE DEUM LAUDAMUS has been for sixteen hundred years or more the Church's stately and courteous way of saying "Thanks be to God." No one knows who wrote it, but eleven hundred years before the Pilgrims landed on Plymouth Rock, one thousand years before Martin Luther nailed his defiance to the church door in Wittenberg, nine hundred years before Columbus saw the palm trees of the New World, five hundred years before the First Crusade, your ancestors were singing the same old hymn *Te Deum Laudamus, Te Dominum Confitemur.* If the barbarians passed by without sacking the cathedral, *Te Deum Laudamus.* If a Saracen fleet of pirate ships were sunk, *Te Deum Laudamus.* If a Pope were crowned, or a little son born to the Emperor; if a war were ended or a royal marriage begun; if the plague had ceased or the crops were abundant, *Te Deum Laudamus, Te Dominum Confitemur*; and always at the end of the year, with its mingled memories, bitter and sweet, its crosses and its crowns, its smiles and its tears, the faithful would see the old year out with a "Thank you, Lord God" on their lips.

Our pagan neighbors have always said it was a sign of our stupidity or cowardice. They have never been able to find much for which they could thank anybody, least of all their God.

But that is not true of us. We have seen widows standing by open graves, men walking the streets in search of jobs, cripples strapped to boards in city hospitals—who could sing *Te Deum* on New Year's Eve. Only last week, at Fordham, we had a Solemn High Mass for the 125 boys who left us it seems only yesterday, to fight for their country, who fought bravely and will not return. It was the Octave of the Immaculate Conception and the Mass was sung in white vestments, with flowers on the altar. They were so young, so fine, so successful, and we felt so grateful to have had them even for a year or two. At Communion time the mothers' faces—and here and there a young widow's—were wet with tears. Whose wouldn't be? But meet them later, and they were calm, resigned, cheerful—no bitterness, no rebellion, perfect understanding. Oh, you and I know plenty of people who can be happy although they have to cry sometimes; people who can be happy because they can hope; people who will be singing the *Te Deum* tonight after three years of dreadful war, singing it for the world's blessings, singing it for their country's blessings and for their own small blessings too.

Some will certainly ask with astonishment what blessings have come to the shattered and bleeding old world this year? Did the future ever look so black before? Was there ever such moral deterioration, such international perfidy, such universal suffering? Can anything, for example, in the annals of Prussia or Tsarist Russia surpass the cynicism with which Poland is being again partitioned? Did we not all agree that Poland was the acid test of our ideals? That by our faithfulness to that gallant Republic which was, after all, the first champion to strike a blow at the Absolute State, a Republic which never surrendered but fought on with tremendous gallantry in Italy, France, Africa and the Soviet—did we not agree that by our faithfulness to Poland could be judged the sincerity of our aims in the present war? Yes, we did. And is it not true that people in the street are now defining an optimist as one who thinks that the fate of the Atlantic Charter is uncertain? Yes, I suppose they are. Then, if our ideals have been slaughtered with our sons on the altar of power politics, where are the blessings for which the world can join in singing a *Te Deum* for 1944? Well, two, at least, of the immense pagan states threatening civilization have had to change their plans. That is something. Whatever Europe does become eventually we know now it will not be a great Nazi fortress; and Australia, New Zealand and the Philippine Islands will not have to bow from the hips to the Emperor of Japan. For that much, *Te Deum Laudamus*. As for gloomy possibilities that could be mentioned—if we needed sobering—they are, after all, future bridges and can wait for crossing until we come to them. Moreover, the Atlantic Charter, while desperately ill, is not quite dead. The United States has not surrendered yet. Who knows—we may never have to bend our necks and dip our flags on this crucial issue? So for the fact that we still have our honor, *Te Deum Laudamus*. As for our native land, its blessings are much more obvious than the whole wide world's. Not a bomb has fallen here. Not a child has been killed. Not one foot of land has felt the tread of a foreign hobnail boot. Our churches, schools and factories are intact. We have plenty of good food and our Navy is the greatest in the history of the world. Moreover, we have learned a great deal—for a price—about the nature of Europe in the last twelve months, some of it disillusioning, perhaps, but invaluable for the future; and we have awakened in the nick of time to the necessity of learning more about South America. *Te Deum Laudamus*. It is true that as a people we have done little to prevent the steady deterioration of our home life. Our record for broken families is, unfortunately, worse than ever —even Japan would be ashamed of it. So the hymn continues, *Salvum fac populum tuum Domine* ("Save Thy people Lord"). But in the midst of this creeping death we find thousands of American men and women who have this year, because of this very war, awakened to a new set of spiritual values and are living their lives now for the glory of God and the good of their neighbor. *Extolle illos*, sings the Church, *usque in aeternum*.

Thus it is always possible to dwell on the bright as well as on the dark side of any year, and we regard it as part of the heritage of our Faith that there has never been in history a year so dark that we could not see the road ahead of us. It is otherwise of course with the poor souls around us who have no faith at all. Self-sufficient men and women who have been living all these years for their own health, culture and comfort can hardly be surprised if life looks today like a rather bitter joke. To them it must seem obvious that most of the people in the world have nothing to live for because for so many many millions there can be no promise of health or culture or the simplest kind of comfort, and even here, where the war has hardly touched us, and even for the few who have every advantage of wealth and position, health, culture and comfort are such terribly fleeting things! That is why the average pagan is so depressed on New Year's Eve; why he needs so much distraction, so much artificial stimulation. There is nothing that he wants to remember. That is why the spirit of the modern world is a spirit of partially concealed despair. That is why you and I are so out of step with the modern spirit. It is not that we are blindly idealistic. We are the genuine realists. We know as much about real trouble as any pagan in the country; much more in fact. For we can see right through trouble to something beyond—we can hope. That is the difference.

So that when we say "Chins up" on New Year's Eve, it is not from any delusion that "all's right with the world" but from the conviction that "God's in His Heaven" which is a very different thing. We know that the times are frequently out of joint—so frequently that each generation thinks its own the worst; we know that good men are always being trampled on and that beasts too frequently wear the ermine—that such has always been the case and always will be. We know that with regard to human progress, there is as much devolution as evolution. We know that without the grace of God man is just as greedy and cruel and dirty as he ever was. Consequently we are surprised at nothing we hear about human depravity in the war. War has always brought out the worst in human nature as well as the best, and always will, and when I say always I mean always. For war will be with us as long as man's will is free and his passions are disorderly.

It should be clear then that we never have to deceive ourselves in order to sing the *Te Deum* on New Year's Eve, we never have to blink the facts. If you and I are in the state of Grace no matter what our other anxieties may be, we can thank God for the greatest gift in His giving His friendship. We can also look out into the dense fog of the future without too much uneasiness, not because we are deluded as pagans say, but rather because we know what it is all about. For we do not expect that everything is going to happen for the best, but that no matter what happens God can always bring good out of evil. We shall not be disillusioned if wrongs are not righted in this life. We know there are some clouds that have no silver lining except what comes to them from the white light of eternity; we know that there are plenty of lifelong roads without any turning whatever. We haven't the heart to tell every poor man we meet that his ship will surely come in some day because it probably will not. Most ships never do; the vast majority of human beings die uncomfortably poor. Yet we sing our *Te Deum Laudamus* because we know that even if men are sometimes dull and stupid and downright wicked and life is too often unfair, there is nothing as stupid, nothing as wicked, nothing as unfair to God as the sin of despair. In a word, we look squarely at life and say, "Life is bitter." Of course it is. "Life is a warfare." But what of it? Who ever believed that this silly round of weeks and months and years with its monotony, its meanness, and its heartbreaks—who ever believed that that was the whole story? Only the fool who hath said in his heart, "There is no God."

So, *Te Deum Laudamus, Te Dominum Confitemur.* On our way out of church tonight we shall shade our eyes from the glare of the city and look into the depths of a winter sky. There planets and stars innumerable marching rank on rank through space will remind us that another year has gone. It is as far beyond recall as 1492. Some things it brought, we shall always remember; some things we shall try to forget. For some things we shall say an act of contrition. What then of the coming year? What of 1945? Will that be in the main prosperity or disaster? Listen. The Universal Church is finishing its ancient hymn with perfect confidence that no matter what comes, we can always avoid the greatest possible disaster: "Deign Lord," we hear it sing, "this day to keep us without sin," and then with solemn fervor as the old chant ends, "Let Thy mercy be upon us Lord, because we have hoped in Thee." *In Te Domine speravi, Non confundar in aeternum* ("In Thee Lord have I hoped, I shall not be confounded forever").

The Most Thrilling Rescue Story in the World

REVEREND HARRY EMERSON FOSDICK, D.D., LL.D.
Minister, The Riverside Church, New York

Dr. Fosdick is one of the great preachers of our time. Whenever he speaks the auditorium of the Riverside Church is filled on Sunday or Wednesday. Protestant visitors to New York feel that they must hear Dr. Fosdick in person after hearing him at home on the radio.

Born in Buffalo in 1878, his ancestry is typically American, a family of hard working people engaged in various trades and professions.

He was educated at Colgate University, Colgate Divinity School, Union Theological Seminary and Columbia University. In recognition of his achievements in the Church, Colgate, New York, Brown, Yale, Glasgow, Princeton,

Boston, Ohio, Columbia, Michigan, Rochester and Harvard universities have conferred the honorary doctorate upon him.

Upon graduation from Union Theological Seminary in 1904, he became pastor of First Baptist Church in Montclair, New Jersey, for eleven years. During part of that time he was instructor in the Department of Practical Theology in Union Theological Seminary, and in 1915 he became Morris K. Jesup Professor of Practical Theology, giving major time to seminary and preaching each Sunday in one of the universities.

During the first World War in Europe he spoke throughout Great Britain under the British Ministry of Information and among American troops under the Y.M.C.A. in France. After the war his professorship in the Seminary was resumed and he became Stated Preacher at First Presbyterian Church, New York, January, 1919, which latter connection was severed on March 1, 1925. He has traveled widely in Egypt, Palestine, China, Japan, England and Scotland, speaking for important conferences in most of these countries.

In October, 1926, he assumed the pastorate of Park Avenue Baptist Church, New York, and some time afterward entered upon the building of the Riverside Church, now one of the most magnificent churches of the entire United States.

His twenty-one books have reached a vast audience and many of them have been translated into French, Danish, Norwegian, Swedish, Spanish, Portuguese, Chinese, Japanese, Hindustani, Arabic and Bulgarian. The Second Mile, The Manhood of the Master, The Meaning of Prayer, Twelve Tests of Character, The Modern Use of the Bible, On Being a Real Person and A Great Time To Be Alive, mark him as one of the great voices of our day.

In this beautiful sermon, preached in the Riverside Church on Palm Sunday, March 25, 1945, Dr. Fosdick brings the story of Jesus' last week in Jerusalem into clear perspective and makes it meaningful to all. His discussion of war and saviorhood, of over-simplified philosophies, and the message of Holy Week are all in his devout presentation of the Christ, the Saviour, and man's need of him.

Sermon Forty

NOTHING is so thrilling as a rescue story. Sometime since, a private soldier badly wounded in the South Pacific and hospitalized home, was still trying to discover the name of a corporal who had saved his life. In a desperate situation, all hope gone, this corporal, whom in his agony the soldier did not recognize, crawled to his help, carried him to safety, and disappeared. Who was he? the soldier wants to know, and always will want to know. For nothing goes deeper with us and takes hold harder than the experience of sacrificial saviorhood when the need is deep.

During that last week of the Master's life in Jerusalem two symbols stand out—palm branches and the cross. The palm branches represent the acclaim of shouting crowds, greeting a Messiah coming to his own; the cross represents tragedy. Why did not Christianity take the palm branch as its symbol, a joyful token to be happy over, with its recollections of hosannas to the conquering Christ? Yet we know well that the Christian Church would never have survived the centuries with only a palm branch over its high altar. The cross goes deeper, oh, much deeper! deeper than anything else into the heart of man's experience—need and deliverance; a rescue story; sin and saviorhood there on Calvary, locked in desperate encounter, with the fate of the world depending on which of those two, sin or saviorhood, in the end shall win.

The central issue of history is this struggle between sin and saviorhood, and the cross of Christ is the climactic exhibition of them both. There on Calvary one sees sin at its very worst, rejecting and slaying the divinest personality that ever came to earth. Yet there on Calvary one also sees sacrificial saviorhood at its best, the supreme rescue story in man's history, one who did not need to do it voluntarily taking on himself the burden of the world's iniquity that he might deliver men and blaze the trail for a kingdom of righteousness on earth. Friends, that's life, the real thing and no fooling, this desperate struggle between sin at its worst and saviorhood at its best!

This should be real to us now. Behind this outward war is a deeper war that no military victory alone will settle, a war not simply between nations but within nations, and within every individual life—sin against saviorhood, and saviorhood against sin. Who now, looking at this world, can doubt the reality of that struggle? Mankind needs a rescue story, saviorhood that can grapple with this sin of ours and overthrow it. Of that tremendous encounter between devilishness and deliverance the cross is the symbol—both there, sin at its darkest, and saviorhood at its best. So from the beginning to the end of the New Testament Jesus is called savior, "Our Saviour, Jesus Christ." We have become used to that, but it is nothing to become used to. Those first Christians thought of him in terms of the redeeming thing he did as vividly as that soldier thinks of the corporal who delivered him from death. Christ, to them, was the thrilling center of a rescue story.

One of the first things that this struggle between sin and saviorhood says to us, is, Don't oversimplify your philosophy of life. We all are tempted to do that, to seek some neat formula that will smooth out, at least in theory, life's disharmonies and conflicts and help us to forget them. Men, for example, adopt a Browningesque optimism, saying,

> God's in his heaven—
> All's right with the world![1]

and so go on to say that evil is not real, but only the shadow cast by good. As the rising sun is real, so is goodness, they say, but all the evil of the world

[1] "Pippa Passes."

is but the passive, transient shade some temporary obstacle casts as the sun rises. That is a childish philosophy! Sin is no mere shadow cast by good, but a demonic, devastating power. It can incarnate itself in a moral maniac who plunges the whole world into such collective agony as mankind has never, in all its history, endured before.

Or men get at this false sense of cheerful harmony in life by working out elaborate philosophies, as Herbert Spencer did, baptizing evolution with optimism and saying—believe it or not, Herbert Spencer did say this— "Progress . . . is not an accident, but a necessity. We are doomed to progress."[2] Well, that too is a childish philosophy! We are not doomed to progress! We do evolve socially into the possession of such scientific power as men never had before, and then diabolical sin lays hold on that power and with it civilization may yet commit suicide. We do evolve socially into a world neighborhood, and then pride and selfishness corrupt all the new contacts and propinquities until the more the possibilities of brotherhood are here, the more the actualities of hatred, prejudice and war are terrible.

Such oversimplified philosophies will no longer do. The Devil is real. I do not mean, of course, that he is an individual, with horns and a tail; he is much worse than that—the symbol of a positive, devastating force in history that can destroy every human hope. Such is the realistic fact, and if it were the only fact pessimism would be the consequence. So Gibbon saw history. "History," he said, "is little more than the register of the crimes, follies, and misfortunes of mankind."[3]

Well, Holy Week brings us another message, a stirring message. All that Gibbon saw in history—crime, folly, misfortune—is here, but something else is here too—saviorhood, voluntarily assuming the burden of the world's needs and redeeming men. The central fact of history is no easygoing harmony but this fierce conflict on which the whole outcome of our human adventure depends—saviorhood against sin.

The story runs that when things were at their worst during the Civil War, hopelessness rampant and Lincoln besmeared with every kind of calumny and abuse, a friend said to him, "Why not resign, and let them sink or swim?" And Lincoln slowly and sadly answered, "If I resign, they perish."[4] How did Gibbon ever miss that factor in history—spirits who will not resign, but shouldering the burden of the world, that they do not need to shoulder, take up their cross and deliver men?

Let us say it to ourselves this Palm Sunday as we see the Master entering Jerusalem amid the crowd's hosannas—saviorhood is in this world. Darkest Africa, but the David Livingstones too; dreadful diseases, but the Pasteurs and their successors too; appalling ignorance, but the Horace Manns and their colleagues too; the Devil and all his representatives, but Christ too.

[2] *Social Statics*, chap. II, "The Evanescence of Evil," p. 80.
[3] *The History of the Decline and Fall of the Roman Empire*, vol. I., p. 33.
[4] As quoted in Leslie D. Weatherhead, *A Plain Man Looks at the Cross*, p. 139.

Lowly and riding on an ass's foal he came to the great city, a savior, and there he did face sin as all saviors do—the sin of ecclesiastics who did not wish their orthodox establishment disturbed, of businessmen wanting no money changers' tables overturned to their profit's hurt, of politicians like Caiaphas playing their clever, selfish games, of cowards like Pilate washing his hands of his responsibility, of Roman soldiers doing whatever cruelty they were commanded, of the crowd persuaded by skillful propaganda to cry, "Crucify him!" So, as always, saviorhood faced sin, but today, nearly two thousand years afterwards, it's not the sin we are celebrating, but the saviorhood. Thank God, that is in the world!

Now, because the central fact of history is this struggle between sin and saviorhood never expect Christianity to pipe down on the reality and terribleness of sin. So long as Christianity is here at all it will be insisting on sin's reality, its power and its catastrophe. Where, for example, is intellectual dishonesty most clearly seen as an evil, and most insistently hated? You had better go to a scientific laboratory for that, for in a scientific laboratory the eyes of men are centered on a great good, indispensable to the progress of the truth—intellectual honesty, objective, disinterested, uncompromising. It is there that the curse of intellectual dishonesty would be most strongly felt and hated. So not in dives and dens and moral slums of life is sin best understood and its diabolical reality most powerfully felt, but in the gospel of Christ, for there the central struggle of human life stands out, no oversimplified Pollyanna philosophy but the real truth—a great conflict, sin against saviorhood, and saviorhood against sin.

Consider further that all deep understanding of Christ's meaning depends on seeing this. It is easy to make a hero of Jesus, as though that category could sum up his meaning. Well, he is a hero! It is easy to describe Jesus as a spiritual genius; his profound influence on human thought suggests that category. Well, he is a genius! It is easy to make an ideal of him; his personal quality, far ahead of us like a pillar of cloud by day and a fire by night, suggests that category. Well, he is the ideal! But when we have called him hero, genius, ideal, or what you will, we must go far beyond that if we are to apprehend his meaning. He is Saviour, the heart and center of a rescue story.

So to the Jews, Moses is a hero, a genius, an ideal. But ask the Jews why all these centuries his name has been their stimulus and strength, and this profounder fact emerges—a slave people in Egypt, hopeless under Pharaoh's tyranny, were emancipated by a savior. What a thrilling experience that is, familiar in our day, as hapless folk long imprisoned in Philippine concentration camps know well, who have heard the incredible good tidings that a deliverer has come!

This Holy Week celebrates that exciting truth at the heart of the Christian gospel. There is saviorhood in this world, and in it is a quality which, really seen, lays hold on us as nothing else ever does. In a rural section of southern

California, we are told, a Mexican mother died, leaving a family of eight children. The oldest girl, not yet seventeen, was a tiny thing and upon her frail shoulders fell the burden of caring for the family. The neighbors watched her as, taking up the task with courage, she kept the children clean, well fed, and in school. One day a friend complimented her on her achievement and she replied, "I can't take any credit for something I have to do." "But, my dear," said the friend, "you don't have to. You could get out of it." The girl paused for a moment, and said, "Yes, that's true. But what about the *have to* that's inside of me?"[5] So! The *have to* that is inside of me! All saviorhood starts there.

Florence Nightingale need not have gone to nurse the wounded in the Crimean War; no outward pressure urged her on; all the circumstances were against her going, the military authorities themselves dubious or antagonistic, and her own family calling her crazy for even thinking of it. But there was that *have to* inside of her. We had better be grateful when we think of this, for all the background of our lives is full of it and every decent and lovely thing we have or hope for has come from it—men and women who needn't have done what they did, but who were compelled by a *have to* inside of them.

Ah, Christ, you had that! That is what took you to the cross. "I lay down my life. . . . No man taketh it from me, but I lay it down of myself."[6] "Greater love hath no man than this, that a man lay down his life for his friends."[7] What a *have to* inside of him! So human life is a struggle between sin—whatever debases and debauches life—and the great succession of the saviors, with the *have to* inside of them. On which side of that issue are we? Let no one spend this Holy Week without facing that question! As the Negro spiritual puts it, "Were you there, when they crucified my Lord?" In one of Rembrandt's paintings of the crucifixion, one's eyes naturally rest at first upon the central figures in the scene; but by and by, in the shadows, one sees another figure—Rembrandt, himself—no doubt about it—Rembrandt himself, helping to crucify Christ. In a world whose central fact is the struggle between sin and saviorhood, on the wrong side of the issue!

Thus our thought brings us inevitably a further step to an intimate personal matter. This struggle between sin and saviorhood is going on inside every one of us. Let's not mince words about that. When we say "sin" we are not meaning little, trivial moralisms, but the gigantic forces of destructive evil that corrupt and devastate the world. Look what sin is doing to humanity today, this most tragic Holy Week mankind ever spent, with such barbarity let loose and such chaos doomed to follow it as earth never before staggered under. And just as all the goodness in human life must first of all

[5] *Reader's Digest*, March, 1945, p. 90: "The Still, Small Voice," contributed by Verna Rallings.
[6] John 10:17, 18.
[7] John 15:13.

be goodness inside people, one by one, so all the sin in human life is first of all evil inside men's souls. This awful spectacle that now confronts us is like a moving picture on a vast screen, but back of it are the small films, the incredibly small films, of individual people in whom all the picture has its origin and its explanation, the world's sin only the enlargement of personal sin. We can't thrust off this struggle of sin against saviorhood and saviorhood against sin as though it were public only; it is private, the central issue of each person's life. As another put it, "No possible rearrangement of bad eggs can ever make a good omelet."

After many years of personal counseling, don't tell me that the Devil, in the sense we mean, is not real in individual experience. See what he does! He approaches a man, saying, Come on, be free; don't be a slave, be free! And a man follows him, free to do as he pleases, until one day he wakes up to the ghastly fact that he is no longer free to stop. Lured by the bait of freedom he has landed in the trap of habit, and the classic words of William James about the man who kept saying, "I won't count this time!" come true. "He may not count it," says James, "and a kind Heaven may not count it; but it is being counted none the less. Down among his nerve cells and fibres the molecules are counting it, registering and storing it up to be used against him when the next temptation comes."[8] Believe me, the power of sin to become habitual is dreadfully real!

Or, again, the Devil says to a man, Here is a pleasure; come on, enjoy it! To be sure, it's wrong, but you can get away with it. What is life for, if not to enjoy yourself? So the man follows him, fascinated in expectation by the indulgence that he plans. But then the day comes when the evil passes from anticipation, through committal into memory, and something momentous and dreadful happens, as the sense of guilt takes hold, settles down, will not let go. Then like a bell buoy on a lonely ocean, tolled by the restless sea, remorse tolls in the man's unquiet soul and will not be stilled. My word, when one deals with real, honest-to-goodness sin, how different the retrospect can be from the prospect!

Or, again, the Devil says to a man, Be yourself! Why this sense of responsibility for everybody else? Live your own life; do as you please! So the man follows him, does as he pleases, and then the day comes when the consequences begin to fall—oh, not upon himself, on someone else—his family, his children, his friends. If only he could keep the consequences of his sin within the confines of his own life and face them there himself, alone! But he cannot. Always the innocent suffer for our sins.

Friends, this thing we are talking about is true. The sin that ruins the world roots back into the sins we personally consent to, and about the whole duty of man is first to accept saviorhood for himself—forgiveness, cleansing, re-established fellowship with God, divine resources of moral power; and,

[8] *Psychology*, chapter X, "Habit" (New York: Henry Holt & Company, 1892), p. 150.

then, to join the saving forces in the world, the men and women with a compelling *have to* inside of them.

The one thing that makes it worth while preaching this sermon is that that dual experience—accepting saviorhood for ourselves and then going out to be saviors—could happen here now to some of us. Well, it had better happen to a lot of people, for, friends, we cannot take civilization for granted any more—not any more! That's what we've been doing through many an optimistic decade—taking civilization for granted. Of course, civilization! As one expected the sun to rise on the morrow, so one expected civilization. But look now at this vast catastrophe and collapse of civilization! Now it is going to be a struggle, the most fateful struggle in human history—sin against saviorhood, and saviorhood against sin—and the saviors must first of all be saved themselves, as Moses met God alone at the burning bush before he confronted Pharoah in the public court. So may some of us this week face the cross of Christ, and seeing there sin and saviorhood locked in that desperate encounter, choose—choose Christ's side!

Take No Thought What Ye Shall Speak

REVEREND J. V. MOLDENHAWER, D.D., LL.D.
Pastor, First Presbyterian Church, New York

Prior to his coming to historic First Presbyterian Church in 1927, Dr. Moldenhawer was, for twenty-two years, pastor of the Second Presbyterian Church in Albany, New York. Through the long years, he has always been a speaker of sincerity and deep insight.

Julius Valdemar Moldenhawer was born in Tavastehus, Finland, in 1877, and was brought to America at the age of two. He was naturalized in 1905, received his college education at Southwestern (now at Memphis, Tennessee), and took his theological studies at Union Theological Seminary, New York. He was ordained in 1900, and his whole ministry has been in the Presbyterian church in the United States of America. The honorary degree of D.D. was conferred upon him by Western Reserve University and by Hamilton College, and the Litt.D. by Southwestern University.

A man of many interests, Dr. Moldenhawer is a trustee of Mackenzie College, São Paulo, Brazil; a director of Union Theological Seminary; a member of the Board of Managers of the Presbyterian Hospital, New York, and a trustee of Sailors' Snug Harbor.

He is deeply interested in books, is widely read, and is the author of Fairest Lord Jesus *and* The Voice of Books.

This sermon was preached on February 25, 1945 and illustrates Dr. Moldenhawer's genius for presenting the Gospel in language which grips men's minds and which troubles their consciences. He fixes attention upon "the great business of the declaration of the Word of God by word of mouth." It is a sermon which Dr. Moldenhawer preached to himself and thus it is a fitting sermon for thousands of other men.

Sermon Forty=one

THE text is in the Gospel according to St. Matthew, the 10th Chapter, a part of the 19th verse:

> Take no thought how or what ye shall speak.

This is one of those extraordinary sayings of our Lord that have moved so many minds to question. Indeed, they have moved many minds to a considerable and unjustified ingenuity of explanation that has more than once resulted in not explaining, but explaining away.

As I shall try to show you, there is something of profound significance in these words that are spoken by our Lord as he sends out the twelve disciples on their mission. How little we know about that mission, and how gladly would we know more about it. How little attention we have paid to it, yet how stirring are many of its familiar phrases.

That advice about choosing the kind of house where the people are glad to receive you! That terrible warning that if they will not hearken, the preacher is to shake off the dust of his feet against them! The prophecy of heavy judgment against those communities that will have nothing to do with the preaching of the Word!

There is more than a little to think about here, and yet how little we know about it. And what a revelation in our Lord's declaration of the true business of discipleship.

Let us consider what that business is. It is the spread of the Gospel by deed and by word. We are by no means to forget the deed. At such a time as this it is particularly easy for us in the Christian Church to remember the significance of the spreading of the Gospel by good deeds. When we think of what has happened in the lands which we call the missionary lands, I suppose it occurs to all of us that at least a good half of the story of what the missionary enterprise has done is in terms of the unceasing good works that have been performed there by the men and women who have been and are our missionaries in those far and often dangerous places.

We never hear, surely any one of us, about what is going on now, without having our minds refreshed with the thought that as in the time of the disciples, so in the time of the service of Christ, even today, it is not forgotten that a great part of the spreading of the Gospel is the spreading of it by the sort of deeds that the Lord Jesus did and that the Lord Jesus loved. And whenever we read the story of another group of persons who have been set free, how glad we are to think that there may be and probably are among those persons many whose stay in foreign parts was for no other reason than that they might continue to serve the people among whom they lived. If there is anything that we as Americans and Christians have a right to be proud of, it is the record of those who have thus spread the Gospel of the Lord Jesus Christ.

Around and underneath and above and interfused with everything I shall say about the declaration of the Word is this—my sure conviction that the service of God through deeds of goodness is of the first importance and must go on even to the end of the story.

Today I mean to fix your attention upon the great business of the declaration of the Word of God by word of mouth. I want you to note that the whole enterprise is conceived as undertaken in the teeth of a sharp hostility. The world is seen as definitely unfriendly to the enterprise on which Christ sends those men out. He does not say to them, even after he says they are to be as wise as serpents and as harmless as doves—he does not say to them, "If you are as wise as serpents and as harmless as doves everyone will be kind to you." Nothing of the sort. What he says is this: "I send you out as sheep in the midst of wolves." A sheep in a world of wolves hasn't much of a chance. That is intended to be the plain description by our Lord of the condition of the men who are going out to proclaim his word.

He says, "Beware of men. They will deliver you up. They will scourge you." Then he goes on, "You shall be brought before governors." The Greek word for "governor" might be easily translated "leader"—making us think at once of Der Führer and Il Duce. Yes, said our Lord, their leaders will take hold of you and you will have to plead your cause before them. And it shall happen, he says, for "my sake." There again, if it is translated literally from the Greek, it has a very sharp sound. Why do they persecute you? "Because of me." "You shall be hated by all men," he says again, "because of my name."

Against this background is his great direction of behavior given. What he says is for the use of Christians when the time comes in which they are challenged to defend their faith; and they are plainly warned that they will be called upon to defend it.

Remember the mounting hostility to Christ in the last days of his earthly mission. Remember that the early Christian Church accepted the fact that the Christian Gospel was in conflict with the world. Before we are fit to respond to the trumpet tones of our Lord's command, we must shed the illusion that the world is naturally friendly to the Gospel of Christ. It is not. The mind of a single man here and there may be naturally Christian, but the mind of the world is not naturally Christian, nor has it ever been. Most of the world, remember—most of that world which we so cheerfully talk about regenerating, about which we with almost fatuous confidence talk about setting on its feet again—that great world about which we say that we are going to make in it a peace that shall be just and lasting—that world, dearly beloved brethren, is still preponderantly non-Christian, and a great part of that non-Christian world is not only non-Christian, it is anti-Christian. And surely we have had lessons enough in the last ten years to see how easy, even in lands which are supposed to be Christian—how dreadfully easy it is for a popular agitator to stir into lively existence emotions and purposes that are deeply anti-Christian.

I beg you to believe that there is nothing that shocks me more, nothing makes me more afraid in this, my own country, than when I hear, as unhappily I do, not infrequently, men echoing here their old, minor reverberations of the hates of the European scene. Every time I hear a man say that something or other "is to be expected of a Jew," and that which he expects is evidently something discreditable, I say, "You have but a little soul!" And I think of "Tomlinson"—and of the devil saying, "but the roots of sin are there."

No, it is not a world that is on the whole friendly to the Lord Jesus Christ.

That being realized, we are prepared to hear and reflect upon the great words, at once so thrilling and so disturbing, which are the text of this sermon. Let me read them again. First comes the direction. "When they deliver you up . . ." Can you think of yourself in such a position? It has happened to thousands of people in Europe who, twenty years ago, never dreamed it could happen. Suppose it happened to you. Suppose it happened to us that a government actually hostile to the whole mind of Christ, like certain of those on the other side, should be established here. Suppose we are brought before the authorities. Then the word comes, "when they deliver you up, take no thought how or what ye shall speak."

There follows the profound reason for this drastic and seemingly perilous piece of advice. "For it shall be given you in that same hour what ye shall speak."

And again the second reason, "For it is not ye that speak, but the Spirit of your Father which speaketh in you."

Now let us go back and take up the direction itself. "Take no thought what ye shall speak." See how it is meant to put rigidity into the spine of a speaker. See how it warns him that no time is to be wasted in conciliating his audience. See how it insists that no attention is to be given to a disgraceful policy of intellectual appeasement.

Think how the leaves of the Bible shine and crackle with the multiplied instances of this uncalculated eloquence of pure fidelity. Think of a scene like that in which a prophet named Nathan, enters the presence of his king, a man whom he loves, to tell that king about his sin. Think of that king having to listen to a prophet who stands before him and tells him the evil he has done in slaying his good servant and taking to himself that good man's wife. "Thou art the man!"

Think of Stephen before the council, and of his bitterly true story of God's patience and of the people's repeated disobedience.

I suppose that was one of the most unpopular addresses ever delivered! Yet that most unpopular address was the introduction to one of the most glorious scenes in the history of the Church, namely, the death of the first Christian martyr. We can well imagine how little forethought Stephen must have given to what he was saying when, after that rushing, historical denunciation he concludes, "Ye stiffnecked, ye do always resist the Holy Ghost: as your fathers did, so do ye. They killed those who prophesied the coming of the Just One, of whom ye have now been betrayers and murderers."

That is the kind of thing that comes out when a man does not calculate too carefully beforehand what he is going to say. Shall we not thank God for it!

Think of the glorious record of reckless loyalty that has accumulated fresh interest throughout history. Think of Anne Askew. I love that story because it is so clear that a great deal of her trial and its irritating quality is due purely to the fact that her inquisitors are dealing with a woman. It irks them no end that she is so terribly quick. It pains them beyond belief that this mere female—and females were supposed to keep quiet before men—that this female should say such telling and such extremely effective things. I think one of the reasons why they finally burned Anne Askew was the mere fact that they couldn't bear to listen to her retorts any longer. And so, in spite of the fact that the Bishop of London, Bonner, who was no softhearted person, did what he could to save her, nevertheless she was not saved.

Again and again, as in the case of Anne Askew and Jeanne d'Arc, it is shown how these apparently helpless and quite inexperienced amateurs in the hands of hardened professionals show fresh and keen and truthful, while their inquisitors are no better than careful and elaborate liars.

That is one of the reasons why the story of the martyrs is such a wonderful story. They are always—as we say in American slang—they are always "speaking out of turn." And in speaking out of turn, merely by not preparing themselves carefully to make as good an impression as they can, they make instead an impression upon the whole course of human events!

I dare say Hugh Latimer could not have even momentarily rehearsed the famous words with which he went to the stake. How they can be repeated without being tired of them! He didn't plan those words. But even as he is on his way to the place where he is to be burned, he thinks of the fire—and he thinks of a light—and he thinks of him who came to bring fire on the earth—he thinks of him who is the Light of the World, and he cries, "Be of good cheer, Brother Ridley, for by the grace of God we shall light in England this day such a candle as will not soon be put out."

These are the glorious, unrehearsed, and unpremeditated sayings.

Then comes the explanation—the first one: "For it shall be given you in that hour what ye shall speak."

There have been, of course, some very foolish applications of this. There are always some odd people in the world who want to make the silliest of applications of very wise sayings. So there are those who have insisted that our Lord meant to advise his preachers that they should never prepare a sermon. The real meaning, of course, has nothing to do with any such futility. It is concerned with the Christian brought to book to defend his faith, and this is what it says. Remember that it may be before an actual authority, that is, an actual authority of the state, as it was in ancient Rome, and as it has been in Germany and as it has been in Japan. Or it may be before the untitled lords of the modern intellectual world, and that, for many of us, is a very hard situation to meet.

Now, hearken and take comfort. If, when challenged by one of these superior persons your whole desire is to speak the plain Christian truth, you need not worry. I am saying this for every one of you because people are being challenged on the right hand and on the left today. If you desire only to speak the pure Christian truth, you need not worry, it will be given you what you shall say. If you are really indifferent to the figure you cut before this or that group of superior persons and speak your natural, plain conviction, it will be given you what you shall speak. If you care only—God grant that we may say "yes" to this—if you care only for the honor of His name, it will be given you what you shall speak. If you wish only to be faithful, the words will be given you, as they were given years ago to a simple-minded minister about whom I heard. He was being twitted by one of his intellectual friends with the brilliant utterances of a famous contemporary scoffer at both religion and morality. The kind of life that scoffer was living came out merely by the way. The good old preacher knew at once the right answer. "Yes," he said, "I can see how the idea of God does not fit in to his scheme of things."

And that is the right answer to more than one scoffer at religion and morality.

Then there is the glorious quality of the second reason. "For it is not ye that speak, but the Spirit of your Father which speaketh in you." What an experience it is, splendid and humble, that of being God's mouthpiece! That queer realization that we are saying not what we thought we were going to say, but something we can't help saying.

Like Balaam, the son of Beor, who was brought out under the tutelage of Balak to curse Israel. Being under the power of God he did not curse, but blessed instead. Remember how he said, "Must I not take heed to speak that which the Lord hath put in my mouth?"

Finally, the inescapable application of all this to those who, like myself, have as their chief duty the proclamation of the Gospel. You will have noted before this that I am preaching one of those sermons that are preached to the preacher. There is a sense in which every sermon is like that, but there are certain sermons that are especially preached by the preacher to himself, and this sermon I am preaching to myself and to all my fellow preachers throughout the world.

He ought not to see those persons before him as I see you now—he ought not to see those persons before him as men and women who are to be pleased or placated. He is to remember the passage in the Book of Ezekiel in which, with bitterness of heart, the prophet says, "And, lo, thou art unto them as a very lovely song of one that hath a pleasant voice. . . . for they hear thy words, but they do them not."

It is so natural, this standing temptation to the preacher to please his audience. He must not do it! What a degradation takes place when a preacher preaches to please.

Think how, on the other hand, Holy Scripture is full of instances of men who pleased God by the simple expedient of not trying to please men, not being concerned about pleasing men.

I think we may say that spiritually speaking the prophets throve on their unpopularity.

I think of a man like Thomas More in his happy days. And when I think of him thus, I can't help thinking how easy it would have been for him to keep happy if his first idea had been to please not the King of kings, but that king, who was so willing to be his friend. Do you remember the scene described of a day—it was enacted not once, but many times—when Henry VIII and Thomas More could be seen walking together in the garden in intimate and friendly converse. The arm of Henry VIII is about the shoulders of his great servant. And the very neck that was circled by the bend of the royal arm was sacrificed later to the insatiate and unbridled egotism of that same king. But if More had wanted to please Henry VIII there might have been a different end.

"O Cromwell, Cromwell," as we hear the sound of one who chose the worldly way—

> O Cromwell, Cromwell!
> Had I but serv'd my God with half the zeal
> I serv'd my King, . . .

Well, there is only one safe way, and that is to desire to serve God, and be careless, infinitely careless about serving the king.

Let me speak, then, as I draw to a conclusion, about the extreme value of the obvious answer when we are hailed before the tribunal of the tall, confident minds of this present day.

I had two experiences like that within the last few weeks. There was one man who said, "Surely it is impossible now for an intelligent being to think of God as a person." Now, that might send anyone into a dither of uncertainty. What are you going to say? I will tell you. How, they ask, can you believe in a personal God, considering all that is happening in the world today? Can you believe in a Being all powerful, all good, concerned for this present world, while all this death and destruction is going on?

There is only one answer, and that is the obvious one. The world has always been full of grief and pain, and they have lived through it best who have relied upon the love of God in spite of everything. They have thrived best who have said, with Job, "Though he slay me, yet will I trust him." Tell them the obvious thing, that you certainly will not make life easier or the world better by getting rid of God.

"Is it possible," said a friend of mine—yes, a friend of mine, brought up in a Christian home—he said it as if he wanted an answer— "Is it possible for a person to be a Christian without believing in a life to come?"

I was so startled for a moment that my words failed me, but when I answered, I had only the obvious answer to give. There was no other possible answer. I couldn't start arguing with him about some complicated metaphysics. I said, "Harry, if your question means, 'Is it possible for a person to live a decent Christian life without that faith,' I answer reluctantly, 'Yes, he can live it for a while as the inheritor of the virtues of his father and mother and grandfather and grandmother. He may last through because of something in them that has been poured into him that he is not now prepared to acknowledge.' But, Harry, if your question means, 'Can a man be a Christian in the sense of holding the essential Christian thought and cherishing the essential Christian faith, and deny or be unconcerned with life out of death,' I say, 'No' "

It is the obvious answer. And if you want to know the reason for that, it is just as simple as two times two. It is this, that it is impossible to conceive of a just and powerful and loving God who would make all these creatures as He has made men, only in order to heap them up in the dust and ashes of the world's scrap heap when they die.

I said, "You can't have God without having a future life if it is a good God you believe in. But, oh, if you will only believe in a good God, if you will only trust in Him and quit arguing! If you will only say, 'Yes, He made us for good and for goodness, He made us for grace and for lovely and courageous and happy living, He made us for life not for a little flickering time of a few burnings of candles, but for a life that shall last."

What have you done? You have simply given the obvious answer

With that, dearly beloved, I end. That is what you have to do. It is what I have to do. You are going to face all manner of questions, all manner of doubts, all manner of studied and even vicious negations. You are going to be made to stand and deliver. They are going to set you up as a sort of a queer Guy Fawkes of the fifth of November, a sort of an effigy, while they do their intellectual dance around you.

There is only one safe way, and that is to remember the words of the blessed Lord when he sent his disciples out in that day: "Take no thought how or what ye shall speak: for it shall be given you in that same hour what ye shall speak. For it is not ye that speak, but the Spirit of your Father which speaketh in you."

O glorious and happy, most satisfying truth. For it may his name be praised.

This Thing Called Religion—What Is It?

REVEREND JOHN HAYNES HOLMES, D.D.
Minister, The Community Church, New York

The sermons of Dr. Holmes hold a unique place in New York, where his congregation has come to look to him for messages which appeal to the intellect.

Born in Philadelphia in 1879, he was educated in the public schools of Malden, Massachusetts, graduated from Harvard College in 1902, and from Harvard Divinity School in 1904. He received the Doctor of Divinity from the Jewish Institute of Religion in 1930 and from St. Lawrence University in 1931.

He began his ministry in the Third Religious Society in Dorchester (Unitarian) in 1904, and remained there three years. In November, 1906, he was called to the Church of the Messiah, New York to succeed Minot J. Salvage, and began his work in February, 1907. In 1919 he left the Unitarian ministry and reorganized his church as an independent society on a community as contrasted with a denominational basis, and changed its name to "The Community Church of New York."

One of the founders of the American Civil Liberties Union in 1918, Dr. Holmes was from the beginning a director, and is now chairman of the Board of Directors. He was a member of a small group which founded the National Association for the Advancement of Colored People in 1909, and since that day has served as vice-chairman. He was chairman of the City Affairs Committee of New York from 1929 to 1938. He went to Palestine in 1929 on a special mission for the Jews, and in recognition of his service was given the annual Gottheil Medal in 1933.

Dr. Holmes has lectured widely in this country, and has traveled extensively in Europe, Russia and the Near East. He is the author of Palestine Today and Tomorrow, Through Gentile Eyes, Rethinking Religion, Out of Darkness, The Second Christmas. *He is editor of* Unity *(Chicago), and associated Editor of* Opinion *(New York), and of* Fellowship *(New York). He is the author of many hymns which have found a place in standard church hymnals in this country and in England.*

Sermon Forty=two

I AM to speak to you upon the question as to what is religion. This is an old question and I doubt if I can say anything that is new. I might best, perhaps, give you a series of the classic definitions of religion, and let it go at that. But I have in mind a somewhat unusual approach to this question. I want to present religion in a relation to human life which is not ordinarily stressed. This will offer, at bottom, nothing new—it will still be the ancient truths that we are considering. But it will give a novel guise to the discussion, and perhaps open up an understanding of religion that we have not had before.

Let me begin by pointing out that religion has always been presented from one or the other of two points of view. That is to say, there have been two theories about religion. One is the supernatural theory. Religion is something that is divinely bestowed upon us from without, or from above. It is an inspired revelation of the mind of God through the mouth of some holy prophet, or the pages of some holy book, or the dogmas of some holy church. In this sense, religion is unique and strange—a miracle that renews itself, from hour to hour, in the soul of the believer. The other theory is the natural theory. Religion is something that belongs to human nature, and therefore has its origin within the soul. It is a part, and the highest part, of man's day to day experience with the world and with his mind. From this point of view, religion is not unique or strange at all, but as normal as sleep at night or waking in the morning—as nourishing as bread, as quickening as water, as wholesome as fresh air. There is nothing miraculous about it, apart from the daily miracle of life itself.

It is needless for me to explain to you that it is this second theory of religion which I accept. My whole approach to this problem is humanistic rather than theological. I start my thought with man and not with God—with this earth and not with heaven—with the facts of human experience and not with the myths of divine revelation. If religion is to be found anywhere, it is to be found in the heart of man—in the joys and sorrows, the dreams and visions of that heart. That it ends there, I do not believe for a single moment. The heart of man is like a key that opens the doors of "many mansions"; the experience of man is the turning of that key. Before we get through, this experience will take us into the very presence of God. Which means that religion has to with God as well as man! But this does not mean that religion suddenly goes supernatural. It remains natural because it begins with the heart of man—and there finds God. Which reminds me of the familiar saying, that "religion is the life of God in the soul of man"!

We begin, therefore, with man—and his experience through many ages upon this earth. What does this tell us about religion?

In the south of France, in the Department of Dordogne, were found some years ago a variety of caves, in which were deposited the bones and skulls of several dozen men and women. These remains were identified as belonging to the Cro-Magnon race of man, which inhabited the southwestern portion of Europe at the close of the Magdalenian epoch. This would be many thousands of years before the birth of Christ.

There were some remarkable things in these caves, besides the bones, which proved them to be the abode of man. None was more remarkable than some freehand drawings upon the walls. Conspicuous among these drawings was a sketch of a wild ox, or steer, which has now become one of the most famous and admired works in the whole history of Western art. The animal as here depicted is so vital, so full of energy, so touched with the beauty of line and feature! Just think of it—here at a time when there was no literature, or even language, when there were no cities or roads or houses, when man was living almost as an animal in caves of the earth and shelters of the rock, when he was himself a rude competitor with the beasts of the field for mere physical survival, at this early moment in his career, man became an artist. He started drawing upon any plain surface that he chanced to find. This work of art was purely gratuitous, or supererogatory. It could have no imaginable relation with the struggle for existence. It represented deeper and finer instincts than any mere hunger of the flesh. It was the beginning of that creative impulse of the inner life which in later ages produced its Raphaels and Michelangelos, and has filled the world with glory.

If we analyze this early Cro-Magnon art, this leaping ox upon the wall, we shall find that it contains at least three elements of expression.

First, there is the outer world of reality—this wild animal which this primitive artist saw and wanted to reproduce. This is what we call experience —this living relationship between ourselves and our environment. In this case, the experience was vivid and accurate in observation. Not only artists come to these caves to study these drawings, but zoologists to see the kind of animals that lived in southwestern Europe so many thousand years ago. This ox is an interesting specimen.

Secondly, there is the soul of the artist, which made this drawing upon the wall of the cave more beautiful than any animal that he actually saw with his own eyes. What he saw without was only the suggestion, or inspiration, of what he conceived within. The animal was a pattern, or design, on which he labored, and from which he drew the lines of beauty which were implicit in what he had seen. This is the function of the artist—to discover the latent beauty that lies within the various objects of nature, and then to disclose it to other and less clairvoyant eyes. No man was ever as beautiful as Apollo of the Belvedere, no woman as beautiful as the Venus of Milo; no mother and child ever revealed such spirituality as "The Sistine Madonna" of Raphael, no peasants such beauty of holiness as "The Angelus" group of Millet. But in ordinary men and women the artists saw these wonders, as in an ordinary wild ox the Cro-Magnon artist saw this marvelous creature scratched upon the wall of his cave. What they saw and recreated was the hidden secret of reality. And this was the work of their own souls.

This leads us to the third element in the Cro-Magnon drawing. I refer to that ideal beauty which the artist strove after but did not attain. As his drawing was actually more beautiful than the animal itself, so the picture that lay within the artist's soul was more beautiful than anything that his rude flint was able to transfer to the rough wall of his cave. His imagination reached beyond his handiwork; the greatest painters and sculptors can reproduce nothing more than a suggestion of that perfect vision which they see "with the mind's eye." For these artists, like pure mathematicians, as Edna St. Vincent Millay has reminded us in her great sonnet, have looked on "beauty bare." Deep down within themselves they have seen the pure essence of aesthetic being. Beauty itself—Beauty written with a capital letter! It is this which is the inspiration of the whole. Though the artist, however wonderful his hand, can never recreate what he sees so perfectly within himself, yet it is the glowing presence of what he sees that gives him the impulse and the decision to do anything at all. It is the vision which creates the work of art.

It is the glory of philosophy, which is man's deepest thought, that in every age it has insisted that the abstract, or absolute, ideal is as real as any object in the physical world. Nay, that the physical world itself has no reality except as it is related to this inner world of vision! It was Plato who first declared this truth of the basic reality of the ideal. There is nothing real, said the great Athenian philosopher, but the ideas, or ideals, which we find present here within our minds. All physical things about us, these physical sensations with which they are interlaced, are the mere shadows, or reflections, of this single reality which exists within the mind. What we conceive as an idea, or imagine as an ideal, this is the substance of the only real world that exists at all. And these ideas, or ideals, are real, as contrasted with the shadow of this earth, because they are themselves the shadows, or reflections, of that all-embracing and eternal Ideal which is God. We do not see the significance of this wild animal in the cave of the Cro-Magnon artist, until we see this truth of the Spirit as the sole reality of life. As we look upon this drawing, we see first the creature that roamed the forests in the ancient day; then we see the artist's recreation of his animal in such lines of beauty as he could master in outward form and symbol; and lastly we see, or ought to see, the vision that lived within the artist's soul—that ideal Beauty which haunted him, and tortured him, and drove him at some fateful moment to his great achievement. This is art—the living witness of the spirit to man's quest of Beauty.

So important is this point of view in our understanding of religion—what it is, and what is its validity—that I am going to tax your patience by giving you another illustration along these same lines. This has to do with music, as my first illustration had to do with art.

There is evidence that music came as early into man's life as painting and sculpture. The evidence is not so good, as man discovered a system of musical notation rather late in his career. Man played by ear for centuries before he played by note. But the early legends of the race tell of music as a potent influence in man's experience. Thus, there is the Greek story of Orpheus, who made such wonderful music that even the rocks and trees were moved by his harmonies. Then there is the Hebrew story of Jubal, who, in the early days of the world, became "the father of all such as handle the harp and organ." From these primitive beginnings developed what we must believe was the glorious music which accompanied the ancient Greek drama—and the sacred harmonies which were heard on sackbut and tabor, to say nothing of great choruses of human voices, in the worship of the Jewish temple. But of all this there is no record. We can only assume that music developed as art developed, and manifested the same three elements of being.

First, the outward world of human experience! Music was undoubtedly first suggested by what man heard with his ear, as painting was suggested by what he saw with his eye. The great god Pan cut a reed by the river and made it into a pipe, because he had listened to the birds and wanted to reproduce their singing. Then there was the sound of the wind in the trees, of the sea upon the shore, of man's own voice as he called to his sheep, or summoned his comrades into battle. As surely as the wild ox in the forest set that Cro-Magnon artist's fingers scrawling upon the wall of his cave, so surely these various sounds of nature stirred men like Orpheus and Jubal to try their hands at making instruments upon which they could play. It is the world, and man's experience therein, that prompts the idea and stirs the impulse.

But the idea and the impulse lie within. Which brings us, with music exactly as with painting, to the soul of the artist as the second element of our problem! No sound in nature is so beautiful as what man hears within, and tries to reproduce upon some instrument. In his process of reproduction he recreates, and thus at last makes music that "never was on land or sea." What is only suggested in the song of the bird and the sigh of the wind his soul elaborates, until he needs a symphony orchestra and an operatic stage to express his feeling. Robert Browning describes his organist, Abt Vogler, as taking a single chord and building a "structure brave, the manifold music," more beautiful than any palace reared by Solomon "to pleasure the princess he loved." For music is not what we hear without, but what we feel within in response to what we hear without. Walt Whitman has the right idea when he writes that "music is what awakens within us when we are reminded by the instruments." So the soul of man is the second element in what we know as music.

[246]

Thirdly, there is the Ideal—that perfect music which even the greatest musician is never able to reproduce. He hears this divine harmony, but it eludes him—like that "lost chord" which the poet said that "only in heaven" should she hear again. We feel this in Beethoven, the most titanic, if not the most perfect, composer who ever lived. Always in Beethoven's work we are conscious of the sense of struggle. He was trying to get hold of those wonderful harmonies which he heard so tantalizingly behind his deafened ears. So that his immortal scores are only the record of his struggles after the Ideal which must remain forever the Unattainable. Even the greatest works of Beethoven—his towering symponies, his mystical quartets—are but a feeble expression of the perfect music with which silently he lived. For Beethoven, like every great musician, had come into the Presence. He had met that ideal Beauty which is the essence of music as it is of art. And this Beauty is real—as real as the music of the spheres in heaven, which we cannot hear but know all the while is there. Browning's hero, Abt Vogler, was trying all his life to get this ideal harmony into his organ, and what he played remained only a "semblance" of what he heard. But he knew that this Ideal, though never played, nonetheless existed more truly than any of the notes which he sounded upon his instrument. You remember the words of his confession:

> Therefore, to whom turn I but to thee, the Ineffable Name?　　3
> 　Builder and maker, thou, of houses not made with hands . . .
> On the earth the broken arc; in the heaven, the perfect round.

I think you will agree with me that this is coming pretty close to what we call religion. And so it is!—for religion is of exactly the same substance in the life of man as art and music. This is the one great point which I want to impress upon your mind—that religion, like art and music, is an expression of man's life upon this planet. As art is the report of what he sees, and music the report of what he hears, then religion may be described as the report of what he is. Art reveals the ideal beauty that resides in all appearance, music the perfect harmony that resides in all sound, and religion the ideal spirit which resides in all being. It is as simple, as natural, as spontaneous as that. Nothing strange about it at all—nothing unusual, or miraculous, or supernatural! When the Cro-Magnon saw that wild animal in the jungle, he felt something instinctively stir within him, and he took up a flint and began to scratch a drawing upon the wall. When Orpheus, or Jubal, or someone else in the early days, heard a bird sing in the morning, or a brook babble at noontide, or the sea moan at night, he was suddenly reminded of something in his soul, and he proceeded to cut a reed, or string a harp, and make the first strains of music. So when man looked upon the vast world of nature, and saw "the heavens," the work of someone's fingers, as he thought, and "the moon and the stars" which someone must have "ordained," he was moved, in awe and wonder, to speculate as to "what is man that thou art mindful of him, or the son of man that thou visitest him." This is religion—like art and music, and poetry and architecture, and love—a groping after the Ultimate, the Eternal, the Ideal, the source of all reality, and therefore composed of the same three elements to which, in the case of art and music, I have referred.

Thus, religion begins with the outer world, and man's reaction upon it. Very early in his career, he encountered forces of which he was afraid— winds, and storms, and lightning, wild animals and the night. These forces, so mighty and so dreadful, seemed to be hostile to his welfare, and he regarded them as enemies to be propitiated and appeased. Other forces in the world were friendly—the light that ushered in the day, the rain that fertilized the soil, the grain that grew and fed the mouth with food—and these he came to regard as friends to be loved and gladly served. And always there were things in the world which stirred awe and reverence within his soul— the mountains, the forests, the sea, the stars, and all the vast pageant of the seasons. It was when he saw these stupendous and beautiful phenomena, and through them the unaccountable marvel of the whole natural creation, that he was moved to kneel, and pray, and erect altars, and worship. What this all meant he did not know—to whom he gave his offerings and devotions, he could not tell—but this was the spontaneous reaction of his life upon the vaster life which compassed him about.

This brings us to the second element of religion, which is the soul within. This soul begins to work upon the world, and try to understand it. In so doing, it begins to recreate the world in ideal forms—just like the soul of the artist and the musician! Thus, man found chaos in the world, and proceeded to put order into it by conceiving laws and relationships. He began to explain to his mind what was going on in this extraordinary place where he was living, and thus brought meaning and purpose into its activites. Above all, man began to discover—or so he thought!—that there were moral values in the world. These dangerous forces which confronted him—these he came to regard as evil. The friendly forces, on the other hand, were helpful and kind, they made it possible and pleasant for him to live, and therefore he thought of them as good. Here, full-blown, was the distinction between good and evil, in relation to the life of man. This meant that man himself must be good or evil in relation to his own words and deeds, and the inner motives of his life. This led to the creation, if I may so express it, of an ethical system, of laws and codes of conduct, of the Ten Commandments, of creeds and rituals, of Bibles and churches and holy sabbaths. Man, in other words, became a moral being. By the sheer impact of his inner life upon the outer world, he conceived of nature, and of the whole vast cosmos of reality, in moral, which is to say in spiritual, terms.

But how did man get this way? What power, or secret, was there within him that led him to such interpretation of his natural environment? How did he bring order out of chaos, if in the world, and in his own soul, there did not already exist an eternal Order? How could he find significance or purpose in the heedless processes of material phenomena, if there was not already a divine Purpose reigning in the heavens, and on the earth? And how could he conceive of good and evil, of right and wrong, of justice and injustice, of love and hate, the whole distinction between the darkness and the light of moral being, unless from the beginning of time there had existed a standard, a value, a law, an eternal Good and an abiding Truth, by which all things could be seen and judged? Surely, there must be a Life within his life, a Spirit above his spirit, an Ideal which moves him and guides him and inspires him to the attainment of what must still lie forever unattainable within the confines of this world.

This brings us in religion, exactly as in art and music, to the third element in our problem. I refer, of course, to that Ideal which is the only real. It is true that there is something in man without which he could never be a man as distinguished from an animal. There is a power within him that takes him beyond himself, and reveals to him those secrets of existence which baffle his mind while they move his heart. What this power is, we do not know. But that it is, we can be sure. A Life which is eternal, and therefore was before all worlds and will be after all worlds are done; a Spirit which is infinite, and therefore pervades all worlds, even as it occupies man's heart; a Truth which is immutable, and therefore is the same yesterday, today, and forever; a Worth, or Value, which is imperishable, and therefore must stand forever as the standard of man's word and work; a Good which is purer than man has ever known; a Beauty which is rarer than man has ever seen; an Ideal which is transcendent beyond all that man has ever dreamed! This is the Presence which we call divine because it is so much more than human. It is the Idea which Plato taught—"the Ineffable Name," of which Browning spoke. Never seen, never perfectly understood, imagined, suspected, felt after but never found, it is yet the realest thing in the world—and the source and secret of everything else. For this Presence is God. Its power is the Will of God, which we must obey if we would truly live. Its work is the Kingdom of God, which some day, by God's will and man's endeavor, shall be established on the earth.

Such is religion—man's creative reaction upon the world, under the impulse and guidance of that spirit which is God! Do you wonder that I classified this interpretation of religion with art and music? Do you not see how religion is as simple, as natural, as instinctive, and as glorious, as these other spontaneous expressions of man's spirit? Do you undertand, perhaps for the first time, why art and music have always been attached to religion, and have done their noblest work in celebrating religion? Where do we turn for the grandest expressions of man's work in wood and stone, if not to the temples and cathedrals and tombs which he has reared in every age—the Parthenon in Athens, the cathedral in Cologne? The greatest sculptures in man's history depicted Jupiter and Apollo and Venus, the deities of the classic world, and Moses and David and the Mater Pieta, the religious saints of Judaism and Christianity. The greatest paintings have been inspired by religious themes

—"The Last Judgment" of Michelangelo, "The Transfiguration" of Raphael, "The Assumption" of Murillo. As for music, it has ever sung the praises of Almighty God, as in the immortal masses of Mozart and Beethoven, the oratorios of Handel, and the vast chorals of Bach. Art and music have frequently been called the handmaidens of religion. They are more truly the comrades and fellow workers of religion. Indeed, may we not say that art and music are themselves religion? Have we not all felt the moving of the spirit as we have gazed at the canvas of some great master, or listened to the symphony of some great composer? Our supreme religious experiences, perhaps, have not been listening to a sermon, but hearing the strains of such a song, let us say, as Schubert's "Ave Maria," or looking upon the face of such a woman as Raphael's "Madonna of the Chair." It is the combination which is the perfect thing! I remember an occasion in the great cathedral of Notre Dame in Paris. The service was conducted with superb pomp and ceremony, and with deep feeling. The towering edifice of carven stone spread like sunlight the glory of its history and the beauty of its architectural splendor. At intervals, from choir and organ, came bursts of music to lift and entrance the soul. Where did religion begin, and art and music end? It was one voice that spoke that day—and it seemed the "great voice out of heaven" that said, "Behold, the tabernacle of God is with men, and he will dwell with them, and they shall be his people, and God himself shall be with them, and be their God."

Thus does religion rank with art and music, among the noblest expressions of man's life. Yet there are those who will not have it so! In this present age, which for various reasons is an unbelieving age, there are many persons, and intelligent persons at that, who insist upon separating religion from all the other experiences of man, and denouncing it as incredible. It is to be said that this is perhaps only a fitting return for the insistence of the Church upon setting religion apart from human uses, and describing it as a miraculous revelation of the divine. But it is nonetheless an extraordinary way in which to read history and to interpret human nature.

It is argued, for example, by way of objection, that religion sprang up in the early period of man's life, and is therefore not to be trusted, or even respected. Since religion is early, it is primitive; since it is primitive, it must be superstitious; since it is superstitious, it must be a sham. Those early years of human history—so many centuries, even aeons, ago—represent the childhood of the race. Man was groping about in a world he did not understand, and therefore imagining all kinds of fantasies and fears. Why should we take these things seriously? "When I was a child," said St. Paul, "I spake as a child, I understood as a child, I thought as a child, but when I became a man, I put away childish things." And so we put away religion!

But it is to be noted that we do not put away art, or music, or literature, for any such reason as this. Art appears as early in man's primitive development as religion, but nobody describes it, for that reason, as superstitious.

The very man who laughs contemptuously at early myths or rites of worship, kneels down in reverence and wonder before the strange Cro-Magnon drawings in the hidden caves in France. Music is perhaps older than religion. Before man knew anything about religious ideas and practices, he was blowing reeds and twanging bowstrings, and trying to make harmonies. But nobody thinks of ridiculing or repudiating these musical activities as childish and therefore to be put away. In our day, scholars are busy hunting out remote and primitive tribes, and making permanent records of their traditional folk songs and dances, so precious do we regard these oldest evidences of man's sense of melody and rhythm. It is one of the beneficent facts of history that man persisted with his early musical experiments until he had created a symphony orchestra and an operatic stage; and persisted with his early artistic endeavors, until he had filled the museums of the world with his masterpieces of color and design; and persisted, likewise, with his religious fantasies and speculations until he had produced the Eight-Fold Noble Path of Buddha, the Ten Commandments of Moses, and the Beatitudes of Jesus. Primitive man, when you come to think of it, was quite a wonderful creature. The whole marvel of our life began with him. He discovered fire, and the propulsive power of wind and water, and the nourishing qualities of food grains; he invented the wheel, the pivot, and the derrick; he domesticated animals, cultivated the soil, and constructed roads; he founded astronomy, mathematics, and medicine; and ceaselessly he observed, and thought, and imagined —saw visions and dreamed dreams! What we have in religion in the early days, exactly as in primitive art and music, is the first awakening of the soul of man to the deeper aspects of reality. Every token of such awakening is infinitely precious. We respect them, or ignore them, at our peril.

As men are troubled these unbelieving days by the early origin of religion, which they regard as evidence of superstition, so they are troubled by the early crudities of religion, and regard these as evidence of error. These early stories, for example, of the genesis of life—these mud pie tales, if I may describe them as such, of God fashioning animals, and even man, out of the dust of the ground, and breathing into them the breath of his own nostrils! These multitudinous gods of earth and sky, quite as many in the shape of animals as of men, and these equally multitudinous devils that delight in pain and evil! These magic rites and ceremonies, and these bloody sacrifices of sheep and goats and even of human beings! What can be more crude, or even horrible, than these paraphernalia of religion, some of which have lasted down even to our own time? Do you mean to say that such silly stories, such gross enormities, are to be respected, or tolerated if they can be gotten rid of? Religion, if we be honest with ourselves, must be seen to be a crude and sometimes dreadful aberration of the human consciousness, from which deliverance is slowly but surely, and happily, being won.

But if religion is thus to be discredited because of its early crudities, why should art and music not similarly be discredited? Most of the primitive drawings of mankind are as crude as the first drawings of a little child. The Cro-Magnon ox is famous, among other things, because it is so rare! Did you ever study the early statues of ancient Greece, for example, and note these straight, stiff, unimaginative, and even ugly figures which were the predecessors of the great works of Praxiteles and Phidias? Did you ever see the swarming statues of early India, with their extravagant multiplication of arms and legs? Did you ever examine the early paintings which appeared in Europe with the first passing of the Dark Ages, and even in the early medieval period—"the primitives," as they are rightly called!—which have no idea of perspective and proportion, no sense of movement, no grace, and only a suggestion of the loveliness which flowered in the later splendor of the Renaissance? These are crudities, even enormities, in the realm of art, but they do not trouble us. We understand them, and appreciate them. And the same must be true of music, though we have no early records. What we have to remember is that all beginnings are crude. Man is awkward in his first endeavors, just as a child is awkward. But he is no more to be despised on that account than a child is to be despised. And the curious thing is that we don't despise these crudities in art and music. Why, then in religion? Which means that, if we despise religion, we are crude! Nay, that we are bigoted! For if our minds were free and fair, we would respect religion in the same way, and for the same reason, as art and music.

One thing more! There is trouble in many minds these days because of the degeneracies of religion. Its cruelties, its persecutions, its ugly evils and corruptions! Some of the darkest ages in human history are those dominated by the Church. How can religion be divine when all too often it is unholy, reactionary, vindictive, bloodthirsty, and tyrannical?

But that's just the point! Religion is *not* divine, in any special, unique, or miraculous sense. Religion, as I have emphasized continually, is human—not supernatural, but natural—a part, and the most fundamental part, of man's experience upon this earth. It is man rising to his highest—and on occasion falling to his lowest. Human nature, being what it is, is doomed at times to fall—but, as Browning puts it,

> . . . fall to rise, . . . baffled to fight better.

We are not troubled when great periods of decline set in in the fields of art and music. We are in the midst of such a period now. Modern art so-called—much of it, at least—is a monstrosity—it reveals an ugliness and sometimes a putridity which could only be matched inside an insane asylum. Modern music also, at least in its dance rhythms, takes us back to the jungle noises of cannibals and head-hunters. But this does not turn us against art and music as corruptions of the inner life of man. On the contrary, we cling the more eagerly to the three R's, Raphael, Rembrandt and Rubens, and to the three B's, Bach, Beethoven and Brahms, and hail anew these immortal masters who revealed to man the abiding mystery of Beauty. And so with religion! Paint religion at its worst; record its persecutions and delusions; describe the long succession of its horrors from the Canaanite invasions of Joshua to the Inquisition crimes of Torquemada, and still stands the pity of the Lord Buddha for all the weaknesses and pains of men, the clear vision of Zoroaster in his eternal distinction between good and evil, the sublime conviction of Jesus that all men are the children of God and brothers one of another. "By their fruits ye shall know them." Not the rotten fruit upon the ground, but the ripe fruit upon the branches!

I return at the end to the point at which I began—the naturalness and humanness of this thing we call religion. It is not something apart by itself— some strange invasion of man's life from mystic and mysterious regions beyond his ken. Rather is it the simple expression of man's own life, the flowering of his innate genius—like art and music, literature, science and philosophy, an expansion and disclosure of the spirit that lies within the flesh.

Every objection to religion proves in the end to be a vindication of its essential character. Does it appear, in starkly primitive fashion, in the earliest periods of man's history?—it is because it is a native instinct of man's being, and an inseparable aspect, therefore, of his human quality. Is religion in the beginning unutterably crude?—it is because man himself was in the beginning crude, and like a child was learning awkwardly to use his fingers, pronounce his words, and disclose the visions that gleamed within his soul. Has religion at times been corrupt and cruel, a veritable disgrace to human nature?—this is because man is himself at times a disgrace, beset by frailty and sin, and dragging down religion, and art, and music, and every other expression of his nobler life, to the low levels of his own momentary degradation. But ever is it man's spirit at work, for better or worse—and steadily, as experience shows, for the better, and at last for the best.

Ralph Waldo Emerson, in his essay on *Art,* has a remarkable passage which I may well use to sum up this discussion of what this thing called religion really is. Throughout this sermon I have argued that religion is akin to art and music, and that all these together are the expression of man's inner life which is akin to God. So says the Concord sage:

> The Gothic cathedrals [he writes], were built when the builder and the priest and the people were overpowered by their faith. . . . The Madonnas of Raphael and Titian were made to be worshipped. Tragedy was instituted for the like purpose, and the miracles of music: all sprang out of some genuine enthusiasm. . . . Beauty, truth and goodness spring eternal in the breast of man. . . . And that Eternal Spirit, whose triple face they are, moulds from them forever, for his mortal child, images to remind him of the Infinite.

A Rising Tide

REVEREND THEODORE P. FERRIS, D.D.
Rector, Trinity Church, Protestant Episcopal, Boston, Massachusetts

*Dr. Ferris was born in Port Chester, New York, in 1908, and was graduated
from Harvard University in 1929 and General Theological Seminary in
1933. While a Fellow and tutor at the Seminary he became assistant to Dr.
Bowie of Grace Church, New York, where he remained until 1937. He
then became rector of Emmanuel Church, Baltimore, which rectorship he
filled until 1942, when he was called to Trinity Church, Boston, as rector.*

*As a preacher Dr. Ferris is winning high praise and great respect from
members of this church, who compare his preaching with that of Phillips
Brooks. It is noted for its clarity and depth of thought; he has his finger on
the pulse of the needs of the day, and preaches to meet these needs. His
belief in the efficacy of preaching is a refreshing note. He is the author of*
This Created World, *the Presiding Bishop's Book for Lent, 1944. "The tide
of the Spirit is rising!" This sermon was preached by Dr. Ferris at the Victory
Service in Trinity Church on Sunday, May 13, 1945.*

Sermon Forty=three

TEXT: Be ye not stiffnecked, as your fathers were, but yield yourselves unto the Lord, and enter into his sanctuary.
II CHRONICLES 30:8

THERE is a rising tide of religion in the land. There was proof of it in
the churches on D-Day and on V-E Day the proof was even more impressive. Letters from every battlefront carry unmistakable signs of it and
the radio is often lifted from its popular levels on the waves of this incom-
ing tide. Churches thronged with people are no sure sign that the people are
filled with thoughts of God. Nevertheless, the fact that the nation as a whole
has interpreted both the dangers of invasion and the triumph of victory as
signs of our dependence on God is a new feature in the landscape of contemporary life. What does it mean? How much is it worth? How deep does
it go and how long will it last? What can we do about it? These are some
of the questions that concern us in the face of the rising tide of religion.

[254]

This rising tide is the surface expression of four discoveries that have been dawning on us during the last decade. They are like the ground swell of which the breaking waves are only the surface evidence. The first discovery is this: *Science, by itself, is not enough.* With the rise of modern science western man began a heroic battle against ignorance and superstition. Further and further back were driven the fear and the darkness that go hand in hand with ignorance. As the achievements of the scientist became more and more universally acknowledged and appreciated, the authority of the scientist grew and grew. He began by being persecuted because he sacrificed everything in the interest of fact. He ended by being idolized because he produced in a world in which it seemed that sacrifice might no longer be necessary. He reached the peak of his prominence by the middle of the nineteenth century, and since then his proclamations have been seldom questioned or challenged.

It is so no longer. Without taking a single gem from the crown of science, thoughtful men and women have been discovering for the past ten years that science, by itself, is not enough. It can air-condition our houses, but it cannot convert them into homes in which families are knit together by loving-kindness and understanding. It can provide penicillin to cure hitherto incurable disease, but it cannot heal the wounds of the spirit or quiet the storms that rage in the mind. It can increase speed and decrease distance, but it cannot develop travelers into men who keep their word. It can give us the figures by which to measure the distance to the moon, but it cannot give us a faith to live by. It can give us machines that the gods of old would have been proud to possess, but it cannot give us the wisdom or the will to control the passions which turn those machines into instruments of the devil. For reasons like these, therefore, science has lost its monopoly on current life. Directors of hospitals are giving chaplains the same rank as physicians and surgeons because they have at last realized that in the care of the body science is not enough. Educators are forgetting their laboratories and lecture rooms for the moment and are turning their minds to the chapels that for several generations have been empty because they have discovered the fact that in the training of a man's mind and spirit, science is not enough. Even the politicians and statesmen are beginning to see that it takes more than blueprints to make a government and more than organization to make a peaceful society. The more clearly men see the limitations of science and its method of procedure, the more surely are they to be overtaken by the rising tide in religion.

In more recent days we have discovered that *Man, by himself, cannot reconstruct the world.* If our task were only to rebuild the buildings that our bombs have destroyed, it would be an expensive and arduous task in mechanics. But, as a matter of fact, that is the smallest part of our task. Our real task is to put together again the broken pieces of a battered world. Economic structures, political patterns, social orders, nervous systems, frames of thought and habits of life. These are the things that have been smashed and these are the things that men, no matter how ingenious they may be, cannot put together again by themselves. By far the largest single task in reconstruction is in the realm of politics. The political units of society must be so rearranged that they will be able to live together without fighting.

It is all too clear that we cannot reconstruct the world along the old lines of absolute national sovereignty. Whether we use those dangerous words or not, we know that unless the nations are willing to surrender some portion of their sovereignty to an authority and ideal that surpass their own particular interests, all the security organizations in the world will avail nothing. When we think what those words mean, we shudder. For they mean that somehow or other Americans will have to be concerned with something more than their forty-eight states, that Britain will have to put its Empire second to the World, and that Russia will have to recognize that the human family is even larger and more comprehensive than the Workers of the World. Is there a possibility of achieving such a thing? Certainly only on one condition, and that is that men find an object of loyalty greater than the family, the clan, the tribe, the nation or the empire; only on the condition that men become the servants of the one God who has made all men, for all of whom He died, and all of whom He loves with an impartial love. Up to this time there have been groups and fellowships that burst their provincial bounds, but they have been few. The Christian Church is one, the fellowship of educated men is another, and the artists, poets and musicians is another. The Red Cross is still another. The outstanding characteristic of each of these international groups is that they spring from sources that are in the realm of the invisible and intangible. Their motive power is in each case spiritual. Politics will travel its own road, to be sure, but the way of reconstruction will be on the way of spiritual loyalties or it will be the way of complete disintegration. Christians may say with neither presumption nor intolerance that in Christ men will find the only object of loyalty universal enough to unite all men in the task of reconstruction, the only incentive powerful enough to induce them to surrender some of their rights and privileges, and the only truth comprehensive enough to insure the permanence of their work.

There is a third discovery. *Man is not the master of history*. Man can make a garden. He can plow it, till it, plant it, water it and cultivate it. But in the long run the garden is at the mercy of the wind and weather, and its future lies in the sun and the rain and in all the mystery of growth. Man can make a garden, but he cannot be its master. So men make history, and make it they do, daily, and bravely, sometimes heroically, they write its pages. They make the courts and councils, they fight the battles and write the treaties, they bridge the rivers and plan new cities, they initiate great movements of thought and idealism, they plan its crusades and suffer the injustices of circumstances. Yet it has become increasingly clear during the last few years that man, while he continues to make history, is never its master. His life, with its curious twists and turns, is never entirely in his own hands.

How did the Allies, for instance, win the victory in Europe? The immediate answer is that they won it by their superiority of men and materials. Undoubtedly they had such a superiority and undoubtedly that superiority cannot be lightly dismissed. But who would say that the victory can be written in terms of superiority alone? What about the dark days when Britain stood alone? She was superior then neither in men nor materials. She had what we call spirit, the spirit that made one man equal to the strength of ten. She had confidence and conviction that real moral issues were at stake and those assurances were her bulwark against the foe. Again, why did Hitler not go straight to England after Dunkirk when he might have wiped the English people off the map? Was it men and materials alone that were the decisive factors?

One ventures to answer these questions only after the most serious thought. Certainly, we do not think of God as playing military favorites, nor can we indulge in that peculiar kind of national pride which sees all the right on our side and all the wrong on the side of the enemy. But neither can we bring ourselves to admit that God is always on the side of the biggest battalions. It is more than men and materials that govern this universe of ours. It is justice and righteousness, freedom and fair play. It is truth and honor. These are the things under which men move and by which they are ultimately controlled. Because they are qualities that we discover only in persons we choose to call these moral governors God. There are some things that the moral universe will not tolerate, that God will not allow. Injustice, oppression, slavery, brutality, murder—these things are finally cast out of a universe that is moral, these things are finally doomed by what we can rightly call the Wrath of God. Hence our victory. It is in this discovery of God as the Maker and Master of our destiny that the rising tide of religion finds its most majestic ground swell.

But there is one more discovery that stands in the same category as these three. *Man is once again on speaking terms with God.* For several generations most of us followed in the steps of the French skeptic: we saluted God, but we did not speak. First we thought we did not need to pray. Then we were ashamed to pray. And finally we forgot how to pray. All the formal religion in the world without prayer is as empty as a bubble. It is like a family in which no one speaks. Now in these latter days, up against the ultimate realities of life and death, men have begun to pray again. Some of their prayers may be little more than reflex action. Some of them no more than childlike cries in a dark wood. But some of them have been more than that. Some of them have been real communications between a desperate man and an infinite God. The important thing is that communications have been re-established. They may not always be on the highest levels or in the finest language, but the fact that the silence has been broken is the all-important thing.

[257]

Whatever a man's religion may be, whatever creed he may formally accept, his religion is real religion to the degree of his nearness to God. If he does not feel that God is near enough to hear what he says, his religion is powerless. It speaks well, may we say, for the future of religion when we can point to men in barracks, in submarines, on rafts, aloft on wings, before and after combat, in fox-holes and in prison camps, and tell the world that they are once again on speaking terms with God.

I have described these four discoveries for two reasons. First, because they give foundation and body to the prevailing interest in religion. These are discoveries that have not yet been made by many, but it is difficult to see how they can be ultimately avoided. Men cannot overtake them without being carried away from the flat marshes of materialism toward the higher altitudes of the spirit. And secondly, because I know how stubborn and stupid we are. Even when discoveries such as these are as plain as the daylight, many of us refuse to recognize them or to pay them any mind. Once men discovered that the world was round, those who continued to live in it as though it were flat were as good as dead. Likewise, once we have discovered that the merciless logic of science is not enough, that the inventive genius of man cannot reconstruct the world, that God, not man, is the master of history, and that man can be in direct communication with God, those who continue to live in a scientifically monopolized, humanly organized, outrageously tyrannized and impersonalized world are worse than dead.

There are words of advice that come to us with great fittingness from the second book of the Chronicles, "Be ye not stiffnecked, as your fathers were, but yield yourselves unto the Lord, and enter into his sanctuary." The tide of the spirit is rising. Let us yield ourselves gloriously to it.

The Indispensable Book

REVEREND DANIEL L. MARSH, PH.D., D.D., LL.D.
A Minister of the Methodist Church; President, Boston University

Boston has great respect for Daniel L. Marsh as educator and man of affairs. He was born in West Newton, Pennsylvania, in 1880, and studied at Northwestern University, Boston University, Garrett Biblical Institute, the University of Chicago, the University of Pittsburgh, the University of Geneva and Oxford University.

He began his career as a Methodist pastor in the Pittsburgh Conference,

*where he served from 1908 to 1913. Then he became general superintendent
of the Methodist Church Union of Pittsburgh until 1926, when he became
president of Boston University. There for twenty years, he has been a
leader in the educational world, and fourteen important institutions have
conferred the honorary doctorate upon him in recognition of his outstanding
achievements.*

*His interests are many and varied and he is prominent in numerous
organizations. He is director of John Hancock Life Insurance Company,
chairman of the Presbyterian Ministers Fund, president of the State Library,
member of the American Council on Education, the Association of American Colleges, the American Association for the Advancement of Science
and the American Academy of Arts and Sciences.*

*Dr. Marsh has a large vision and sticks to a project long enough to get big
things done. His plan for a unified university on the bank of the Charles
River, the great College of Business Administration, and his dream of education for the minds and hearts of young men and women mark him as one
of America's truly great leaders.*

Among his thirty-eight books are: The Challenge of Pittsburgh; The Faith
of the People's Poet; Higher Education Plus the Highest Education; Bell,
Benefactor of Mankind; The Patriotism of a Mature Mind; Freedom of
Discussion Indispensable to Democracy; *and* The American Canon.

*In this sermon he presents his views on the Indispensable Book in educa-
tion. It was preached as the baccalaureate sermon for the University on May
20, 1945, and created something of a sensation at the time.*

MILLARD L. ROBINSON

Sermon Forty=four

TEXT: Open thou mine eyes, that I may behold wondrous things
out of thy law. PSALM 119:18

THERE is one thing that I have felt for twenty years should be said to
every person entering the university in quest of an education, and to
every person graduating and going out in the belief that he has an education.
And I am now going to say it in this my twentieth consecutive baccalaureate sermon at Boston University, namely: that a full-orbed education,
whatever else it requires, demands that you have an acquaintanceship—at
least that you be on speaking terms—with one certain Book.

There are many different definitions of an educated person. It would be
impossible to secure unanimous acceptance of any one definition; but
nearly everybody would agree that to get an education you must do some

[259]

reading. Travel, experience, practical knowledge, and reflection all need to be supplemented by reading.

There is no dearth of books. "Of the making of many books there is no end." Long ago, Francis Bacon opined that "reading maketh a full man." But what is a man to read? Bacon preceded this quoted sentiment by saying: "Some books are to be tasted, others to be swallowed, and some few to be chewed and digested."

While the intellectual interests of one person, the professional needs of another, the taste of another, and the desire to "keep up with the Jones's" in another will prompt them to read different books, yet there are a few books— relatively, very few—that must be read by everybody who aims to be educated in any sense of the term, or even to be moderately well informed. One of these bears such a vital relationship to our culture, our mores, that a knowledge of it is absolutely indispensable to anyone who desires to feel intellectually at home in the American scene. That book is the Bible. No wonder that our recent "Committee on the University in the Post-war World" recommended the establishment of an undergraduate department of Bible!

It is a theorem of geometry that through any three points, not in a straight line, a circle can be drawn. A circle is a symbol of completeness. Let me name three points, not in a straight line, through which we can draw the circle of the complete indispensability of this Book.

A knowledge of the Bible is indispensable to anyone who would understand the genius of America, and who would be equipped to defend and perpetuate true Americanism. It is our nation's Sacred Book, as the Koran is the sacred Book of the Moslem world, or the Vedas of Hindu India. The Supreme Court has declared the United States to be a Christian nation. This does not mean that we have, or can have, an established church, or a tax-supported church; but it does mean that the Bible is the cornerstone of our national life.

During Queen Victoria's reign, a prince from India sent her a letter in which he asked her the secret of England's glory. In reply, the good Queen sent him a Bible, on the flyleaf of which she had written: "This book is the secret of England's glory." The same is more strikingly true of America. The early discoveries and explorations of this continent were made for the most part by men whose dominating motive was the dissemination of the religion of the Bible. Practically every charter given for colonial grants in North America contained some clause indicating the same purpose. The early settlers all bore in their very van the Bible, as Israelites of old bore the Ark of the Covenant.

Practically the only textbook the children of the Puritan settlers of New England had for the first hundred years of their public school system was the Bible. Naturally, they became the moral lawgivers of the continent! The Declaration of Independence marks the beginning of our separate national existence: It is the symbol of our national life. President Calvin Coolidge indicated for us its real origin when he said that in its great outlines the Declaration of Independence was the result of the religious teachings of the preceding period. He said that he had made extended research which clearly showed that the intellectual life of our forefathers "centered around the meetinghouse. They were a people who came under the influence of a great spiritual development and acquired a great moral power. No other theory is adequate to explain or comprehend the Declaration of Independence. It is the product of the spiritual insight of the people"—an insight gained by strict attention to the teachings and authority of the Bible.

When the march westward began, and the slavery question was up,' it was on the plains of Kansas that the civil struggle first came to the fore, and it was to those plains that the pioneer went with an open Bible in his hands, and the fire kindled by it burning in his heart. To the early settler, the building on the hilltop was at once fort and church, where arms were stacked for defense and the Bible preached for salvation.

The relation of this Book to the very genius of America was accurately expressed by Andrew Jackson, the "Old Hickory" of hero worshipers, who, when dying, placed his hand upon the Bible and said: "That Book, Sir, is the rock on which our Republic rests." The same idea was tersely stated by another soldier-statesman, U. S. Grant, when he declared: "The Bible is the sheet anchor of our liberties." A hundred quotations from prominent national leaders could be given in support of this thesis, as, for example, the sententious utterance of Daniel Webster: "If we abide by the principles taught in the Bible, our country will go on prospering and to prosper; but, if we and our posterity neglect its instruction and authority, no man can tell how sudden a catastrophe may overwhelm and bury all our glory in profound obscurity."

The objectives for which the allied nations waged World War II, if those objectives have been correctly stated by our leaders, grow out of, and are supported by, the teachings of the Bible concerning the supreme importance of the individual. In a dictatorship or a totalitarian system, the individual is only a cog in a wheel of a ruthless machine that grinds and grinds for the corporate state, but in a democracy the individual is altogether important. A democratic government secures its authority from the individual citizens, and must always be regarded as their servant, not their master.

Our American democracy rests upon the Biblical doctrines of the sacred worth of human personality, the equality of individual rights, brotherhood as interpreted by the Golden Rule, and service as the standard of greatness. All these foundation principles of Democracy are quarried from that bedrock which we call the Bible.

I hold that the *Genesis*[1]—the "In the beginning"—of American democracy is the Mayflower Compact, and it opens with the words, "in the name of

[1] This paragraph is based upon *The American Canon*, by Daniel L. Marsh.

God, Amen," and the writers declare that what they are doing they do for "the glory of God." The *Exodus* of American democracy is the Declaration of Independence—it marks our going out from the land of bondage to the promised land of liberty and self-government—and it makes a fourfold appeal to Almighty God. Our *Book of the Law* is the Constitution of the United States, and in the Constitutional Convention, when it seemed utterly impossible for the delegates to devise any instrument for the more perfect union which they were contemplating, Benjamin Franklin arose and moved that the Convention should be opened each morning with prayer. The speech in which he made the motion is one of the most powerful of his distinguished career, and it is replete with Scriptural quotations and allusions. Our *Major Prophecy* is George Washington's Farewell Address, in which he says: "Of all the dispositions and habits, which lead to political prosperity, religion and morality are indispensable supports. In vain would that man claim the tribute of patriotism, who should labor to subvert these great pillars of human happiness, these firmest props of the duties of men and citizens." Abraham Lincoln's Second Inaugural Address is the *Gospel of Americanism*. Its Scriptural cadences are freighted with a moral intensity. In it, Lincoln affirms and reaffirms his faith in the justice of his cause and in the righteousness of God. The last article Woodrow Wilson ever wrote, entitled "The Road Away From Revolution," I have called *An Epistle to the Americans*. In it, Wilson pleads for "a Christian conception of justice," and declares: "The sum of the whole matter is this, that our civilization cannot survive materially unless it be redeemed spiritually. It can be saved only by becoming permeated with the spirit of Christ." Our *Psalm of Americanism* is "The Star-Spangled Banner." Not often do we think of it as a religious hymn, and yet note the spiritual passion and the religious phraseology of the last stanza:

> Oh! thus be it ever when freemen shall stand
> Between their loved homes and war's desolation!
> Blest with victory and peace, may the heaven-rescued land
> Praise the Power that hath made and preserved us a nation!
> Then conquer we must, when our cause it is just,
> And this be our motto: "In God is our Trust."
> And the Star-Spangled Banner in triumph shall wave
> O'er the land of the free and the home of the brave.

A knowledge of the Bible is indispensable to an adequate comprehension of the great literature of the world. The Bible is itself our supreme literature. The King James translation has exercised a more determinative influence upon the English language than any other book ever written. Truthfully did Lord Macaulay once declare: "The English Bible,—a book which if everything else in our language should perish, would alone suffice to show the whole extent of its beauty and power."

A knowledge of the Bible is a prerequisite to a proper appreciation of the matchless works of English literature. For instance, the writings of Shakes-

[262]

peare alone contain 550 Biblical quotations or allusions. Take such a sentence as this from his *King Richard II*:

> Some of you with Pilate wash your hands
> Showing an outward pity,[2]

or this:

> As hard to come as for a camel
> To thread the postern of a small needle's eye.[3]

Such quotations will mean one thing to a person acquainted with the Bible, as Shakespeare was, and something entirely different to one who does not know their original source and setting. The poetry of Tennyson contains 330 Biblical quotations or references. How immeasurably more meaningful it is to the student of the sacred volume than to an ignoramus!

Bunyan's *Pilgrim's Progress* has always been given a place of primacy by competent scholars for its influence upon the modern English tongue, and it is steeped with Biblical language and symbolism.

The speeches of our most persuasive orators—name any of them at random: Burke, Bright or Gladstone in Britain; Webster, Lincoln, Bryan or Wilson in America—their finest orations are interlarded with Scriptural references. Can anyone who is ignorant of the Bible get the full force of Lincoln's speech about the "house divided against itself," or of his Second Inaugural, which contains two direct and several indirect Biblical quotations? Or, for instance, how can one who is ignorant of the Bible get the full value of the figures of speech in Daniel Webster's eloquent tribute to the work of Alexander Hamilton: "He smote the rock of the national resources, and abundant streams of revenue gushed forth. He touched the dead corpse of Public Credit, and it sprung upon its feet"?

As has oft been pointed out, the Bible is in itself a marvelous Library containing sixty-six books, written by some forty or fifty different authors over a period of at least thirteen hundred years, and even then including material that had been handed down by word of mouth from generation to generation for long stretches of time antedating its first writing.

If you wish to read old books that have stood the test of time, you cannot afford to neglect the Bible, nor dare you ignore it if your aim is only to keep up with the most popular books. In 1944 33,400,000 copies of the Bible or portions of it were issued and sent out to the world. Compared with these figures, the tooted "best sellers" of a decade—*Gone with the Wind*, *The Robe*, *Anthony Adverse*, or any others—pale into insignificance. In fact the advertised "best sellers" are all gone with the wind in a few years, while the Bible continues to be *the* "best seller" century after century.

If you like to read history, you can find nothing more exciting than the history contained in this Library. Reading it, you hear the clash of battle,

[2] See Matt. 27:24.
[3] See Matt. 19:24.

the shock of sword on sword and sword on shield, the wail of defeat, and the shout of victory. Reading it, you behold as in a glass the shaping and molding of desert tribes through all kinds of vicissitudes into a nation that makes a contribution of immeasurable worth to the human world. The most important institution in the history of human progress is the Christian Church, and in the brief book of Acts, you have the story of its founding and its history for the first thirty years of its existence.

If you like to read biography, you will find nothing more stimulating anywhere than the colorful vignettes in this Library. Here heroes are made to stand forth vividly in all their strength and in all their weakness, their virtues presented without gloss, and their defects depicted without apology.

If you like to read works of travel, then nowhere in all the travel literature of the world can you find anything more thrilling than the travel stories related here—the story of Abraham, who "went out, not knowing whither he went"; or of Moses, who led the children of Israel on a trek from the land of night to the land of light, wandering through the wilderness en route for forty years; or of Paul, who traveled over the whole known world, scattering the seeds of Christianity and founding an empire that was to reach beyond the bounds of Rome.

If you enjoy tracing durable institutions back to their source, read the account of the beginnings of government by law in the eighteenth chapter of Exodus, where Moses undertakes to judge every case of dispute among the Israelites, and then, at the suggestion of his father-in-law, devises a complete judicial system. Or read the account of the giving of the Ten Commandments, where the thing was so dramatic and powerful that it seemed to the writer as though the chariot of God had stopped for a moment on Mount Sinai, and its granite summit smoked; or as though God had seized Mount Sinai for a pulpit, and the mountain reeled and tottered. Justinian, Charlemagne and Alfred the Great each began his more modern code of law by quoting the Ten Commandments—the constitution of the world in ten articles.

If you like to read poetry, then you must read the Bible. Whether we judge it in terms of poetic conception, or moving cadences, or glowing imagery, its poetry is unexcelled. The wild, capricious lyrics of life are here. The thoughts and feelings, the irrepressible yearnings and anticipations of the human soul are set forth in unforgettable phrases, in rhythmic beat with nature's heart. Lean and listen to the lilt of David's harp, and then sing with him, "The Lord is my shepherd; I shall not want."

If you like high drama, read the Book of Job in the Old Testament, and you will be caught up in the whirlwind of its dramatic power; or read the Apocalypse in the New Testament, and you will join your voice with the voices of "ten thousand times ten thousand, and thousands of thousands, saying, 'Worthy is the Lamb that was slain to receive power, and riches, and wisdom, and strength, and honor and glory and blessing.'"

If your preference is for stories, you will find the masterpieces of all the ages in this Library. The story of Joseph, with his coat of many colors; the jealousy of his brethren; their deceitful selling of him into slavery; Joseph carried into Egypt; Joseph honoring God, and God honoring Joseph, until by and by he becomes food administrator for Pharaoh's government. And all the while back home, troubles thicken upon the family. Drought vexes the land until dust foams at the mouth of the well. Then when the famine is at its worst, the brothers go down into Egypt to get food. They appeal to Joseph as food administrator, without recognizing him, albeit he recognizes them. They say that their father is an old man, and they have come to get food for him, and then Joseph, still concealing his identity, says: "The old man of whom you spake, the old man, your father, is he well?" Read the story for yourself! It will draw its tribute of tears from the eyes of far-off generations long after the names of today's secular "best sellers" will have been forgotten.

If you like love stories, you must read the story of Ruth, sweet, idyllic, beautiful, so compassionate that we have made the word "ruth" a common noun in the English language, the definition of which is "compassion for misery."

If you wish to read the sweetest story ever told, read of Joseph's girl-wife, Mary, in the stable of the Bethlehem inn, holding in her girlish hands the little unshod feet of her Baby, and stroking the silk-soft hair, and kissing the eyelids drooping down in earth's first helpless sleep, while the air above Judea's hills pulsated with the angel's song of peace on earth, good will to men. If you would like to read the saddest story of all the ages, read the account of the uplifted cross on a barren Judean hill, outside the city wall, where a thorn-crowned Sufferer paid "the last full measure of devotion" to a cause immeasurably more significant for humanity than any for which men ever sacrificed themselves on battlefields. And if you would care to read the most triumphant story of all time, read the story of the first Easter—and while you read, your heart will sing the Easter hymn exultant.

A knowledge of the Bible is indispensable to a proper understanding of the most vital source of the inspiration of great works, noble deeds, and victorious lives. This inspirational value is not limited to the field of literature. It has subdued rude and boisterous minds, and has exercised a creative influence upon those polished arts which have thawed out the ice-locked harbors of human feelings. Music? A whole galaxy of musicians whose names shine on the pages of history like stars blazing in the night found here the inspiration for their greatest works. Architecture? The old cathedrals of Europe are the optimum of architectural splendor, so sublime that Friedrich von Schelling described them as "music in space, as it were a frozen music"—and they are but the materialization of the aspiring moods created by a study of the Bible. Sculpture and painting? The old masters imbibed at the same fountain the motive for their greatest achievements. Archaeology? The sacred volume sends men to study in libraries and archives; to unearth cities long buried; to inspect tombs of ancient kings.

The Bible energizes as well as inspires. One of the historic "Articles of Religion" declares that "the Holy Scriptures contain all things necessary to salvation." This is true concerning both personal salvation and social redemption. Huxley says that the only true education is that which enables a man to do what he knows he ought to do, regardless of the consequences. More than any other book ever written, the Bible communicates power, enabling man to keep step with the commandments of the Almighty against all kinds of opposing forces. No other book so tones up one's personal life as the Bible. It denounces and condemns selfishness and sin, makes resolute the weakened will, wings the faith of the discouraged, comforts the sorrowing, gives hope to the despairing, refines judgment, clarifies reason, purifies imagination, and disturbs the indolent with divine discontent. Worthy of acceptance by everybody is the advice which Abraham Lincoln gave his friend, Judge Speed, namely: "Take all of this Book that you can by reason, and take the rest of it by faith, and you will live and die a better man."

The Bible is not a textbook of science: It is a book of religion. It does not aim to give us scientific speculation: It gives us heavenly wisdom, which relates to the proper conduct of life and the education of the highest faculties of our being. It is a unique repertory of moral and spiritual truths, and such truths are self-attesting to minds able to realize them. The Bible is God's disclosure of Himself along the way and through the life of a tragic people. It is a revelation of God not only, but also of God's dealing with man, and of our duties and relationships with God and with one another. All the entrancing stories and biographies and history and poetry are but the shell: The kernel is the life-giving revelation it contains of man's need and God's love. Those other things are but the scaffolding to build a Book of conduct and character. They are the bodily vesture: The immortal soul within is the revelation of a right relationship between God and man, and between man and man.

The teachings of the Bible, if heeded, will avail not only for personal salvation, but also for social redemption—for political purity, civic righteousness, economic justice, and even for the cure of war, the most terrible of all social and international sins. Not long ago I was called to Chicago to deliver an address at a banquet of city-wide interest, held in the Palmer House. I was seated by the side of Dr. Arthur H. Compton, one of the most distinguished scientists of this generation, a Nobel prize-winning physicist. The subject of war naturally came into our table conversation. We were both apprehensive lest the stage was being set for another war in the next generation, when the means of death and destruction will be even more horrible than in this war. I asked Dr. Compton for his best thought on the prevention of this final disaster to our civilization, and was profoundly impressed by his answer; for instead of expressing the opinion that the remedy is to be found in science, as

attention immediately and then how he begins his message promptly. This sermon was preached in his church on the Sunday following the premature announcement of the surrender of Germany.

Sermon Forty=five

TEXT: Ye know not what manner of spirit ye are of. For the Son of man is not come to destroy men's lives, but to save them. LUKE 9:55-56

YESTERDAY we thought victory had come. For a brief period we were thrilled with the news of the unconditional surrender of Germany. Then came the announcement that it was all a mistake, and we felt terribly let down. In this hour of expectancy and tension, we have been given the chance to better prepare our minds and hearts through worship for the day of victory when it does arrive.

There are two stories in the New Testament that serve as the basis for our thinking today. The first is taken from the ninth chapter of Luke. It is the story of Jesus sending messengers into a Samaritan town to find lodging for Himself and the disciples for the night. When the group found no hospitality there, James and John wanted Jesus to call down fire from heaven to destroy the people. Whereupon, our Lord rebuked them saying, "Ye know not what manner of spirit ye are of. For the Son of Man is not come to destroy men's lives, but to save them."

The other story is from the tenth chapter of Acts. In this story Peter sees the vision of the unclean beasts which devout Jews were forbidden by law to eat but which Peter in the vision was commanded to eat. Peter, not understanding the vision, was soon faced with its application. He had to decide whether or not to accept a Gentile, Cornelius, into the Christian fellowship. This created a situation which finally led him to say, "Of a truth I perceive that God is no respecter of persons; but in every nation he that feareth him, and worketh righteousness, is accepted with him."

These two stories remind us that Jesus was sent into the world not only to reveal what *God* is like, but also to reveal what *men* must be like, if they are ever to create a social order in which justice and truth shall prevail, and in which the opportunity to realize one's best is possible for every man. God revealed in Jesus Christ not only *His* attitude; He also revealed the kind of attitude that *men* must have if ever this dream of a better world is to come true. No wonder our Christian faith has such great significance today. There can be no permanent world peace, no stable social order until the barriers that separate us from our fellow men are broken down.

[269]

The decision of people like you will finally determine the course of action of our nation in the days that follow victory. You are a part of that group of our citizens who have confessed Jesus Christ as Lord and Saviour and who have given a pledge of allegiance to the things for which the Church of Christ stands. There are enough people like you in our nation to change the future of civilization for the next thousand years, if only your decision and theirs is made in harmony with the basic truths of our religious faith. Whether or not our religion will be made relevant and effective in this crisis now remains to be seen.

When Jesus was crucified, He *did* reveal God's love, a love that went all the way to the Cross to save men. But that is not the final word. On the third day God raised Jesus from the dead that we might forever have confidence in the *living* power of God that can and does work in and through human personality. During the forty days following the Resurrection Jesus convinced His followers that He was alive, but in a spiritual form, so that forever after they and we could be assured of His presence and His power. Then during the period that followed Pentecost a reluctant group of disciples had to be shown just what was needed to be done by this spiritual power. God revealed to those early Christians and all who came after them, that spiritual power was given to enable men to break down the barriers that separate them from their fellow men. Before the truth of Christ's death and resurrection could be given to the world there were boundaries to be crossed over and walls of separation broken down. Unfortunately these barriers have not yet been completely broken down, and today you and I, and our world, need this same power of the living Christ to break down the barriers that still divide us.

The story of Jesus and John at the Samaritan village and the sequel to this story brings us one illustration of the power of the living Christ to break down barriers. While on a journey John and James went into a Samaritan village and asked for lodging for the night for their friend Jesus. Now, the Samaritans and the people who lived in Galilee and in Judea had nothing to do with each other. You remember this from the story of Jesus and the woman of Samaria in the fourth chapter of John's gospel. When Jesus, a Galilean, asked the Samaritan woman at the well for a drink, the woman looked at Him in surprise and said, "Why do you ask me? You are a Jew. I'm a Samaritan. You know the Jews have no dealings with the Samaritans." So bitter was this feeling, in fact, that when people who lived in Galilee started to Jerusalem in Judea, they did not even *walk* through the country of Samaria if they could help it. They preferred the long way round this despised country.

It is easy to understand how John felt therefore when, standing outside the Samaritan village he faced the fact that these hated "foreigners" would not let Jesus spend the night there. He probably said to himself, "Isn't that just like the scoundrels? They aren't worth being allowed to live. The world ought to be rid of them." Then turning to Jesus he said, "Why don't you call down fire and destroy them?" The reply of Jesus needs to be remembered by Christians today. "Ye know not what manner of spirit ye are of. The Son of Man is not come to destroy men's lives, but to save them." And may have added, "This desire of yours to destroy the people of this town because they have treated us shamefully is the very spirit I came to destroy. That's the manifestation of the spirit that has been blocking God's plan all these years. If this spirit you reveal were not in the world, there would have been no need for me. If you are to be a follower of mine, you've got to acquire a different spirit."

Now look for the sequel to this story in Acts the eighth chapter and fourteenth verse. Here we find that the first appointment John received after Pentecost was to preach the gospel *in Samaria*! Can't you imagine John saying, "The very idea of sending me to preach to those barbarians, the Samaritans! I can preach the gospel to my kind of folks, but not to 'foreigners.'" But the Spirit said, "You either go, or you lose the power. The gospel is *not* just for the people that live around Jerusalem. This gospel is for the world, for all of God's children everywhere." So John went to Samaria and preached the gospel, whereupon, to his amazement, the Holy Spirit came upon all believing people there also. Thus the spirit of the living Christ spread across national boundaries, and the barrier that separated those two nations was broken down. Nothing but the power of Christ had ever been able to accomplish this miracle.

So far, so good, but the task of revealing the power of the spirit is not yet completed. National boundaries are bad enough, but there was another barrier even worse—that of race—which must be broken down. The person selected for this demonstration was Simon Peter. He was a Jew, and proud of it. God had revealed Himself in Jesus, born of a Jewish mother. This gospel must be for the Jews, the chosen people. Why worry about the Gentiles? It's strange, isn't it, that those among us who are so prejudiced against the Jews forget that the problem in those early days was not how to keep the Jews out, but rather how to get the Gentiles into the fellowship. Those early Christians were confronted by the barrier between Jew and Gentile, and Peter was the man chosen by the Spirit of God to break that racial barrier down.

In the tenth chapter of Acts we read that Peter was asleep on the housetop of Simon the tanner in Joppa. He saw the vision of the animals that according to his religious beliefs were not to be eaten. The Voice said, "Rise, Peter, kill and eat." Then Peter said, "I can't do it. I've never touched anything unclean or common." But the Voice continued, "What God hath cleansed, call thou not common." After this had happened three times, there came a knock at the door, and a message arrived from a Gentile named Cornelius. The message was, "Please come over and share this gospel with us." Peter started to tell the messengers just what he would have said the day before, "This gospel is for my kind of folk, not for you." Then he remembered the vision and its meaning became plain to him. So Peter went with the messengers and preached to a group of Gentiles in Cornelius' house, and the Spirit of the living Christ became manifest in them. Proud Jew, though he was, Peter was now convinced of the divine purpose revealed in the message he had received, and said, "God is no respecter of persons." Thus this religion of ours broke across the barrier that separated racial groups, thank God, or you and I could not be here in a Christian church this morning.

Still the job was not yet finished. The strongest barrier of all was the one that exists between religious groups, and it still is. Opening the closed mind of a religious bigot is the toughest job God ever tackled. He has an easier time opening the mind of a nationalistic or a racial fanatic than He does that of a religious bigot. Paul was the one selected for this job. Paul, who was at first called Saul, and was a Pharisee of the Pharisees. He had been persecuting the Christians because he thought it was his duty. What terrible crimes have been committed by those who have thought it was their religious duty to persecute anybody who disagreed with them! These early Christians were sharers of Saul's own religious faith, but they had acquired some new ideas that to him were heretical. They talked about God's love and mercy revealed in Christ. They said that Christ died to save all men everywhere. They said that God raised Christ from the dead and that this living Christ daily gave them power through this fellowship. Saul, the strict religionist was disturbed and said, "This is a bad state of affairs. They are endangering our holy faith, but we'll settle it. We'll kill them." And he set about persecuting those who held this new faith.

Now, we had better not get self-righteous about what Saul did before his experience on the Damascus road because we've had something of that same attitude in our own nation. For example, there was an official high in the United States government, who in a public address just two weeks ago said about the same thing. Speaking of the Japanese, he said, "Exterminate them! Kill them!" And when someone asked for a further explanation after the speech, he added, "I didn't mean kill the soldiers and sailors only, I meant kill all of them." Well, if there was ever an absurd idea advanced that is it, isn't it? That is, it's absurd if we are in earnest about building a world order that can endure.

Yet that was just the idea Saul had about the early Christians. He had started out to kill a few more of them, when on the Damascus road a voice said to him, "Saul, Saul, why persecutest thou me?" This surprised Saul, who must have said to himself, "What do you mean, persecute *you*, Lord? I'm not persecuting you. I'm doing your business. I'm just ridding the world of some worthless people whose religious ideas are dangerous."

It was a hard job to bring Saul to the point where he could see that the God he was faithfully serving was the same God who had spoken through

Jesus on a Galilean hillside saying, "Inasmuch as you did it unto the least of these, my brethren, you did it unto me." It took a long time after Saul became Paul for him to be really convinced that the spirit of the Lord was in these people that he had been persecuting because he was such a religious bigot. In fact, it took nine years to bring this miracle to pass. Two years he spent in Arabia and then seven more he waited while he thought through the implications of these new ideas. When Paul finally decided he had better do something about the mission which the Spirit had been pressing him to undertake, he became the greatest evangelist of the early Church. Today, as in Paul's day, the barrier of religious differences holds back the flood tide of evangelistic fervor. The power of the living Christ can break down that barrier if only we will put our common devotion to Him in the center of our thinking.

Here we are today in a dangerous era, a time for making peace. We know how to make war. When will we learn how to make peace? We have men now at San Francisco engaged in building the framework of world peace, but this is no hope unless we have enough people who can think straight about this matter of religion and the future peace of the world, supporting their efforts. Our world is hopelessly committed to war unless we have men and women who are committed to the application of religious principles to international problems, whatever they may cost.

Of course your minds and hearts are tempted to resentment and the desire for retaliation and revenge for the barbarities that the Germans have perpetrated on defenseless men and women. The sons of some of you have died at their hands. If you allow this feeling to control your actions, however, you are no better than a pagan. You are no contributor to the future stability of the world if you let that passion betray you into believing that we can remedy the situation by being as cruel as they are. Destroy the Japanese people? Exterminate the Germans? How absurd! You cannot kill an idea with a machine gun bullet. You cannot build with bombs. Neither can you heal by barbarism the wounds of our world that were caused by barbarism.

The problem is this: either the people of this world will learn how to live together in justice and peace and brotherhood, or our grandchildren are going to die in World War III. There must be a great deal of sacrificial work done if a new type of world order is ever to be built, and this work must be done by many people of different nations, creeds and races. It cannot be done overnight—it may take hundreds of years. How long it will take we cannot know and need not know, but it must be done.

The real task before us is to break down the barriers that separate us today. For this we need the power of the living Christ. The power of material force is self-defeating. Until a man or woman or a nation joins *voluntarily* in building a better world order, something is lacking. God needs the voice of every man, regardless of his nation or his race, if the Hallelujah Chorus is ever to be sung as He wants it sung.

The diplomats seeking to solve the problems of peace around a Conference table are facing on a world scale the same problems you and I face in our national life, and in our personal experiences. How can we expect our world problems to be solved if we cannot adequately handle the same difficulties when they confront us locally.

There are barriers today that separate the thirteen million Negro citizens of our nation from the rights and privileges that belong to our white citizens. Does the Holy Spirit your religion believes in use you for a willing instrument for breaking these barriers down? There are barriers today that separate four and a half million Jewish citizens of our nation from full fellowship with the majority group. A new wave of anti-Semitism can already be felt in our nation, similar to the one that followed the first World War. We who live in Texas are well aware of the barriers that prevent our citizens of Mexican parentage from entering fully into our national heritage. Barriers between races, classes and men of varying creeds exist now, at our very doors. If we are not driven by our religious faith to break these barriers down at home, what grounds for hope have we of a permanent peace on a world scale?

Those among us who would deprive the Negro of his rights as an American citizen or would ostracize the Jew as one of an alien breed or would sit complacently by while any of God's children among us are mistreated or exploited, need to hear again the voice of Jesus saying, "Ye know not what spirit ye are of. . . ."

Thank God, John and Peter and Paul became empowered by a different spirit. They learned the lesson which Jesus taught. They learned what the power of Christ can do to break down the barriers which hinder the spread of His message. We need that same power. We must have the power of His spirit to break down the religious barriers that separate us and keep us from co-operation. We must have the power of His spirit to bring us into a creative fellowship with our fellows in the effort to realize in our social order these great truths of God. I believe that God is trying in this day as never before to bring to us this power. We have the best chance any generation has ever had to help forward the Kingdom of God, but we shall fail if we do not let those who lead us hear our voice, the voice of United Christendom saying, "For God's sake and for the sake of future generations, don't give us a peace dictated in a spirit of revenge and retaliation."

"Oh, so you advocate a 'soft peace,'" someone will say. Well, what is a *soft* peace? Certainly a peace that is based upon a theory of revenge and retaliation is a *softheaded* peace. It's a hardheaded peace plan that thinks in terms of justice and fairness, and in terms of protecting the world's interests, not the interests of some favored nations only. It is a hardheaded peace that plans a constructive program of education, discipline and development. That's the plan that was used with China after the Boxer Rebellion. We demanded reparations then and were paid them for the damage the Chinese had done.

Then we turned around and put those millions of dollars back into the hands of the Chinese leaders for use in building better relationships between China and America. They built such ties through these years that China is today the best friend we have in the Far East. Was that soft? No, it was a sensible and religious way of looking at things.

Our world needs a rebirth of the power which breaks down the barriers which separate men, the power which made possible the spread of Christianity. "Ye know not what manner of spirit ye are of. For the Son of Man is not come to destroy men's lives, but to save them." I had rather be a worker for Christ and with Christ during the next ten years than in any generation since Pentecost.

Attaining Spiritual Maturity

REVEREND DAVID ALEXANDER MacLENNAN, D.D.
Minister, Timothy Eaton Memorial Church, of the United Church of Canada, Toronto, Ontario

Dr. MacLennan was born in Boston, Massachusetts, in 1903, the son and grandson of Scottish Presbyterian ministers. Ordained in the Presbyterian Church, U. S. A., he had two brief pastorates in Hyde Park, Boston, and Faith Presbyterian Church, Baltimore. In 1930 he succeeded Dr. J. W. G. Ward as minister of Emmanuel Church, Montreal. Since 1936 he has been senior minister of one of the largest congregations in the Dominion, despite the fact that he came to his metropolitan pulpit while still junior in age to his local contemporaries. Dr. MacLennan was educated at the University of Manitoba, Manitoba College (Winnipeg), and the United Theological College, Montreal. During his first pastorate he did graduate study at Harvard. In 1943 Victoria University, the University of Toronto, conferred the honorary degree of doctor of divinity upon him. In prewar summers he preached in City Temple, London, England, and in St. George's West Church of Scotland, Edinburgh. In recent years he has been a guest in Dr. Sizoo's pulpit in New York, at Syracuse University and in several other American centers.

During World War II, Dr. MacLennan served as chairman of the council of social workers of the Toronto community chest; chairman of Toronto's church committee "for Troops in Training"; and as chaplain of the second battalion (reserve) of the Irish Regiment of Canada. He is the author of two booklets, A Week's Rations, *and* The Healing of His Seamless Dress—

Meditations for the Sick now in its tenth edition. Within the United Church of Canada he serves on the Committee of Worship and Architecture, and on the Board of Evangelism and Social Service.

The late Principal Richard Davidson of Emmanuel College, Toronto, who presented Dr. MacLennan for his honorary degree at the university convocation, said: "David MacLennan's preaching is of a piece with his father's and grandfather's, continuing a great evangelical tradition as he proclaims the Gospel with Celtic warmth and Celtic concreteness and Celtic sense of mystery." The sermon which follows was preached in Timothy Eaton Memorial Church, Toronto, on Sunday morning, October 21, 1945.

Sermon Forty=six

TEXTS: And it came to pass in those days, when Moses was grown, that he went out unto his brethren, and looked on their burdens . . . EXODUS 2:11

And when he was full forty years old, it came into his heart to visit his brethren the children of Israel. ACTS 7:23

HOW would you characterize a grownup? On what basis do you judge a person to be mature? The obvious measurements frequently fail. Full physical stature, for instance; at a distance our teen-age children make us look like adolescents! Age is not a reliable index. A man may have reached manhood by the calendar, may be adjudged legally to be an adult, undertake business responsibilities and yet exhibit an infantile response to certain situations. Intellectual equipment of itself furnishes no proof of true maturity: many an academically educated individual has been unable to put away childish attitudes and habits.

Last week our American neighbors read what one of their magazine editors called the "shocking news about themselves" in an official report that approximately 12 per cent of all men examined for military service were not grown up sufficiently to be accepted for the army or navy of the republic. They were "too inept, stupid, or illiterate" for adult action. We Canadians read the announcement with feelings akin to superiority—until our own figures were published! Our army rejections reached the astounding proportion of 48 per cent of the men examined, the larger proportion having been rejected for mental retardation. If such disquieting figures disturb our apathy and arouse us to comprehensive "national fitness" programs, the disclosure of our deficiency will prove salutary.

Clearly, we have fairly scientific measurements for intelligence. But no such technique exists for measuring spiritual capacity and achievement. If we could discover our "S. Q."—our spiritual quotient—we might be shocked to learn that we suffered from arrested spiritual development. In the second chapter of the second book of the Bible, the book of Exodus, there is one significant test of maturity. It is part of the story of Moses:

> And it came to pass in those days, when Moses was grown, that he went out unto his brethren, and looked on their burdens.

Moses had been brought up in the palace, but no royal patronage had retarded his growth, at least not past his fortieth birthday! If you read St. Stephen's last sermon, recorded in the seventh chapter of the book of the Acts of the Apostles you will learn that when Moses "was full forty years old, it came into his heart to visit his brethren the children of Israel." I know what some of you would like to say: life begins at forty even for Moses! It did begin for him, not because a particular birthday marked an access of creative living, but because when he was forty Moses moved out of the balcony into the arena. He began to see beyond the walls erected by privilege. He joined the human race. As Halford Luccock once put it, "he escaped from the royal routine of 'peace, perfect peace' into a labor struggle." Mature, useful life could begin at twenty, at thirty, fifty, or seventy for some of us if we would go out unto our brethren, and become aware of the loads they carry and of our obligation to share them.

Doubtless there are other tests of spiritual maturity; the ability to adjust to reality, the power to exercise independent judgments, the resource of emotional stability—all derived from, and nourished by, a deep confidence in the Christlike God. Such marks reveal the mature Christian personality. But this social vision and spiritual insight credited to the ancient leader of the Israelites is essential to mature character.

Here is a truth, commonplace but commonly ignored, to keep before us in these trying days of postwar reconstruction: *Spiritually mature persons alone can solve the problems of our time.* Does it sound as platitudinous as saying, sunlight and rain are essential to the growth of crops? Be patient for a moment! During the pressures of total war most citizens behaved admirably. Complaints about individual rights being ignored in the common effort to defeat the enemy were seldom heard. With brave men dying overseas it seemed childish to talk about our deprivations. Moreover, while we may have indulged in silly antics in the name of patriotism, we did take the maintenance of morale seriously. The majority of us kept true to the old fidelities. Family sanctities and personal decency held firm for most of us, however alluring the temptations to moral experimentation. Admittedly, numbers of men and women did not keep honor bright, but the majority did. Again, in our attitudes toward other racial and national groups there was a commendable maturity. Race prejudice was reduced; anti-Semitism was viewed as dangerously near treason. Were not the Jews the chief victims of the evil forces we fought against? As for the Russians, well, we assumed that dislike of political and economic features of their internal economy offered no valid excuse for withholding admiration of their heroic struggles against the common foe, or material equipment for their fight. Think of Stalingrad, we said; of what they keep from us. As for religious sectarianism, in war it was simply irrelevant. For the first time, many secularized citizens looked with new respect on the religion of brotherhood as they witnessed the brotherhood of religion. Take it all in all, we did achieve adult attitudes and grownup behavior in many areas of living under the terrific impact of war. "And it came to pass in those days . . . that *we* went out unto our brethren, and looked on their burdens" and tried to do something about what we saw and felt.

What of the brief period since the war ended? It would be unfair to charge us with wholesale degeneration. But however we may squirm, let us face the fact that we have slipped back into childishness in many relationships where spiritual maturity is desperately needed. What do I mean? For one thing, we are beginning to whine a little too audibly and pettishly about our sacred rights. Of course, we believe in liberty, and in its extension to every man. The restoration of the democratic rights which we willingly suspended for the war's duration ought to be a serious concern of every citizen. But this whimpering about our rights, and higher returns for diminishing effort becomes infantile in a shattered world. In the ranks of both capital and labor, it drowns out the "still, sad music of humanity," hungry, ill-clothed, frightened by the specter of want as the first winter after our victory approaches. Is it not infantile to produce a prolonged tantrum of temper because, as we say, we do not intend to be pushed around by anybody, anywhere, for any reason?

As for morale, its close connection with morality tends to be utterly ignored by men and women who ought to know better. A man or woman affirms, without even citing the specious arguments of a now obsolete behavioristic psychology, that there are certain inalienable rights of personality. Indeed, there are! And the bill of rights applies to others as well as to ourselves. We have responsibilities too. Call it the backwash of war, if you like, but this letting down of moral standards built up through the long experience of mankind, and validated by the revelation of Sinai and Calvary, is actually a "regression to the infantile." In the field of racial and international conflict, the growing suspicion of erstwhile allies, the increasing resentments among once intimate friends and comrades, parallels the egocentric displays sometimes seen in nursery-age children! Across the centuries I hear the Strong Son of God asking us to be men and women worthy of our sires, worthy of the Perfect Man who called us his brothers and his friends. As for those of us who profess and call ourselves Christian, we are not exempt from the charge of being childish. Once militant, the Church catholic and reformed now appears hesitant. To be sure, Christian unity is on the agenda of most ecclesiastical conferences, but no longer has it priority or power. We talk impressively about settling the vexatious matter of "orders," by which we mean ordination to the ministry of the Word and Sacraments. Have we forgotten that more important in the eyes of our blessed Lord are our "marching orders"—that he commands still "Go ye into all the world, and preach the Gospel to every creature"? St. Paul might feel he had better readdress his letter to Corinth, if he could observe our factious spirit. You remember the letter in which he penned this blistering line: "I fed you with milk, not with meat; for ye were not able to bear it . . . for whereas there is among you jealousy and strife." Prejudice and partisanship in Corinth or in Toronto, in Canterbury or in New York, prolongs babyhood. The Church of Christ was created to produce new men in Christ, not babes in the woods.

Shall we ever grow up? We have matured with incredible speed in scientific inventiveness. Modern man has demonstrated extraordinary capacity for progress along some lines. As Paul Scherer observed not long ago, "He can turn out a future to suit himself. He has a radio, an airplane, and a thirty-five ton machine up at Harvard that thinks nothing of multiplying twenty-three numbers by twenty-three other numbers in five seconds, calculating logarithms in fifty-nine seconds, and working out trigonometric functions in eighty-eight seconds flat!" There is scientific maturity for you! Tremendous creations by Homo sapiens, 1945 model, and no mistake. "No mistake?" Unless, perhaps, a flaw in the moral mechanism of control, in the spiritual composition of the inventor. Atomic bombs in our hands at last—and we toss them up and down, wondering if we dare let our playmates have them too, like so many youngsters playing with a pretty red ball! It was a mighty Russian thinker who declared that "human life becomes truly terrible when there ceases to be anything above it." Indeed it does, and atomic energy must be handled by the hands and minds of adults who dedicate their newly-found powers to the service of the great God who is above our human life as the sky above the earth.

Spiritually mature persons alone can solve the problems of our time. Agreed; how can immature men and women handle the cosmic powers now tapped? Only those who put away the childish things of selfishness, of skepticism concerning God and man, duty and destiny, can be adequate. And yet, even a brief review of contemporaneous conduct discloses little evidence of growing spiritual maturity. Here is where the New Testament enters with hope abounding! For this is true also: *We can grow up until, as the apostle Paul would say, we become spiritually mature "in Christ."* Listen to this "little man" of three cubits' height who yet touched the sky:

till we should all attain the unity of the faith and knowledge of God's Son, reaching maturity [the phrase sounds as if it had been borrowed from a modern textbook in child psychology!], reaching the full measure of development which belongs to the fulness of Christ—instead of remaining immature, blown from our course and swayed by every passing wind of doctrine . . . we are to hold by the truth, and by our love to grow up wholly into Him.[1]

[1] The Bible: A New Translation, by James Moffatt. Harper & Brothers, publishers.

Mark that clue to great living—"by our love to grow up." You think of the miracle of transformed character worked by a Christian social worker in one of our hostels for difficult girls. One of the "problem children" (God forgive us for making the problem!) refuses to grow up. Her reactions—to use one of our blessed modern words—are those of a much younger child. She is difficult, recalcitrant, and in various ways sufficiently bad to try the patience of a saint. But not this modern saint, this patient, hopeful housemother. The girl changes; she grows up! What worked the miracle? By the housemother's love, the love that hopeth, endureth, believeth all things, the girl enters into useful young womanhood. By our love for God in Christ, by his love for us, we grow up. And the evidence of our maturity consists in this, that we "love the brethren." "When Moses was grown . . . he went out unto his brethren." When you and I grow up we too go out unto our brothers, be they ever so difficult or repulsive, in rags or riches, in our pale skin or in rich colors of black or brown or yellow. We join the human race. Otherwise we pay the cruel price exacted by life for arrested development. We become victims of hardening of the sympathies, and find our most godlike qualities disintegrating. "When Moses was grown . . . he went out unto his brethren, and looked on their burdens." Are you sufficiently grown to do that? In Europe, in Asia, are hungry, ill-clad brothers and sisters of yours; can you see them? Can you see the burdens of those who are being strangled by "Egyptian" brutes called Hunger, Disease, Despair?

Does someone wish to protest that a generation exposed to realism may be excused for being a little impatient with this kind of romantic idealism toward the alleged burdens of others? Surely no such belated mind remains among us, at least not in a Christian church, who believes that seeing the burdens of others and desiring to help relieve them is romantic idealism! Harry Emerson Fosdick recently told us of the Gambia mosquito of Central Africa. Have you ever heard of that particular insect? I confess I did not until I read Dr. Fosdick's reference to it. It seems that the Gambia mosquito is one of the species responsible for malaria. Until 1930 nobody on this continent worried about it. Buzzing around in Central Africa, how could it affect us? But in 1930 a new airline joined Central Africa and Brazil. Gambia mosquitoes were among the unlisted passengers; malaria came through a new carrier to the Western Hemisphere. So today in Africa, American and Canadian scientists (Canada's contribution is through a Toronto scientist at present working in Egypt on this project) are working to rid the people of Africa of this plague. "We are members one of another," and we cannot have health here until they have it there. When we go out to our brothers and see their burdens of disease, of poverty, of war, and do something about them, we help ourselves in the only effectual way we can be helped.

You need no preacher to indicate the specific burdens our brothers carry here in our own favored community and nation. Heaviest of all the loads our fellow pilgrims shoulder are those imposed by life's sorrows and frustrations, and the memories of personal moral failure and spiritual brokenness. Do you see these burdens? Christ was always opening the eyes of the blind. He restores vision and sharpens insight still. "And it came to pass in those days, when Moses was grown, that he went out unto his brethren, and looked on their burdens."

Inevitably, by logic and by living we come to this fact of faith and of experience: *Christ is the Standard and the Power by which we attain spiritual maturity.* He was the Perfect Man, the Representative and Typal Adult, even as he was the supreme embodiment of the invisible God. Concerning him, it is the merest justice to say that "when he was grown, he went out unto his brethren, and looked on their burdens." He looked with compassion on them. He identified himself completely with all "that labour and are heavy laden," and in him as in no other they found, and find, rest. His spirit matures our spirits until we find ourselves increasingly adequate for the responsibilities of adult life in an exacting but splendid world. When this Son of Man confronts the enemy of our peace and usefulness, his weapons are strangely unlike those of Moses. For this Man destroys the power of the enemy through his redemptive love. He gets beneath the burden by carrying the Cross. Upon the Cross, he lifts us from our littleness into the greatness of life hidden with Christ in God, and found through Christ in our brothers everywhere.

Do you remember that beautiful play of American Negro religion of an earlier day, *The Green Pastures?* If you saw it, you will not forget the final scene. The play's theme is revealed, that God can only save men through forgiveness, and that forgiveness can be brought about only through suffering; that God must love men to the death to save them. Gabriel listens to God as He tells him "somethin' de Boy tol'" Him, "somethin' 'bout Hosea, and himself. How dey foun' somethin'." Gabriel asks, "What, Lawd?" "Mercy. 'Through sufferin','" he said. "Yes, Lawd. I'm tryin' to find it too. It's awful impo'tant. It's awful impo'tant to all de people on My earth. Did He mean dat even God must suffer?" Then in the distance there are heard cries: "Oh, look at Him; Oh, look, dey goin' to make Him carry it up dat high hill! Dey going to nail Him to it! Oh, dat's a terrible burden for one man to carry!" Beyond the audience, in the dim background, is enacted the mysterious tragedy and triumph of the Cross. God Himself in the Son of His Love joining His children, the little brothers of His Son, bears their burdens in the "terrible burden" of the Cross. This is the height of manhood, of womanhood; aye, let me say it in deep reverence, this is the height of Godhood, that we should join Christ in lifting the burden of mankind's cross.

PRAYER: *O Divine Redeemer and Eternal Friend of all the friends of men, keep our minds alert to Thy demands in the least of these our brethren. Keep our hearts humble, compassionate, and overflowing with Thy love for them. Lead us to make our service to those who travail and are heavy laden as gracious and beautiful as Thine own. For Thy Kingdom's sake we ask it. Amen.*

God on a Battlewagon: The Four Directions

CHAPLAIN JAMES V. CLAYPOOL
*Captain, U.S.N.R. (Methodist), Chaplains' Corps,
Naval Operating Base, Norfolk, Virginia*

During World War II Chaplain Claypool was on the famous U.S.S. "South Dakota" (known as "Battleship X" and "Old Nameless"), at the battle of Santa Cruz on October 26, 1942, and at Guadalcanal on November 14 and 15, 1943, and when she was attached to the British Home Fleet during the summer of 1943.

In World War I, he was a private first class in the First and Seventh Regiments, U.S. Marine Corps, and it was while in the Marine Corps at Guantanamo Bay, Cuba, he felt a call to enter the ministry, when he attended a service conducted by a naval chaplain from the U.S.S. "Pennsylvania," who a score of years later he learned was Boynton Merrill. After the war, he attended Brown, Boston and Temple Universities and was ordained a Methodist minister. Brown University recognized his work with the honorary Doctor of Divinity in 1945.

At present he is senior chaplain, Naval Training Station and senior chaplain, Naval Operating Base, Norfolk, Virginia, and is second in seniority of the chaplains on active duty.

In his work at the Operating Base at Norfolk, Captain Claypool has worked to insure religious services for men of all faiths, daily communion in the Protestant Chapel, special Lenten services, Sunday School (sailors do attend Sunday School), and a Service Men's Christian League. Special Catholic services provide three Masses daily, confessions before all Masses on Sunday, for four and a half hours on Saturday, and Monday through Friday during all evening Masses.

In 1944 he published God on a Battlewagon, a reprint of stories syndicated by the Chicago Tribune, from which the title of this sermon was taken. In this he shows his understanding of the fighting men and their problems. His sermon was preached at the Naval Operating Base at Norfolk, for his men, on January 21, 1945, and by popular request was later preached at Marble Collegiate Church, New York, and in other churches.

Sermon Forty=seven

TEXT: Get thee hence, and turn thee eastward. . . . I KINGS 17:3

SAILORS are traveling more these days during the war than at any other time in naval history. This is due to several factors. One factor is the speed with which task forces and fleets can operate. It is due more, however, to the fact that never have we been engaged in naval activities that require so much in the way of manpower, north, south, east and west all at the same time.

When someone says, "My ship traveled 80,000 miles in the last one and a half years and was in dry dock four times," we think it must have been under way a good deal. Another sailorman retorts, "We cruised 150,000 miles in fifteen months." And then somebody else tells a taller tale than that, but most of these accounts are true.

Many of the places where sailors stop these days they are not likely to have the opportunity to see again. Some of them they do not ever want to see again. The amount of travel that is being and has been done is enormous, and it is going to make some change, unquestionably, in the thinking of American manhood.

There are four directions, in the main, that we can take in our mind, or that we can cause our spirits to go. It is not the gale, but the set of the sail that determines where our lives are directed. When you are choosing the aim of your life and the direction you should give to your own personal thought, then you start your course on one of four routes.

The first is to the westward. The place of the setting sun and the evening star brings beautiful memories, and memories are lovely if you don't dwell there and try to enjoy them too much. There is prone to be a touch of melancholia when we travel in a westerly direction most of the time. We think of things that we would like to have done but have not done, and things that we have done that we ought not to have done—the times we have missed the mark, the times we have failed, the times we have been disappointed—and we don't always feel too happy. Some of us when we have started out on life's journey have repeated these words of promise and declaration of achievement:

> Out of the night that covers me
> Black as the pit from pole to pole
> I thank whatever gods may be
> For my unconquerable soul.

[283]

In the fell clutch of circumstance
I have not winced nor cried aloud
Under the bludgeonings of chance
My head is bloody but unbowed.

Beyond this place of wrath and tears
Looms but the horror of the shade;
And yet the menace of the years,
Finds, and shall find me unafraid.

It matters not how strait the gate,
How charged with punishments the scroll,
I am the master of my fate;
I am the captain of my soul.[1]

You look back now and you find you haven't been the master of your
fate and there have been situations where you can't say you have been the
captain of your soul. It is like the old farmer whose horse was compelled to
take him across the creek when the stream was very swollen. After they came
back, the water had subsided, but old Dobbin didn't want to cross over, and
the farmer said to him, "Dobbin, your memory is better than your judgment."
That sometimes happens to us when we look at the past, too. We see that we
aren't where we expected to be, and we become unhappy because of where
we are now.

I am thinking of a friend who is a university professor in the Middle West,
a Rhodes scholar. He is very successful in his department, has no family
cares, nothing in his life, so far as I know, but happiness. But he thinks that
in the past he had a whole string of mishaps. One of them is that when he
was at Oxford he didn't make the Lacrosse team. What does that matter now?
He looks backward too much for his own happiness, particularly to the good
old days. Of course, there never were any good old days. We see changes
today which are difficult to get adjusted to; we see changes socially and
economically. That is dangerous—that is not good—to look to the westward
and to look backward. We consider that we might be hermits and go off by
ourselves. But there are few who can do that; there are few farmers even
who can farm anywhere and farm completely by themselves.

The whole mood of turning to the west is expressed in

Sunset and evening star,
And one clear call for me!
And may there be no moaning of the bar
When I put out to sea.
But such a tide as moving seems asleep,
Too full for sound and foam,
When that which drew from out the boundless deep
Turns again home.

[1] "Invictus," from *Poems* by *William Ernest Henley*. Copyright by Charles Scribner's
Sons, New York.

Twilight and evening bell,
And after that the dark,
And may there be no sadness of farewell
When I embark,
For, though from out our bourne of time and place,
The flood may bear me far,
I hope to see my Pilot face to face
When I have crossed the bar.

The sentiment of Tennyson's lines is beautiful, and true, but the western road is not the place to live.

Some people would like to take the southern road, to travel personally in a southerly direction all the time. The journey south is languid, lovely, pleasant, and supposedly brings easy living, but it is tinged with boredom. There are no mighty rivers to cross, there are no tunnels to build, no valleys to bridge, no ridges to climb, no mountains to scale, no rough seas to sail. A man soon gets tired of that.

I am among those who are sorry that so many young folk, particularly in the haste of wartime, in getting married assume that marriage is the southern route, that everything will be easy, that you don't have to think any more, that the virtues of charity and kindness and the Golden Rule don't have to be taken into account because perfection has arrived. That would be great if true. Wedded life is a most happy, enchanting experience. But to assume that a person doesn't have to use brains any more after marriage is just assuming that he can travel the smooth road south and it will always be both pleasant and easy.

Then there is the road that goes north. It is a very popular one these days too. It is dark and dreary, tinged with pessimism, wars and rumors of wars, persecution, sadness, disappointment, sorrow, and yet it is an appealing road in this generation. There are many people who if they are going to write the word "realist" and put an equalizing word alongside it, feel that the word must be "cynic," people who have come to believe that if you face reality it can mean nothing beyond cynicism. A person who faces facts and endeavors to deal with the truth need not be a cynic. There are still times when "all's right with the world." Nothing in human experience in the past or the present justifies this assumption that a person who measures up to reality must scowl and be sour.

Some of us like Hamlet feel the times are out of joint, and echo, "O cursed spite, that ever I was born to set them right." We wish we had been born a little too soon for the draft, or hadn't been born yet. We begrudge the time taken from our lives by conscription. But the interruptions and interludes in our lives that God allows are the working out of His will, and our heavenly Father wants us to do our best in it. No, the west road, the south road, the north road are not the way to go.

[285]

In those long centuries about a thousand years before Christ, when Elijah was alive, people were taking all three of those roads. The people in Jerusalem took the west road. They looked back upon the Golden Age of King Solomon which had passed, and were undoubtedly weeping longingly before their Wailing Wall. They thought of the prosperous men and successful leadership under King Solomon and the stalwart virtues of a few generations before.

But the rulers of the kingdom thought otherwise and were appealed to by a southerly direction. Ahab and Jezebel didn't care about the glories of the past or their heritage. They were interested only in the southern road—the voluptuous, self-satisfied, easy life. They were not interested in the spiritual world, nor the prophecies of God, nor the truths of Moses and the Ten Commandments; they wanted only to take the southern route and exercise their hope to enjoy everything.

Then Elijah came, the opposite extreme. He traveled the north road, where often he sulked under the jutting juniper tree. He saw no hope for the children of God. He despairingly lamented that he alone kept the faith and was true to Jehovah. Some Christians are still like that. It is quite hard when any of us chaplains have to deal with well-meaning but divisive folks who think they are the only ones who have seen the Gospel light.

To all three of these groups of people—the common people looking back to the western past, the rulers looking only to the southern pleasure, and Elijah looking to the bleak north, came this message from God, "Get thee hence, and turn thee eastward." The new life Elijah received will in similar fashion come to us. Then will ascend a new hope, an expanding world, the glory of the dawn. "Heed well the salutation of the dawn. Look to this day, for it is life, the very life of life. Yesterday is but a dream, tomorrow is but a vision, but today well-lived"—that is what you have. Tomorrow may not come—yesterday is gone, but today we have, and today we will live—that is what we have as we are traveling the easterly direction, the road we find bright and beautiful.

The Apostle Paul certainly was a realist. He seemed to get sort of sour in spots when writing letters to some of the early Christian congregations. He was a realistic saint, all right, but he never abandoned his road toward the East, his confidence and expectation in the God in Whom he lived and moved and had his being. This Divine Father lights the life of every man that cometh into the world. That light continues in all of us.

Paul recorded for everyone:

Whatsoever things are true, whatsoever things are honest, whatsoever things are just, whatsoever things are pure, whatsoever things are lovely, whatsoever things are of good report; if there be any virtue, and if there be any praise, think on these things . . . and the God of peace shall be with you.

That is the way to travel—the way to the East.

I didn't realize it when meditating on this sermon, but it could be a New Year's sermon—not to take the north road, the west road, or the south road, but to take the east road and meet the New Year with hope and confidence. Likewise, it could be a Christmas sermon— "We have seen his star in the east, and are come to worship him"—this star of your ideals and decisions and ambitions which you will follow as long as you live. The star that you follow cannot be seen by any kind of route—not west or south or north, but you needs must take the east.

> To every man there openeth
> A Way, and Ways, and a Way,
> And the High Soul climbs the High Way,
> And the Low Soul gropes the Low,
> And in between on the misty flats,
> The rest drift to and fro.
> But to every man there openeth
> A High Way and a Low,
> And every man decideth
> The Way his soul shall go.[2]

The Returning Veteran and the Church of the Future

CHAPLAIN NEWELL DWIGHT LINDNER
Lieutenant, Chaplains' Corps, U.S.N.R.;
Rector, St. Mark's Protestant Episcopal Church, Islip, New York

This sermon grew out of Chaplain Lindner's convictions after eighteen months on a tour of duty with the U.S.S. "South Dakota" in the Pacific when most of the action there was taking place. He saw men die bravely; he spent long hours discussing every variety of subject with boys and men from all walks of life, for this wartime Navy of ours was a "civilian" Navy in the sense that it was made up largely of new men drawn from offices and farms and factories and colleges and high schools. The Chaplain got to know the men well and listened to their problems, their "beefs" and their joys.

He believes that the Church can attract the returning service men, but that the men will want a more vital religion than many churches offered in the years between the two world wars. "They are all interested in religion," he says, "but not in the old clichés. They want something that is real, honest and sincere, and until we clergy realize this we will make little impression. The Church faces a crisis in the next quarter century but there is also an

[2] From Gentlemen—the King! by John Oxenham (Boston: The Pilgrim Press).

equally great opportunity. Every man I ever talked with is interested in God but not too many are concerned with present-day presentations of Him. Too much unchristian competition and narrowness of outlook regarding other denominations leaves him cold and, not unlike people in the Orient, he sees little Christian love on the part of self-professed Christians to make him want to do anything but avoid it. I am afraid we have to cleanse our own temple before we can hope to cleanse society as a whole!"

Chaplain Lindner has had three churches, Christ Church, Bellport, New York, from 1934 to 1938; St. John's, Mt. Pleasant, Michigan, from March, 1938, to October, 1939, when he became rector of St. Mark's at Islip. On December 3, 1942, he entered the Navy as a chaplain, saw 30,000 WAVES go through Hunter College, then went to active duty on the U.S.S. "South Dakota," was with the Bureau of Naval Personnel in Washington after the peace, and returned to his parish on December 1, 1945. He was educated at Princeton, Union Seminary and Berkeley Divinity School. This sermon was preached in St. Bartholomew's Church, New York, on September 9, 1945, and attracted attention for it attacked the problem facing the churches and the service men in hard-hitting Navy style.

W. N. THOMAS

Sermon Forty=eight

SO MUCH has already been written about the returning veteran and the Church, and so many capable speakers have given the general public the benefit of their thinking and experience in this matter, that one hesitates to broach the subject anew, for fear of exposing himself to the charge of repetition. Be that as it may, one cannot serve for three years in the Navy, with half that time spent on a ship, without drawing some conclusions. When life is reduced to its simplest terms, as it is in continuing combat, and there is nothing to be gained by a man thinking otherwise than as he really does within the innermost recesses of his being, there is ample opportunity to gain insights of character at such moments. Such insights every chaplain who knew and loved his men secured and, in the passing of them on to interested people, there may be, and often is, much that is not palatable. If it is discovered that the speaker's observations fall into this category, he asks, not your forgiveness, but only your understanding of what is at stake.

What about our returning service man with particular reference to his relation to the Church of the future? Will he be friendly toward it? Will he despise it? Or will he tolerate it, much as you and I tolerate ideas and institutions in which we are no longer interested?

First of all, before we try to answer such questions, let us seek to understand the nature of the veteran, particularly the one who has seen extended combat duty. When he was inducted or enlisted, he was a normal youth just like any other youth. The segment of society from which he came may have been affluent or destitute; he was a civilian with a normal civilian outlook. The military service went to work on him with a will to make a fighting man out of him, and if he lacked the qualifications deemed necessary for such, he was weeded out and placed elsewhere. Overnight he became a unit in a very large organization, and his individuality was obliterated by force of circumstances. He even lost his name, for all practical purposes, and became a serial number. He fell in with other men from totally different walks of life from his own—different ideas, different ideals, different habits, different everything. He found that some men were made of sound stuff and some men were very earth, earthly. He found that some men were worth cultivating as friends, and some were to be avoided like the plague. The religious convictions he brought with him into the service were scant in most cases. He had attended Sunday school for a few years and then may have gone to church once or twice a year with his parents. But religion had never been a very large part of his consciousness.

In due time this lad of ours became an expert killer. His indoctrination served him extremely well and his instructors looked on him as an efficient fighting unit. Then came the day when he went overseas, east or west, and from then on, it was his life or the enemy's. In the long hours of inaction, when there were moments to think, and particularly after an action in which his buddy beside him had been blown out of this world into some other world, his mind drifted backward for fleeting glances at more pleasant scenes. Loneliness can be a horrible thing, even when thousands of men are around you. And our lad did not escape this, either. He perhaps was too ashamed to mention it to his friends, but he felt it nevertheless. Did not God's own Son feel this on the cross? Yes, our lad felt it but he was too proud to give way to it, except perhaps to his chaplain in a moment when no one else was near. In such moments do the insights spoken of come; but they are brief and, half in shame, half in satisfaction, the soul is bared.

This lad who left us a stripling comes home now a man. He is much wiser in the ways of the world than when he left; he has had to be to survive. He is very cocky, and why not? He has been on a winning team, a team which never lost a single game. We all know that nothing in this world succeeds like success. And there is a chip on his shoulder, too. All the resentment that has been stored up these many months comes pouring out. "How much money did you make while I was away? Where were you all the time? Who has my job now? And my girl—why did she have to marry somebody else as soon as my back was turned? And whoever put the idea of a divorce in my wife's head when I was not even here to defend myself?" These are just a few of the questions which serve as props to hold the chip on the shoulder. What are we to do with this attitude? How shall it be met?

I think the question is best answered in a negative way. Do not argue with it. Do not combat against it. Accept it! To do anything else, no matter how well taken or logical, will serve only to harden it into something which not even time can mellow. Accept it for what it is and try to understand whence it comes. And, too, in all probability, the conduct of our returning veteran will in many instances offend us. He will do and say things which we deem highly objectionable. But do not condemn him too quickly, friends. Remember, hell has been his living place these many, many months past. Remember that he was conditioned to be what he is. It took time to make him that way. He was a civilian and they made him an efficient fighting man. It will take longer to make him a civilian again, and in the interim you must exercise every bit of patience and understanding and love of which you are capable. Sincere love of persons is the best antidote to all kinds of human poisons. We have Christ's own example for that.

Perhaps the most practical thing we can do for our young veteran as he returns is to get him out of uniform as quickly as possible. If we can do that, we shall have won half the battle already. But as long as he is in uniform with the war over, there is a psychological difference between himself and his friends, and only the donning of civilian clothes will make him feel that he is really back in society again.

The relation of the veteran to the Church of the future is in reality only one phase of the much deeper problem of the veteran in general. It goes without saying, does it not, that the millions of men who return to civilian life within the next year will have a loud voice in the destiny of the country they fought for. It takes no prophet or seer to make that clear. Anyone who thinks at all and is conscious of life even in the smallest degree knows that these returning millions will largely fashion our education, our politics, our economics and our entire culture for many, many years to come. It is extremely doubtful if their thinking can be done for them by those who do not understand them, and even more doubtful if they can be adjusted to follow once again the old familiar patterns of thought. Whether we like it or not, they hold the future in their hands.

A backward glance over the years should refresh our memories. You recall that after the last war, first in Russia, then in Italy, then in Germany, and finally in Spain, it was the veterans who provided the foundation for totalitarian thinking and action. It was they who provided the social ferment in their respective countries because democratic leadership was too timid to satisfy the veteran type of thinking.

What kind of spiritual leadership can the Church provide to do its share in meeting this kind of thinking? How alive are our ecclesiastical leaders to the explosive nature of the situation we face in the immediate future? Of course, the usual commissions, committees and boards have been established by many denominations to study this problem. But I strongly doubt if any appreciable number of our ecclesiastical leaders of any importance are really aware of what the future holds in store.

The Church is face to face with a new mentality, a veteran mentality, that will dominate the national scene for many years to come, a mentality that labors under no illusions whatsoever and has known for several years that the only reality was a miserable death, or at best, a consuming loneliness in some foreign land thousands of miles from home and kin. The men who return have been to no Sunday school picnic, and it is going to be a terrific task to convince them that Christianity has any relevancy whatever to their lives.

Is this attitude, you say, the sole result of the war through which we have just passed, or is there something more to it? Yes, there is much more to it, much which the war has served merely to reflect with utter tragedy—much which the war, not unlike some chemical agent, has caused to rise to the surface of our consciousness. For centuries we have told ourselves with pride that ours is a part of Western civilization, that we are part of the heritage which civilized Europe after the Dark Ages. We have repeated this to ourselves so often that we have completely forgotten what Western civilization was or is. We have overlooked the very important fact that Western civilization was Christian civilization with all the implications inherent in that term. We have tried to maintain a Christian civilization without ourselves being Christian and have justifiably opened ourselves to the charge of hypocrisy.

Can you think of any more materialistic country than ours, where the machine is the object of so much reverence and worship? As you look back and think about it, can you not understand now how Henry Adams felt when he gazed upon the dynamo at the Paris Exposition? Do you know of any place where there is more emphasis in the entire educational system on mastery of materials and processes, on production and consumption, on statistics and averages, with an apparent assumption that no man does live by bread alone?

The sad and basic truth is that the war just ended was but the complete manifestation of the spirit of materialism that has infected the world these many centuries. As always, war is a result, not a cause; and again, as always, it is within ourselves that we must look for the answer. We must begin from within. Like Isaiah in the temple we must admit before God that we are a people of unclean lips, dwelling in a world of unclean hearts. There is no other answer.

So the fundamental task of the Church today is in reality no different from what it has always been: to convict man of his desperate need of God and to lead man to repentance. This is the crux of the matter, the point of success or failure of the Church of the future. Oh, how ancient and yet how modern that program is! It is so modern and so recent that innumerable men in the service never heard about it until some chaplain spoke of it in a brief moment before an action. Certainly back home, after a few years in the Sunday school, the local church meant nothing. It became something far removed from their daily experience and went its own way satisfied with its own importance. The Church went asleep and, God help us, still slumbers on. How else, friends, can you explain the fact that less than 5 per cent of the men in the service ever heard from their church back home? How else can you explain the fact that a letter from the local parish was always an object of curiosity? You judge a tree by its fruit and, like the fig tree which Jesus caused to wither, we have borne no fruit. The common answer I have always received from men relative to hearing from the local parish has invariably been, "I guess they don't care." Don't care! "God so loved the world that he gave his only begotten Son." If this returning veteran of ours has only contempt for the Church of the future, let us put the blame where it belongs, on the Church. What a victim of ecclesiastical indifference he has been!

The main question is this: How can the Church salvage the future and convince this veteran mentality of which we have been speaking that Christianity does have a relevancy to life—to its life? Only by mercilessly exposing and attacking the philosophy of life now widespread in America; only by first cleansing itself of its pride and its prejudice, can it hope to attract followers later. The attack of the Church of the future must come from two directions—the intellectual and the emotional simultaneously. We need today as never before some intellectual giant who can do for our age what Aquinas did for his of the thirteenth century. We need some giant, thoroughly trained in theology, in science, in philosophy, and in religion, to create a synthesis of our knowledge as we have it today; and then we need the courage and the conviction to broaden our spiritual and religious horizons. The heart and the mind must conspire together to give a new direction and a new meaning to a kind of life now unfit for a child of God to endure; and the only source from which this leadership can come is the Church of God.

The Church of the future will find, too, that the old competitive denominationalism is a luxury it can no longer afford. Such men in the service who have been brought to the reality of God and the sense of His presence have been brought thither by Christian ministers, whose only designation was "Chaplain." I doubt very much if any appreciable number of veterans who show any interest in the Church of the future will be interested in denominational labels. Are those of us already in the Church daring enough to accept this, or will we continue in the old competitive, "dog eat dog," unChristian philosophy? Are we ready to approach this problem with sincere hearts and minds, laying aside all malice and distrust for each other? Pray God that we are, because the future of the Church lies somewhere along this road.

The Church of the future will find, too, that she must insist upon a higher caliber of servant to represent her. She must no longer be content to send forth representatives into the world who are half-baked intellectual and spiritual specimens. She needs men: tall, sun-crowned men, men who are not afraid of the world, men who can carry the message of the love and hope of the Church to the teeming millions throughout the world, men whose thinking is clear, whose hearts are on fire with the love of God and the love of humanity, upright men, simple men, God-fearing men, men whom the world cannot crush, men who are harmless as doves and wise as serpents in carrying out her work. The Church of the future must be sure that a man is a man, because no less will be accepted, even before she begins her training to fit him for his life's work. Oh, the Church of the future must rededicate herself from within to the salvation of human society, and only then can we expect God to bless her work.

Finally, to those of you whose homes now possess an empty chair through the sacrifice of a son on the altar of his country's need, may I say this: There is a hole in your heart and in your home which no amount of words, no matter how sincere, can change. Through bitter experience on too many occasions I have learned of the complete inadequacy of words at such times. To look into the faces of loving fathers and mothers and wives, and tell them that their loved one is no more, is an experience that never loses its stark reality no matter how often undergone. From birth, what hopes you had for that boy, what a brilliant future he had, and how you hoped and planned to help him make his mark. He has made his mark already, but certainly not as you intended. His mark perhaps is a simple white cross in a quiet place somewhere in a distant land, and the cry of lament which rends your heart makes you a kinsman with Job!

In all this let us keep our thinking straight, regardless of how difficult that may be. God never willed any man's death before his time, and your son is no exception. God can do only one thing, love; and all that is not love in this world is not of Him or of His nature. To each of His children God has given the terrible responsibility of free will, and no matter how we exercise it, God can do only one thing—love us. God could do no more for His Son as he hung upon the cross, and if Jesus was permitted to go down to seeming defeat before the forces of cruelty and evil of his day, can we expect more in ours—more, that is, as long as the same hatred, the same cruelty, the same evil which nailed him to the cross still remain in the world today because we continue to misuse the responsibility which God has given us? Of a certainty Isaiah expressed eternal truth when he wrote: "Surely he hath borne our griefs, and carried our sorrows: . . . he was wounded for our transgressions, he was bruised for our iniquities." God was a stricken Father, too. Let us never forget that! He, too, knows grief and heartache and shares our sorrow as our hearts open to receive Him.

That boy of yours is forever beyond the sordidness of this world. Never again must his life be sullied by the cruelty of wicked hands, the hatred of poisoned minds, or the meanness of small people. The daily hurts which you and I must continue to endure can no longer touch him. God has assigned him to other tasks. There is no waste. There he can grow and develop and mature into that spiritual perfection which God's love alone makes possible. And in that final day when God shall wipe away all tears and all earthborn shackles shall have been burst asunder and we look once again into the face of our beloved, then will our lament be forever stilled and the peace which passeth all understanding be ours.

The grave is a beginning, not an end, and may our faith in the moral integrity of God be the kindly light that leads us to our ultimate rendezvous with Him. Until then, take courage—take courage in the words of the hymn writer who knew so well the depth of our common human sorrow when he wrote:

> Must Jesus bear the cross alone,
> And all the world go free?
> No, there's a cross for everyone,
> And there's a cross for me.

Let us pray:

Our Heavenly Father, King Eternal, immortal, invisible, Thou only wise God our Saviour; hasten, we beseech Thee, the coming of Thy Kingdom upon the earth and draw the whole world of mankind into willing obedience to Thy blessed reign. Overcome all the enemies of Christ and bring low every power that is exalted against him. Cast out all the evil things which cause wars and fightings among us, and let Thy spirit rule the hearts of men in righteousness and love. Restore the desolations of former days. Rejoice the wilderness with beauty and make glad the city with Thy law. Establish every work that is founded on truth and equity, and fulfill all the good hopes and desires of mankind. Manifest Thy will, Almighty God, in the brotherhood of man and bring in universal peace; through the victory of Jesus Christ Thy Son, our Lord. Amen.

We Shall Remember Them

REVEREND JOSEPH R. SIZOO, D.D.[1]
Minister, St. Nicholas Collegiate Church (Reformed), New York

Dr. Sizoo is one of the great preachers of our day. His sermons have a historical perspective which make his religious interpretations doubly valuable for men and women in our troubled times.

[1] Sermons by members of the Advisory Committee were contributed at the special request of the editor and are included on his responsibility. It was preached November 22, 1945.

Born in the Netherlands, he was educated at Hope College and New Brunswick Theological Seminary. He has been a minister of the Dutch Reformed Church all his life except for twelve years as minister of the famous New York Avenue Presbyterian Church in Washington, D.C. It was here that diplomats, senators, businessmen and people from ordinary walks of life crowded his church to hear his brilliant preaching.

The Collegiate Church of St. Nicholas called him to New York, where he has won recognition and great respect for the substantial character and spiritual quality of his sermons. This church is the oldest Protestant congregation in New York City with a continuous ministry and was originally organized at the Battery as "the Church in the Fort." Theodore Roosevelt attended St. Nicholas Church when he was a boy and his pew is now identified with a memorial tablet. All of the Collegiate Churches are part of the historic Dutch Reformed Church.

In 1942 he was president of the General Synod of the Reformed Church in America, served a term as president of the Greater New York Federation of Churches, as vice-president of the Protestant Council, and as chaplain of the Twelfth Regiment of the New York Guard. His books have been widely accepted. Three of them, Make Life Worth Living, Not Alone *and* On Guard, *have had a great influence. During the war he visited army and navy bases and spoke to the enlisted men and chaplains. In the sermon given here he discusses the historical significance of Thanksgiving as an American religious institution, showing clearly that the early founders of this country intended it to be a Christian country in faith and practice.*

Sermon Forty=nine

TEXT: Wherefore seeing we also are compassed about with so great a cloud of witnesses. . . . HEBREWS 12:1

NOVEMBER is one of those months in the calendar year when the past crowds in on us. On All Saints' Day, Armistice Day and Thanksgiving Day we live over again the great moments of yesterday and think of those into whose inheritance we have entered. We are here to keep alive a tradition: to give thanks to God for the past and to dedicate ourselves to their unfinished task. In that we set a good example. We are so casual with tradition. It is so easy to conclude that nobody in the past had significance until we came. It is good for a people to halt every now and again and go over the road they have traveled. If we knew history better we would not be so disturbed today. A nation is judged by the kind of men it honors in the past.

In the far past there are the Pilgrims landing upon New England's broken coast. They sailed in the "Mayflower," a ship no larger than the life boats on the "Queen Mary." They tumbled and tossed through a green, angry sea over an uncharted course for thirteen weeks. There were one hundred and two in all when they landed. One-half their number was dead within six months and they were buried in graves made level with the ground so that they would not be desecrated by the hostile Indian. The remainder endured pestilence and hunger and cold and loneliness. They lived on the unaccustomed diet of dried fish, ground nuts and corn. They worked for seven long years to pay back to London bankers the loan which made possible their adventure. And yet, when their work was done they had established here this government under God into the inheritance of which we have entered.

In the near past there is another company who, by the mercy of God and their own gallantry, maintained the freedom which the Pilgrims established. They fought a war they neither wanted nor created. They came from many homes: rich and poor; humble and educated; from the Avenue and from the other side of the tracks. It was not without cost that this freedom was maintained. There are faces we shall never see again; there are hands we shall never grasp again; there are voices we shall never hear again. There are eyes that will never see again; there are limbs that will never grow again; and there are minds that will never think again. We remember them in gratitude before God—the great and the good who bore the testimony of a good conscience, who fought a good fight, who finished their course, who kept the faith, who endured, "as seeing Him who is invisible," who conquered in the fight, for whom the trumpets have already blown on the other side.

But going back has its peril, too. The traditionalist is always in danger. It is so easy to live in the past, rather than by the past. When an idea becomes frozen into a form it is so easy to think more of the form than the idea. Sooner or later convictions fall into a pattern. In times like that we are so disposed to worship the pattern rather than the conviction. Many conceive of an inheritance as some lovely bundle wrapped up in colored cellophane, bound up in red, white and blue ribbons which the past has put into our hands. Twice a year—on July Fourth and Thanksgiving we bring it out of its hiding, dust it off carefully, carry it in a procession, while onlookers sing, "God bless America." Then we put it back into hiding for another year. You see, it is so easy to live in the past, rather than by the past. What the past asks of us is not to be remembered, but to be satisfied. They carried their torch into the night, but there is still darkness left. They laid the foundation of a new order, but have put into our hands their working tools with which to complete the superstructure. So the question is, how can we make the past effective in the life of the present? How can we make yesterday meaningful in today? What must we do to live, not in the past, but by the past?

Someone has said that history is the record of what man thinks of himself, of others and of God. Movements and institutions which have outlasted time have always been built upon these three convictions. Nothing is permanent in any world order unless it is rooted and grounded in these three: integrity, understanding, reverence; personal initiative, social responsibility and spiritual sensitiveness.

1. History is the record of what man thinks of himself. Movements and institutions will live and last when they are registered in character. At the rock bottom of any enduring order is integrity. It is one thing to fall in the esteem of others, but it is far more terrible to fall in one's own esteem. It is a dreadful thing to lose your reputation, but it is much worse to lose your self-respect. And yet, integrity is almost a forgotten word in our present-day vocabulary. One doesn't often hear it. Above all other things that is the supreme need of the hour.

Well-meaning, but misguided people are living today with a pleasing illusion; and because the illusion is so pleasing it is all the more deadly and fatal. It is this: that the enthusiasm for unselfishness and high idealism generated by the war will be permanent. Many have made themselves believe that the high levels of patriotic devotion, social restraint and self-discipline which the war forced upon us will continue in peace. That is a dreadful illusion because history holds no such warrant. The Civil War was followed by a period of unbelievable political corruption which struck an all time low in the Tweed Ring. The first World War which we fought to make democracy safe for the world was succeeded by an era of the so-called new freedom: obey that impulse, let yourself go, express yourself. We never asked if we had a self worth expressing.

High moral effort is always followed by moral lassitude and indifference. Just look around you today and see the flagrant violation of the law, the vulgar indecencies of stage and screen, the dreadful juvenile delinquency and an increase in the crimes of violence. Out of every one hundred crimes committed in our country forty-one are by young people eighteen years of age. But I am thinking of this moral lassitude in the broader aspects. In our national life there are signs of moral instability. As I go up and down the country and listen to thoughtful people, they do not ask, are we turning to the right or to the left of center, but have we a center left? They wonder if there is still some moral beam by which we sail the course of the ship of state. They wonder if there is some ethical standard by which everything is evaluated. These are days of expediency. Those in control of the affairs of the nation are so apt to let, I will, wait upon I would, traveling the primrose path of dalliance. There is a danger that we shall accommodate ourselves to all kinds of pressure groups. Altogether too many send up a trial balloon to find out which way the wind is blowing before they cast their ballot. It is so easy to gyrate from one side of the street to the other in all manner of compromise. How our time needs to hear again,

[297]

> To thine own self be true
> And it shall follow as the night the day
> Thou canst not then be false to any man.

2. History is the record of what man thinks of others. Movements and institutions which last must express themselves in understanding. Life to be great must have its setting in the framework of the community. To personal integrity there must always be added compassionate understanding. It is only when the sense of social responsibility is joined to personal initiative that a nation is safe. Civilization is not a lonely journey of a lonely soul upon a lonely God. It is a pilgrimage on a crowded highway on which we learn to live together for the common good. We are all God's children and the Almighty plays no favorites. Just as it is impossible for families to achieve happiness while brother hates brother and sister disavows parent, so in the family of nations wherever ill will and suspicion abound, peace is utterly unthinkable.

That needs saying today because we are living in a world with a new kind of frontier. There was a time when the boundaries of nations were determined by geography. The barriers between races and nations were larger natural barricades: a mountain range, a wide river, a sea or a belt of swamp land and forests. As long as these frontiers stood nations thought themselves secure. No one from without could come in and no one from within could go out. Then came modern science and suddenly frontiers became imaginary lines and natural barriers became meaningless. We can tunnel any hill, we can bridge any river, we can sail any sea and we can fly a plane over any hump. Indeed, there are not two places in all the world more than fifty or sixty flying hours apart. You can fly around the whole world in one hundred and fifty hours. Natural frontiers are meaningless. So it has come to pass that nations are building a new kind of frontier much more impenetrable and impregnable. These new frontiers are invisible: they sink so deep before you are aware of their existence. They are the frontiers of the mind: the frontiers of suspicion, hate, fear and power.

Not long ago I asked a leader of the underground of one of the liberated countries of Europe what was the attitude of his country toward us. "Frankly," he said, "we do not like you." When I reminded him that we had just finished fighting and dying for their liberation he said, "That is true, but you are so powerful, we are afraid." The new frontier of suspicion. So one could go on to multiply the examples of these new frontiers. As long as they stand we can never hope to achieve peace on earth. It will take all the patience, all the forbearance, all the tolerance and all the grace of God we can possibly muster to live even with a reasonable contentment in such a world.

What is true in our attitude to others is equally true in our attitude to ourselves. There is nothing more magnificent in American history than the sense of unity which came to us through the war. We set aside our differences and our disagreements. We walked the way of linked arms through the struggle, but now that the war is over it is so easy to tumble apart. There is something strange about human nature: we are welded together by adversity, but we soon disintegrate when that danger passes away. Already there are too many signs of this disintegration. We are falling apart into brittle groups each seeking some advantage at the expense of the other.

What this age needs is men and women who will live with an adventurous good will. It may be that much out of the past is crumbling. It ought to crumble, because it was not good enough and mankind was entitled to something better. We have a chance, it may be our last chance, to build a better world without pain, without panic, without disease; a world in which childhood shall not be forgotten, old age not abandoned and womanhood not neglected; a world in which man shall come before the machine and personality before profits; a world in which man's inhumanity to man shall be supplanted by the higher law that we are our brothers' keeper; a world in which the four horsemen of the Apocalypse shall never ride again. We need people who have imagination, who are creative, who will adventure with this good will. Dr. Santayana, the distinguished New England savant, was lecturing one day to a group of students at Harvard University. During the course of his lectures he said, "If it were given to me to look into the heart of a man and found there no good will, I would say, 'you are not an American.'" God grant it may ever be so. Movements and institutions which last must express themselves in understanding.

3. History is the record of what man thinks of God. Movements and institutions which have outlasted time have always been founded on spiritual forces. It is possible for a man to have personal initiative, and even to have a sense of community-mindedness and still make a wreck of the universe. Germany and Japan were resourceful, had imagination and courage, were dominated by a sense of national responsibility, but look what happened to them and what they did to the world. Unless to integrity and understanding there is added reverence, a civilization cannot long survive.

How all that needs repeating I need hardly suggest. Oftentimes we have been asked, how did the world get this way? And what has happened to us that times like these should come to pass? Of course, we always had the answer. We talked about economic maladjustment in the world, social injustice in groups, political chicanery, diplomatic double talk and crackpot ideologies. It is true that all these had a part in the darkness which has settled upon the world; but they do not go to the root of the matter. These times have come because we lost our moral awareness and the importance of spiritual values. We thought that the absence of faith was a sign of intellectual vigor. We supposed that man was great in proportion as the sense of mystery vanished. We treated the idea of God so casually. We thought of religion as one of the take-it-or-leave-it affairs. We suddenly discovered that the seeds of national decay are never in a political technique or social structure, but in the character of its people. A nation can be no better than the level of the soul of its people. A new world can only come to pass through new people. The hope of the world rests essentially in the reconversion of the human spirit. All the ingenious devices for international good will, all the painstaking, meticulous arrangements for world peace will come to nothing if they are placed in the hands of men who are unreliable and untrustworthy.

Just before the war ended I was at an Army camp. Early one morning at dawn two regiments marched out to the edge of a hill to listen to a lecture by an officer on how to take a military objective. I marched out with them and in the early morning we sat down in the tall, wet grass. At the foot of the hill stood the officer. He first described the wrong way to reach the objective and then he demonstrated it by the use of troops. After that he described the right way of reaching a given goal. To demonstrate it there were a group of well-seasoned soldiers on their hands and knees hugging the earth, holding fast to the grass. You could hardly see them. As they advanced toward their objective the officer called out somewhat casually, "If you advance on your knees you are always safe." That sentence should be carved upon the threshold of every school and on the doorpost of every home. It is still true that that nation alone is great whose God is the Lord. The same God who gave us eyes to see and ears to hear and lips to speak, gave us knees to bend. When we lay hold of that fact we shall have something which no experience can impeach and no temptation can imperil. History is the record of what man thinks of God.

What Do You See? (see p. 85)

THE VERY REVEREND CHESTER BURGE EMERSON, D.D.
Dean, Trinity Cathedral, Protestant Episcopal, Cleveland, Ohio

Dean Emerson was born in Massachusetts in 1882 and was educated at Bowdoin College and Union Theological Seminary. Bowdoin and Kenyon College honored him with the Doctor of Divinity.

He was ordained to the Congregational ministry in 1909 and assumed the pastorate of First Parish, Saco, Maine, which he held for four years. In 1913 he was called to North Woodward Church, Detroit, where he remained until 1932. He was made canon residentiary of Trinity Cathedral, Cleveland, from January to November, 1933, and became its dean in November, 1933.

During the first World War, Dr. Emerson served with the Y.M.C.A. in

France. His varied activities cover civic as well as religious and educational fields. Besides having served as president of the board of trustees of the Michigan Conference, member of the executive committee of the Commission on Missions of the National Council of Congregational Churches, he is a member of the executive committee of the State Board of Congregational Churches, overseer of Bowdoin College, member of the board of directors of Chicago Theological Seminary, trustee of Hampton Institute, member of Arts and Crafts Society of Olivet College, Founders Society of the Art Museum of Detroit, Fine Arts Society, and a past director of the Detroit Symphony Orchestra.

Dean Emerson believes that a man's personality, his presence, his voice and his style of speaking have a vast influence in the impression that his sermon makes, and that, therefore, some sermons read infinitely better than they sound when spoken, while others, although great and inspiring when delivered, don't read well when put in print. This sermon shows how man's vision comes from within as well as from the things around him.

Sermon Fifty

TEXT: What went ye out . . . for to see? LUKE 7:24

THAT is a very searching question. For life is pretty much what you yourself make of it. It depends upon your point of view. If you are enthusiastic about living and happy in what you are doing, that is largely to your credit. But if you are unhappy, finding little interest in what you do, and little hope for the morrow, that is partly to your discredit. Satisfaction in life depends very largely upon what a man is in himself, his wants, his outlook, his will to be and to do.

All this is only another way of saying that a man's philosophy is the most important thing about him. It determines what he does today and is likely to become tomorrow. It gives shape and size to his thoughts, scope to his ambition, let or hindrance to his emotions. A wrong philosophy of life is bound to work itself out into an unhappy career. A wise philosophy equally will work itself out into a useful career, regardless of how little or how much it is regarded in the things of this world.

So the world is much as you think it to be. Certainly it is a various place with the makings of undreamed of things, and equally the makings of all manner of lives.

What do you see in it? The adaptability of the earth is conditioned only by the power of vision that marks a man; in a way it makes him; it gives him

[301]

reaching power. And this truth holds in every realm of the world from the making of machines to the discernment of deity.

Someone dreamed a dream and out of it fashioned a fact. So has it always been and will be always in the achievements of humanity.

One man dozed by a singing kettle. Watts dreamed an engine drawing heavy loads.

One man dodged a falling apple in the yard. Newton discovered a natural law.

One man closed his eyes in terror at the lightning. Franklin snared it for his use.

One man stumbled against a block of granite. Rodin chipped "The Thinker" with his skillful hands.

One man paid three francs for a piece of canvas and a little paint. Millet brushed in "The Angelus."

One man heard the noisy tuning of instruments. Strauss tuned from them "Death" and "The Transfiguration."

One man tossed aside the record of a sordid murder trial. Browning read out of it "The Ring and the Book."

One man saw an eagle flying low against the sun. Robert Coffin pulled a poem from beneath its wings.

One man lost his way in the mist upon a mountain. Moses met God face to face and gave a world the moral law.

One man passed a Carpenter on the road. Paul kneeled before the living Christ.

There is something men call sight and something they call insight. The difference is in themselves. What do you see?

Maurice Maeterlinck wrote a very thoughtful book called *Wisdom and Destiny*. In it he says:

> Let us always remember that nothing befalls us that is not of the nature
> of ourselves. There comes no adventure but wears to our soul the shape of
> our everyday thoughts; and deeds of heroism are but offered to those who,
> for many long years, have been heroes in obscurity and silence. And whether
> you climb up the mountain or go down the hill to the valley, whether you
> journey to the end of the world or merely walk round your house, none but
> yourself shall meet you on the highway of fate. If Judas go forth tonight, it
> is towards Judas his steps will tend, nor will chance for betrayal be lacking;
> but let Socrates open his door, he shall find Socrates asleep on the threshold
> before him, and there will be occasion for wisdom. Our adventures hover
> around us like bees round the hive when preparing to swarm. They wait till
> the mother-idea has at last come forth from our soul, and no sooner has she
> appeared than they all haste to you; love, and adventures will flock to you,
> throbbing with love. They seem to be all on the watch for the signal we
> hoist from within. . . .

"What went ye out . . . for to see?"

The difference between a clod and a cloud is a difference of element and elevation. The difference between a clodhopper and a seer is the same thing —element and elevation. The clod is of the earth earthy, so is the clodhopper. The cloud is of Heaven heavenly, so is the seer. However his feet are set his soul is forever established.

So with a man's attitude toward the earth. For the earth is full of treasures and generously kind to all. There is enough and to spare for all her children, if only men would conquer their greed and work together for mutual benefit. The universe can be trusted, and she will pay in kind for any distrust. She will feed him who digs into her resources, she will starve him who does not seek her gifts. Co-operation between her children is both easy and practical; generosity begets generosity, consideration is rewarded with kindliness. If only men will stop their cruel competition one with another, and give themselves together in common service for all, then will the earth give forth her increase, not only in full measure but running over.

So with a man's attitude to humanity. One man looks upon the other man as a competitor, one looks upon him as a neighbor. To one he is a curious biped sprung from dust and speeding back to dust, at best enlarging for a little while his fund of knowledge, perhaps controlling his instincts for greater effectiveness, learning to associate with others like himself for the sake of convenience, here for a little, and then no more.

Yet to another man, he may be all that but infinitely more. He is a spirit emerging from darkness to light, plodding the long road upward from beasthood to manhood; he is a soul dwelling in a body and climbing slowly to the estate of a son of God. He learns truth by degrees and through bitter experience, "catching at mistake as midway help, until he reach fact indeed."

He finds other souls working like himself for self-expression, so he loves the other man and works with him, prays with him, struggles forward with him, laughs and weeps with him, blesses him, calls him "brother." And presses on by superlative courage and fortitude to an end which calls him, though he sees it not. At last he stumbles into an open doorway where One in Whose face dwells the eternal dawnlight gathers him to His bosom, saying, "Come unto me, all ye that labour and are heavy laden, and I will give you rest. . . . rest unto your souls."

So it is likewise with this great issue of world unity. There really never has been a separate heartbeat under the sun. For hunger and cold and thirst and pain and sorrow are common to all mankind, and every wise voice out of every tribe in every tongue has begged mankind to tear down its fences, all of the fences that hem one group from another, to demolish all the obstacles to mutual understanding and co-operation. Our inventions do not speak in separate languages, not one of them. The Chinese can fly as well as Americans. The Russian will find the atomic bomb only a little later than the Anglo-Saxon. The estrangements that exist between the peoples have nothing to do with nature. They are man-made.

God is one God and nature is one nature. So is human nature. There is but one root language in all of the earth—the language of human need and divine grace. The spirit of man is one. He is estranged neither in his ideal for this world nor in his hope for the other. In one of his books years ago, Newell Dwight Hillis used these descriptive words:

> By ten thousand cables and electric threads God is binding the nations together in weaving one warp and woof—a world people.
>
> Physically Providence has distributed his needs so that no nation is a full nation. He gives wheat to the north, cotton to the south, tea and spices to the east, sugar and coffee to the tropics. No man is a full man, because of the distribution of the intellectual gifts. God took the ideal man and broke him up into fragmentary men, so that they would have to unite their gifts through brotherhood to produce a civilization, just as God broke up the light and distributed it in fragmentary stars and then bound the stars together into one cosmic system. He gives religion to the Hebrew, law to the Roman, culture to the Greek, the love of detail to the German, wit and beauty to the Frenchman, colonization to the Englishman, practical invention to the American, mental alertness to the Japanese, patience to the Chinese, endurance to the Russian. The world is the Father's house and all men brothers.

Now all these things of which we have spoken are plainly set forth in the teachings of our Lord. The earth to him was the good gift of our heavenly Father. All men were His children. If some were in greater need then those in greater abundance must come to their help. If there be evil in the earth, then because they are the children of God with an inheritance of righteousness, must they feel the responsibility to band together to demolish that evil. Knowledge they must pool, since no one mind is a full mind, and wisdom is diffused among the peoples, not concentrated.

Together they must dream dreams and see visions of a more productive earth and a more co-operative humanity, and those who have seen that vision must covenant together to bring it to pass, however great may be the cost "in blood and sweat and tears."

So life to him and through him to all men is full of worth and meaning. Run over the events and experiences of his own tragic yet matchless life. He was a carpenter's son, living in a provincial village, dedicated to the service of his neighbors, but rejected by them and at last crucified by those whom he had blessed. Worth-while? Yes. Because of the contribution he could make to the general livableness of life and for the satisfaction he gained in his own soul in doing his Father's will, and in the job itself being well done.

So with our own lives as we look back upon them from the vantage point of age, or as we look forward to them in our youth by the light that shines from the experience of our fathers and mothers, or our older friends. Well might we say with John Percyfield:

> Our dear ones die, our affairs get tangled, our powers wane, life and youth are spent, the hearing dulls, the eye weakens—it may be a losing game. But when one's interests are concentrated on something bigger than the imme-

diate personal career, upon the social good, upon the purified soul, it is possible to be eternally youthful and happy. No selfish idling can bring it, no dangling in museums and libraries, no aimless wanderings by the mountains and the sea—no selfish pursuit of any kind whatever. It comes only through human service and human sympathy, and human outreaching toward that which is eternal and divine.

Such a vision of the worth of man and the worth of life is essentially spiritual. It is not ascetic—it loves all that is beautiful and good and true and joyous. It is not aristocratic—it mingles with crowds in sympathy, understanding and appreciation. But it is spiritual in outlook.

And it is this spiritual outlook that helps us to set the things of this world in their proper places, to get a true sense of proportion, to put first things first and keep secondary things in subjection. There is nothing that can keep one from the sordid spirit, which in the end hardens our sensibilities to all truth and goodness and beauty, like this vision of ourselves as the children of God, and the world as the place for our habitation.

"What went ye out . . . for to see?" It depends, I repeat, what you want to see, and what you have learned to see by the light of Christ that is lit in your own mind, and the love of Christ which has been kindled in your own heart. These are the things that every wise man will learn from him about life. Namely, the dignity and worth of man, the worth and livableness of life, the unity of the world in the purposes of God, and above all, God's mercy and loving-kindness to the children of men.

Even if we see God's hand in nothing but His judgment on the world in these terrifying times, we still see Him. He is saying to humanity, "when will you be as wise as you know how to be wise; when will you be as good as you know how to be good; when will you be as kind and honest and unselfish as you know how to be? You know enough to have a better world! You can have it when you are willing and obedient enough to follow the light that has been given you. You cannot disobey the moral law which I have written in your heart and escape the consequences. You cannot scramble and clutch and fight and have either plenty or peace in the earth. You cannot make your bed in hell and complain about it when you could as well make it in Heaven and enjoy it."

"What went ye out . . . for to see?" Nothing that is not in your own mind and heart. God grant we see what Christ saw and feel as he felt, and above all else, want what he wanted—a civilization, not a chaos; a brotherhood of man, not a jungle.

World's End

REVEREND ADOLPH KELLER, D.D., LL.D.
*A Minister of the Reformed Church; Professor of Theology in the
Universities of Geneva and Zurich, Switzerland*

Dr. Keller is one of the great men of our day in the religious world. He is recognized as one of the foremost Christian leaders, a teacher of unusual ability and a preacher of breadth and power. He has traveled widely in Europe, made twelve journeys to America, was in Egypt for three years, and was part of the famous scientific expedition up Mt. Sinai to collate manuscripts in the Monastery of St. Catherine to prepare a new Greek edition of the New Testament from which James Moffatt made his famous version.

He was one of the early pioneers of the ecumenical movement and is still active on the Committee of the World Council of Churches. As professor at the Universities of Geneva and Zurich, he was the first to introduce ecumenical theology in the curriculum of the theological faculties. He was the founder of the Ecumenical Seminar at Geneva to which he invites some of the prominent American theologians. He serves thus as an interpreter of highest value of one continent to the other. For twenty-five years he was director of the European Central Bureau for Relief to Suffering Churches, which is now amalgamated with the World Council of Churches, adding its wealth of knowledge and experience to this new ecumenical work for relief and reconstruction.

He has written extensively in English, German and French, including Protestant Europe *(with George Stewart),* Religion and Revolution, Karl Barth and Christian Unity, Five Minutes to Twelve, Church and State on the European Continent, Christian Europe Today, American Christianity Today *(in German and French).*

Edinburgh, Yale and Geneva have honored him with the doctorate and he is sought by Christian groups everywhere for his insight into religious problems. His understanding of the world situation and the world need for Christ is clearly revealed in this sermon. He has a world view and world feeling.

Sermon Fifty=one

TEXT: Lo, I am with you alway, even unto the end of the world.
MATTHEW 28:20

WE ARE really going through a world end. It is not merely one of those political or social earthquakes which from time to time make the cultural and moral structure of our society tremble. It is an *end*. We feel the shock in our politics as well as in science, in our moral and religious life. An end may not always be total destruction. Many large forests in the Ardennes, in France, in Poland and Prussia seem destroyed, but the trees already begin to put on new branches and leaves. Their life is continuing and the battlefield will soon be covered by green meadows and flowers. But what happened in the human soul and in human society is something different. Two impressions give us the feeling of an end: What was passing over our life and thinking was not simply the cyclone of the murderous battles, the cataclysm of the downfall of whole cities, the ghastly harvest of human lives death is still gathering in. But a judgment, a verdict, a majestic and imperative No! spoken by an invisible voice over the misdeeds of whole nations. "World History is Judgment," says Schiller. The Angel with the fiery sword barred not simply the way back to Paradise, but seems to bar any way into the future.

And this is the second impression which gives us the feeling that we have reached an end: Looking back, we do not see in the life and traditions of the last generation those germs which are promising a continuity or an evolution, a fresh start and a future. I once saw a house burning. The frightened owner tried to save what was at hand. I saw him running out of the burning house with something in his arms. But it was not some hidden treasure, or a bed or clothing or a loaf of bread. It was a bundle of straw which he laid down near the fire engine. It was futile and foolish to save it while the real values were being destroyed in the fire. But are we not also trying to save from a world fire such bundles of straw: unessential half- or non-values, all kind of paraphernalia, ornaments and pleasures of life while we are losing what makes life worth living? The sense of life, its promise and eternal aim.

The war is over. But we did not save even a ragged peace. Rather we are entering into an era of deep conflicts, controversies and dilemmas. No whole is left whole—everything is disintegrating. It is as if human personalities and the very cells of society were bombed like the atoms by some mysterious, demonic cyclotron which is menacing the whole structure of our existence by a gigantic explosion. We have no longer a common human language or

[307]

religion or social creed. The end is perhaps not so much destruction as such, but disruption, dissolution of our civilization into its ultimate conflicting elements or atoms, no longer held together by natural cohesion, by the laws of creation.

It would be superfluous to give examples. Everybody can find them in our political assemblies and conferences. Where two or three are together, even if they are two or three mighty of the earth—lo, there is strife and disunity.

What from a moral and religious angle is more important than the perception of such disintegration, is the realization in our feelings and conscience that we are really passing through such an *end*, that the world is under a judgment which is not hitting this or that nation, but the world, as a whole in the Biblical sense of the word, ourselves, our family and church life, our inner self. It is for millions as if the great flood was again passing over them, and there seems to be no ark, no shelter, no comfort, the mere nihil, the deadly vacuum alone left.

It must be difficult for the victorious nations to have this feeling. It should hit those who, by the dire law of retaliation, deserve not only ruined homes, death and downfall, but just such humiliating feelings of shame, despair and severe judgment. In a country like America it would be preposterous to expect such feelings of inner failure and despair. So that even in our confession of sins a voice, deeper and more severe than our own would have to remind us, "Lest we forget," that we are all under God's judgment, the whole world and nobody, no nation, no political group can stand it.

If the world forgets, the dire potentialities of the atomic bomb will remind it. Such humiliating experiences are particularly felt among the peoples of the tragic and unfortunate continent which is Europe today. They know over there what a little world end came over their political, social and religious life. If they are Christians, they know also that in the middle of such a breakdown no hope is left to us except that which our text gives us: "Lo, I am with you alway, even unto the end of the world."

How shall the Christian Church bring home such comfort to a despairing world filled with horrors of hatred and starvation? After Judgment Day we hear today the challenge of the prophet: "Comfort, comfort ye my people." But how and with what? Surely bread is comfort, is help. No doubt we can save thousands of children by medical care. But suppose we would just send bales of clothing, tons of flour and condensed milk, vitamins, barracks for sheltering homeless wanderers, suppose we would do it anonymously, invisibly, without a presence, without letting them feel a hand is tendered, that a heart beats in these expressions of helpfulness, that comfort, compassion, personal sympathy is reaching them in and through these gifts? Suppose we could help without being present with our heart, without making an effort to be there, personally, standing side by side near these unfortunates, with our heart and conscience! Do you think such help would really be very valuable or uplifting to a smashed life or encouraging to a despairing heart? No!

A real presence is needed such as Christ promised to those who lose everything. He did not say: Lo, I am with you alway, in a doctrine, in the devotional exercises of a church group, in a correct theology—but "Lo, I am with you." I—the living Christ, the divine presence of God's personal Love and Grace. We have here again that mysterious and paradoxical personalism which is so commonly repudiated by the world and yet so characteristic of the Biblical message. It is the relationship between an I and a Thou which allows and commands confidence, faith, personal confrontation and responsibility, compassion and that holy conversation which is prayer. The Christian religion will remain impersonal, cold objectivity, historic tradition, or psychological subjectivity as long as this personal element is not infused into our belief, into our theology and into our worshiping, to quicken and vivify our faith.

What is happening today in the spiritual life of Christians, trembling under God's judgment and simultaneously uplifted and comforted by this Grace is just this quickening of that personal element in our faith which Christ tried to awake in us when he promised his presence. Where he is, everything becomes personal, concrete, directly related to the living presence of Christ. We have to come down from the stratosphere of our abstractions into which we escape so often. We have to give up that irresponsible aestheticism which allows us to sit on a balcony, as spectators looking down, indifferent, on the arena of real life which challenges a personal decision. Even if we sit in hell, as Psalm 139 says, it is not a blind Fate, an unconscious, automatic machine which tortures us—but "Thou art there also"—Thou, God. In the midst of the cruelties of an impersonal, heartless world, we experience the personal presence of a superhuman heart and will. The pious men of the Old Testament were living in this personal omnipresence of the terrible and holy God. We as Christians are allowed to live in the personal presence of our loving divine friend and Redeemer, Jesus Christ.

It is an invisible presence. We are enveloped in the invisible. In so far as we are parts of nature we are held together by the atomic energies. They are working in us as that constituent power which binds us together as a whole, an entity dangerous to be split and disintegrated. It is an invisible presence. Truly, we are frightened by it, by such a hidden presence of dangerous forces. So many discussions show us today only that the world did not know what it let loose when the first explosions of the atomic bomb happened. We let loose Death itself, the final destructive power, and knew only that we had escaped ourselves, for the moment, a possible end of our world. We resemble that rider who in a winter night rode without knowing it over the frozen lake of Constance. Snow had fallen on the ice, and he rode believing that his horse had solid ground under its hooves while he rode over the fathomless depth of the water. When he learned at the other end of the lake what fate he had escaped, he fell, in the safety of firm ground, dead from his horse. The invisible omnipresence of Death killed him when he learned afterward that he had unconsciously faced it. We are in the midst of this deadly, invisible presence every hour, and pay no attention to it. We had better think of it sometimes. Your boys creeping through Indian jungles or German minefields knew about this ubiquity of the invisible, of the deadly powers menacing them from all sides. I spoke with a soldier returning from the solitude of the Pacific into the crowded streets of New York. He had experienced in his soul the presence of sinister powers around him all the time when he was away. But he was frightened, in the deepest sense, only when in the streets and cafes of New York he saw that people knew nothing of this invisible presence, and are living a life of easygoing indifference without knowing that the tentacles of ubiquitous, ghastly forces are already touching them. What is frightening in such experiences is the impersonal character of blind, pitiless forces. That we should be in the hand of soulless, destructive energies—this, we can hardly stand. Even the silence of the limitless skies above us, as Pascal said, may frighten us because there seems to be no voice, no heart, no consciousness, nothing but this impersonal immensity and infiniteness of cosmic forces.

In the midst of this glacial silence we hear this amazing voice: Lo, *I* am with you. What? An I, an invisible Ego, in the midst of this soulless, terrible *It*? A personal presence in the midst of the roaring thunder of an impersonal universe? Dare we believe it, listen to it without being suspected of frivolous credulity? There was no place in the scientific thought of the last generation for such personalism. The impersonal matter seemed to be more understandable than the personal spirit. But lo, suddenly what we thought understandable—a solved problem—matter—a conglomerate of atoms—became a mystery. Matter, energy is mystery today. Great physicists tell us today that the universe appears to resemble more an idea than a machine, as we thought, and therefore a thinking mind, or a consciousness which conceives or creates ideas and makes itself felt as an invisible presence.

Well for us, it is more than an idea or a kind of cosmic reason. It is Christ, the living and personal incarnation and presence of God's Love. He is with the abandoned children over in Europe and China and Japan. He is with the millions of refugees who will never find homes, with your lost, isolated sons standing guard on a Pacific island. He is with the starving and dying human beings who have lost everything except this presence, everywhere, always, until their end, until the end of the world. They understand better today, in such moment, the contrast between a world which comes to an end and the life and presence of a divine person who is not involved in the maelstrom of a dying world, falling like a Niagara into an unknown abyss where Space and Time end. He stands there "always." It means not a given moment in Time, with certain conditions of our cognition, the word always means the eternal background behind a transitory world. This background is not a laboratory of destructive forces, but the living presence of a just and merciful God above and beyond all History, revealing himself in and through History in the person of Christ, belonging to Time and History likewise. We need such a message at a moment when the smashed, the unfortunate, those in despair over there are looking for such an ultimate presence. They resemble a shipwrecked mariner on his raft, who, despairing and hopeful, waves a handkerchief in order to be seen and saved. Passengers traveling comfortably on one of our palatial ships are not on such a lookout. They feel secure. It is a fatal security because those comfortable passengers have not the eye for seeing the distress neighboring all the time and the salvation visible in the one who stands here, near us, always. The possible end of the world has come forth from dreamland and is no longer a utopian idea. It might happen here in America as well as in Europe. The end is menacing us everywhere today—this is the meaning of the bomb. But the constructive personal force of the Creator is everywhere also wherever the message is heard, "Lo, I am with you." This is the meaning of Christ: God's merciful, creative presence. In letting loose the bomb with its destructive forces, we helped the devil, the destroyer and enemy of mankind. In listening to Christ and following him, we help God himself create a new world.

The world cannot save the world. Man cannot save himself. Only Christ on the Cross has salvation, for the Cross precedes the resurrection. Today the pillars of human confidence have broken down. European countries recently saw their securities break. Resignation, despair, or defeatism are on many sides. But the Christian Church still has the message men need, for she sees that God is still at work in His world. God still *is*. It is the task of the Church and the ministers as His prophets to open the people's eyes so that they may see that all the evils and ills in the world find their end in God's judgment and in His grace. Here the new world begins.

Memoirs of Joseph of Arimathea

Reverend Ferdinand Q. Blanchard, D.D.
Minister, Euclid Avenue Congregational Church, Cleveland, Ohio;
Moderator, Congregational-Christian Churches

Pastor of the Euclid Avenue Congregational Church in Cleveland, Dr. Blanchard still finds time to live in the realm of the spirit and create sermons that paint lasting spiritual impressions on the mind and heart. Moderator of the Congregational-Christian Churches for the past two years and interested in the social agencies of his city, he does not lose sight of the real job of the Protestant Minister—to preach and care for the souls in his congregation.

He was ordained as a minister of the Congregational church in 1901 and has been at the Euclid Avenue Church for the last thirty years. Amherst and Oberlin have recognized his work with the honorary doctorate.

His writings reflect a combination of the imaginative, the spiritual and the uplifting. Among his books are For the King's Sake, The Authority of Jesus, How One Man Changed the World *and* Jesus and the World's Quests. *He wrote the hymn, "O, Child of Lowly Manger Birth."*

"Memoirs of Joseph of Arimathea" was preached in Euclid Avenue Church, Cleveland, and caused considerable comment and discussion. It has a spiritual message much needed in this time and shows Dr. Blanchard's ability to clothe the Christian story in words which grip the modern imagination.

Sermon Fifty=two

IT SO happened that one day about the year A.D. 75 a young man entered the ample hall of the building which housed the library of Alexandria and nodding in friendly fashion at the librarian who at that moment was on duty to assist readers, he was about to seat himself in a favorite niche to which he resorted for study. But the librarian detained him.

"Demetrius," he said, "would you be interested in something we have just received? Since the Romans well nigh destroyed Jerusalem they have been cleaning up the wreckage. There was not much left to save, you may be sure."

Demetrius nodded. The story of the demolition inflicted on the ancient

[312]

capital of Jews after the desperate siege was well known throughout the Roman world.

"However," the other man continued, "there was an officer with extra common sense who tried to save whatever manuscripts turned up in his job and shipped the lot to us here. I have been looking over the stuff. Not much is valuable but I came across yesterday what looks like the memoirs of some high-up Jewish official. You like these little tidbits on life here and elsewhere. It is not long. So I saved it for you. Take it with you and see if you don't agree with me the story is worth a half hour of your time."

That is why if you and I could have stood behind the chair of the young man called Demetrius we might have read as follows:

It seems to me it will be worth while to record for my children and their children the strange experiences I had some years ago. The end of them all is not yet, I believe, disclosed. I shall tell only one chapter of what may be a long story someday.

It is of no great interest to the world, but you for whom I am writing have heard me tell of my boyhood in the little village of Arimathea and of my coming as a young man to Jerusalem. You know, too, how by much hard work I became a well known lawyer and finally was chosen a member of the Sanhedrin. Thus it happened that when I was about fifty years old I could count myself one of the chief men in Jerusalem.

It was no doubt a group of able men who made up the Sanhedrin, but the head of it was one for whom I had no liking, a hard opinionated man, a politician before he was scribe or priest. My closest friend came to be Nicodemus, a kindly spirit as well as able councilor.

Alone with me one day Nicodemus said,

"Joseph, I have had an experience which has disturbed me much. I met a young Galilean who was in the city for the Passover. He was talking with a group in the temple courts. I stopped to hear what he said and I was so impressed that that evening I looked him up where he lodged and we talked for hours. He is a man of great insight, but unless I am mistaken he is going to get into trouble if some of our colleagues hear what he is saying. But I believe his views are sound. I am going to watch his career."

Our conversation went further but I need not stop to detail it. What happened next in my story is that a business matter took me into Galilee some months later. There I found the country chattering eagerly about this young man, Jesus. Wherever he went he was arousing interest. I made it a point to follow him about. I saw and heard him talking to hundreds. I also was present when he was speaking in small groups. I met people whom he had helped physically. It was strange. Acquaintances I had among the Pharisees were mostly very critical. The common people heard him gladly. Finally, I got hold of him for a quiet personal talk. He impressed me as he had Nicodemus. He made God very real. He made men seem very important. He sensed a better society than we had. He seemed to know the way into it.

[313]

The strength of the opposition he was meeting did not frighten him though he was aware that almost any time it might endanger not only his freedom but his life. I had no thought of making myself conspicuous by joining his followers. I thought my position would not warrant that. But I did assure him that if he should come to Jerusalem I wanted to see him again.

And now I must go on to the Passover some months later. At that time the Roman governor was Pontius Pilate. He had made himself unpopular by his harshness and had impressed no one with his integrity. The Sanhedrin thought it expedient to play along with him. Each disliked the other and yet was dependent on the other. Such was the state of politics in Jerusalem.

On the first day of that week in which the Passover was held, as I was about some business in the city, I heard a considerable hubbub in the streets leading up to the temple. I was interested to see what caused it. With hundreds of pilgrims there for the festival anything unusual might happen.

Just then I caught sight of a considerable crowd surging towards me.

"What is going on?" I inquired of a passerby who like myself seemed interested.

"Some Galileans," he answered, "seem to be making a stir over some man out of their province. They have formed a procession for him over the Mount of Olives."

At once my mind went to Jesus. Then before I had a chance to gather what was happening I caught sight of him. A considerable company was about him waving palm branches and shouting out "Hosanna. Blessed be He that cometh in the name of the Lord." He was riding an ass; not, you will think, a very impressive way to arouse enthusiasm. I followed. He reached the temple area, passed through into the outer courts and there paused and looked about him. You may not know that in those days a great abuse had crept into the temple. The business of exchanging currency to provide the temple tax, and of selling doves for offerings at the altar, had turned the courts into a clutter of petty business. But it all paid a commission to the priests and so was permitted.

Jesus had no doubt seen it all before, but that day he had behind him a large group of enthusiastic followers. He could act. With quick impetuous energy he swept down on the traders, overthrew the tables with their heaps of coin and broke up the cubicles where the doves were sold.

Then with a clear ringing voice he called out,

"Is it not written, My house shall be called of all nations the house of prayer? but ye have made it a den of thieves."

It was all over in a few minutes leaving me gasping in surprise. I could applaud his courage, but I wondered if he knew the danger. Neither the traders nor their backers would permit this attack to go unrebuked. For the moment they could not act but they would plan their revenge at once.

[314]

That day I had no chance for a private word with Jesus. But on each of the succeeding days I found an opportunity. My heart went out to this daring young man. I admired his courage. I believed he had placed his finger on ills that afflicted our life and he pointed truths that seemed so true if so simple. But more than his words was the man himself. Quiet, serene, but intense, he seemed to fear nothing. He had the simplicity of a child, the courage of a hero, the wisdom of a saint.

"I shall not be in the city tomorrow," he told me in our last interview, "but I shall keep the Passover here. After that we may meet. I am not telling my plans lest my enemies seek to end the work I feel given me by God to do."

On the day of the Passover I kept the feast with the family as usual. That evening I received an urgent summons to a special meeting of the Sanhedrin. I went thither with forebodings in my heart. Well were they justified! I found Jesus a prisoner before them. Only later did I learn how he had been arrested through the treachery of one of his intimate followers. That long night through he stood before us. Caiaphas beset him with every conceivable query and before the trial ended he suffered even physical violence. Only Nicodemus and I defended him. In the end we were outvoted and matters passed out of our hands into those of Pilate who alone had power to decide his fate.

I need not repeat here the story of those morning hours when Jesus faced the crafty cruel Roman, bent only on avoiding an out-and-out conflict with the Sanhedrin and in the end willing to sacrifice a man he knew to be guiltless. Surely it has been truly written of Jesus, "Never man spake like this man." Never man faced his fate in more calm and dauntless courage. Before noon the pretense of the trial was over. I knew that Jesus was to die.

And now the part I played in that tragic event developed. Some years before I had purchased a stone-walled tomb just outside the city wall and close by the hill known as Calvary. It came to me suddenly that the poor Galileans who had followed Jesus to the city had no place to lay his body. No mark of respect or tenderness would be paid it in that circumstance. Had I been, I asked myself, too reluctant in my loyalty? At least I determined to be so no longer.

As soon as I learned that the pain on the cross had ceased in death I forced my way (it came to just that) into Pilate's presence. He was in a mood of fierce resentment against the priests with the following of the crowd who had badgered him into the execution. Probably he was angry with himself for the sinning against his own sense of decency. When the priests had complained about the inscription over Jesus' cross, he had driven them out of his presence with a curse. But I would not be denied and as a high Jewish official I could not be summarily dismissed. And when I persisted in face of his first inclination to refuse, he granted my request. I asked that the body of Jesus be given over to me that I might bury it in my own tomb. It offended no law. Perhaps Pilate thought it would further anger the priests whom he hated. I sought out Nicodemus with utmost speed. Together we prepared the linen and the spices for the body, and when it was lifted from the cross we found those at hand to bear it down the hill to the tomb.

Was that the end? I thought so that evening. Now you know it was not so. Ere another week had passed, from one to another had gone the word, "He is not dead, but living." The rest is history. That bewildered group in Jerusalem, the scattered pilgrims that dispersed into Galilee, were the seeds of an ever enlarging company who now have set the outposts of our faith from Jerusalem to Rome. I buried a broken body. A spirit with eternal life lives and reigns over the hearts of an ever mightier host.

On the day after Jesus died a friend said to me as we met, "Joseph, you are a fool to link your name with that of Jesus. He taught what men may believe but will not practice. He dreamed of a kingdom. But there is no place for it among the kingdoms of this world."

I wonder. No place among the kingdoms of this world? Yes, that is true. But this I believe. There is a place above the kingdoms of this world. The pilgrims acclaiming him were right. "Blessed is He who cometh." Aye and to the end of time, blessed is he who followeth him that came.

INDEX

[318]

[319]

You may be able in your theological treatises from the pulpit to dust away a few cobwebs from the corners of his theological living room, but he will go on having primarily his own theology — when he was born it was a part of his nature. You must reach his heart (see sermon beg. 287)

"God's Dynamite" — p 87

On done — p 88